Lecture Notes in Computer Science

Lecture Notes in Computer Science

Edited by G. Goos and J. Hartmanis

186

Formal Methods and Software Development

Proceedings of the International Joint Conference
on Theory and Practice of Software Development
(TAPSOFT)
Berlin, March 25–29, 1985

Volume 2:
Colloquium on Software Engineering (CSE)

Edited by Hartmut Ehrig, Christiane Floyd,
Maurice Nivat and James Thatcher

Springer-Verlag
Berlin Heidelberg New York Tokyo

Lecture Notes in Computer Science

Edited by G. Goos and J. Hartmanis

186

Formal Methods
and Software Development

Proceedings of the International Joint Conference
on Theory and Practice of Software Development
(TAPSOFT)
Berlin, March 25–29, 1985

Volume 2:
Colloquium on Software Engineering (CSE)

Edited by Hartmut Ehrig, Christiane Floyd,
Maurice Nivat and James Thatcher

Springer-Verlag
Berlin Heidelberg New York Tokyo

Editors

H. Ehrig
C. Floyd
Technische Universität Berlin
Fachbereich 20, Informatik, SWT FR 5-6
Franklinstr. 28/29, D-1000 Berlin 10, FRG

M. Nivat
L.I.T.P., U.E.R. de Mathématiques
Université de Paris
2, Place Jussieu, F-75251 Paris Cedex, France

J. Thatcher
Math. Department IBM, T.J.W. Research Center
Yorktown Heights, NY 10598, USA

CR Subject Classification (1982): D, D2, F3

ISBN 3-540-15199-0 Springer-Verlag Berlin Heidelberg New York Tokyo
ISBN 0-387-15199-0 Springer-Verlag New York Heidelberg Berlin Tokyo

Printing and binding: Beltz Offsetdruck, Hemsbach/Bergstr.
2145/3140-54321

PREFACE

TAPSOFT is an international <u>Joint Conference on Theory and Practice of Software</u>
<u>Development</u>. The idea for TAPSOFT originated when it was suggested that the 1985
annual Colloquium on Trees in Algebra and Programming (CAAP) should be held in
Berlin. In view of the desired interaction between theory and practice, it was
decided to supplement CAAP with a corresponding Colloquium on Software Engineering
(CSE), and an advanced seminar connecting both parts. The overall aim of the conference is, to bring together theoretical computer scientists and software engineers
(researchers and practitioners) with a view to discussing how formal methods can
usefully be applied in software development.

TAPSOFT is being held from March 25-29, 1985 at the Technical University of Berlin.
It is organized by the Technical University of Berlin, the Gesellschaft für Informatik,
and the European Association for Theoretical Computer Science. The general organizers
are Hartmut Ehrig (TU Berlin), Christiane Floyd (TU Berlin), Maurice Nivat (Université de Paris VI) and Jim Thatcher (IBM Research, Yorktown Heights).

TAPSOFT comprises three parts:

- <u>Advanced Seminar on the Role of Semantics in Software Development</u>
  The aim of this advanced seminar is to bring together leading experts in the fields
  of formal semantics and software engineering so as to enable them to present their
  own work and views on the role of semantics in software development, and to provide a forum for discussions between seminar speakers and all other conference
  participants.

  The seminar consists of invited lecturers and a panel discussion chaired by
  W. Turski and entitled "Formalism - or else?". Each lecture is followed by a brief
  response, giving a critical appraisal, and by a general discussion.

  The invited speakers are

J. Backus (USA)	H.D. Mills (USA)
M. Broy (Germany)	U. Montanari (Italy)
R.M. Burstall (UK)	P. Naur (Denmark)
A.P. Ershov (USSR)	D.L. Parnas (Canada)
J.J. Horning (USA)	J.C. Reynolds (USA)
C.B. Jones (UK)	D. Scott (USA)

The invited lectures are arranged in three sections:

Concepts of Semantics with a View to Software Development
The Role of Semantics in Language Design
The Role of Semantics in the Development of Software Systems

with a considerable overlap between the concerns of the contributions to the different sections.

- **Colloquium on Trees in Algebra and Programming (CAAP '85)**

The previous Colloquia on Trees in Algebra and Programming were held in France and Italy as autonomous conferences. CAAP '85 is integrated into the TAPSOFT conference.

Following the CAAP tradition, papers accepted for CAAP '85 cover a wide range of topics in theoretical computer science. In line with the theme of the TAPSOFT conference, special emphasis is given in the CAAP '85 program to problems arising in software development.

The selected papers are organized in six sections:

Algorithms and Combinatorics
Rewriting
Concurrency
Graph Grammars and Formal Languages
Specifications
Semantics and Data Types.

The program committee for CAAP '85 consists of:

A. Arnold (France) M.C. Gaudel (France)
G. Ausiello (Italy) H.-J. Kreowski (Germany)
E. Blum (USA) B. Mahr (Germany)
W. Brauer (Germany) U. Montanari (Italy)
R. Cori (France) M. Nivat (France)
M. Dauchet (France) G. Plotkin (UK)
H.D. Ehrich (Germany) G. Rozenberg (Netherlands)
H. Ehrig (Chair, Germany) E. Wagner (USA)

- **Colloquium on Software Engineering (CSE)**

CSE focusses on the relevance of formal methods to software development. It tries to answer the following questions:

- Can notions of software engineering be clarified with the help of formal concepts?

- Can concepts of formal semantics be applied in practical software development? Which supporting tools are needed?
- What experiences have been gained using formal methods and how are they related to the claims of their proponents?
- What alternatives to formal methods can be proposed?

These questions are taken up by researchers presenting concepts together with their realisation, and by practitioners reporting on industrial experience with methodical approaches. This session is supplemented by invited lectures given by experts from leading computer and software companies.

The selected papers are presented in the sections listed below:

Concepts and Methods in Software Development

Tools and Environments

Rigorous Approaches to Programming

Abstract Data Types in Software Development

Views of Concurrency

Industrial Experience

The program committee for CSE consists of:

C. Floyd (Chair, Germany)   P. Löhr (Germany)

C. Haenel (Germany)   P. Naur (Denmark)

P. Henderson (UK)   M. Sintzoff (Belgium)

H.-J. Hoffmann (Germany)   J. Thatcher (USA)

C.B. Jones (UK)   W. Turski (Poland)

G. Kahn (France)   H. Weber (Germany)

W. Koch (Germany)   J. Witt (Germany)

C.H.A. Koster (Netherlands)

The TAPSOFT conference proceedings are published in advance of the conference in two volumes. The first volume includes the first two sections of invited papers for the Advanced Seminar and the final versions of 19 papers from CAAP '85, selected from a total of 54 papers. One additional selected paper from CAAP '85 was withdrawn by the authors because of an error in the proofs. The second volume includes the third section of invited papers from the Advanced Seminar, the final versions of 20 papers from CSE, selected from a total of 62 papers, together with three invited papers on industrial experience.

We would like to extend our sincere thanks to all program committee members and referees of CAAP '85 and CSE, as well as to the subreferees for CAAP '85 listed below for their care in reviewing and selecting the submitted papers:

E. Astesiano, M. Bellia, G. Berthelot, B. Biebow, M. Bidoit, P. Boehm,
L. Bonsiepen, L. Bradley, G. Brebner, B. Buchberger, H. Carstensen, C. Choppy,
H. Cohen, A. Corradini, B. Courcelle, E. Dahlhaus, P. Degano, V. Diekert,
K. Drosten, J. Engelfriet, W. Fey, P. Flajolet, L. Fribourg, M. Gogolla,
V. Goltz, U. Grude, J. Gruska, A. Habel, H. Hansen, K.-P. Hasler, D. Haussler,
C. Kirchner, H. Kirchner, W. Kowalk, K.-J. Lange, G.A. Lanzarone, M. Lightner,
U. Lipeck, S. Maaß, M. Main, C. Montangero, R. de Nicola, H. Oberquelle,
R. Orsini, P. Padawitz, F. Parisi-Presicce, J.C. Raoult, M. Simi, F. Simon,
W. Struckmann, R. Valk, B. Vauquelin, M. Venturini Zilli, G. Violal-Naquet,
F. Voisin, H. Wagner, E. Welzl, K.-J. Werner, A. Wilharm and K. Winklmann.

We gratefully acknowledge the financial support provided by the following institutions
and firms:

Deutsche Forschungsgemeinschaft

Senator für Wirtschaft und Verkehr, Berlin

IBM Europe

Arthur Andersen & Co., Hamburg

Softlab GmbH, München

Cray-Research GmbH, München

Siemens AG, München

Epsilon GmbH, Berlin

We wish to express our gratitude to the members of the Local Arrangements Committee:
Wilfried Koch, Bernd Mahr, Ulrike Niehaus and Christoph Oeters and to all members of
the Computer Science Department of the TU Berlin who helped in the organization, in
particular: G. Ambach, P. Bacon, H. Barnewitz, M. Bittner, D. Fähndrich, W. Fey,
A. Habel, H. Hansen, K.-P. Hasler, K. Kautz, W. Köhler, R. Kutsche, M. Löwe,
H. Pribbenow, M. Reisin, K. Schlicht, H. Wagner and K. Wohnhas. Without their help
the conference would not have been possible.

Finally, we would like to thank the Springer Verlag, in particular Mrs. I. Mayer for
her friendly cooperation in preparing the proceedings.

Berlin, March 1985

Hartmut Ehrig
Institut für Software
und Theoretische Informatik
Technische Universität Berlin

Christiane Floyd
Institut für Angewandte
Informatik
Technische Universität Berlin

Maurice Nivat
U.E.R. de Mathematiques
Université de Paris VI

James Thatcher
IBM T.J.W. Research Center
Yorktown Heights

CONTENTS OF VOLUME 1

CONTENTS OF VOLUME 2
page

INTRODUCTION

ON THE RELEVANCE OF FORMAL METHODS TO SOFTWARE DEVELOPMENT

Christiane Floyd

TU Berlin
Sekr. FR 5-6
Franklinstr. 28/29

D-1000 Berlin 10

Motivation

As hostess of the practice-oriented part of the TAPSOFT conference, I would like to
welcome you as participant in a discussion which we wish to promote both at the conference itself and beyond it. This discussion should focus on a central theme: the
relevance of formal methods for practical software work. This leads to a series of
questions: Under what circumstances and for what purposes should these methods be
used? What gains may be expected? What resources and tools are needed? Which claims
are founded or unfounded? What issues are or are not addressed by formal methods?
What other kinds of techniques are required, and how can they be combined with formal methods, if desired?

We feel that this discussion is urgent in view of the many still unresolved problems
in software development and the widely recognized need for higher quality; and that
it needs to be encouraged because the general tendency is for authors developing formal approaches to operate in fairly closed circles, thus reinforcing each other's
views, while many potential method users are left out. Some do not see the potential
benefit of such methods to their work, or they feel that they cannot articulate their
needs. Others are discouraged by the amount of learning involved, or, if they are interested, they do not know how to select the method best suited to their production
situation. The technical contributions as well as the generous support given to our
conference by several industrial firms indicate clearly that the topic is considered
highly relevant by some institutions, while other practitioners flatly state that they
consider our topic too theoretical and not worth their time. Perhaps this is related
to the fact that the introduction of formal methods consumes considerable resources
and that the   use of formal methods will inevitably create yet another kind of spe-
cialist within a given community of DP specialists, which is undesirable in organizations producing application software for their own needs only. Thus, we are mainly
addressing firms producing software on a large scale and therefore able and willing
to consider a sizeable extra investment in methods.

In this introduction my aim is to clarify basic concepts and sketch out some lines of argumentation so as to prepare the ground for the discussion and to stimulate your thoughts on the topics taken up in detail in the seminar lectures and colloquium papers. In these contributions, the central theme of the conference is approached from various sides:

- Several papers focus on <u>concepts of formal semantics and their application</u> to specific tasks in software development, such as the specification of modular programs, the derivation of programs from formal specifications and the treatment of concurrency. These papers encourage us to think of programs in abstract, mathematical terms, and emphasize program correctness, correctness being understood in a very technical sense as a property which can, and should, be proved formally on the basis of a given specification, while the relation of the specification itself to what is needed in reality remains open.

- A second group of papers present <u>software tools to support the application of formal approaches</u>. Typically, the tools facilitate the formulation of syntactically correct specifications; they perform consistency checks and partially automate the transition from specifications to programs or the generation of test data on the basis of a given specification. Since the use of formal approaches tends to lead to considerable extra work involving bulky documents, which have to be kept up to date over a long period, the convenience offered by such tools has a decisive influence on the usability of the underlying method. Of particular importance in practical work is the possibility of making changes conveniently and consistently in all documents.

- In other papers the scope is widened to <u>methods for software development as a whole</u>. They report experiences with more or less formal methods gained in projects and in introducing methods in industrial settings. We can see here that methods are not well-defined "things" which can be mechanically applied to produce predictable results; rather, the introduction of a method in any given setting involves complex processes of learning, gaining experience and method adaptation, in which the original method as presented by its author serves as an inspiration and is eventually transformed to meet the actual needs of its users. Strictly speaking, there can be no formal method for software development as a whole because software development involves other issues besides formalization.

- Finally, the scope of <u>applicability of formal methods and the claims put forward by their proponents are critically examined</u>; in one case, by pointing to specific problems in software development which can or cannot be aided by formalization in the widest sense; in another, by showing how all formal approaches, in the end, depend on intuitive insight, so that in software development, as in all other human activities, our basic aim must be to go along with and strengthen our own intuition. As an essential requirement for formal methods themselves, it follows that they must be suitable as aids to our intuition.

We hope that the various partial views presented by some of the leading authors in our field will enable you to better ascertain your position in relation to others. We would like to enable practitioners to see what the approaches offer, how they should be applied, and what their benefits and their limitations are; to enable teachers to gauge to what extent training in software engineering should be geared to such formal approaches, given their relevance; and to enable researchers to get feedback on the usefulness of their methods with a view to making them increasingly workable.

For all of us, I hope that we shall improve our understanding of how aspects that can be formalized interact with others that cannot, and how this can be taken into account by methods. Perhaps Wlad Turski had something like this in mind when he suggested "Formalism - or else?" as the title for the panel discussion.

I will devote the rest of my introduction primarily to the question of formal methods and their relevance to software development as a whole. In doing so, I have to combine the role of hostess in a controversial discussion aiming at mutual understanding with a strong viewpoint of my own, which I do not wish to hide. I will, therefore, base my arguments on my own views, without wishing to impose these views on you, and you are invited to disagree.

To clarify positions, I will attempt to sketch out a "formalist" standpoint, summarizing the key arguments of proponents of formal methods, as I know them, and a "counter-formalist" standpoint criticizing this line of argumentation. I consider myself a moderate counter-formalist. There is, however, no one coherent counter-formalist position. My own critique is based on a process-oriented view of software development, which I will contrast with the formalist position.

What do we mean by "formal"?

The underlying convictions of formalists and counter-formalists can be illustrated by examining various meanings of the term "formal" as given in the Oxford English Dictionary, which I have excerpted from a much longer, numbered list of usages:

formal

1   Of or pertaining to form, in various senses
   a) pertaining to the form or constitutive essence of a thing: essential
      (opposed to material) .....

c) pertaining to the outward form, shape, or appearance (of a material object); also, in immaterial sense, pertaining to the form, arrangement, external qualities .....

d) Logic. Concerned with the form, as distinguished from the matter of reasoning .....

5 Done or made with the forms recognized as ensuring validity; explicit and definite, as opposed to what is the matter of tacit understanding .....

9 Marked by extreme or excessive regularity or symmetry; stiff or rigid in design; wanting in ease or freedom of outline or arrangement

b) in immaterial sense: having a 'set' or rigorously methodical character.

In my opinion, several of these meanings of "formal" are implied when different people, in varying contexts, speak about formalization in software development, without this becoming explicit. In particular, formalists and counter-formalists use this term differently. I would like, therefore, to point out some important types of differences between the various usages:

- <u>How is form seen to be connected with matter or substance?</u>

In 1 a) form appears as constitutive essence, while in 1 c) it is reduced to outer appearance. Substituting "contents" for "matter" in our immaterial world of software development, I think formalists would tend to argue that the choice of formalism used to express our specifications (for example) will have constitutive influence on the contents to be expressed, while their critics will hold that the formalism chosen will influence the external appearance of these contents.

- <u>What values are associated with issues of form?</u>

In 5, obeying given rules of form inspires confidence, because they are perceived as ensuring the validity of results. By contrast, in 9 form has distinctly negative connotations, such as restricting freedom in design and behaviour.

I think that both of these views are to be found in our context, too; promoters of formal methods, in particular, are highly confident that formalization will lead to greater systems quality, while their critics usually think of design as a creative process in which an initial vision of the whole system is gradually refined and improved on the basis of a critical evaluation of preliminary proposals and in which formalisms may appear as a hindrance.

- To what extent is form considered on its own?

Again, in 1 a) form and matter seem inextricably linked; in 1 d), however, which is the usage most directly related to what we mean by "formal" in the expression "formal semantics", form is explicitly severed from the contents of reasoning and considered on its own. While this may be fine for logic, I consider it dangerous in the development of software systems, which are not abstract games, but intended to affect, by their contents, other peoples' lives.

Also, in 5 formal is seen to be opposed to what is a matter of tacit understanding. But all our understanding, knowing and communicating fundamentally rests on tacit understanding, which stems from the context of common action and experience. Therefore, for formal descriptions to be meaningful to people, they should not be opposed to, but explicitly rooted in, what is a matter of tacit understanding. In software development, all discussions ultimately rest on tacit understanding, referring to the intended application context. For a formal document to be meaningful, we have to ensure, by suitable informal procedures such as the careful reconstruction of concepts, as used in the relevant application area, or by arguments giving the context and the decisions that have led to the specific formal model, that it relates to our tacit understanding.

Formal methods

A method offers guidelines, consisting of techniques, tools and forms of organization. In a formal method, the techniques and tools centre around the use of a formalism, for example a language with a formal syntax and formal semantics. By contrast, languages (and methods using them) are called semi-formal if they have a formal syntax but no formal semantics. People also speak about informal methods, but, in my opinion, this term is only fit for colloquial use, since it indicates the absence of formalism but not the presence of anything else.

I see important differences between formal and semi-formal languages in their use as communication media between people (for example, when writing specifications):

- Semi-formal languages can be used for partial, incomplete descriptions arranged in a formalized manner, whereas whatever is described with the help of formal semantics must be complete and unambiguous; this is normally required only for texts which are to be machine-processed.

- Semi-formal languages do not provide the basis for formal correctness proofs, claimed to be one main advantage associated with the use of formal methods.

In discussing the relevance of formal methods to software development, we have to distinguish between methods on two levels: global methods addressing software development as a whole, and components of such methods supporting specific tasks with local applicability. Formal methods can only appear as component methods, to be combined with other component methods offering semi-formal languages and techniques for writing prose-texts, as well as informal methods to be discussed later. For formal methods to be useful, their combination with other method components and their embedment in software development as a whole must be carefully designed since, surely, it is the process as a whole, and not the local use of any particular method, that determines the quality of the resulting product.

The formalist argument and its critique

As far as I am aware, formalists, in advocating their methods, rely on the following view of software development:

Software development starts from fixed requirements, which are given but, as yet, not usually formally expressed (it is to be hoped, from the formalists' point of view, that suitable formal techniques will soon be available for handling requirements). The task of the software developer is to transform these fixed requirements into a correct (and efficient) program. This transformation occurs in several steps. First, we need to specify WHAT the program does in abstract, mathematical terms without regard to HOW the program is implemented. Then, for any given programming language, the corresponding program can be derived in one or more steps which themselves can, and should, be formalized. As opposed to conventional programming, the resulting program can be proved correct with formal proof techniques. If needed, it can subsequently be transformed into a more efficient solution.

In the view of formalists, the use of formal methods leads to important gains:

1. The process of formalization (abstraction) in the early stages of software development will promote the finding of errors, inconsistencies and missing elements in the requirements.

2. On the basis of the specification, software developers will be able to answer questions on the intended functionality of the program at a very early stage.

3. Programs can be proved correct with respect to their specifications.

4. Specifications can be transformed into programs according to fixed rules ("mechanically").

5. In some methods, specifications can be executed and thus serve as a prototype for the future system.

In giving a critique of the formalist position, I will disregard questions of training, motivation, resources and tools. I will confine myself to the questions: To what
extent is the formalist standpoint relevant to software development? Are its assumptions valid? Are its claims justified?

In doing so, I will draw on a different, process-oriented view of software development, which can be summarized as follows:

Software development consists of processes of learning, creative cooperation and communication involving people of differing backgrounds and interests. Its object is not
so much a product derived from fixed requirements, but a change in human work processes involving the use of this product. While there is a class of well-defined functional requirements, which may be determined in advance and perhaps even formalized, this
does not hold for those aspects that determine the suitability of a program as a tool
for human users: the distribution of functions between man and machine, the matching
of system functions to work-steps, the possibility of human intervention in the case
of system errors, and the handling of errors in the context of human work. These aspects are not amenable to formalization since they cannot be described completely and
unambiguously in advance. Furthermore, software requirements change with the needs of
the user organization.

Therefore, software development must be understood in cycles of (re-)design, (re-)im-
plementation and (re-)evaluation in which processes of software development leading
to system versions are interleaved with processes of system use; since software quality
is determined in using software, the development and use of software must be considered together.

In this view, formal methods fail to address key issues in software development:

- finding out what are the relevant requirements and how they relate to each
  other;

- designing system functions and software architecture taking into account both
  the informal context of the system's use and the specific properties of the
  underlying base machine;

- making software systems suitable as tools for people;

- adapting existing systems to meet new needs.

Against this background, several benefits of formal methods, as claimed by their proponents, appear doubtful:

- ad 1.   Formalization is only one activity that will lead to finding errors and

missing elements, and it is not necessarily the most reliable one. In particular, it does not point to discrepancies between the requirements as
formulated and the real needs of the application context.

- ad 2. "Understanding" system functions on the basis of a formal specification
means understanding their abstract mathematical properties; it does not
enable us to answer reliably questions pertaining to the use of these
functions in human work or problem-solving.

- ad 3. Proofs essentially rest on argumentation; they are established, found convincing or revised in a social process involving learning and constructive
criticism; formal proofs are subject to the same errors as programs and
would themselves have to be proved by informal argumentation; therefore,
it is not obvious what is gained by formal correctness proofs of programs;
moreover, it is not clear what is gained by a "correct" program since the
specification rests on shaky ground, being the formalized version of the
result of an unreliable communication process early in software development.

- ad 4. I know of no case where a programmer has derived a program mechanically
from a specification, and I think there are good reasons why programmers
proficient in formal methods, after having written the specification, have
to make a design which takes the specification into account, but cannot be
derived from the specification by any fixed rules. There are large parts of
programs which are beyond the scope of formal specifications: details of
man-machine interaction, formats of input and output data, communication
mechanisms with peripheral devices and software utilities; they also obey
different quality criteria, such as efficiency and storage economy; a new
design will, therefore, lead to better results.

- ad 5. A specification that can be executed by a computer is a program; it may
well be that improved programming languages based on formal semantics will
constitute an improvement on existing languages, but this leaves open the
problem of specifications that are useful for humans; such a specification
cannot be a formal document only, and it must be geared to the actual needs
in communication between the people involved, rather than to the prerequi-
sites of mathematical theories.

Towards a balance between formal and informal methods

The purpose of this conference is not, of course, to confront two irreconcilable
positions, but to work towards a harmonious interplay between process and form at all
levels in software development. Therefore, the two standpoints sketched out above
need to be seen as complementary rather than contradictory.

Even in the process-oriented view, we work at any point in time towards a product whose requirements are considered fixed. On the other hand, every formalist will readily agree that formal methods are applied in a context of changing human needs. Furthermore, while both views can be applied to all software systems, their relative importance depends on the type of system to be constructed and how it is embedded in its usage context. For example, compilers for a given programming language have a well-defined desired functionality and are therefore vastly more amenable to formal approaches than interactive application systems where the interleaving of computer-supported and other work-steps of predominantly lay users is a major concern. There-fore, not all points of the critique of the formal argument carry equal weight in all situations.

As a sceptic with respect to formal methods, I can nevertheless see their usefulness in several important respects:

- to clarify concepts underlying our software work, as has happened in the case of abstract data types and modules, which have emerged, as a result of work in for-mal semantics, as vehicles for focussing our thoughts and discussions in software design and which can be studied and practised on the basis of small examples; personally, I find this help immensely valuable, and I believe that a large por-tion of the positive experiences reported by users of formal methods is due to this effect;

- for literal application in well-defined sub-problems, where concerns of function-ality and reliability take precedence over concerns of usability and where re-quirements can be expected to remain stable; in my view, the treatment of con-currency falls into that category;

- to serve as an inspiration or guidance for organizations developing their own methods; I feel that the emphasis here must be on retaining the spirit of the method while deliberately omitting the literal use of some of its more formal elements and adding suitable informal elements geared to supporting processes of learning and creative cooperation;

- to standardize solutions in problem classes which are already well understood and where the problem of designing new systems in a creative process can, to some extent, be replaced by the use of known solutions;

- to provide new ways of programming with the help of languages based on formal semantics, which may well avoid the serious shortcomings of existing programming languages while at the same time permitting the formulation of programs at a higher level.

On the other hand, I feel strongly that processes of learning, communication and creative cooperation cannot, and should not, be formalized, although attempts at doing so are wide-spread amongst authors of software design methods, for example when structuring criteria like "top-down" are applied to the design process as it takes place in time, rather than to the form of its result. In my own experience as a software designer and project adviser, processes cannot be entirely formalized, and attempts at doing so prove positively harmful.

Such attempts to reduce process to form are based on a serious misunderstanding of the nature of processes. Processes are irreversible; they take place in time. By their very nature, they cannot be fully understood and described in advance; they can only be understood by the people involved in these processes as they happen. Here, people act in open situations, on the basis of their needs and commitments, pursuing changing goals as they go along and revising their understanding in the event of new insights. If we wish to understand the nature of such processes, we have to develop a new theory drawing largely on concepts that are useful for studying living systems, as they exist in nature and society, and language as it is used in communication between people.

Though no such theory is available at present, we can nevertheless suggest concrete informal methods to support processes of communication, which are in wide use:

- working out relevant examples, taking into account the application context

- taking care in the choice of basic concepts used in software development so as to enhance common understanding

- constructive criticism of partial solutions or partially formalized solutions on the basis of transparent criteria

- carrying out controlled experiments, for example in the form of prototypes, which can be evaluated

- using psychological methods for improving the communication between groups of people enacting different roles.

Whether or not formal methods are applied, these informal procedures may be expected to bring enormous benefits.

I should like to close this introduction with a few personal words. My involvement in the TAPSOFT conference must be understood in terms of my friendship with my colleague Hartmut Ehrig, which is based on great mutual respect at a personal level, while at the same time we most heartily disagree: he is a powerful advocate of formal methods, whereas I remain an undaunted sceptic in this respect. However, because of our friendship, it has not been possible for us to dismiss each other's viewpoints as irrelevant; so, instead, we have carried on a continual heated discussion over several years. As a result, I now have a fairly good appreciation of what algebraic specification can or cannot do for me, under what circumstances and for what purposes I would use it in software development, and how it could be embedded in the overall approach which I favour. I am sure, too, that Hartmut has a better appreciation of the importance of those aspects of software development which cannot be formalized. Yet, I continue to work without feeling any compulsion to become proficient in algebraic specification, while he continues to "abstract from" those unpleasant aspects of software development which are not amenable to formal approaches, in order to make progress in elaborating his specification technique. Thus, our disagreement is not resolved, and it cannot be, since it rests on both sides on differing fundamental convictions. And yet, as we share a common concern for greater quality in software development, the basic question in my mind is how these two viewpoints can fruitfully interact and be combined to produce workable approaches.

I have borrowed the phrase "a balance between formal and informal methods" from Don Knuth. In his enlightening paper on "Literate Programming" he writes: "I owe a great debt ..... to Peter Naur for stressing the importance of a balance between formal and informal methods". I owe Peter Naur a much greater debt in this respect, since he has for years been my main support in developing my own ideas in a context where contrary views were for a long time the predominant ones.

COMBINING ALGEBRAIC AND PREDICATIVE SPECIFICATIONS IN LARCH

J. J. Horning
Systems Research Center
Digital Equipment Corporation
130 Lytton Avenue
Palo Alto, CA 94301 U. S. A.

Abstract

Recently there has been a great deal of theoretical interest in formal specifications. However, there has not been a corresponding increase in their use for software development. Meanwhile, there has been significant convergence among formal specification methods intended for practical use.

The Larch Project is developing tools and techniques intended to aid in the productive use of formal specifications. This talk presents the combination of ideas, both old and new, that we are currently exploring.

One reason why our previous specification methods were not very successful was that we tried to make a single language serve too many purposes. To focus the Larch Project, we made some fairly strong assumptions about the problem we were addressing.

Each Larch specification has two parts, written in different languages. Larch interface languages are used to specify program units (e.g., procedures, modules, types). Their semantics is given by translation to predicate calculus. Abstractions appearing in interface specifications are themselves specified algebraically, using the Larch Shared Language.

A series of examples will be used to illustrate the use of the Larch Shared Language and the Larch/CLU interface language. The talk will conclude with notes on the key design choices for each of the languages, and for the method of combining the two parts of a specification.

Introduction

I would like to begin with three general observations about the field of formal specification:

Theoretical interest: It is clear that formal specification has captured the interest of a signficant group in the theoretical computer science community. The program for this joint conference gives evidence of the vitality of the research area. Similar evidence will be found in a dozen other recent conferences and in numerous journals. Sound theoretical foundations are being given for more and more different kinds of formal specification languages, and subtle semantic problems are being explored to ever-greater depth, particularly in such areas as parameterization and concurrency.

Adoption: It is equally clear that this interest has not been matched by the use of formal specifications in software development. Several attempts—and even some successes—have been reported. But formal methods have not swept the programming community (at my employer, or in the world at large) in the same way that higher-level languages did in the decade after FORTRAN. In retrospect, perhaps this should have been expected, for a variety of reasons. Many of the theoretical results are not presented in a form accessible to practitioners. It is not obvious how some of the theoretically appealing methods deal with many problems of practical importance. Formality is not inevitable in specifications— there are more alternatives for human/human communication than for human/machine communication. Few of the formal specification languages have come with the quality of computer support that even the original FORTRAN did.

Convergence: As developers of formal specification methods confront the problems of practical software development, many distinctions that formerly seemed clear-cut are becoming blurred. Everyone seeks to combine the advantages traditionally associated with each method, while mitigating its disadvantages. Good ideas are borrowed freely and hybrid methods are tried. It is difficult to track "intellectual ancestry," and generalizations about the limitations of classes of methods are quickly falsified.

In this talk, I would like to share the particular combination of old and new ideas that we are currently exploring in the Larch Project. We do not yet have much experience with their use in practical software development, and the supporting tools are not yet available. But we are pleased with the way the pieces seem to be fitting together. We hope that software developers will assess their promise for dealing with practical problems, and that developers of other specification methods will consider including some of them in their own schemes.

Context: The Larch Project

The Larch Project at MIT's Laboratory for Computer Science and DEC's Systems Research Center is the continuation of more than a decade of collaborative research with John Guttag and his students in the area of formal specification. It is developing both a family of specification languages and a set of tools to support their use, including language-sensitive editors and semantic checkers based on a powerful theorem prover [Lescanne 83][Forgaard 84].

Larch is an effort to test our ideas about making formal specifications useful. We tried to analyze the reasons why our previous specification methods had not been as useful (and hence not as widely used) as we had hoped they would be [Guttag, Horning, and Wing 82]. We identified several problems to be solved before we could confidently offer our methodology to software developers. To focus the project, we made the following assumptions, which strongly influenced the directions it has taken:

Local specifications: We started with the belief that programming-language-oriented behavioral specifications of program units could be useful in the near future. No conceptual breakthroughs or theoretical advances seemed to be needed. Rather, we needed to use what we already knew to design usable languages, develop some software support tools, and educate some system designers and implementers.

Sequential programs: We focussed on specifications of the behavior of program units in nonconcurrent environments. We are aware of the importance of concurrency, and of many of the additional problems it introduces. However, we find it quite hard enough to deal adequately with the sequential case. A successful framework for dealing with concurrency will still need a method for specifying the atomic actions of the concurrent system.

Scale: Methods that are entirely adequate for one-page specifications may fail utterly for hundred-page specifications. It is essential that large specifications be composed from small ones that can be understood separately, and that the task of understanding the ramifications of their combination be managable. For large specifications, the "putting together" operations [Burstall and Goguen 77] are more crucial than the details of the language used for the pieces of which it is composed.

Incompleteness: Realistically, most specifications are going to be partial. Sometimes incompleteness reflects abstraction from details that are irrelevant for a particular purpose; e.g., time, storage usage, and functionality might be specified separately. Sometimes it reflects an intentional choice to delay certain design decisions. And sometimes it reflects oversights in the design or specification process. It is important to detect the latter kind of incompleteness without making the other two kinds awkward.

Errors: Our experience suggests that the process of writing specifications is at least as error-prone as the process of programming. We believe that it is important to do a substantial amount of checking of the specifications themselves. The ultimate tool for error-detection is the understanding of human minds. However, we have found that—by designing the specification language to incorporate useful redundancy—some surprisingly effective mechanical checks are feasible. We have chosen to supplement checking analogous to a compiler's syntax and type checking with a number of semantic checks that rely on a theorem prover.

Tools: A serious bar to practical use of formal specifications is the number of tedious and/or error-prone tasks associated with maintaining the consistency of a substantial body of formal text. Tools can assist in managing the sheer bulk of large specifications, in browsing through selected pieces, in deriving interactions and consequences, and in teaching a new methodology. Thinking about such tools has changed our ideas about what it is important to include in specification languages.

Handbooks: It is inefficient to start each specification from scratch. We need a repository of reusable specification components that have evolved to handle the common cases well, and that can serve as models when faced with uncommon cases. It is no more reasonable to keep reinventing the specifications of priority queues and bitmaps than to axiomatize integers and sets every time they are used. A rich collection of "abstract models" is a step in the right direction, but the collection should be open-ended, and include application-oriented abstractions, as well as mathematical and implementation-oriented ones. We expect the most useful parts of specification handbooks to be written in the Shared Language.

Language dependencies: For many years we tried to write specifications in languages that were completely free of bias towards any programming language. We now think that effort was misdirected, at least for local specifications. The environment in which a program unit is embedded, and hence the nature of its observable behavior, is likely to depend in fundamental ways on the semantic primitives of the programming language. Any attempt to disguise this dependence will make specifications more obscure to both the unit's users and its implementers. On the other hand, many of the important abstractions in most specifications *can* be defined in a language-independent way.

We have adopted a two-tiered methodology [Wing 83]. Each specification has two parts, written in different languages: specifications of program units are written in a Larch interface language that is tailored to a programming language; these specifications use programming-language-independent abstractions, which are specified separately in the Larch Shared Language. Some important aspects of the Larch family of specification languages are:

Composability: The Larch Shared Language is oriented towards the incremental construction of specifications from other specifications.

Emphasis on presentation: To make it easier to read and understand specifications, the composition mechanisms in the Larch Shared Language are defined as operations on specifications, rather than on theories or models.

Interactive and integrated with tools: The Larch languages are intended for interactive use. Tools are being constructed for both interactive construction and incremental checking of specifications.

Semantic checking: The semantic checks for the Larch languages were designed assuming the availability of a powerful theorem prover. Hence they are more comprehensive than the syntactic checks commonly defined for specification languages.

Shared Language based on equations: The Larch Shared Language has a simple semantic basis taken from algebra. However, because of the emphasis on composability, checkability, and interaction, it differs substantially from the algebraic specification languages we have used in the past.

Interface languages based on predicate calculus: Each interface language is a way to write assertions about states, that can be translated to formulas in typed first-order predicate calculus with equality. Programming-language-specific notations deal with constructs such as side effects, exception handling, and iterators. Equality over terms is defined in the Shared Language; this provides the link between the two parts of a specification.

Example Specifications in the Larch Shared Language

The following series of examples is intended to give the flavor of the Larch Shared Language. A complete description of the Larch Shared Language is contained in [Guttag and Horning 85a], and extensive examples of its use are given in [Guttag and Horning 85b].

The *trait* is the basic module of specification. A trait may specify an abstract data type, but frequently traits are used to capture general properties that may be shared by many types. Such traits may be included in other traits that specify particular types.

Consider the following specification describing tables that store values in indexed places:

> TableSpec: **trait**
> > **introduces**
> > > new: → Table
> > > add: Table, Index, Val → Table
> > > #∈#: Index, Table → Bool
> > > eval: Table, Index → Val
> > > isEmpty: Table → Bool
> > > size: Table → Card
> > **constrains** new, add, ∈, eval, isEmpty, size **so that**
> > > **for all** [*ind1, ind2:* Index, *val:* Val, *t:* Table]
> > > > eval(add(*t, ind1, val*), *ind2*) = **if** *ind1* = *ind2* **then** *val* **else** eval(*t, ind2*)
> > > > *ind1* ∈ new = false
> > > > *ind1* ∈ add(*t, ind2, val*) = (*ind1* = *ind2*) ∨ (*ind1* ∈ *t*)
> > > > size(new) = 0
> > > > size(add(*t, ind1, val*)) = **if** *ind1* ∈ *t* **then** size(*t*) **else** size(*t*) + 1
> > > > isEmpty(*t*) = (size(*t*) = 0)

This example is similar to a conventional algebraic specification in the style of [Guttag and Horning 80]. The part of the specification following **introduces** declares a set of *operators* (function identifiers), each with its *signature* (the *sorts* of its domain and range). These signatures are used to sort-check *terms* (expressions) in much the same way as function calls are type-checked in programming languages. The remainder of the specification constrains the operators by writing equations that relate sort-correct terms containing them.

Each trait defines a a set of well-formed formulas (wff's) of predicate calculus that is closed under inference. The theory associated with a simple trait written in the Larch Shared Language is defined by:

Axioms: Each equation, universally quantified by the variable declarations of the containing **constrains** clause, is in the theory.

Inequation: ¬ (true = false) is in the theory. All other inequations in the theory are derivable from this one and the meaning of equality.

Predicate calculus: The theory contains the conventional axioms of typed first-order predicate calculus with equality, and is closed under its rules of inference.

The next example is an abstraction of those data structures that "contain" elements, e.g., set, bag, queue, stack. It is useful both as a starting point for specifications of various kinds of containers, and as an assumption for generic operators. The crucial part of the trait is the **generated by**. By indicating that any term of sort C is equal to some term in which new and insert are the only operators with range C, it introduces an inductive rule of inference that can be used to prove properties of terms of sort C.

> Container: **trait**
>   **introduces**
>   new: → C
>   insert: C, E → C
>   **constrains** C **so that** C **generated by** [new, insert]

The next example builds upon Container by assuming it. It constrains the new and insert operators it inherits from Container, as well as the operator it introduces, isEmpty. The **converts** clause adds nothing to the theory of the trait. It adds checkable redundancy by indicating that this trait is intended to contain enough axioms to adequately specify isEmpty. Because of the **generated by**, this can be proved by induction over terms of sort C, using new as the basis and insert(c, e) in the induction step.

> IsEmpty: **trait**
>   **assumes** Container
>   **introduces** isEmpty: C → Bool
>   **constrains** isEmpty, new, insert **so that for all** [c: C, e: E]
>   isEmpty(new) = true
>   isEmpty(insert(c, e)) = false
>   **implies converts** [isEmpty]

The next two examples also assume Container. Like **converts**, the **exempts** clauses are concerned with checking, and add nothing to the theory. They indicate that the lack of equations for next(new) and rest(new) is intentional. Even if Next or Rest is included into a trait that claims the convertibility of next or rest, the terms next(new) and rest(new) don't have to be converted.

> Next: **trait**
>   **assumes** Container
>   **introduces** next: C → E
>   **constrains** next, insert **so that for all** [e: E]
>   next(insert(new, e)) = e
>   **exempts** next(new)

> Rest: **trait**
>   **assumes** Container
>   **introduces** rest: C → C
>   **constrains** rest, insert **so that for all** [e: E]
>   rest(insert(new, e)) = new
>   **exempts** rest(new)

The next example specifies properties common to various data structures such as stacks, queues, priority queues, sequences, and vectors. It augments Container by combining it with IsEmpty, Next, and Rest. **Includes** indicates that this trait is intended to inherit their operators, and to constrain them further. Specifically, the **partitioned by** clause constrains new, insert, and isEmpty by indicating that they are a "complete" set of observer functions. I.e., if two terms are different, this difference can be observed in the value of at least one of these functions. Since little other information has been supplied about these operators, the **partitioned by** does not yet add much to the associated theory.

> Enumerable: **trait**
> > **includes** Container, IsEmpty, Next, Rest
> > **constrains** C **so that** C **partitioned by** [next, rest, isEmpty]

The next example specializes Enumerable by further constraining next, rest, and insert. Sufficient axioms are given to convert next and rest. The axioms that convert isEmpty are inherited from the trait Enumerable, which inherited them from the trait IsEmpty.

> PriorityQueue: **trait**
> > **assumes** TotalOrder with [E for T]
> > **includes** Enumerable
> > **constrains** next, rest, insert **so that for all** [q: C, e: E]
> > > next(insert(q, e)) = **if** isEmpty(q) **then** e
> > > > **else if** next(q) $\leq$ e **then** next(q) **else** e
> > > rest(insert(q, e)) = **if** isEmpty(q) **then** new
> > > > **else if** next(q) $\leq$ e **then** insert(rest(q), e) **else** q
> > **implies converts** [next, rest, isEmpty]

The next example illustrates a specialization of Container that does not satisfy Enumerable. It augments Container by combining it with IsEmpty and Cardinal, and introducing two new operators. Container and IsEmpty are **included** because the trait further constrains operators inherited from them. Cardinal is **imported**; this indicates that this trait inherits Cardinal's specification, but is not intended to further constrain any of its operators. The theory associated with Cardinal can thus be understood independently, and will not be enriched by MultiSet. **Imports** and **includes** yield the same theory, but stronger checks are performed for **imports**.

The **partitioned by** indicates that count alone is sufficient to distinguish unequal terms of sort MSet. **Converts** [isEmpty, count, delete] is a stronger assertion than the combination of an explicit **converts** [count, delete] with the inherited **converts** [isEmpty].

> MultiSet: **trait**
> > **assumes** Equality with [E for T]
> > **imports** Cardinal
> > **includes** Container with [MSet for C, {} for new], IsEmpty with [MSet for C]
> > **introduces** count: E, MSet $\rightarrow$ Bool
> > > delete: E, MSet $\rightarrow$ MSet
> > > size: MSet $\rightarrow$ Card

constrains MSet **so that**
> MSet **partitioned by** [count]
> **for all** [*c:* MSet, *e1, e2:* E]
>> count({}, *e1*) = 0
>> count(insert(*c, e1*), *e2*) = count(*c, e2*) + (**if** (*e1* = *e2*) **then** 1 **else** 0)
>> size({}) = 0
>> size(insert(*c, e1*)) = size(*c*) + 1
>> delete({}, *e1*) = {}
>> delete(insert(*c, e1*), *e2*) = **if** *e1* = *e2* **then** *c* **else** insert(delete(*c, e2*), *e1*)
> **implies converts** [isEmpty, count, delete]

An Example Specification in Larch/CLU

Theories are all very well, but what is their connection to software development? In Larch, the theories associated with specifications written in the Shared Language are used to give meaning to operators appearing in specifications written in Larch interface languages. It is these interface specifications that actually provide information about program units.

Interface languages are programming-language dependent. Everything from the modularization mechanisms to the choice of reserved words is influenced by the programming language. At present, there is only one moderately well-developed Larch interface language, the Larch/CLU language [Wing 83][Guttag, Horning, and Wing 85]. The semantics of Larch/CLU incorporates semantic constructs from CLU. For example, the meaning of **signal** in Larch/CLU derives from the meaning of **signal** in CLU—which is different from the meaning of SIGNAL in PL/I or MESA. Correspondingly, Larch/CLU uses CLU-like syntax for constructs in common, e.g., procedure headers. Other interface languages would use concepts and terminology based on their programming languages.

I will present just one short specification written in a version of Larch/CLU to give the flavor of the language. The specification defines a type, ten_bag, together with four procedures. It would be implemented by a CLU *cluster*.

> ten_bag **mutable type exports** singleton, add, remove, choose
>> **based on sort** MSet **from** MultiSet **with** [int **for** E]
>
> singleton = **proc**(*e:* int) **returns**(*b:* ten_bag)
>> **modifies nothing**
>> **ensures** new(*b*) $\land$ *b* = insert({}, *e*)
>
> add = **proc**(*b:* ten_bag, *e:* int) **signals** (too_big)
>> **modifies at most** [*b*]
>> **ensures normally** b_{post} = insert(b_{pre}, *e*)
>>> **except signals** too_big **when** size(b_{pre}) = 10
>>>> **ensuring modifies nothing**

remove = **proc**(*b*: ten_bag, *e*: int)
    modifies at most [*b*]
    ensures b_{post} = delete(b_{pre}, *e*)

choose = **proc**(*b*: ten_bag) returns(*e*: int)
    requires ¬ isEmpty(*b*)
    modifies nothing
    ensures count(*b*, *e*) 0

end ten_bag

The specification of each procedure can be straightforwardly translated to a predicate over two states in the style of [Hehner 84]. The **requires** clause, if present, represents a precondition that may be assumed by the implementation, and must be ensured by any caller. The **modifies** clause places a bound on the objects the procedure is allowed to change. The **ensures** clause is like a postcondition, but may reference values of objects in both the pre and post states.

The names in a Larch/CLU specification tie it to two other kinds of formal text: traits in the Shared Language, and programs in CLU. Operators (e.g., insert), sort names (e.g., MSet), and trait names (e.g., MultiSet) provide the link to a theory defined by a collection of traits. Names of procedures (e.g., add), formal parameters (e.g., *e*), types (e.g., int), and signals (e.g., too_big) provide the link to programs that implement the specification. The primary job of an interface language is to bring these two together. For example, the **based on** clause connects type names and sort names. The **requires** and **ensures** clauses contain operators, formal parameters, and signal names. These are used together to constrain the relationship between the values of the actuals on entry to a procedure and their values on exit from the procedure.

Each procedure's specification can be studied in isolation—in contrast to traits, where the core of the specification involves the interactions among operators. Of course, to understand or reason about the type, it is still necessary to consider the specifications of all its procedures. CLU's type-checking ensures the soundness of a data type induction principle for this type. This would enable us to prove that the size of any ten_bag value generated by a non-erroneous program is less than or equal to 10.

Induction over the procedures of a data type is distinct from induction over the generating operators of a sort, and is used to prove theorems about values in a different space. Each value of type ten_bag can be represented by a term of sort MSet, but not every term represents a value that can be obtained using the procedures of the type. For example, induction over {} and insert can be used to prove that for every term of sort MSet there is term representing a larger MSet. This is not in conflict with the proof mentioned in the previous paragraph.

Choose is probably the most interesting procedure in this example. Its specification says that it must return some value in the ten_bag it is passed, but doesn't say which value. Moreover, it doesn't even require that different invocations of choose with the same argument produce the same result. Choose is an example of nondeterminism, and therefore cannot be specified by equating its result to a term.

This specification can be satisfied by a CLU cluster implementing one type, ten_bag, with four procedures, singleton, add, remove, and choose. The specification says nothing about "implementing" sorts (such as MSet) or operators (such as {} and insert). These auxiliary constructs are defined solely for the purpose of writing interface specifications; they do not exist in programs.

Execution errors, on the other hand, are properties of programs; they do not exist in traits. **Requires** clauses and **signals** provide means to specify two different ways of dealing with erroneous conditions. For example, add must raise a signal if adding another element would make its argument too big, whereas the implementor of choose is allowed to assume that it will not be called with an empty ten_bag. Note that this precondition cannot be checked at runtime by a program using the type ten_bag. The size operator is available for reasoning about procedures, but the interface (as specified) does not supply any corresponding procedure. Ensuring that execution of a program using this type is error-free would thus require some sort of (formal or informal) proof about the program.

Notes on the Larch Shared Language

Why Algebra? This question really expands into two questions: Why not an operational or abstract model approach? and Why not full predicate calculus? The short answer is that we find equations to be a convenient notation for stating properties of many abstractions useful in programming. A more detailed answer would cover such issues as the ease with which partial specifications can be combined to yield stronger specifications, the ease with which partial specifications can be read and understood, the descriptive power of the technique, and the suitability of the formalism for efficient theorem-proving using rewrite rules.

The Shared Language is perhaps more notable for what it leaves out than for what it includes. We tried to keep it simple. However, before omitting a feature found in other algebraic specification languages, we had to convince ourselves that the gain in simplicity of the language was worth the cost in expressive power or increase in the complexity of specifications written in the language.

A key assumption underlying our design was that specifications should be constructed and reasoned about incrementally. This led us to a design that ensures that adding things to a trait never removes formulas from its associated theory. The desire to maintain this monotonicity property led us to construe the equations of a trait as denoting a first-order theory. Had we chosen to take the theory associated with either the initial or final interpretation of a set of equations (as in [ADJ 78] and [Wand 79]), the monotonicity property would have been lost.

In a trait that defines an "abstract data type" there will generally be a distinguished sort corresponding to the "type of interest" of [Guttag 75] or "data sort" of [Burstall and Goguen 81]. In such traits, it is usually possible to partition the operators whose range is the distinguished sort into "generators," those operators which the sort is **generated by**, and "extensions," which can be converted into generators. Operators whose domain includes the distinguished sort and whose range is some other sort are called "observers." Observers are usually convertible, and the sort is usually **partitioned by** one or more subsets of the observers and extensions.

While we expected that many traits would correspond to complete abstract data types, we expected that even more would not. This led us to introduce **generated by** and **partitioned by** as independent constructs. **Generated by** is used to close the set of constructors of a sort, and **partitioned by** to indicate that a set of observers is complete. Separating these constructs affords the specifier some useful flexibility.

The ability to substitute for any operator or sort identifier appearing in a trait, using a **with** list, is very powerful. In effect, all such identifiers are formal parameters. An earlier version of the Larch Shared Language had explicit lambda abstraction in traits. However, we discovered that our assumptions at the time when a trait was written about which names should be parameters too often limited their applicability. We often wished to substitute for a name that had not been listed as a parameter. Even more often, we found ourselves using the same identifier for the actual as the formal, because most of the potential parameterization was not needed for a specific use.

It is the trait's text that is effectively parameterized by sort and operator identifiers, rather than the associated theory. This allows us to completely sidestep the subtle semantic problems associated with parameterized theories, theory-valued parameters, and the like—some of which are dealt with in other presentations at this conference.

We have chosen not to use "higher-order" entities in defining the Larch Shared Language. Traits are simple textual objects, combined by operations defined on their text. We have found that such operations are much easier to explain to readers of specifications than are operations on theories or models. Of course, for each of our combining operations on traits, there is a corresponding operation on theories such that the theory associated with a combination is equivalent to the combination of the associated theories, so the difference is largely one of exposition.

Notes on Interface Languages

Why predicates on two states? It should scarcely be necessary to justify the use of predicate calculus in program specification, since it crops up in so much work dealing with precise descriptions of programs—starting from Turing and von Neumann, and running through Floyd, Hoare, Dijkstra, and many more—uses this notation. But we have followed Hehner and Jones in using predicates over two states, rather than one. This seems to work out well both as a tool for describing the semantics of programming languages and as a tool for stating requirements on particular programs. In practice, we have found our specifications easier to write and to read since we adopted the two-state notation, but I know of no formal justification for this.

Notes on Combining an Algebraic and a Predicative Language

This section touches on some of the more important ramifications of the way Larch Shared Language and Larch interface language specifications fit together.

The style of specification used in Larch resembles that used in operational specifications built upon abstract models. It differs, however, in several important respects. The Shared Language is used to specify a theory rather than a model, and the interface languages are built around predicate calculus rather than around an operational notation. One consequence of these differences is that Larch specifications never exhibit "implementation bias."

The semantic bases of Larch interface languages tend to mirror the semantic bases of the programming languages from which they are derived. In general, this means that the semantics of an interface language is rather complex. But it does allow us to be quite precise about what it means for an implementation to "satisfy" a Larch specification.

The semantics of the Larch Shared Language is quite simple, largely as a consequence of two decisions:

Operators and sorts appearing in traits are auxiliary and are not part of the implementation.

Issues that must be dealt with at the interface language level are not tackled again at the Shared Language level.

As a result of the first decision, there is no mechanism to support the hiding of operators in the shared language. The hiding mechanisms of other specification languages allow the introduction of auxiliary operators that don't have to be implemented. These operators are not completely hidden, since they must be read to understand the specification and are likely to appear in reasoning based on the specification. Since none of the operators appearing in a Shared Language specification is intended to be implemented, the introduction of a hiding mechanism could have no effect on the set of implementations satisfying a Larch specification.

As a result of the second decision, there is no mechanism other than sort checking for restricting the domain of operators. Terms such as eval(new, i) are well-formed, even though there are no equations that allow them to be simplified. Furthermore, no special "error" elements are introduced to represent the "values" of such terms. Preconditions and errors are handled at the interface language level.

Similarly, nondeterminism is left to the interface language. Nondeterminism in an interface should not be confused with incomplete specification in a trait. We often intentionally introduce operators in traits without giving enough axioms to fully define them. That is to say, there are distinct terms that are neither provably equal nor provably unequal. However, it is always the case that for every term t, $t = t$. The whole mathematical basis of algebra and of the Larch Shared Language depends on the ability to freely substitute "equals for equals." This property would be destroyed by the introduction of "nondeterministic functions." It is also not generally true for "functions" in most programming languages.

Issues of name scoping are also left to the interface language level. The Larch Shared Language does not "qualify" operator or sort names with the traits in which they are introduced or defined. Thus, within a trait, all such names (including those acquired from other traits) are "global." This is extremely helpful when combining a number of traits to specify a single type, but raises the possibility of accidental "collisions." Although we do not have a lot of experience yet, we expect two features of the language to keep this from becoming a serious problem: an operator's signature is treated as part of its name, so that two operators with different signatures can never collide; and imports checking ensures that a trait does not add new constraints to operators being acquired.

A Larch Shared Language trait does not have block structure, and there is no "hierarchy" in its associated theory. We do not expect this to be a problem, because the traits needed to specify single program units should be relatively small.

While the semantic basis of Larch/CLU is considerably more complicated than that of the Larch Shared Language, its static semantics is considerably simpler. In the Shared Language, there are several mechanisms for building a specification from other specifications and for inserting checkable redundancy into specifications. Corresponding mechanisms are not present in Larch/CLU. Interfaces are specified in terms of traits, not in terms of other interfaces.

We wish to encourage a style of specification in which most of the structural complexity is pushed into the Shared Language part of specification. We feel that specifiers are less likely to make serious mistakes in this simpler domain. Furthermore, it should be easier to provide machine support that will help specifiers to catch the mistakes that they do make. Finally, by encouraging specifiers to put effort into Shared Language specifications, we increase the likelihood that parts of specifications will be reusable.

Concluding Remarks

The ideas behind the Larch Project are more important than its details, except to the extent that the details must be gotten right in order to fit the pieces together. A useful methodology is more than a collection of separately good ideas. Thus the issue of combination re-occurs on the meta-level. There is not much that I can offer in the way of solid advice, other than the warning that it is harder than it looks to get all the details right.

It is too soon to draw any conclusions about the utility of Larch in software development. We have written a significant number of Larch Shared Language specifications. On the whole, we were pleased with the specifications, and with the ease of constructing them. While writing them, we uncovered several design errors by inspection; we are encouraged that many of these errors would have been uncovered by the checks called for in the language definition. However, until we have the tools that will allow us to gain experience with automated semantic checking, it is impossible to know just how helpful these checks will be.

We have not yet written any large specifications in Larch interface languages. Small examples seem to work out well. The Larch style of two-tiered specification leads to specifications that looks like they will "scale" well. We are presently in the process of documenting Larch/CLU, and are using it to write more substantial interface specifications. That experience should give us a much firmer basis for evaluating the Larch Shared Language, Larch/CLU, and—most importantly—the Larch style of specification.

Acknowledgements

The work that I have been describing was done in collaboration with John Guttag and his students at MIT—especially Randy Forgaard, Ron Kownacki, Jeannette Wing, and Joe Zachary. John's influence has been all-pervasive.

My ideas about formal specification have been shaped over the years by so many people that I hesitate to give an incomplete list. However, I am especially indebted to IFIP Working Group 2.3 (Programming Methodology), both for a continuing education and for being a constructively critical sounding board. I vividly recall getting key ideas during discussions with Jean-Raymond Abriel, Rod Burstall, Cliff Jones, Bill McKeeman, Doug Ross, Mary Shaw, Jim Thatcher, and Steve Zilles.

Jeannette Wing, Butler Lampson, and Soren Prehn have been especially helpful in improving the exposition.

The Larch Project has been supported at the Massachusetts Institute of Technology's Laboratory for Computer Science by DARPA under contract N00014-75-C-0661, and by the National Science Foundation under Grant MCS-811984 6, by the Digital Equipment Corporation at its Systems Research Center, and by the Xerox Corporation at its Palo Alto Research Center.

References

[ADJ 78] J. A. Goguen, J. W. Thatcher, and E. G. Wagner, "Initial Algebra Approach to the Specification, Correctness, and Implementation of Abstract Data Types," in R. T. Yeh (ed.), *Current Trends in Programming Methodology, Vol. IV, Data Structuring*, Prentice-Hall, Englewood Cliffs, 1978.

[Burstall and Goguen 77] R. M. Burstall and J. A. Goguen, "Putting Theories Together to Make Specifications," *Proc. 5th International Joint Conference on Artificial Intelligence*, Cambridge, MA, 1977, 1045–1058.

[Burstall and Goguen 81] — , "An Informal Introduction to Specifications Using CLEAR," in R. Boyer and J. Moore (eds.), *The Correctness Problem in Computer Science*, Academic Press, New York, 1981, 185–213.

[Forgaard 84] R. Forgaard, "A Program for Generating and Analyzing Term Rewriting Systems," S.M. Thesis, Laboratory for Computer Science, Massachusetts Institute of Technology, MIT/LCS/TR-99, 1984.

[Guttag 75] J. V. Guttag, "The Specification and Application to Programming of Abstract Data Types," Ph.D. Thesis, Computer Science Department, University of Toronto, 1975.

[Guttag and Horning 80] — and J. J. Horning, "Formal Specification as a Design Tool," *Proc. ACM Symposium on Principles of Programming Languages*, Las Vegas, Jan. 1980, 251–261.

[Guttag and Horning 83] — , "Preliminary Report on the Larch Shared Language," Technical Report MIT/LCS/TR-307 and Xerox PARC CSL-83-6, 1983.

[Guttag and Horning 85a] — , "Report on the Larch Shared Language," *Science of Computer Programming*, to appear.

[Guttag and Horning 85b] — , "A Larch Shared Language Handbook," *Science of Computer Programming*, to appear.

[Guttag and Horning 85c] — , "An Overview of the Larch Family of Specification Languages," in draft.

[Guttag, Horning, and Wing 82] — , and J. M. Wing, "Some Notes on Putting Formal Specifications to Productive Use," *Science of Computer Programming*, vol. 2, Dec. 1982, 53–68.

[Guttag, Horning, and Wing 85] — , "Preliminary Report on the Larch/CLU Interface Language," in draft.

[Hehner 84] E. C. R. Hehner, "Predicative Programming, Parts I and II," *Comm. ACM*, vol. 27, Feb. 1984, 134–151.

[Lescanne 83] P. Lescanne, "Computer Experiments with the REVE Term Rewriting System Generator," *Proc. ACM Symposium on Principles of Programming Languages*, Austin, Jan. 1983, 99–108.

[Musser 80] D. R. Musser, "Abstract Data Type Specification in the Affirm System," *IEEE Transactions on Software Engineering*, vol. 1, 1980, 24–32.

[Nyborg 84] *Proc. Workshop on Combining Specification Methods*, Nyborg, May 1984, Springer-Verlag.

[Wand 79] M. Wand, "Final Algebra Semantics and Data Type Extensions," *Journal of Computer and System Sciences*, vol. 19, 1979, 27–44.

[Wing 83] J. M. Wing, "A Two-Tiered Approach to Specifying Programs," Ph.D. Thesis, Laboratory for Computer Science, Massachusetts Institute of Technology, MIT/LCS/TR-299, May 1983.

THE ROLE OF PROOF OBLIGATIONS IN SOFTWARE DESIGN

Cliff B. Jones
Department of Computer Science
University of Manchester
Manchester, ENGLAND

Abstract

This paper presents certain "proof obligations" which can be used to establish the correctness of software design. The design of both sequential and parallel programs is considered. The position is taken that an understanding of formal results of this kind can aid practical software development.

Introduction

Other papers in this volume discuss the use of formal semantics in language design. The, so-called, "VDM" work in this area is discussed in [Bjorner 82] and a recent application is contained in [Welsh 84]. This paper is concerned with the use of "VDM" in the design of general software. It outlines a revision of the method proposed in [Jones 80] and some extensions to cope with parallelism.

The concluding section presents a position statement on the role of such formal methods in software design.

Functional Specification

The *functional specification* of a system must define the required input/output behaviour. For simple sequential operations, such specifications can be formalised by pre- and post-conditions written as logical expressions. More complex systems comprise a collection of operations. There are two contrasting ways of recording the specifications of such a collection. In the "property oriented" approach, the meaning of the operations is fixed by writing equations in terms of several operations. This approach appears to be well suited to basic data types such as lists.

In the alternative - "model oriented" - approach, each operation is defined in

terms of an underlying state. Such a state is chosen to capture the information
which is essential to a system. The state is normally defined in terms of basic
data types like sets and lists. There is an intuitive notion that certain states
are more abstract than others; this notion can be formalized so that it is possible
to prove that there is no *bias* towards certain implementations. (The paper by
Horning in this volume discusses the property and model oriented approaches.)

A simple function, which locates those indices of an Array (modelled here by a
map) which are mapped to elements satisfying 'p', can be specified by writing its
signature and pre- and post-conditions:

findp: map N to X → N
pre-findp(m) ≙ ∃i∈domm . p(m(i))
post-findp(m,r) ≙ r = mins({i∈domm | p(m(i))})

where:

mins: set of N → N
pre-mins(s) ≙ s ≠ {}
post-mins(s,r) ≙ r∈s ∧ ∀i∈s . r≤i

N set of natural numbers

Such specifications clearly show the assumptions on the arguments to functions
(pre-conditions). The post-conditions show the required relationship between
results and arguments. One advantage of such specifications can be seen in
'post-mins'. It is frequently clearer to write a specification by recording
separate (conjoined) properties. It is also possible to write a specification
which does not precisely characterize a result. For example:

post-findp(m,r) ≙ p(m(r))

would permit an implemntation to return any index – rather than the minimum – with
the required property. One view is that such specifications under-determine
implementations. With parallel programs, the implementations themselves can be
non-deterministic.

A proposed implementation of the 'findp' specification is written as a function
definition. If the implementation is correct, the following logical expression can
be proved to follow from the definitions:

∀ m ∈ map N to X . pre-findp(m) ⇒ post-findp(m,findp(m))

(The axiomatisation used is that of the "Logic of Partial Functions" described in
[Barringer 84a].)

The preceding sequent is a *proof obligation* which establishes that the function
definition *satisfies* the given specification. Clearly, it would be possible to
write "specifications" which are unimplementable. There is, therefore, a proof
obligation on the specification itself that it be *implementable*. In this case:

m ∈ map N to X, pre-findp(m) ⊢ ∃r∈N . post-findp(m,r)

The ideas on functions apply directly to operations which transform states. The
experience with writing large "VDM" specifications has, however, prompted a number
of abbreviations which make it easier to define the dependance on, and changes to,
the state. Each operation lists those parts of the state to which the operation
has *external* access; read only (rd) or read/write (wr) access is marked for each
component. The names of such state components are written in upper case letters;
the values are referred to in the logical expressions using lower case letters; in
post-conditions, the value prior to the operation is marked with a hook while the
final value is undecorated.

An operation 'FINDP' can be specified.

FINDP
ext rd M: Array
    wr R: N
pre true
post satp(m,r) ∧ ∀i∈{1,...,r-1} . ~p(m(i))

where:

satp(m,i) ≙ i≤N ⇒ p(m(i))

```
Array = map N to X
where
inv(m) ≙ dom m = {1,...,N}

p: X → B
N (∈ N) a given constant
```

Notice that the pre-condition needed on the function has, here, been obviated by allowing 'FINDP' to return a number greater than 'N'.

In this small example, where only one operation is being considered, the advantage of this notation may not be clear - the larger examples in [Jones 80] benefit from such notational conventions.

Sequential Design Steps

An implementation can be proved correct with respect to a formal specification. In the design of large programs, errors can be made early in the design process. Attempts to detect errors by test cases are known to be unreliable. Even if the construction of proofs were a good way of detecting errors, it would share with running test cases the defficiency that such late detection of errors can result in the need to replace work based on erroneous design decisions.

A development method would therefore provide greater benefit if it could be used to establish the correctness of early (high-level) design decisions before proceeding to more detailed design. This observation applies equally to formal and informal design methods. Techniques for "inspections" or "structured walkthroughs" aim to increase the chance of detecting any errors in early design decisions before design goes further.

If the assumptions about the more detailed design are recorded formally, a proof can be produced that the high-level design decision is correct. The consequence of the foregoing discussion is that a formal development method must satisfy the following *requirement*:

> If a design step introduces sub-problems, its correctness can be established solely in terms of their specifications.

This requirement is relatively easy to satisfy for sequential programs; the equivalent problem for parallel programs is less well understood.

A large specification might consist of an abstract state model and a number of operations. It is normally the case that the early steps of design involve refining, in one or more stages, the abstract state into data structures which can be easily represented in the implementation. One set of proof obligations for *data refinement* is built around the idea of providing a retrieve function (homomorphism) from the representation to the abstraction:

retr: Rep → Abs

The *adequacy* proof obligation concerns the states alone and establishes that there is at least one representation for each abstract state:

a∈Abs ⊢ ∃r∈Rep . a = retr(r)

Two proof obligations must be discharged for each operation. If the operations on the abstract state are 'OPAi' and those on the representation 'OPRi', the *domain* proof obligation is:

r∈Rep, pre-OPAi(retr(r)) ⊢ pre-OPRi(r)

The *result* proof obligation is:

$\overleftarrow{r}$,r∈Rep, pre-OPi(retr($\overleftarrow{r}$)), post-OPRi($\overleftarrow{r}$,r) ⊢ post-OPAi(retr($\overleftarrow{r}$),retr(r))

The requirement on development methods is satisfied since subsequent steps of design rely only on the representation and its operations.

Large examples of such data refinements are published elsewhere (e.g. [Fielding 80], [Jones 83b], [Bjorner 82], [Welsh 82]).

The process of data refinement brings the specification closer to an implementation, but post-conditions still define what has to be done rather than how to do it. *Operation decomposition* splits such implicitly specified operations into small steps. These smaller (sub-)operations may either be represented by specifications or be available operations of the implementation (hardware, language or other supporting software).

Proof obligations for operation decomposition must exist for each construct in a programming language. The original proof rules of [Hoare 69] concerned post-conditions of the final state alone; the first attempt in [Jones 80] to handle post-conditions of two states was unnecessarily clumsy; the more tractable proof obligations given in [Jones 83b] were suggested by Peter Aczel (cf.[Aczel 82]). These rules again satisfy the requirement on a development method: sub-components can be developed solely from their specifications and can ignore the context in which they are used.

A very simple example is to show that the sequential composition of 'INIT' and 'SEARCHES' satisfies the earlier specification of 'FINDP':

INIT
ext wr R: N
pre true
post r = N + 1

SEARCHES
ext rd M: Array
    wr R: N
pre satp(m,r)
post consid(m,r,Ind) ∧ satp(m,r)

where:

Ind = {1,...,N}
consid(m,i,s) ≙ ∀j∈s . p(m(j)) ⇒ i≤j

The sequential composition rule in this case does little more than check that the post-condition of 'INIT' establishes the pre-condition for 'SEARCHES'. A slightly more interesting example would be the decomposition of 'SEARCHES' into a loop. Examples of the use of these rules are given in [Jones 83a], [Jones 83b].

Parallel Decomposition Steps

The decomposition of operations into sub-operations which can execute in parallel must now be considered. The difficulty is to meet the development method requirement. Here, shared variable parallelism is considered. The first observation is that the pre-/post-condition form of specification is not rich enough. It is easy to construct examples where the behaviour of two operations running in parallel is not goverened by their separate post-conditions. The *interference* which the operations exert on each other influences the final result.

The research results reported in [Francez 78], [Lamport 80] and [Jones 81] each attempt to solve this problem by extending the notion of specification to capture some aspects of the interference. The last of these methods is described here. The approach proposed is to face the issue of interference throughout development; to reflect its existence in the specification; and to recognise that it must be checked at each design step.

Specifications of interfering operations are extended with assertions (rely-conditions), which express the assumptions that can be made about the interference which can be tolerated, and assertions (guarantee-conditions), which constrain the interference which may be caused. More precisley, a *rely-condition* is a predicate of two states which defines the relationship which can be assumed to exist between the external variables in states changed by other processes. Thus the implementor of an operation, although not able to assume that the implementation will run in isolation, knows some limit to the state changes which other processes can make. For example the rely-condition:

$$x = \overset{\leftarrow}{x}$$

expresses the assumption that the (value of the) external variable 'X' will not change; but:

$$t \leqslant \overset{\leftarrow}{t}$$

accepts the possibility of change but requires that 'T' never increases in value. The rely-condition:

$$x+y = \overset{\leftarrow}{x}+\overset{\leftarrow}{y}$$

requires that the sum of two values remains unchanged. (This example and the next imply some notion of indivisible operations in the implementation.) The role of a switch to control changes can be given in a rely-condition:

$$\overset{\leftarrow}{sw}=FULL \twoheadrightarrow buf=\overset{\leftarrow}{buf}$$

Rely-conditions, like pre-conditions, are recording assumptions for the implementation; the commitments (cf. post-conditions) relating to interference are recorded in *guarantee-conditions*. These are again predicates of two states which all state transformations must respect. The expessions above could occur in guarantee-conditions. A process which was to *coexist* with one whose rely-condition was as in the last equation, might have only read access to 'SW' and use:

$$\overleftarrow{sw}=EMPTY \rightarrow buf=\overleftarrow{buf}$$

as a guarantee-condition.

It is possible to think of a rely-condition, for say 'OP', as a post-condition of an operation which may be executed between any two atomic steps of 'OP'. The guarantee-condition can be thought of as the post-condition for the atomic steps of 'OP'. (Although this explanation refers to "atomic steps", the level of atomicity is not fixed.)

The *Sieve of Eratosthenes* is used as a first illustration of the extended specifications. The idea of using two parallel processes was proposed in [Hoare 75]. The solution is extended here to use more processes. The overall task can be achieved by storing the set of all integers between 2 and N in a variable and then invoking SIEVE:

S := {2,...,N}; SIEVE

SIEVE
ext wr S: set of N
rely s = $\overleftarrow{s}$
post s = s − U{mults(i) | i∈{2,...,sqrt(N)}}

mults(i) ≙ {i*m | m∈{2,...,N}}

Notice that interference on 'S' is excluded in the specification. Suppose 'SIEVE' is to be implemented by executing in parallel many instances of a process 'REM' — one instance for each 'I'. What should the specification of the 'REM' process be? The beginning is straightforward:

REM(I: N)
ext wr S: set of N

If the post-condition were:

$$s = \overleftarrow{s} - mults(i)$$

the overall post-condition would follow from the conjunction of those for each
'REM(I)'.   This would be acceptable if each instance of 'REM' were run in
isolation.   The equality sets an upper and lower bound on changes to 'S'.   This is
too restrictive in the case that other parallel interfering processes are changing
'S'.   ('REM(2)' might, for example, run at a time when 'REM(3)' removes the value
'9' from 'S'.)   The lower bound on the effect of 'REM' can be defined in the
post-condition:

$$\forall j \in mults(i) \ . \ j \notin s$$

However, the conjunction of such post-conditions will not yield the overall
post-condition.   The proof rule for realization by parallel processes is given
below (in a form suggested by Peter Aczel in [Aczel 83]).   The overall
post-condition can be a consequence of information about interference.   In this
case it is clear that for any state which can arise a value which has been removed
must be a multiple of one of the process indices.   Formally:

$$\forall c \in (\overleftarrow{s} - s) \ . \ \exists i \in \{2, \dots, N\} \ . \ c \in mults(i)$$

Since the states which can arise are all created by the steps of the instances of
'REM', this must follow from the transitive closure of the guarantee-condition for
'REM'.   Thus the guarantee-condition must include:

$$\forall c \in (\overleftarrow{s} - s) \ . \ c \in mults(i)$$

Another way to see the need for this guarantee-condition is to observe that the
post-condition would be satisfied by a process which set 'S' to the empty set!

Furthermore, the 'REM' process can only ensure that elements will not be in the
final value of 'S' if no other (interfering) process can reinsert values   (e.g.
'REM(2)' will remove the value '6' once - if 'REM(3)' were to reinsert the value,
the post-condition would not be satisfied).   Thus a rely-condition of:

$$s \subseteq \overleftarrow{s}$$

is required.   Since multiple instances of 'REM' will run in parallel, this must
also be conjoined to the guarantee-condition.   Thus the overall specification for
'REM' becomes:

```
REM(I: N)
ext wr S: set of N
pre true
rely s ⊆ ̄s
quar s⊆̄s ∧ ∀c∈(̄s-s) . c∈mults(i)
post ∀j∈mults(i) . j∉s
```

Returning to the 'FINDP' problem, the overall specification might have rely-and guarantee-conditions:

```
rely m=m̄ ∧ r=r̄
quar true
```

The operations 'INIT' and 'SEARCHES' require similar, trivial, extensions. The extended form of the sequential proof rules is given in [Barringer 84b].

Suppose that 'SEARCHES' is now to be implemented by the parallel execution of 'T' processes 'SEARCHi' (for i∈{1,...,T}) where each such process is responsible for checking a set of indices given in a map:

```
GS: map {1,...,T} to (set of Ind)
```

The each 'SEARCHi' process is specified:

```
SEARCHi
ext rd M: Array
    wr R: N
pre true
rely m | gs(i) = m̄ | gs(i) ∧ r ⩽ r̄
quar r≠r̄ ⇒ r<r̄ ∧ satp(m,r)
post consid(m,r,gs(i))
```

where the map restriction operator yields that portion of a map whose domain is in the set:

```
m | s = [d ↦ m(s) | d∈(dom m ∩ s)]
```

A specification now consists of four predicates:

P   pre—condition of one state

R   rely—condition of two states

G   guarantee—condition of two states

Q   post—condition of two states

The proof rule for the decomposition to two parallel processes is:

S1 __sat__ $(P,R \lor G2,G1,Q1)$,

S2 __sat__ $(P,R \lor G1,G2,Q2)$

$(S1 \mid\mid S2)$ __sat__ $(P,R,G1 \lor G2,Q1 \land Q2 \land (R \lor G1 \lor G2)^*)$

The generalisation to 'n' processes is:

$\&_i(Si$ __sat__ $(P,R \lor \lor_j G_j,G_i,Q_i))$ $i \neq j$

$(\mid\mid Si)$ __sat__ $(P,R,\lor_i G_i,\&_i Q_i \land (R \lor \lor_i G_i)^*)$

where $\&_i / \lor_i$ are generalised (finite) conjuctions and disjunctions.

To show that the parallel decomposition of 'SEARCHES' is correct, a number of proof obligations must be discharged.

$\&_i(pre\text{-}SEARCHES \rightarrow pre\text{-}SEARCH_i)$

is vacuously true;

$\&_i(rely\text{-}SEARCHES \lor \lor_j guar\text{-}SEARCH_j \rightarrow rely\text{-}SEARCH_i)$

is straightforward;

$\lor_i(guar\text{-}SEARCH_i) \rightarrow guar\text{-}SEARCHES$

is vacuously true;

$pre\text{-}SEARCHES \land (\&_i post\text{-}SEARCH_i) \land$
      $(rely\text{-}SEARCHES \lor \lor_i guar\text{-}SEARCH_i)^* \rightarrow post\text{-}SEARCHES$

requires:

$$satp(\overleftarrow{m},\overleftarrow{r}) \wedge \&_i \; consid(m,r,gs(i)) \wedge m\overleftarrow{=}\overleftarrow{m} \wedge r\overleftarrow{\neq}\overleftarrow{r} \twoheadrightarrow satp(m,r) \twoheadrightarrow$$
$$consid(m,r,Ind) \wedge satp(m,r)$$

which follows provided that the distributed union of the range of 'GS' is equal to 'Ind'.

In [Owicki 76] a parallel implementation of this problem is given using one process each for the odd and even indices. In [Jones 83c] it is shown how this can be developed from the 'SEARCHi' specification. (Basically by a specialization to two processes and a data refinement of 'R' onto an expression.) The key requirement of a development method is again met in that it is not necessary to reconsider the earlier stages of design. (The same paper discusses a maximal parallel solution with one process per index.)

The method outlined above illustrates that it might be possible to find a way of developing interfering programs which meets the requirement. The expressiveness of the rely-/guarantee-conditions is, however, inadequate for many problems. Recent research (e.g. [Lamport 83], [Barringer 84], [Barringer 85] – for overview see [de Roever 85]) has moved to using Temporal Logic. This author has some hesitation in following this step! It must be realized that even the sequential rules discuss the temporal changes to states. The contribution of the Naur/Floyd/Hoare techniques is that the proof obligations themselves hide this fact. The rely/guarantee idea was an attempt to regain this situation in spite of the more complex environment. The next step should be work on a number of examples using such temporal rules (e.g. [Sa 84]); if patterns of specification and proof can be isolated, perhaps we can again confine temporal arguments to the justification of proof rules which then do not use temporal logic. (A general overview of approaches to parallelism is given in [Barringer 84b].)

Position

These advanced seminars are considering the relevance of formal methods in software development. This section contains a number of *claims* which indicate this author's position.

1. Formal specifications tend to focus on the functional apsects of systems – questions like the need for a system are not normally considered. (The separation

of performance issues should not cause surprise.)

2. Formal specifications have been written for (the functional apsects) of significant software, and hardware, systems.

3. There is a need to develop techniques to aid checking that the specifications of large systems meet the user's intentions.

4. A specific area where formal specification is, at the moment, less helpful (than simulation) is so-called "Man-Machine Interfaces". (Some work in this are is reported in this conference - [Marshall 85].)

5. A formal specification can provide a precise and (relatively) concise model of a system prior to construction. Such a specification can both deepen understanding of the intended system and provide a correctness criteria for implementation (and design).

6. The skills required to write such specifications are not yet widely available - education is likely to be the limiting factor in the use of formal methods.

7. Support tools (cf. [Madhavji 85], [Snelting 85] in this conference) are required - there is a danger that such tools could force "mathematics as a specification language" to develop into Ada-like syntactic quagmires.

8. Formal development methods focus on correctness issues and leave somewhat aside the intuitive aspects of how to choose a good design (cf. [Naur 85]).

9. Application of formal methods to the early steps of design can reduce the possibility of undetected errors - it is these errors which damage the "productivity" of the program design process.

10. The decision as to the appropriate degree of formality to be used in design verification is difficult. It is, as yet, unrealistic to use completely formal (machine checked) proofs for large systems. It would appear that the earlier stages warrant more formal treatment than the later ones. A crucial step towards greater machine support would be the development of "theories" about commonly used data structures.

11. Formal methods will certainly not solve all problems concerned with

software development. It is, however, a valid research area.

12. Experiments are needed to improve the ease of access and style of formal documents. Perhaps some of the research effort which appears to develop mathematics for its own sake could benefit from more application to actual computing problems.

13. Formal methods, even in their evolving state, have a contribution to make to current problems (see reports from industry at this conference).

References

[Aczel 82] **A Note on Program Verification**, P.Aczel, *manuscript*, January 1982.

[Aczel 83] **On an Inference Rule for Parallel Composition**, P.Aczel, *manuscript*, February 1983.

[Barringer 84] **Now You May Compose Temporal Logic Specifications**, H.Barringer, R.Kuiper and A. Pnueli, *Procs. of 16th ACM Symposium on Theory of Computing*, May 1984.

[Barringer 84a] **A Logic Covering Undefinedness in Program Proofs**, H. Barringer, J.H. Cheng and C.B. Jones, ACTA *Informatica*, Vol 21 Part 3, pp251-269, 1984.

[Barringer 84b] **A Survey of Verification Techniques for Parallel Programs**, H.Barringer, *to be published, LNCS, Springer-Verlag*.

[Barringer 85] **A Compositional Temporal Approach to a CSP-Like Language**, H.Barringer, R.Kuiper and A.Pnueli, *IFIP Working Conference on "The Role of Abstract Model in Information Processing"*, Vienna, January 30th - February 1st, 1985.

[Bjorner 82] **Formal Specification and Software Development**, D.Bjorner and C.B.Jones, *Prentice-Hall International*, 1982.

[Fielding 80] **The Specification of Abstract Mappings and their Implementation as** B^+**-Trees**, E. Fielding, *Oxford University, Monograph PRG-18*, 1980.

[Francez 78] **A Proof Method for Cyclic Programs**, N.Francez and A.Pnueli, *ACTA Inf.* Vol 9 No 2, pp133-157, April 1978.

[Hoare 69] **An Axiomatic Basis of Computer Programming**, C.A.R.Hoare, *CACM*

[Hoare 75] **Parallel Programming: An Axiomatic Approach**, C.A.R.Hoare, *In Computer Langs, Permagon Press*, Vol 1, pp 151-160.

[Jones 80] **Software Development: A Rigorous Approach**, C.B. Jones, *Prentice-Hall International*, 400 pages, 1980.

[Jones 81] **Development Methods for Computer Program Including a Notion of Interference**, C.B.Jones, *Oxford University, Monograph PRG 25*, June 1981.

[Jones 83a] **Specification and Design of (Parallel) Programs**, C.B.Jones, *(invited* paper), *IFIP 1983, Paris, North-Holland*, pp 321 — 332, September 1983.

[Jones 83b] **Systematic Program Development**, C.B.Jones, *Symposium 'Wiskunde en Informatica', Amsterdam, to be published in the Mathematical Centre Tracts*.

[Jones 83c] **Tentative Steps Toward a Development Method for Interfering Programs**, C.B.Jones *ACM Trans. Program. Lang. Syst.*, <u>Vol 5 No4</u>, pp 596 — 619, October 1983.

[Lamport 80] **The "Hoare Logic" of Concurrent Programs**, L.Lamport, *Acta Inf.*, <u>vol 14 no 1</u>, pp21-37, June 1980.

[Lamport 83] **What Good Is Temporal Logic?**, L. Lamport, *North-Holland, Proc. of the IFIP 9th World Computer Congress, Paris*, pages 657–668, 1983.

[Marshall 85] **A Formal Specification of Line Representations on Graphics Devices**, L.S.Marshall, *TAPSOFT Joint Conference on Theory and Practice of Software Development*, Berlin, March 1985.

[Madhavji 85] **Software Construction Using Typed Fragments**, N.H.Madhavji, N.Leoutsarakos, D Vouliouris, *TAPSOFT Joint Conference on Theory and Practice of Software Development*, Berlin, March 1985.

[Naur 85] **Intuition in Software Development**, P. Naur, *TAPSOFT Joint Conference on Theory and Practice of Software Development*, Berlin, March 1985.

[Owicki 76] **Verifying Properties of Parallel Programs: An Axiomatic Approach**, S.S.Owicki and D.Gries, *Comm. ACM*, <u>Vol 19 No 5</u>, pp 279–285.

[de Roever 85] **The Quest for Compositionality — a Survey of Assertion-based Proof Systems for Concurrent Programs**, W.P.de Roever, *IFIP Working Conference on "The Role of Abstract Models in Information Processing"*, Vienna, January 30th — February 1st., 1985.

[Sa 84] **Temporal Logic Specifications of Communication Protocals**, J.Sa, *Manchester University*, 1984.

[Snelting 85] **Experiences with the PSG-Programming System Generator**, G.Snelting, *TAPSOFT Joint Conference on Theory and Practice of Software Development*, Berlin, March 1985.

[Welsh 82] **The Specification, Design and Implementation of NDB**, A. Welsh, *M.Sc. Thesis, Manchester University*, October 1982.

[Welsh 84] **A Database Programming Language: Definition, Implementation and Correctness Proofs**, A. Welsh, *Ph.D. thesis, Manchester University*, October 1984.

FUNCTIONAL SEMANTICS OF MODULES

John Gannon
University of Maryland

Richard Hamlet
Oregon Graduate Center

Harlan Mills
University of Maryland

October, 1984

Abstract

Because large-scale software development is a struggle against internal program
complexity, the modules into which programs are divided play a central role in software
engineering. A module encapsulating a data type allows the programmer to ignore both the
details of its operations, and of its value representations. It is a primary strength of
program proving that as modules divide a program, making it easier to understand, so do
they divide its proof. Each module can be verified in isolation, then its internal details
ignored in a proof of its use. This paper describes proofs of module abstractions based on
the functional semantics, and contrasts this with the Alphard formalism based on Hoare
logic.

Authors' addresses: Dr. Hamlet, Department of Computer Science, Oregon Graduate
Center, Beaverton, OR 97006; Drs. Gannon and Mills, Department of Computer Science,
University of Maryland, College Park, MD 20742. Research of Drs. Gannon and Hamlet
was partially supported by the Air Force Office of Scientific Research under contract
F49620-80-C-0004.

1. Introduction

Modules that encapsulate complex data types are perhaps the most important sequential programming-language idea to emerge since the design of ALGOL 60. Such a module serves two purposes. First, in its abstraction role, it allows the programmer to ignore the details of operations (procedural abstraction) and value representations (data abstraction) in favor of a concise description of their meaning. Second, encapsulation is a protection mechanism isolating changes in one module from the rest of a program. The first role helps people to think about what they are doing; the second allows program changes to be reliably made with limited effort.

Modules have their source in practical programming languages beginning with SIMULA [1], and their theory has developed in two directions, based on program proving by Hoare [2], Wulf, London, Shaw [3] and others; and on many-sorted algebras by Guttag [4], Goguen, Thatcher, Wagner, Wright [5] and others. This paper reports on a new proving theory using functional semantics [6].

The essence of data-abstraction is captured by a diagram showing the relationship between a *concrete* world, the objects manipulated directly by a conventional programming language, and an *abstract* world, objects that the programmer chooses to think about instead of the more detailed program objects. Within each world, the items of interest are mappings among the objects. The two worlds are connected by a *representation* function that maps from concrete to abstract.

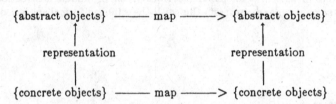

A data-abstraction theory must define *correctness*, intuitively the property that the concrete maps programmed do properly mirror the abstract maps in our minds. A theory following Hoare's example also defines a *proof method*, a means of establishing the correctness of any particular module.

2. Functional Semantics of Modules

A *denotational* or *functional semantics* associates a meaning with certain fragments of a program. Denotational definitions are mathematically precise, but do not always obviously capture the intuitive meaning of programs. In this paper we do not demonstrate that our denotational definitions agree with operational intuition, although that argument can be given [7]. We treat only a subset of Pascal needed for the example of Section 4.

The most fundamental meaning function is the *state*, mapping program identifiers to their value sets. This function may be undefined when an identifier has no value; the situation can arise for syntactically correct programs only in the execution interval

/ between declaration and assignment of the first value.

Expressions have as meaning mappings from states to values. The meaning of an integer constant in state S is the (mathematical) integer whose representation in base 10 the constant is (as a string). The meaning of an identifier V in state S is its value, that is, S(V). On this base the meaning of integer expressions can be defined inductively. If the expression is X + Y, then in state S its value is the value of X in state S plus (integer addition) the value of Y in state S. It is convenient to have a notation for meaning functions, and we adopt a convention similar to one used by Kleene: the meaning function corresponding to a programming object is denoted by a box around that object. Using this notation, we have

$\boxed{c}$ for integer constant c is the constant function for which c represents the base-10 value.

$\boxed{V}$ (S) = S(V) for identifier V and state S.

$\boxed{X + Y}$ (S) = $\boxed{X}$ (S) + $\boxed{Y}$ (S)

(and similarly for subtraction, multiplication, and integer division).

For Boolean expressions it is almost the same. For example,

$\boxed{X > Y}$ (S) is *true* iff $\boxed{X}$ (S) > $\boxed{Y}$ (S) and *false* iff $\boxed{X}$ (S) ≤ $\boxed{Y}$ (S).

Since it is possible for the value functions on identifiers to be undefined, expression functions may inherit this property.

This inductive definition hides the parsing that must actually be done to assign a meaning function to an expression. In an expression with more than one operation, the operator precedence must be followed in applying the definition. The use of the mathematical operations in these definitions ignores the possibility of overflow. A precise definition could be given for any particular Pascal implementation, but it would complicate our proofs.

Program statements are given meanings of state-to-state mappings. The meaning of assignment

$V := E$

is

$\boxed{V := E}$ = {(S, T): T = S except that $\boxed{V}$ (T) = $\boxed{E}$ (S)}.

The meanings of other program constructions are inductively defined; for example

$$\boxed{\text{BEGIN } A;\ B \text{ END}} = \boxed{A} \circ \boxed{B}\ ,$$

where o is functional composition, written in the order the functions are applied. (Again, the parsing necessary to isolate the compound statement is ignored.)

A more complex example is

$$\boxed{\text{IF } B \text{ THEN } S} = \{(u, \boxed{S}(u)): \boxed{B}(u)\} \cup \{(u, u): \neg\, \boxed{B}(u)\}$$

for the conditional statement with Boolean expression B and nested statement S.

The loop has a less obvious definition:

$$\boxed{\text{WHILE } B \text{ DO } D} = \{(T, U): \exists\, k \geq 0, \text{ such that } \forall\, 0 \leq i < k$$
$$(\boxed{B}(\boxed{D}^{\,i}(T)) \wedge \neg\, \boxed{B}(\boxed{D}^{\,k}(T)) \wedge \boxed{D}^{\,k}(T) = U)\}.$$

In words, the loop function is undefined for state S unless there is a natural number k (the number of times the loop body is executed) for which the test fails for the first time following k iterations. Then S is transformed to the k-fold composition of $\boxed{D}$ on S. This definition is not constructive, so a characterizing theorem is needed to allow practical proofs to be carried out. It is:

THEOREM (WHILE statement Verification): Let W be the program fragment

> WHILE B DO D.

Then

$$f = \boxed{W}$$

if and only if:

1. domain(f) $\subseteq$ domain($\boxed{W}$)
2. $f(T) = T$ whenever $\neg\, \boxed{B}(T)$
3. $f = \boxed{\text{IF } B \text{ THEN } D} \circ f$.

(The proof is given in [7].)

This theorem implies a proof method for loop W as follows: First, guess or work out a trial function f, say by reading program documentation, or by examining representative symbolic executions of W. (f would be already given if W is the code that implements a stepwise refinement of a design.) Then use the three conditions of the if-part of the theorem to check that the trial function is correct.

A comparison between this method and that of Floyd/Hoare is revealing. The function f corresponds to the Floyd/Hoare loop assertion, but unlike an assertion, it must be exact, it cannot merely be sufficiently strong to capture necessary properties of the loop. This is both the strength and weakness of the functional method, because exact functions are sometimes easier to find and state than assertions, yet sometimes much harder to work with than the weak assertions that suffice for strong initial conditions of the loop.

The definition of statement meaning culminates with the procedure-call statement: the meaning function of a call is the function for the declared body, after textual substitutions (based on the ALGOL 60 copy rule) have been made to accommodate parameters and identifier conflicts. When there is one VAR parameter X in the declaration of procedure P, whose body is T, the meaning of a call on P passing parameter A is:

$$\boxed{P(A)} = \boxed{T \leftarrow A \backslash X}$$

where $T \leftarrow A \backslash X$ means that each occurrence of X in T is replaced by A. Students of ALGOL 60 will recognize the semantics of call-by-name; in the absence of arrays this is the same as Pascal's strict call-by-reference. A similar copy-rule substitution can be used to define the meaning of call-by-value parameters. This definition hides a great deal of parsing: to find the meaning of P(A) actually requires locating the definition

PROCEDURE P (VAR X: ...)

and extracting the declared body.

In practice it is convenient to calculate the meaning of a procedure in terms of its formal parameter, and for each call later substitute the actual parameter identifier. That is, to calculate $\boxed{P(A)} = \boxed{T \leftarrow A \backslash X}$ instead calculate $\boxed{T} \leftarrow A \backslash X$.

The definition assumes there are no conflicts between local and global identifiers; its generalization to multiple parameters is straightforward if there is no aliasing. Each restriction imposed for simplicity can be lifted (and call-by-value parameters handled) in this theory, in contrast to the Floyd/Hoare theory. When there is recursion, the definition leads to a fixed-point equation whose least solution is the defined meaning, and a theorem similar to the WHILE verification theorem is needed for practical proofs [7].

The meaning function for a procedure call gives precise form to the concrete portion of the diagram for a data abstraction. The concrete objects are states, and the concrete mapping is the meaning function for a procedure call. The abstract level is more difficult to capture. Its objects and transformations are mental constructions, things a programmer finds convenient to think about. A mathematical theory is seldom available to describe them. There are, however, well defined identifiers and states in the abstract world, formed using type identifiers in place of their component identifiers. The final element in the picture is the correspondence between a typical concrete object and its abstract counterpart, the representation function. This mapping is often many-to-one, because the concrete realization is not unique.

In the data-abstraction diagram:

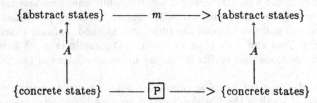

the abstract mapping is m, the representation mapping is A, and the concrete mapping is the meaning of some procedure P. We say that the diagram *commutes* iff beginning in the lower left corner and passing in both possible directions always gives the same result, that is $A \; o \; m = \boxed{P} \; o \; A$.

3. Proof Method

When using a module, a programmer begins with objects that are not of the module's type. These may have come from the external world, or may have been created internally. They cannot be of the module's type because details of the representation are the module's secret. What the programmer possesses is raw information necessary to construct a value of the module type, and the first call on a module is therefore a conversion call: the calling program passes the component information, and within the module it is placed in the secret internal form. Succeeding invocations of the module make use of the value thus stored, transforming it according to the operations defined within the module. Finally, the transformed value must again be communicated to the world outside the module, converted back to externally usable form. The process is a familiar one: from the very beginning programming languages have had secret representations for integers, reals, characters, etc., and compilers have performed conversions from external to internal forms and back.

For example, in a module implementing complex numbers, the raw data might take the form of two REAL values, one for magnitude and the other for angle. The COMPLEX module's input conversion routine would have a declaration like

    PROCEDURE InComplex(Mag, Ang: REAL; VAR Val: COMPLEX)

and a programmer might begin by reading in the pair of REAL values, or by creating them (e.g., for the constant i with:

    InComplex(1.0, pi/2, Eye)

to place the result in the variable Eye). Similarly, a routine declared

    PROCEDURE OutComplex(VAR Mag, Ang: REAL; Val: COMPLEX)

would be called to obtain answers, while ones like

```
PROCEDURE AddComplex(A, B: COMPLEX; VAR Result: COMPLEX)
```

would implement operations of the type. Of course, if the implementor chose the radix form for complex numbers internally, the code for `InComplex` and `OutComplex` would be trivial; however, if there is a great deal of addition and not much conversion, an implementation using real and imaginary parts would be better, and in that case these routines make actual conversions.

In any application of a module, its users will reason about its actions "in the abstract." That is, they will imagine it performing a mapping involving objects that do not really exist, those of the intuitive type it implements. For example in `COMPLEX`, they will think of `AddComplex` as performing the mathematical operation of complex addition, etc. Here the input- and output-conversion operations have a special role: they are thought of as maps between the built-in language values and the intuitive values of the type being defined. Thus

```
InComplex(1.0, p1/2, Eye)
```

intuitively gives `Eye` the value $1.0 \times e^{i\pi/2} = i$. The reasoning represented by this equality is an example of "in the abstract:" it in no way depends on the implementation of the module, only on mathematical properties of complex numbers.

The objects whose values are the raw data from which type values can be constructed, exist in the concrete world, which for these objects is also the abstract world. That is, the representation function for such objects is required to be identity. If the abstract function for the input conversion of `COMPLEX` is C, the diagram is

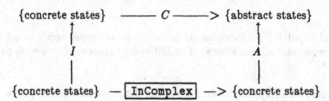

showing identity on the left instead of the representation mapping. Or, the left side could be collapsed to identify the two worlds, producing a triangular diagram. Here for example:

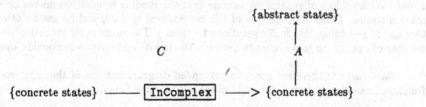

Thus the programmer has in mind abstract functions for each operation of a module. These map between values of the module's type, and other values that may be built in, or defined by other modules. In reasoning about the program using a module, the programmer will employ these abstract functions. Intuitively, the module implementation is correct if and only if such reasoning is safe. In terms of the operation diagrams, a sequence of operations is thought of on the top: beginning with a triangular diagram whose left side does not involve objects of the module's type T, an object of type T is created by the abstract operation InT, then used by abstract operations m_1T, m_2T, ... and finally converted back to known values by (another triangular diagram) OutT. The abstract view of this sequence of diagrams is that abstract (non-module) values are transformed to other abstract values by the function

$$\text{InT } o \text{ } m_1T \text{ } o \text{ } m_2T \text{ } o \text{ ... } o \text{ OutT}$$

with the intermediate values being the abstract ones of the module's type.

Of course, the actual calculation proceeds across the bottom of the diagrams. The implementation begins with values and successively transforms them, at no time leaving the built-in types of the language. If the procedures for the example functions above are PInT, Pm1, Pm2, ..., POutT, the actual function computed in the sequence is

$$\boxed{\text{PInT}} \text{ } o \boxed{\text{Pm1}} \text{ } o \boxed{\text{Pm2}} \text{ } o \text{ ... } o \boxed{\text{POutT}} \text{ .}$$

Correctness then means that any extended diagram, a sequence with triangular diagrams at the extremes, commutes. That is, in the general example above,

$$\text{InT } o \text{ } m_1T \text{ } o \text{ } m_2T \text{ } o \text{ ... } o \text{ OutT} = \boxed{\text{PInT}} \text{ } o \boxed{\text{Pm1}} \text{ } o \boxed{\text{Pm2}} \text{ } o \text{ ... } o \boxed{\text{POutT}} \text{ .}$$

The strange feature of this defining equation is that the representation function does not appear!

To be useful in software development, however, proofs must apply to operations in isolation, not to sequences of operations. The following theorem allows such proofs to be given.

THEOREM. A module's implementation is correct if there is a representation function A such that each operation's diagram commutes using A, and A is the identity I on built-in types.

Proof. Without loss of generality, assume that the module in question makes no use of other modules. (This must be true of the lowest-level module, and its use by others can be thought of as adding "hidden" operations to them.) The proof is by induction on the number of operations in a sequence between the input- and output-conversion operations.

Base case. If there are none, the extended diagram consists of the input-conversion function immediately followed by the output-conversion function:

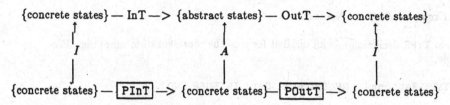

In the notation above, we must show that

$$\mathrm{InT} \; o \; \mathrm{OutT} = \boxed{\mathrm{PInT}} \; o \; \boxed{\mathrm{POutT}} \; .$$

Suppose it were not so, for the point x, i.e.,

$$\mathrm{OutT}(\mathrm{InT}(x)) \neq \boxed{\mathrm{POutT}} \; (\; \boxed{\mathrm{PInT}} \; (x)).$$

The diagram for the input-conversion function commutes, and a special case is

$$\mathrm{InT}(x) = \mathrm{A}(\boxed{\mathrm{PInT}} \; (x)),$$

which substituted on the left side above gives:

$$\mathrm{OutT}(\mathrm{A}(\boxed{\mathrm{PInT}} \; (x))) \neq \boxed{\mathrm{POutT}} \; (\; \boxed{\mathrm{PInT}} \; (x)).$$

That is, there exists a y $= \boxed{\mathrm{PInT}}$ (x) such that

$$\mathrm{OutT}(\mathrm{A}(y)) \neq \boxed{\mathrm{POutT}} \; (y).$$

But this violates the assumption that the diagram for the output-conversion function commutes. Hence the two diagrams commuting imply that the extended diagram commutes, as required.

Induction step. Suppose then that for all diagrams with less than k > 0 operations between input and output conversions, the component diagrams commuting implies that the overall diagram commutes. Consider a diagram with k operations between conversions. Reasoning similar to that used in the base case shows that if the extended diagram fails for some point x, then the diagram formed by stripping off its last operation would also fail for x. But that contradicts the inductive hypothesis. QED.

The verification of a module may therefore be accomplished in isolation by selecting a proper representation function, calculating the meaning of each procedure, and then showing that each operation's diagram commutes for the intended abstract function, calculated meaning, and chosen representation function.

4. An Example: Rational Numbers

A Pascal **TYPE** declaration is an implicit form of the representation mapping. For example,

    TYPE Rational = RECORD Num, Den: INTEGER END

suggests the abstract world of *rational numbers*, where concrete states contain pairs of integer values (N, D), and the corresponding rational value is the fraction with numerator N and denominator D, defined only if N and $D \neq 0$ are defined. The representation mapping A_{rat} from concrete state S to abstract state T is thus

$A_{rat} = \{(S,T): x.\text{Den} \neq 0$ and $T = S$ except that identifiers of the form $x.\text{Num}$ and $x.\text{Den}$ are replaced by x, with the corresponding rational value$\}$.

The procedure **ExpRat** given below is intended to raise a rational number R to the power N. The comment describes this intention in the abstract ("abs") and concrete ("con") worlds. The comment notation combines concurrent assignments with alternative relational guards to describe functions in the syntax of programs. For example, the "abs" part would be more conventionally expressed:

$\text{ExpRat}_{abs} =$
$\{(S, T): \boxed{N} (S) \geq 1 \wedge T = S$ except that $\boxed{R} (T) = \boxed{R} (S) \overset{\boxed{N}}{} (S)\}$
$\cup \{(S, S): \boxed{N} (S) < 1\}$.

Similarly, the "con" comment describes $\boxed{\text{ExpRat}}$.

```
PROCEDURE ExpRat(VAR R: Rational; N: INTEGER);
 {abs: (N>=1 --> <R> := <R**N>) | (N<1 --> < > := < >)
  con: (N>=1 --> <R.Num, R.Den> := <R.Num**N, R.Den**N>) |
      (N<1 --> < > := < >) }
 VAR
  T: Rational;
  I: INTEGER;
 BEGIN {ExpRat}
  T.Num := R.Num; T.Den := R.Den;
  I := 1;
  WHILE I < N
  DO
   BEGIN
    I := I + 1;
    T.Num := T.Num * R.Num;
    T.Den := T.Den * R.Den
   END;
  R.Num := T.Num; R.Den := T.Den
 END  {ExpRat}
```

To demonstrate the correctness of this procedure, we must calculate $\boxed{\text{ExpRat}}$ (see Appendix), and prove that the following diagram commutes:

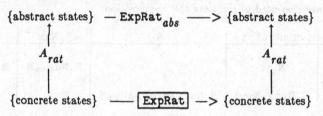

That is:

$$A_{rat} \circ \text{ExpRat}_{abs} = \boxed{\text{ExpRat}} \circ A_{rat}.$$

The composition of A_{rat} with ExpRat_{abs} is:

$$(R.Den \neq 0 \rightarrow <R> := <R.Num/R.Den>) \circ$$
$$((N \geq 1 \rightarrow <R> := <R**N>) | (N < 1 \rightarrow < > := < >))$$

The *trace table* [8] is a device for organizing the calculation of program meanings, particularly useful when there are many cases introduced by conditional statements. It is essentially a symbolic execution of the program. Two trace tables, corresponding to the two cases of ExpRat_{abs}, are used to compute the composition:

part	condition	R	R.Num	R.Den
A_{rat}	R.Den$\neq$0	R.Num/R.Den		
ExpRat$_{abs}$	N $\geq$ 1	(R.Num/R.Den)$_{**}$N		

part	condition	R	R.Num	R.Den
A_{rat}	R.Den$\neq$0	R.Num/R.Den		
ExpRat$_{abs}$	N < 1			

The resulting function is:

$$(\text{R.Den}\neq0 \text{ AND } N\geq1 \rightarrow <R> := < (\text{R.Num/R.Den})_{**}N >) \mid$$
$$(\text{R.Den}\neq0 \text{ AND } N<1 \rightarrow < > := < >)$$

The composition of ExpRat with A_{rat} is:

$$((N\geq1 \rightarrow <\text{R.Num, R.Den}> := <\text{R.Num}_{**}N, \text{R.Den}_{**}N>) \mid$$
$$(N<1 \rightarrow < > := < >)) \; o \; (\text{R.Den} \neq 0 \rightarrow <R> := <\text{R.Num/R.Den}>)$$

Two trace tables are also used to compute this composition:

part	condition	R	R.Num	R.Den
ExpRat	N$\geq$1		R.Num$_{**}$N	R.Den$_{**}$N
A_{rat}	R.Den$_{**}$N$\neq$0	R.Num$_{**}$N/R.Den$_{**}$N		

Since R.Den$_{**}$N$\neq$0 implies R.Den$\neq$0, this part of the composition can be rewritten as:

$$N\geq1 \text{ AND R.Den}\neq0 \rightarrow <R> := < \text{R.Num}_{**}N/\text{R.Den}_{**}N >$$

Turning to the second case, we have the following table:

part	condition	R	R.Num	R.Den
ExpRat	N<1			
A_{rat}	R.Den$\neq$0	R.Num/R.Den		

Thus the result of the second function composition is:

$$(N\geq1 \text{ AND R.Den}\neq0 \rightarrow <R> := < \text{R.Num}_{**}N/\text{R.Den}_{**}N >) \mid$$
$$(N<1 \text{ AND R.Den}\neq0 \rightarrow <R> := < \text{R.Num/R.Den} >)$$

which is identical to the first composition. Hence the diagram commutes, and ExpRat is correct.

5. Comparison with Related Work

Just as the functional method of program proof is close in spirit to the Floyd/Hoare method, so the treatment of modules given here is little more than the application of denotational-semantic definitions to Hoare's initial formalization of SIMULA classes. However, we believe that the choice of the concrete and abstract domains as sets of *states* containing variables connected by the representation mapping is an improvement over the Alphard methodology that is also based on Hoare's work. The states allow the representation to include not only the value correspondence, but an identifier correspondence as well. When a data abstraction is used, the calls on its operations occur in states that include the abstract variables, and our proof method allows the abstract function whose correctness has been established by the proof of a module to be used directly in such a state.

In the Alphard methodology things do not work quite so well. For example, consider the procedure **ExpRat** proved in Section 3. In Alphard terms, its abstract pre- and postconditions would be

$$\beta_{pre} \equiv R = R' \quad \text{and} \quad \beta_{post} \equiv R = R' \mathrel{**} N$$

where the ghost variable R' has been introduced to represent the initial value of the parameter. The concrete input and output assertions are similarly:

$$\beta_{in} \equiv R.Num = R.Num' \bigwedge R.Den = R.Den'$$
$$\beta_{out} \equiv R.Num = R.Num' \mathrel{**} N \bigwedge R.Den = R.Den' \mathrel{**} N$$

with ghost variables $R.Num'$ and $R.Den'$. Proof of a usage requires

$$C(x) \bigwedge \beta_{pre}(A(x)) \supset \beta_{in}(x)$$

where C is the concrete invariant and A the representation function. With the invariant $R.Den \neq 0$ this is

$$R.Den \neq 0 \bigwedge R = R' \supset R.Num = R.Num' \bigwedge R.Den = R.Den'$$

which cannot be proved, since the concrete representation is not unique. Nor can the invariant be strengthened to allow the proof. The trouble is that the correspondence between abstract and concrete state is not precise enough to pull implications about the latter from facts about the former.

In expression-based (functional) programming languages, values do not necessarily require names. But assignment-based (procedural) languages manipulate distinct named values, and their abstract data types require these names.

References

1. O.-J. Dahl, B. Myhrhaug, and K. Nygaard, The SIMULA 67 common base language. Norwegian Computing Center, Oslo, Publication Nr. S-22, 1970.

2. C. A. R. Hoare, Proof of correctness of data representations, *Acta Informatica* 1 (1972), pp. 271-281.

3. W. A. Wulf, R. L. London, and M. Shaw, An introduction to the construction and verification of Alphard programs, *IEEE Trans. Software Engineering* SE-2 (1976), pp. 253-265.

4. J. Guttag and J. Horning, The algebraic specification of abstract data types, *Acta Informatica* 10 (1978), 27-52.

5. J. A. Goguen, J. W. Thatcher, E. G. Wagner, and J. B. Wright, Initial algebra semantics and continuous algebras, *J. of the Assoc. for Comp. Mach.* 24 (1977), pp. 68-95.

6. R. G. Hamlet and H. D. Mills, Functional semantics, University of Maryland Computer Science Technical Report 1238, 1983.

7. *Ibid.*, Functional Analysis of Programs, Oregon Graduate Center Technical Report CS/E 84-006, October, 1984.

8. Linger, R.C., Mills, H.D., and Witt, B.I., *Structured Programming: Theory and Practice,* Addison-Wesley, 1979.

Appendix

To determine $\boxed{\text{ExpRat}}$, we compose the functions computed by the three initial assignment statements, the WHILE statement, and the two final assignment statements.

```
(<I, T.Num, T.Den> := <1, R.Num, R.Den>) o
((I<N → <I, T.Num, T.Den> :=
             <N, T.Num*R.Num** (N-I), T.Den*R.Num** (N-I)>) |
 (I>=N → < > := < >)) o
(<R.Num, R.Den> := <T.Num, T.Den>)
```

The result of the compositions is:

$$((1 < N \rightarrow \; <I, \; T.Num, \; T.Den, \; R.Num, \; R.Den> :=$$
$$<N, \; R.Num_*R.Num_{**}(N-1), \; R.Den_*R.Den_{**}(N-1),$$
$$R.Num_*R.Num_{**}(N-1), \; R.Den_*R.Den_{**}(N-1)>) \; |$$
$$(1 >= N \rightarrow \; <I, \; T.Num, \; T.Den> := \; <1, \; R.Num, \; R.Den>)$$

Simplifying and ignoring the effects on local variables yields the function:

$$((1 < N \rightarrow \; <R.Num, \; R.Den> := \; <R.Num_{**}N, \; R.Num_{**}N>) \; |$$
$$(1 >= N \rightarrow \; < \; > := \; < \; >)$$

This is identical to ExpRat :

$$(N >= 1 \rightarrow \; <R.Num, \; R.Den> := \; <R.Num_{**}N, \; R.Den_{**}N>) \; |$$
$$(N < 1 \rightarrow \; < \; > := \; < \; >)$$

since for N=1, R.Num = R.Num**N.

The functions for the sequences of assignment statements were obviously chosen correctly. However, we still must establish the correctness of the function chosen for the WHILE statement.

```
WHILE I < N
DO { (I<N --> <I, T.Num, T.Den> :=
                <N, T.Num*R.Num**(N-I), T.Den*R.Den**(N-I)>) |
    (I>=N --> < > := < >) }
  BEGIN
    I := I + 1;
    T.Num := T.Num * R.Num;
    T.Den := T.Den * R.Den
  END;
```

Using the WHILE Statement Verification Theorem, the intended function F, which appears as a comment on the WHILE statement, and WHILE I < N DO S are identical if:

1. domain(F) $\subseteq$ domain(WHILE I < N DO S)
2. F(T) = T whenever ¬ I < N (T)
3. F = IF I < N THEN S o F

The domain of F is:

I<N OR I≥N = true

If I≥N, the WHILE statement is skipped so termination is assured. If I<N, the WHILE statement is executed, I is incremented, and the eventual termination of the statement is

assured because the value of I approaches N. Thus the first condition is satisfied.

The second condition requires F to be the identity if the WHILE condition does not hold. This is exactly the final case in the definition of F.

Finally, we can work out the right side of the third condition. The function of the IF statement

IF I $<$ N DO S

is

$(I<N \rightarrow <I,T.Num,T.Den> := <I+1,T.Num_*R.Num,T.Den_*R.Den>)$ |
    $(I\geq N \rightarrow < > := < >)$

The composition $\boxed{IF\ I\ <\ N\ THEN\ S}$ o F is:

$((I<N \rightarrow <I,T.Num,T.Den> := <I+1,T.Num_*R.Num,T.Den_*R.Den>)$ |
    $(I\geq N \rightarrow < > := < >))$ o
$(I<N \rightarrow <I,T.Num,T.Den> :=$
         $<N, T.Num_*R.Num_{**}(N-I), T.Den_*R.Den_{**}(N-I)>)$ |
    $(I\geq N \rightarrow < > := < >)$

There are four cases to consider.

Execution Table 1

Part	Condition	I	T.Num	T.Den
IF	I$<$N	I+1	T.Num$_*$R.Num	T.Den$_*$R.Den
F	I+1$<$N	N	T.Num$_*$R.Num$_*$R.Num $_{**}$(N-(I+1))	T.Den$_*$R.Den$_*$R.Den $_{**}$(N-I+1)

Simplifying some of these expressions yields:

I$<$N AND I+1$<$N = I+1$<$N
T.Num$_*$R.Num$_*$R.Num$_{**}$(N-(I+1)) = T.Num$_{**}$R.Num(N-I)
T.Den$_*$R.Den$_*$R.Den$_{**}$(N-(I+1)) = T.Den$_{**}$R.Den(N-I)

Thus this part of the composition is:

I+1$<$N $\rightarrow$
    $<I,T.Num,T.Den> := <N,T.Num_*R.Num_{**}(N-I),T.Den_*R.Den_{**}(N-I)>$

Execution Table 2

Part	Condition	I	T.Num	T.Den
IF	$I<N$	$I+1$	$T.Num*R.Num$	$T.Den*R.Den$
F	$I+1\geq N$			

The condition is:

$I<N$ AND $I+1\geq N$ = $I+1=N$

For $I+1=N$, we observe:

$T.Num*R.Num**(N-I) = T.Num*R.Num$
$T.Den*R.Den**(N-I) = T.Den*R.Den$

Thus this part of the function is:

$I+1=N \rightarrow$
   $<I,T.Num,T.Den> := <N,T.Num*R.Num**(N-I),T.Den*R.Den**(N-I)>$

Execution Table 3

Part	Condition	I	T.Num	T.Den
IF	$I\geq N$			
F	$I<N$	N	$T.Num*R.Num**(N-I)$	$T.Den*R.Den**(N-I)$

The condition $I\geq N$ AND $I<N$ cannot be satisfied, so this part contributes nothing to the composition.

Execution Table 4

Part	Condition	I	T.Num	T.Den
IF	$I\geq N$			
F	$I\geq N$			

Thus this part of the function is:

$(I\geq N \rightarrow < > := < >)$

Putting the four part functions together:

```
(I+1≤N → <I,T.Num,T.Den> :=
            <N,T.Num*R.Num**(N-I),T.Den*R.Den**(N-I)>) |
  (I≥N → < > := < >)
```

Since I+1≤N = I<N, the composition of the four part functions is identical to F, establishing the third condition.

INTUITION IN SOFTWARE DEVELOPMENT

P. Naur
Datalogisk Institut
Copenhagen University
Denmark

Abstract

A characterization of the pervasiveness of intuition in human conscious
life is given, followed by some remarks on successes and failures of
intuition. Next the intuitive basis of common notions of scales, logic,
correctness, texts, reasoning, and proofs, is described. On this basis
the essential notions of data models of human activity and of software
development, as built on human intuition, are discussed. This leads to
a discussion of software development methods, viewed as means to over-
coming the hazards of intuitive actions. It is concluded that programmers' experience and integrity are more important than their use of
methods.

1. Introduction

The purpose of the present discussion is to clarify the manner in which
software and some of the notions and techniques entering into producing
it are grasped by the human being involved. More particularly, an attempt will be made to make clear that immediate human apprehension, or
intuition, is the basis on which all activities involved in software
development must build.

The immediate reason for taking up the question of intuition is
that in current discussions of programming there is a clear tendency to
speak of intuition as an inferior human trait which is the cause of
major difficulties in program development and whose influence on programming therefore should be eliminated. In the view to be presented
here such a notion is based on a fundamental fallacy. What will be
claimed is that intuition enters directly into any of the mental activities that together constitute software development. This holds in particular for the use of techniques such as special notations and modes
of argumentation, which do not eliminate the influence of intuition,
but rather must be regarded as aids by which certain risks of errors of
intuitive insight may sometimes be reduced.

The questions to be taken up here are peculiar in that while they
relate mostly to matters that, it must be supposed, are experienced by

every mature human being continually during all his or her waking hours,
yet tend either to be ignored or overlooked, or when they are taken up
for scrutiny to lead to controversy.

In the present discussion the notion of intuition will first be
taken up for clarification. This is followed by discussions of several
notions that enter into software development, such as scales, classifi-
cations, logic, correctness, syntax, semantics, and proof. This leads
to a final discussion of software development and software development
methods.

2.   The notion of intuition

Intuition is explained by dictionaries in such words as "immediate apprehension by the mind without reasoning; immediate apprehension by
sense; immediate insight". Thus it is used with two different, but related, senses, either about something happening, or about insight obtained as a consequence of that kind of happening.

Intuition tends to be overlooked because it is so all-pervasive, a
so basic constituent of anything a person does, and works so smoothly
and effectively. As we go through our lives, we see, hear, feel the touch
of, things and persons around us, continually, throughout our waking
hours, recognizing them and reacting to them. Only upon reflection will
we realize that by far the most of the actions and insights involved in
these transactions are intuitive, according to the definition. In fact,
a person's intuition embraces his or her experience, knowledge, and memory. Each of these items of the person's mental possession are intuitive
in so far as they are readily available to the person himself or herself

Part of our intuitive ability is to make sense of the impressions
that we receive through our senses. However, the intuitive insight or
grasp we have of our surroundings cannot be separated from that of
language and of theories, nor can it be separated from our consciousness
or world view.

A person's intuitive insight changes throughout life, by additions
and modifications. One important part of a person's life is to add to
his or her fund of intuitions, to the kinds of things that he or she can
recognize intuitively.

Because of its pervasiveness, intuition tends to be referred to only
when it is unexpected. For example, when some people talk about "feminine
intuition" they clearly refer to insight had by women where they expect
none. In quite another context, intuition is referred to by Medawar [1]
in talking about "the generative act in scientific enquiry, 'having an
idea'.[...] Intuition takes many different forms in science and mathemat-

ics, though all forms of it have certain properties in common: the sud-
denness of their origin, the wholeness of the conception they embody,
and the absence of conscious premeditation". Popper [2] expresses himself similarly: "My view of the matter, for what it is worth, is that
there is no such thing as a logical method of having new ideas, or a
logical reconstruction of this process. My view may be expressed by
saying that every discovery contains 'an irrational element', or 'a
creative intuition', in Bergson's sense. In a similar way Einstein
speaks of the 'search for those highly universal laws ... from which a
picture of the world can be obtained by pure deduction. There is no logical path', he says, 'leading to these ... laws. They can only be reached by intuition, based upon something like an intellectual love ('Ein-
fühlung') of the objects of experience'".

The view that intuition can refer only to extraordinary situations
is so common that Quine [3] finds it necessary to defend himself against
it: "Twice I have been startled to find my use of 'intuitive' miscon-
strued as alluding to some special and mysterious avenue of knowledge.
By an intuitive account I mean one in which terms are used in habitual
ways, without reflecting on how they might be defined or what presuppo-
sitions they might conceal".

3. Successes and failures of intuitive insight

As perhaps the most important characteristic of intuition, with normal,
adult persons it is enormously successful. In the course of their lives
such persons perform vast numbers of actions and interactions with the
world, each involving huge numbers of muscular and nervous activities
in incredibly complicated interplay. All this goes on day after day, and
for by far the greater periods of time each human organism manages quite
successfully in the activity at hand. We stretch out our hands, get hold
of things, handle them; we move our body about among the multitute of
other people and things, quite successfully; through our senses we get
in contact with more distant parts of surroundings, recognize things and
people known or unknown, without trouble most of the time.

But our intuition is not perfect, occasionally it does let us down,
make us drop the cup we are holding, bump into something, make a mistake
in recognizing a face, or in dialing a telephone number. Such failures
can be taken as a warning that unaided intuition may lead us astray.

A further reason for distrusting intuition is that it is so temptin-
ly convenient. Making the reaction or giving the answer that comes first
to our mind is bound to be less troublesome than any other procedure.

An additional complication is that over a large range of a person's

reactions to certain common situations of life it is impossible to clas-
sify them as either successes or failures. There may thus be no basis
for criticizing the reaction that comes to us intuitively. This holds
particularly for reactions that involve understanding of language. Our
understanding is, primarily, entirely intuitive, and furthermore develops throughout life, partly so as to keep up with the development of
the communal language itself.

4. Bounding the failures of intuition

A main point of the present discussion is that all human activities must
always remain entirely dependent on intuition, and that failures of intuition cannot be entirely eliminated. At best the ill consequences of
them can be reduced. In the present section some basic patterns of how
to achieve such reduction will be discussed.

Certain failures of intuition are in themselves irreversible, for
example dropping a cup so as to break it. Other failures, such as dialing a wrong telephone number, can usually be put right by a simple cor-
rective action. Even just these two examples suggest two important general issues in making our intuitions successful, first the recognition
of the difference of importance between different kinds of failures, and
second, the procedure, in certain situations, consisting of reaching a
certain goal by repeating an action until success is achieved. Other
action patterns along this line are achieving success by repeating a
certain action and comparing the outcomes for sameness, doing actions
carefully and slowly, and having other people check the outcome of an
action.

What should be noted about these patterns of actions is that in
their meaningful application they all depend on intuitive insight into
the wider context of the action with which they are concerned. Thus one
may say that they indicate ways in which intuitive insight can be made
to support other intuitive insight, in other words a self-conscious mode
of proceeding. Thus they conform directly to the scientific manner, described by Quine [3] in the words "science is self-conscious common
sense". Closely related, they depend on self-criticism and an undogmatic
attitude, with readiness to admit the limited validity of any insight.

5. Intuition, scales, logic, and correctness

The previous discussion of intuition has deliberately been phrased in
terms of the vague concepts success and failure, without any attempt to
clarify more precisely what these stand for. In this manner of speaking
it is suggested that in our intuitive apprehensions we are perfectly

capable of dealing with the world and its quality without basis in criteria or scales of values.

It is further suggested that any kinds of well-recognizable categories, counts, and measures, in their application to the world depend entirely on our intuitive understanding. This means in particular that we may accept the application of certain categories, counts, and measures, without it being clear what their limitations are, neither with respect to their clarity of definition nor the scope of their application. This holds in particular for binary categorizations, such as right and wrong. For example, when we go on a trip we may say that we got on the right train and reached the right city, since trains and cities usually, although not always, are distinct enough. However, we are not normally prepared to say whether the weather turned out to be right or wrong, or whether the kindness of the population was agreeable or disagreeable, or even just put the quality of the weather and the kindness of the population on any kind of scale. Even so our notions of the weather and the kindness are perfectly meaningful intuitively.

These considerations show that any description of the world in terms of strict categories and scale values is no better than our intuition will make it. From this it further follows that such human failures or errors that depend in their very notion on strict categories are, in a sense, produced by the making of the categories as much as by the particular erroneous human action. Thus if there is no highway code there can be no traffic misdemeanour.

In using logic on matters of the real world we find the same dependence on intuition. This can be illustrated by looking more closely at a common logicians' claim, that our knowledge is made up of predicates. Take for example the statement, Paris is the capital of France. The logician will claim that this is essentially a predicate, that is something that may be true or false. As everyone knows, as part of our intuitive knowledge, the statement means far more than that. If we ask for a justification why we accept the statement, we do not ask for a proof. Rather we may mention many different kinds of evidence for the validity of the statement, without ever claiming neither their necessity nor their sufficiency. For example, the president of France is resident in Paris, the ministeries of the French government are located there, as is the chamber of the Deputies, every book about France will say that Paris is the capital, etc. etc.

In ordinary use of language we rarely deal with something close to the logician's truth and falsity. To claim that our knowledge of the fact that Paris is the capital of France is equivalent to accepting the truth of a predicate is misleading. Our intuitive knowledge, which extends without a clear bound into scientific knowledge, is a connected whole of innumerable items of insight and knowhow, continually adjusting us to the changing situation. Our acceptance of the statement is connected with our knowledge of how human beings arrange themselves into cities and states and may be supported by our having a theory of government and the significance of capitals. With this knowledge we will be able to give reasons why we find the statement acceptable, and might also indicate circumstances under which it would cease to be so. In this there arises no question of truth or falsity, in the intuitive sense. Such a question is relevant only in certain specialized situations, where the issue is whether someone has told a lie.

The dependence of logic on intuition is not confined to logic in its application to the world, but extends right into logic itself. In fact, even the notions of the best established formal theories depend on their being grasped intuitively by a human being. Thus as mentioned by A.N. Whitehead [4, page 266] the most basic constituents of formal logic, such as Proposition, are used with many different meanings in treatises written by highly acute modern logicians. This statement itself, it may be noticed, depends entirely on human intuition, since sameness of meaning has no sense independent of its being decided intuitively.

The situation of correctness is similar to that of truth. We do not ordinarily refer to the manner of operation of mechanisms we deal with by the word correct. We do not ask whether a car works correctly, but rather we may say that it is working order. This does not imply a set of sharp criteria to be satisfied, and indeed is compatible with our awareness that it has minor defects. What it means is that the car is in such a state that under a reasonably wide class of circumstances it will provide the kind of service we expect from a car. If we try to make the matter more precise we will find that we cannot. To a large extent the performance of the car depends on characteristics that do not admit such sharp limits that are needed in order to formulate sharp criteria. Again, if we adopt arbitrary limits on characteristics so as to establish a criterion, this does not guarantee that a car which is perfect according to the criteria will not be found to break down under certain conditions of stress that the user still would call normal.

This observation nas relevant bearing on the question of program correctness. The situation may be described as follows. The user of a program clearly wants the program to work, that is to give the right results when it is used. However, this desire is not, and cannot be made, the basis of a once-for-all strict description of user requirements. Indeed, while there will undoubtedly be results of the program that the

user would unhesitatingly describe as correct or incorrect, most commonly there will be whole classes of results or reactions from the program
to which the user would be unprepared and uncertain. To a considerable
extent the user might, with good reason, respond to queries concerning
such cases with the suggestion that many of them ought never to arise
and so are irrelevant.

In response to this state of affairs some computer scientists insist that where no usable criterion of correctness is at hand it is the
programmer's task to introduce one. For this purpose the programmer will
describe the action of the program to be developed in terms of a set of
strictly defined specifications. A program is then "correct" if its actions satisfy the specifications, a matter which is strictly defined.
However, this matter of operating does not alter the dependence of the
compatibility of texts and other circumstances of the world on being
intuitively grasped. Thus the extent to which the texts of the specification and the matters of the world that are of concern to the user are
compatible, remains a question that can only be ascertained intuitively.

6. Intuition and text

Software development to a considerable extent depends on the programmer's use of texts, where text is understood to include any data on readable form, including ordinary language prose, programs, and formulae of
any kind.

As one of its important functions in the present context, text may
serve as an aid to reducing the hazards of intuition, being a relatively
stable record of something the unaided memory might not retain. This
function of text directs our attention to the manner in which text is
intuitively comprehended, or made to influence the knowledge had by a
person.

In much recent discussion of text and language there is a strong
tendency to take for granted that in dealing with texts one has to distinguish between things called syntax and semantics, and a corresponding
unquestioned belief that the reading of a text must involve separate
syntactic and semantic analyses. In computer oriented environments such
a notion is further supported by the fact that in both the design and
the structure of compilers for programming languages a division into
syntax and semantics makes useful sense. From this background it would
appear to be obvious that the distinction between syntax and semantics
must likewise appear in some way in the manner human reading of texts
takes place.

It must be pointed out that the assumption of an inherent distinction between things like syntax and semantics rests on several doubtful claims. First, that in analyzing a text it is generally possible to perform a syntactic analysis independent of the semantic analysis. Second, that the intuitive, human reading of a text is based on such a distinction

On the first of these issues it should be noted that the concepts syntax and semantics, and several others, primarily have been introduced as aids to a scientific description of language phenomena. However, what concepts to use for describing any particular language is by no means given in advance. Rather, the choice of concepts will be a matter of descriptional simplicity and convenience in relation to the particular language at hand, and will moreover reflect the point of view adopted by the linguist. For example, Jespersen in his classical description of English [5] mentions that "grammar is usually divided into two parts: *accidence* - also called morphology - i.e. the doctrine of all the forms (inflexions) of the language, and *syntax*, i.e. the doctrine of sentence structure and the use of the forms." But he then goes on to explain his reasons why this type of division has been disregarded in his book.

More generally, the essential point about such concepts as syntax and semantics is that they are not issues in terms of which a language may first be presented to a person. Rather, they may, at best, serve to bring out aspects of a language to someone who already has the language, intuitively. Applied to the analysis of a text of the language the concepts can make sense only to someone who already understands the text. This point, as related to the teaching of mathematics, has been made Kline [6], who says: "The proper pedagogical approach to any new subject should always be intuitive. The strictly logical foundation is an artificial reconstruction of what the mind grasps through pictures, physical evidence, induction from special cases, and sheer trial and error. The theory of the calculus is about as helpful in understanding that subject as the theory of chemical combustion is in understanding how to drive an automobile."

The unity, or wholeness, of the manner in which a human being's intuitive grasp of a text takes place may be illustrated strikingly by the success of reading even in situations where an application of rules would fail. For example, the title of a film on show in Copenhagen at the time when this is written appears in the newspaper advertisement as follows:

En Russer i New York

Presumably any normal Danish reader will grasp this immediately to say, in Danish, "A Russian in New York". However, clearly any analysis of the text by means of rules would stumble even at the level of recognition of the single letters, since the first letter of the second word is not a Danish letter at all. The proper, intended understanding of the text depends on an interplay of what in an analysis by means of rules are entirely different levels, in addition to recognition of similarity or analogy which lies beyond any rules.

The essential unity of a person's intuitive comprehension of a piece of text is confirmed in the study by Ledgard et al. [7] on interfaces of an interactive text editor. As emphasized by the authors of this report, the subjects in the experiment "made no distinction between syntax and semantics. They simply could not conceive of editing power or function as something different from the appearance of the actual commands. To them, the actual commands embodied the editor to such an extent that many were surprised when told after the experiment that the two editors were functionally identical".

The most important point of the present discussion is to make clear how deeply a person's reading of a text depends on intuition, which cannot be understood in terms of applications of rules, such as rules of syntax. This point can be brought out most clearly if it is realized that a person's reading of a text can only be understood as one indivisible action, where the decisions that what is present before the eyes is in fact a text, that that text is relevant to the purpose at hand, say, the development of a piece of software, and that the text contains such and such statements, or formulae, or whatever, these decisions cannot be separated, as premises of an argument, but rather are consequences of the intuitive insight. The justification of this claim is best based on the well-known infinite regress of rules which would be invoked if the decisions had to be made separately, from rules. For example, take the first decision, that what is present before the eyes is in fact a text. If there were to be separate rules behind this decision the question would immediately arise how to decide that those particular rules are actually relevant. This new decision problem would then raise yet another need for rules about how to decide what rules are relevant, etc. in an infinite regress. Since this is absurd the initial assumption that the decision that a text is in view can be rule-based must be dropped.

The conclusion to be drawn from the discussion of the present section is that for the effective comprehension of a text by a person no particular aspect of the text can in general be said to be more important than any other. Thus, in particular, the common use of the designation syntactic sugar to denote a certain aspect of a notation suggests a contrast to matters supposedly more important that tends to be misleading. Consequently in evaluating the merit of a language or notation for use in supporting software development, the full range of its actual application by the actual programmers must be considered. In other words, the criterion that the notation works cannot be replaced by any criterion based on scale values or formal characteristics.

7. Reasoning, proof, and intuition

For the present discussion a crucial issue is the connection between reasoning, proof, and intuition. Reasoning, according to the dictionary, is the activity of forming or trying to reach conclusions from premisses by connected thought, silent or expressed. A proof, correspondingly, is the result of a successful piece of reasoning. A main point of the present discussion is that reasoning and proof, far from excluding or being opposed to intuition, are completely dependent on intuition. For a person to do reasoning and for someone to grasp the resulting proof, it is necessary that he or she has intuitive knowledge of each of the premisses, of their mutual connections, and of the total pattern by which they support the conclusion. This is in addition to an intuitive understanding of what a proof is. Thus a proof is an expression of intuitive insights patterned so as to show the reasoning supporting a conclusion.

As an illustration of a proof concerning such real matters as are also the concern of applied software, consider the following proof that there are now four apples in the basket. Proof: a minute ago I saw that the basket was empty; since then I have seen first Susan and then Barbara each put two apples into it, and nothing else has happened; and twice two make four.

This illustration, simple as it is, demonstrates all that goes into a proof about matters of the real world, and in particular exhibits the dependence on intuition throughout. Thus there is only intuitive insight behind deciding the emptiness of the basket, behind seeing the two girls with apples in their hands, behind relating that sight to the natural numbers, and behind the knowledge that the operation of multiplication is relevant to the situation. In a more careful analysis one might ask for an enumeration of the conditions for the validity of the proof. One may then be told that the basket is supposed to be an ordinary one, without a hole in the bottom, and that the validity is limited in time, until one of the apples has rotted away. But a very cautious respondent may want to add that the proof depends basically on the assumption of a certain continuity of the world which is entirely beyond enumeration.

As also shown by the illustration, the proof depends on having a logical model of an aspect of the world, in this case amounting to using the whole numbers for counting such items of the world as apples. This model and the implied correspondence between certain things, apples in this case, and the logical constructs numbers can only be known intuitively. Part of this intuitive knowledge is that the model applies to apples, at least under certain circumstances. That this is significant insight may be seen from the fact that a similar model will not always work. It does not work for drops of water, for example. If we let first two and then again two drops of water fall into an empty cup it is unlikely that we will then find four drops in the cup.

Proofs concerned exclusively with the properties of mental constructions, such as those of mathematics, have a special character in so far as, since mental constructions may be endowed with eternal unchangability, they may establish results of eternal validity. This of course is a unique quality in a world which otherwise has nothing but inconstancy. This quality does not make the corresponding proofs less dependent on intuition, however. Both the mental items entering into the proof and their connections have to be grasped intuitively for the proof to be established.

While reasoning is entirely dependent on intuition, intuitive insight is only incidentally dependent on reasoning and proof. Throughout our lives our intuitive knowledge develops incessantly, the impressions from our senses combining with the knowledge already had to form ever new insight. Predominantly the combination of the new insights and observations with the previous knowledge is felt to follow without special effort, without appeal to laws, principles, or algorithms. Even so, if examined closer the activity involved cannot be distinguished sharply from that of reasoning. We speak of reasoning when the number of relevant circumstances and their connections is not too small and the conclusion follows only through their somewhat subtle combination, to such an extent that the formulation of the proof seems a worthwhile effort.

Making oneself familiar with a proof may contribute to adding the insight into the conclusion to one's intuitive knowledge, but is neither necessary nor sufficient for that purpose. One may accept the steps of a proof and yet fail to grasp the conclusion intuitively. Conversely, one may accept a statement without proof. Sometimes one may retain a conclusion, but have forgotten the proof of it. For example, to someone who has taken certain elementary courses of mathematics the statement "a quadratic equation has at most two different roots" may well have

become part of the intuitive knowledge, but the person may have forgotten how to prove it. On the other hand, in order to understand the
statement the person must necessarily have an intuitive knowledge of
such items as quadratic equations, roots, differences between roots, in
addition to the knowledge of numbers.

Intuitive knowledge acquired with some aid from a proof is not essentially different from such knowledge that has not been connected
with a proof. What the proof may contribute is intuitive knowledge about
the connections between certain items of intuitive knowledge. Insight
into the manner in which the premisses are connected together in a proof
is significant in its own right. This follows from the fact that a person may be fully aware of all premisses and yet fail to draw the conclusion. This is a common failure, even in activities that put high
premium on invention.

In summary, reasoning and proof do not provide insight independently of intuition, being in fact intuitive insights patterned in special
manners.

8. Data models of human activity

Software is developed with the purpose of supporting human beings in
their activity. Although the manner of support may take many forms and
be concerned with many different aspects of human life, a common underlying principle of software solutions is the use of a model of the human
activity in the form of data and data processes. As a way of showing
the connection between the notions of data, data processes, specifications, data representations, formalization, and proof, a human activity
and its support by a model will be briefly sketched. The activity chosen, although simple, will be found to bring out most of the typical
problems arising in designing data models.

The activity to be considered as illustration is stockkeeping in
an ordinary household. In one manner of solving this problem all kinds
of supplies are obtained at regular intervals, once in every shopping
cycle. This means that the shopper of the household in each shopping
trip must undertake two main actions, first, establish the shopping
needs on the basis of the remaining stocks and the expected consumption
for the period of the following shopping cycle, and second, buy the
goods needed and bring them home. In implementing the shopping according
to this general manner it may be helpful to make use both of specifications and formalized descriptions. The stocks that should be established
in each shopping trip can be specified as a stock plan, that is a list
giving the minimum and maximum amount for each kind of goods, determined

from the average consumption of the household, the storability of the
kind, and the storage capacity of the household. In the first action
of the shopping trip the shopper will combine this specification with
data on the remaining stock of each kind of goods and so produce a shopping list, that is a formal description showing what kinds of goods to
be bought and how much of each. In the second action of the shopping
trip the shopping list is used in selecting the goods from the shelves
of the shop.

An examination of principles and actions of this household stocking procedure will show that human intuition has to be brought in at
all stages of both the design and execution of it. One may want to claim
that the procedure can be derived systematically from one single, overall requirement, such as that the household must at no time run out of
supply of any kind of goods. In stating this it should be noted, however, that in its very statement the requirement definition depends on
an intuitive understanding of the total situation of the household and
such items as supplies and kinds of goods. In establishing the principles of the procedure to be applied at each shopping trip we depend
on an intuitive understanding of the consumption of goods in a household and the relevance of the formal concept average consumption. This
intuitive understanding in particular is necessary in establishing the
connection between the shopping procedure and the overall requirement
of the procedure. It is further decisive in determining the limitation
of the validity of procedure, and in designing margins and safeguards
in the procedure, so as to make it valid even for certain classes of
abnormal situations. At the same time it must be obvious that no procedure will be able to ensure the satisfying of the requirement under
any conceivable circumstances. For example, if the household stock of
any particular kind of goods disappears from theft or is destroyed by
fire, then at that moment the requirement ceases to be satisfied.

During the execution of the household stocking procedure intuition
enters every time a human being deals with an item of goods in any manner whatsoever, first of all in identifying it, and possibly in determining it more closely with respect to quantity and quality. The intuitive insight obtained by this direct contact with the goods may then,
again intuitively, be related to the formal descriptions of the stock
plan or the shopping list.

The possible application of a formal proof as part of the design
of the household stocking procedure again depends on intuitive insight
in several ways. For example, the design might include an algorithm for
determining the minimum and maximum amount of goods, for use in establishing the stock plan. The design might include a proof that the over-

all requirement is satisfied when this algorithm is used. For this step
in the design to be valid it must be intuitively clear that the proof
criteria do indeed justify the conclusion drawn from the proof. Moreover, the proof will undoubtedly depend on premises that express restrictive conditions on the situation. It will be a matter for the intuitive insight of the designer to establish whether or to what extent
these restrictive conditions are or can be satisfied.

9. Software development

For the present discussion of the importance of intuition in software
development, a vital issue is the proper view of the development process
considered as an interplay of intuitive knowledge had by the programming
person and the real world accessible to that person, which includes the
texts used or produced by the person. In the following discussion the
word knowledge will be used to indicate intuitive knowledge had by a
person. A major source of difficulty, and possibly of confusion, is the
need to talk of parts of that knowledge at the same time as it must be
recognized that a person's knowledge at any time is an indivisible whole.
In the following discussion this recognition is reflected in that the
identifiers used to indicate the person's knowledge, K1, K2, ..., refer
not to parts of that knowledge, but to that total knowledge as it is
increased in the software development process.

The real world, which is open to inspection by the programmer and
other persons, will be denoted W. Certain parts of it are recognized
intuitively by the programmer and other persons as having the special
nature of texts of some language or notation and will be denoted WT1,
WT2, ...

The simplest conceivable software development activity can now be
described in terms of the following items:

W.   The real world, as accessible for inspection to several
     people.
WT1. Text describing the programming language.
WT2. Text describing the problem to be solved by the program to
     be developed.
WT3. Text of program and its documentation.
K1. Knowledge of the world, of ordinary language, and of the
     programming language to be used.
K2. K1 with the addition of knowledge of the problem to be solved.
K3. K2 with the addition of knowledge, or theory, of the program-
     med solution.

The software development activity or process typically proceeds as fol-

lows. Initially the programmer has K1, and W and WT1 are available.
Here K1 and WT1 must be assumed to have a certain close relation of intuitive compatibility, in the sense that the person, having K1, upon
inspection of WT1 will find at least most of it familiar and understandable. On the other hand, it would be misleading to claim that K1 includes merely a kind of copy of WT1. In acquiring K1 the person may have
used WT1 as an aid in getting to know the programming language, but
establishing K1 has also depended to a large extent on previous knowledge of programming and of the world and language generally, and on
the accessibility of W.

The software development activity may be initiated by making WT2
available to the programmer. This will be a decisive source in the programmer's acquiring K2, which, however, inevitably will also depend
strongly on K1. Indeed, even just understanding a problem of programming
depends on the person's having a background knowledge of programming
and of a programming language.

Of similar importance, in acquiring K2 the programmer must relate
the contents of WT2 to his knowledge of the world, which is part of K1,
and may also have to refer to W. These combinations of parts of the real
world and knowledge are only conceivable as manifestations of intuitive
insight. Indeed, a text, such as WT2, can be related to the world, W,
only through on the one hand, understanding and interpretation of the
text, and on the other hand, selection of and assignment of significance to the features of the world. All of this can only make sense if
understood as elaborate, purposeful actions undertaken by the programmer, depending on intuitive insight at every turn.

The actual software development, if pursued strictly as a sequence
of phases, consists in the programmer's forming the theory of the solution, and thus in acquiring K3, and then in the writing of WT3, the
text of the program and its documentation. On such a view the program
text, WT3, is produced purely from the fully formed knowledge K3, as an
expression of a certain aspect of that intuitive knowledge.

Probably software development will rarely, if ever, proceed by the
phases suggested in the previous paragraphs. Correspondingly, the strict
distinction between K2 and K3 probably rarely is possible. Rather, the
development will proceed as a continued interplay between the programmer's growing insight, both into the problem and its solution, and the
real world items, W, WT2, and WT3. The growing, intuitive insight will
tend to be supported by the gradual production of the documentation and
program, WT3, and at the same time new uses of the accessible W and WT2
will contribute to forming K2. Occasionally the programmer may also need
to refer to WT1, the description of the programming language, although

to be at all effective he or she must be able to rely mostly on K1 for knowledge about the programming language.

Whether the software development proceeds more closely as a sequence of distinct phases or as one more complicated phase, the overwhelming importance of the programmer's intuition must be clear. At all stages the activity depends on combining items of the world that have no inherent affinity apart from the programmer's intuitive understanding interpretation, and notion of purpose and significance.

10. Software development methods and intuition

In the discussion of this section a software development method is any set of rules designed to influence how the programmer proceeds in his or her task, beyond the rules inherent in the development activity described in the previous section. The rules of a method will normally be mutually dependent and supporting. The matters of concern of a method can be divided into three major areas, as shown below.

1. <u>Activity</u>. Rules about what should be done or produced, in addition to what is covered by the minimal software development actions. Typical items under this heading are: produce descriptions of variables; produce assertions of invariant properties of the variables of the program execution; produce descriptions of the program logic in other forms than the program itself, such as for example specifications of the relation between input and output; produce proofs of the consistency or compatibility of certain expressions; perform particular check operations; perform walk-throughs.

2. <u>Forms of expression</u>. Particular notations or languages that should be employed for various purposes in the software development.

3. <u>Ordering of activities</u>. Imposition of particular orders in which the activities of the software development should be undertaken, such as top-down, or stepwise refinement.

A major issue of any particular software development method is the extent to which it is effective, i.e. whether and how much it contributes to improving the software development in which it is adopted. In principle it would be desirable to have the effectiveness of methods determined empirically, by means of observations of actual software development activities. In practice such an approach meets difficulties of several kinds: In trying to detect improvements, what software development activity can be taken as basis for the comparison? How can the improvements be evaluated or measured? How is it possible to make sure that such improvements that are in fact detected are the result of using the method? Quite generally, any empirical study of a method de-

signed to improve conditions of a poorly developed kind of activity is
faced with a difficulty described by Bernard Shaw [8] under the heading
The Surprises of Attention and Neclect: when an activity is in a state
of neglect, any attention given to it, even such that are based on entirely misguided notions, is likely to improve matters. Clearly, under
such circumstances an improvement brought about by the application of
a method is no sure evidence of the efficacy of the method.

As an alternative or supplement to empirical evaluations, software
development methods will here be evaluated on the basis of their relation to intuition. What can be noted, first, is that, as is the case
for all other software development activities, the use of the rules of
a method depends directly on the programmer's intuition in deciding when
each rule of the method applies and how.

As the second major issue, the various kinds of rules of methods
must be related to the shortcomings of the programmers' intuitive insight and behaviour. These shortcomings are of two kinds: (1) *omissions*
to do what the programmer is intuitively aware should be be done, and
(2) *flaws* in the actions taken intuitively.

Considering first omissions, the first area of concern for methods,
activity, clearly is highly relevant and potentially useful. Even just
a simple check list of activities that experience shows may be relevant
in software development may be effective in avoiding omissions. Having
such a check list and insisting that it is used might well be part of
a methods in the area of activity. The second area of concern of methods,
forms of expression, is of no direct importance to omissions. The third
area, ordering of activities, is slightly relevant, in so far as even a
very simple activity aid, such as a check list, must be used at not too
late stages of the software development, if it is to be useful at all.

Turning to flaws in the actions taken intuitively, the activities
prescribed by a method are highly important in so far as they insist on
the programmer performing checks. The checks may be just that, doing
the same work another time and verifying that the results are the same.
However, the aspect of check is implicit in several other kinds of activities, including the production of descriptions of the program logic
in other forms than the program itself. Comparing direct and implicit
checks, each kind has its merits and limitations. The advantage of direct checks, based on repetition of actions, is that there is no question about what it is they verify. The limitation is that if done by
the same person there is a strong risk that the same flaw of intuition
will repeat itself. This limitation may be overcome by having the check
done by another programmer. Implicit checks avoid repetition of flaws
of intuition, but pose new problems of the extent to which they are ef-

fective in verifying solutions. Usually only certain aspects of a solution will be verified, and typically such aspects as the spelling of variable names is left almost wholly unchecked.

The relation between flaws of intuition and the imposition of particular forms of expression of a method is a complicated one. The claim is often made that certain forms, or formalizations, will guarantee the absence of flaws of arguments. What seems to lie behind such claims is the fact that by the use of certain kinds of formalizations it is possible to formulate the connections between statements corresponding to a proof in terms of rules for manipulating the statements. While this property is of great interest as a matter of principle, and also is the necessary basis for mechanical proof construction and verification, and occasionally is used in the reasoning carried out by people, it provides no guarantee for the absence of flaws in the arguments used in software development making use of formalizations. In fact, the compatibility of descriptions used in developing a piece of software and the matters of the world that are supposed to be modeled by them remains a matter for human intuition in any case. Avoiding flaws in that modelling undoubtedly depends to some extent on the form or language used for the description. However, what is the most suitable form or language for any situation will depend not only on the degree of formalization of the description, but equally on the character of the aspect of the world to be modelled and the background experience of the programmer who has to establish the description. Thus to claim, for example, that the mathematical properties of a form of notation have to be decisive in choosing it for software development, implies a gross disregard for the importance of human intuition. It must further be concluded that rules of a mathod that impose the use of particular, restricted forms of expression on the programmer may in fact contribute to introducing flaws in the software product. For further discussion of this issue, see [9].

Relating, finally, flaws of intuition to the third area of concern of methods, ordering of activities, it seems likely that imposed orderings will not help to avoid flaws and may in fact contribute to them. Indeed, the task of software development involves the programmer's dealing with complicated patterns of interconnected restrictions and concerns and deriving new, relevant conclusions from them, intuitively. Avoiding flaws of such derivations depends to a considerable extent on the programmer's concentration in retaining complicated patterns. Such concentration may well be disturbed or interrupted by externally imposed demands on the ordering in which certain matters should be attended to.

As a summary of the above discussion of methods and the failures of intuition, methods appear to be useful primarily by providing check lists that may help programmer's to avoid flaws of omission, while the rules of methods in the areas of form of expression and ordering of activities are of doubtful utility.

The conclusion just suggested raises additional questions concerning the most pressing problems of software development. Indeed, in evaluating a method the question is not only what advantages might accrue from using the method, but also how can one make sure that the programmers in a particular project do in fact follow the rules of it? And more generally, how can one make sure that the programmers make proper use of relevant, well-known results and techniques? The question may be asked whether the flaws of software systems are caused primarily by lack of methods, or perhaps rather by failures to make proper use of such techniques that are generally well known, by simple neglect. The suggestion implied in this question gains some support from experience gained in other large scale human construction activity, such as the construction of buildings. For example, an investigation made in 1984 of buildings constructed in the year 1979 in Denmark reveals a large number of flaws of construction that predominantly are such that could have been avoided by application of perfectly well established techniques, which have been neglected from sloppiness.

The indication of such experience supports the above discussion of intuition in the conclusion that the problem of high quality software development cannot be solved by rules and methods, which essentially assume that the programmer acts like a machine for producing programs. As an alternative it will here be suggested that the primary task of the programmer is to build theories of the way the problems at hand can be aided by a computer program, an idea discussed in more detail elsewhere [10].

11. Conclusions

The major conclusion of the present discussion is that software development in all its phases, and irrespective of the techniques employed in its pursuit, must and will always depend on intuition.

The fundamental way of reducing failures of human intuition is to apply multiple work and check. Rules for guiding the software development depend on intuition to decide where and how they apply. Consequently a view of software development that makes the application of rule--based methods and notations the basic issue is misguided. The deeper problem of software development is the programmer's building of theories of the computer-based solutions.

Finally, to the question of this conference, what is the role of semantics in software development? Answer: neither that of the composer, nor of the librettist, the conductor, the hero, or the heroine, but that of the prompter, who does nothing but tell the actors things they know already, but that may momentarily have slipped from their minds.

References

1. Medawar, P.: *Pluto's republic*. Oxford University Press, Oxford 1982

2. Popper, K.R.: *The logic of scientific discovery*. Hutchinson, London, 1959.

3. Quine, W.v.O.: *Word and object*. M.I.T. Press, Cambridge, Massachusetts, 1960.

4. Whitehead, A.N.: *Adventures of ideas*. Pelican Books, Harmondsworth, Middlesex, England, 1942.

5. Jespersen, O.: *Essentials of English grammar*. George Allen and Unwin, London, 1933.

6. Kline, M.: *Why the professor can't teach*. St. Martin's Press, New York, 1977.

7. Ledgard, H., Whiteside, J.A., Singer, A., Seymour, W.: The natural language of interactive systems. *Comm. ACM* 23 (10), pp. 556-563, 1980.

8. Shaw, B.: *The doctor's dilemma*. Penguin Books, Harmondsworth, Middlesex, England, 1946.

9. Naur, P.: Formalization in program development. *BIT* 22 (1982), 437-453.

10. Naur, P.: Programming as theory building. Microprocessing and Microprogramming, in preparation.

A RATIONAL DESIGN PROCESS: HOW AND WHY TO FAKE IT

David L. Parnas
Department of Computer Science
University of Victoria, Victoria BC V8W2Y2 Canada
and
Computer Science and Systems Branch
Naval Research Laboratory
Washington DC 20375 USA
and
Paul C. Clements
Computer Science and Systems Branch
Naval Research Laboratory
Washington DC 20375 USA

ABSTRACT

Software Engineers have been searching for the ideal software development process: a process in which programs are derived from specifications in the same way that lemmas and theorems are derived from axioms in published proofs. After explaining why we can never achieve it, this paper describes such a process. The process is described in terms of a sequence of documents that should be produced on the way to producing the software. We show that such documents can serve several purposes. They provide a basis for preliminary design review, serve as reference material during the coding, and guide the maintenance programmer in his work. We discuss how these documents can be constructed using the same principles that should guide the software design. The resulting documentation is worth much more than the "afterthought" documentation that is usually produced. If we take the care to keep all of the documents up-to-date, we can create the appearance of a fully rational design process.

A RATIONAL DESIGN PROCESS: HOW AND WHY TO FAKE IT

David L. Parnas
Computer Science Department
University of Victoria, Victoria BC V8W 2Y2 Canada
and
Computer Science and Systems Branch
Naval Research Laboratory
Washington DC 20375 USA

and

Paul C. Clements
Computer Science and Systems Branch
Naval Research Laboratory
Washington DC 20375 USA

I. THE SEARCH FOR THE PHILOSOPHER'S STONE: WHY DO WE WANT A RATIONAL DESIGN PROCESS?

A rational person is one who always has a good reason for what he does. Each step taken can be shown to be the best way to get to a well defined goal. Most of us like to think of ourselves as rational professionals. However, to many observers, the usual process of designing software appears quite irrational. Programmers often appear to make decisions without having reasons. They start without a clear statement of what they are going to build. They make a long sequence of design decisions with no clear statement of why they do things the way they do. Their goals are never defined; their rationale is rarely explained.

Many of us are not satisfied with such a design process. That is why there is research in software design, programming methodology, structured programming and related topics. Ideally, we would like to derive our programs from a statement of requirements in the same sense that theorems are derived from axioms in a published proof. All of the methodologies that can be classified as "top down" are the result of our desire to have a rational, systematic way of designing software.

This paper brings a message with both bad news and good news. The bad news is that, in our opinion, we will never find the philosopher's stone. We will never find a process that allows us to design software in a perfectly rational way. The good news is that we can fake it. We can present our system to others as if we had been rational designers. The further good news is that it pays to do so.

II. WHY WILL A SOFTWARE DESIGN "PROCESS" ALWAYS BE AN IDEALISATION?

We will never see a software project that proceeds as suggested above. Some of the reasons are listed below:

1. In most cases the people who commission the building of a software system do not know exactly what they want and are unable to tell us what they do know.

2. Even if we were to know the requirements, there are many other facts that we need to know to design the software. Many of the details only become known to us as we progress in the implementation. Some of the things that we learn invalidate our design and we must backtrack.

3. Even if we were to know all of the relevant facts before we start, experience shows that human beings are unable to fully comprehend the plethora of details that must be taken into account in order to design and build a correct system. The process of designing the software is one in which we attempt to separate concerns so that we are working with a manageable amount of information. However, until we get to that point, we are bound to make errors.

4. Even if we could master all of the detail needed, all but the most trivial projects are subject to change for external reasons.

Some of those changes may invalidate previous design decisions.

5. Human errors can only be avoided if one can avoid the use of humans. No matter how rational our decision process, no matter how well we have collected and organised the relevant facts, we will make errors.

6. We are often burdened by preconceived design ideas, ideas that we invented, acquired on related projects, or heard about in a class. Sometimes we undertake a project in order to try out or use a favourite idea. Such ideas may not be derived from our requirements by a rational process; they may arise spontaneously from other sources.

7. Often we are encouraged, for economic reasons, to use software that was developed for some other project. In other situations, we may be encouraged to share our software with another ongoing project. The resulting software may not be the ideal software for either project, i.e., not the software that we would develop based on its requirements alone, but it is good enough and will save effort.

For all of these reasons, the picture of the software designer deriving his design in a rational, error-free, way from a statement of requirements is quite unrealistic. We believe that no system has ever been developed in that way, and probably none ever will. Even the small program developments shown in textbooks and papers are unreal. They have been revised and polished until the author has shown us what he wishes he had done, not what actually did happen.

III. WHY IS A DESCRIPTION OF A RATIONAL IDEALISED PROCESS USEFUL NONETHELESS?

What we have said above is quite obvious, known to every careful thinker and admitted by the honest ones. In spite of that we see conferences whose theme is the software design process, working groups on software design methodology, and a lucrative market for courses purporting to describe logical ways to design software. What are these people trying to achieve?

If we have identified an ideal process but cannot follow it precisely, we can still write the documentation that we would have produced if we had followed the ideal process. Someone reading the documentation would have the benefit of following a rational explanation of the design. This is what we mean by "faking a rational design process".

Below we list some of the reasons for such a pretense:

1. Designers need guidance. When we undertake a large project we can easily be overwhelmed by the enormity of the task. We will be unsure about what to do first. A good understanding of the ideal process will help us to know how to proceed.

2. We will come closer to the ideal process, and to a rational design, if we try to follow the process than if we proceed on an ad hoc basis. For example, even if we cannot know all of the facts necessary to design an ideal system, the effort to find those facts before we start to code will help us to design better and backtrack less.

3. When an organisation undertakes many software projects there are advantages to having a standard procedure. It makes it easier to have good design reviews, to transfer people, ideas, and software from one project to another. If we are going to specify a standard process, it seems reasonable that it should be a rational one.

4. If we have agreed on an ideal process, it becomes much easier to measure the progress that a project is making. We can compare the project's achievements with those that the ideal process

would call for. We can identify areas in which we are behind (or ahead).

5. Regular review of the project's progress by outsiders is essential to good management. If the project is attempting to follow an ideal process, it will be easier to review.

IV. WHAT SHOULD THE DESCRIPTION OF THE DEVELOPMENT PROCESS TELL US?

We believe that the most useful form of a process description will be in terms of work products. For each stage of the process, we describe:

- what we should work on next;

- what criteria that work product must satisfy;

- what kind of persons should do the work;

- what information they should use in their work;

Management of any process that is not described in terms of work products can only be done by mindreaders. Only if we know which work products are due and what criteria they must satisfy can we review the project and measure progress.

V. WHAT IS THE RATIONAL DESIGN PROCESS?

In this section, we describe the rational, idealised software design process that we follow. Each step is accompanied by a detailed description of the work product associated with that step.

The description of the process that follows includes neither testing nor review. This is not to suggest that we ignore either of those. In this paper we are describing an ideal process; testing and review belong in the real process, not the ideal. When we apply the process described in this paper, we include extensive and systematic reviews of each work product and testing of the executable code that is produced.

A. Establish and document requirements.

If we are to be rational designers we must begin knowing what we must do to succeed. We record that in a work product known as a requirements document. Completion of this document before we start allows us to design with all the requirements in front of us.

1. Why do we need a requirements document?

- We will be less likely to make requirements decisions accidentally while designing the program.

- We will avoid duplication and inconsistency. Without this document, many of the questions it answered would be asked repeatedly throughout the development by designers, programmers and reviewers. This would be expensive and would often result in inconsistent answers.

- Programmers working on a system are very often not familiar with the application area. Having a complete reference on externally-visible behaviour relieves them of any need to decide what is best for the user.

- It is necessary (but not sufficient) for making good estimates of the amount of work and money that it will take to build the system.

- It is valuable insurance against the costs of personnel turnover. The knowledge that we gain about the requirements will not be lost when someone leaves the project.

- It provides a good basis for test plan development. Without it, we do not know what to test for.

- It can be used long after the system is in place to define the constraints for future changes.

- It can be used to settle arguments; we no longer need to be, or consult, application experts.

Determining the detailed requirements may well be the most difficult part of this process because there are usually no well-organised sources of information. Ideally, it would be produced by representatives of the future users. In fact, it is probably going to be produced by software designers who must get it approved by the users' representatives.

2. What goes into the requirements document?

The definition of the contents of the requirements document, in the idealised design process, is simple: it should contain everything you need to know to write correct software, and no more. Of course, we may use references to existing information, if that information is accurate and well organised. The general rules for an ideal requirements document include:

- every statement should be valid for all acceptable products; none should depend on implementation decisions.
- the document should be complete in the sense that if a product satisfies every statement, it should be acceptable.
- where information is not available before development must begin, the areas of incompleteness are indicated, not simply omitted.
- the product is organised as a reference document rather than an introductory narrative about the system, because this is the most useful form. Although it takes considerable effort to produce such a document and is more difficult to read than an introduction, it saves labour in the long run because the information that is obtained in this stage is recorded in a form that allows for easy reference throughout the project.

We obtain completeness in our requirements document by using separation of concerns to obtain the following sections:

- a specification of the machine on which the software must run. The machine need not be hardware -- for some systems this section might simply be a pointer to a language reference manual;
- a specification of the interfaces that the software must use in order to communicate with the outside world;
- for each output, a specification of its value at all times in terms of the software-detectable state of the system;
- for each output, how often or how fast the software is required to recompute it;
- for each output, how accurate it is required to be.
- if the system is required to be easy to change, the requirements must contain a definition of the areas that are considered likely to change. You cannot design a system so that everything is equally easy to change, and programmers should not have to decide which things are most likely to be altered.
- the requirements must also contain a discussion of what the system should do when, because of undesired events, it cannot fulfil its full requirements. Most requirements documents ignore those situations; they discuss what will happen when everything works perfectly but leave to the programmer the decision about what to do in the event of partial failures.

We hope it is clear that correct software cannot be written unless each of those requirements is defined, and that once you have succeeded in specifying each of those things, you have completely specified the requirements for your system.

To assure a consistent and complete document, there must be a simple mathematical model behind the organisation. Our model is motivated by our work on real-time systems but because of that it is completely general. All systems are real-time systems.

We assume that for real-time control systems the ideal product is not a pure digital computer, but a hybrid computer consisting of a digital computer that controls an analogue computer. The analogue computer transforms continuous values measured by the inputs into continuous outputs. The digital computer brings about discrete changes in the function computed by the analogue computer when discrete events occur. The actual system is a digital approximation to this hybrid system. As in other areas of engineering, we write our specification by first describing this "ideal" system and then specifying the allowable tolerances. In our requirements document we treat outputs as more important than inputs. If we get the value of the outputs correct, nobody will mind if we do not even read the inputs. Thus, the key to the first stage in the process is identifying all of the outputs. The heart of our requirements document is a set of mathematical functions in tabular form. Each function specifies the value of a single output as a function of external state variables that are relevant to the application. An example of a complete document produced in this way is given in [9] and discussed in [8].

B.   Design and document the module structure

Unless the product is small enough to be produced by a single programmer, one must now give thought to how the work will be divided into work assignments, which we call modules. The document that should be produced at this stage is called a module guide. It defines the responsibilities of each of the modules by stating the design decisions that will be encapsulated by that module. A module may consist of submodules, or it may be considered to be a single work assignment.

We need a module guide to avoid duplication, to avoid gaps, to achieve separation of concerns, and most of all, to help an ignorant maintainer to find out which modules he must work on when he has a problem report. Again, we see that the document that records our design decisions is the same one that will be used during the maintenance phase.

If one diligently applies information hiding or separation of concerns to a large system, one is certain to end up with a great many modules. A guide that was simply a list of those modules, with no other structure, would help only those who are already familiar with the system. Our module guide has a tree structure, dividing the system into a small number of modules and treating each such module in the same way until all of the modules are quite small. For a complete example of such a document, see [3]. For a discussion of this approach and its benefits, see [15,6].

C.   Design and document the module interfaces

Efficient and rapid production of software requires that the programmers be able to work independently. The module guide defines responsibilities but it does not provide enough information to permit independent implementation of the modules. Precise interfaces must be specified for each module. A Module Interface Specification is written for each module; it must be formal and provide a black box picture of each module. They are written by senior designers and reviewed by potential implementors together with the programmers who will use those interfaces. An interface specification for a module contains just enough information for the programmer of another module to use its facilities, and no more. This is also the information needed by the implementor. The document we produce is used by both.

While there will be one person responsible for each such document, they are actually produced by a process of negotiation between
those who are expected to implement the module, those who will be
required to use it, and others interested in the design, e.g.,
reviewers. The main content of these specifications consists of:

- a list of programs to be made invokable by the programs of
  other modules, (called "access programs");

- the parameters for those access programs;

- the effects of these access programs on each other;

- timing constraints and accuracy constraints, where necessary;

- definition of Undesired Events (forbidden happenings).

In many ways this module specification is analogous to the
requirements document. However, the notation and organisation used is
more appropriate for the software-to-software interfaces with which we
are concerned at this stage in the process.

Published examples and explanations include [11], [2], [1], [5].

D.   Design and document the module internal structures

Once a module interface has been specified, its implementation
can be carried out as an independent task except for reviews. However,
before we begin coding we want to record the major design decisions in
a document that we call the module design document. This document is
designed to allow an efficient review of the design before the coding
begins and to explain the intent behind the code to a future maintenance programmer.

In some cases, the module is simply divided into submodules and
the design document is another module guide, in which case the design
process for that module resumes at step B above. In other cases, we

begin by describing the internal data structures; in some cases these data structures are implemented (and hidden) by submodules. For each of the access programs, we include a function [10] or LD-relation [14] that describes its effect on the data structure. For each value returned by the module to its caller, we provide another mathematical function, known as the abstraction function, which maps the values of the data structure into the values that are returned. For each of the undesired events, we describe how we check for it. Finally, we provide a "verification", an argument that programs with these properties would satisfy the module specification.

We continue the decomposition into, and design of, submodules until each work assignment is small enough that we could afford to discard it and begin again if the programmer assigned to do it left the project.

If we are unable to code in a readable high level language, e.g. if no compiler is available, we include pseudo-code as part of the documentation. We have found it useful to have the pseudo code written by someone other than the final coder, and to make both programmers responsible for keeping the two versions of the program consistent [7].

E.   Design and document the uses hierarchy

The uses hierarchy [13] can be designed once we know all of the modules and their access programs. It is conveniently documented as a binary matrix where the entry in position (A,B) is true if, and only if, the correctness of program A depends on the presence in the system of a correct program B. The uses hierarchy defines the set of subsets that can be obtained by deleting whole programs and without rewriting any programs. It is important for staged deliveries, fail-soft systems, and the development of program families [12].

F.   Write Programs

After all of this design and documentation has been carried out, we are ready to write actual executable code. We find that this goes quickly and smoothly. We believe that the code should not include comments that are redundant with the documentation that has already been written. It is unnecessary and makes maintenance of the system more expensive while increasing the likelihood that the code will not be consistent with the documentation.

VI.   WHAT IS THE ROLE OF DOCUMENTATION IN THIS PROCESS?

A.   What is wrong with the current documentation? Why is it hard to use? Why isn't it read?

It should be clear that documentation plays a major role in the design process that we are describing. Most programmers regard documentation as a necessary evil that is done as an afterthought, and done only because some bureaucrat requires it. We believe that documentation that has not been used before it is published will always be poor documentation.

Most of that documentation is incomplete and inaccurate but those are not the main problems. If they were they could be corrected simply by adding or correcting information. In fact, there are underlying organisational problems that lead to incompleteness and incorrectness and are not easily repaired:

- poor organisation. Most documentation today can be characterised as "stream of consciousness", and "stream of execution". Stream of consciousness writing puts information at the point in the text that the author was writing when the thought occurred to him. Stream of execution writing describes the system in the order that things will happen when it runs. The problem with both of these documentation styles is that people other than the authors cannot find the information that they seek. It will therefore not be easy to determine that facts are missing, or to correct them when they are wrong. It will not be easy to find all the parts of the document that should be changed when the software is changed. The documentation will be expensive to maintain and, in most cases, will not be maintained.

- boring prose. We find lots of words to say what could be said by a single programming language statement, a formula or a diagram. We find certain facts repeated in many different sections. This increases the cost of the documentation and its maintenance and leads to inattentive reading and undiscovered errors.

- confusing and inconsistent terminology. Any complex system requires the invention and definition of new terminology. Without it the documentation would be far too long. However, the writers of software documentation often fail to provide precise definitions for the terms that they use. As a result, the terms are not used consistently. Careful readings reveal that there are many terms used for the same concept and many similar but distinct concepts described by the same term.

- incompleteness. Documentation that is written when the project is nearing completion is written by people who have lived with the system for so long that they take the major decisions for granted. They document the small details that they think they will forget. Unfortunately, the result is a document useful to people who know the system well but impenetrable to newcomers. There are always newcomers on large software projects.

B.   How to avoid these problems?

Documentation in the ideal design process meets the needs of the developers and the needs of the maintenance programmers who come later. Each of the documents mentioned above records design decisions and is used as a reference document for the rest of the design. However, they also provide the information that the maintainers will need.   Because the documents are used as reference manuals throughout the building of the software, they will be mature and ready for use in the later work. They will always be up to date. The documentation in our design process is not an afterthought; it is viewed as one of the major products of the project. There are checks that can be applied to increase completeness and consistency.

One of the major advantages of this approach to documentation is the amelioration of the Mythical Man Month effect [4]. When new programmers join the project they do not have to rely on the old staff for their information. .They will have an up-to-date and rational set of documents available.

We avoid "stream of consciousness" and "stream of execution" documentation by spending a great deal of effort designing the structure of each document. We define the document by stating the questions that it must answer; we carry that discipline down to individual sections. We try to have a place for every fact that must be contained, and make sure that there is only one such place. Only after we have determined the structure of a document do we begin to write it.   If we write many documents of a certain kind, we write and publish a standard organisation for those documents [5].   All of our documents are designed in accordance with the same principle that guides our software design, separation of concerns.   Each aspect of the system is described in one section and nothing else is described in that section. When our documents are reviewed, we review them for adherence to the documentation rules as well as accuracy.

The resulting documentation is not easy or relaxing reading, but it is not boring. We make use of tables, formulae and formal notation to increase the density of information. Our organisational rules prevent the duplication of information. The result is documentation that must be read very attentively but rewards its reader with detailed and precise information.

To avoid the confusing and inconsistent terminology that pervades conventional documentation we use a system of special brackets and typed dictionaries. Each of the many terms that we must define, is enclosed in a pair of bracketing symbols that reveals its type. For each such type we have a dictionary that contains only definitions of that type. Although beginning readers find the presence of !+terms+!, %terms%, #terms#, etc., disturbing, regular users of our documentation find that the type information implicit in the brackets makes the documents easier to read. The use of dictionaries that are structured by types makes it less likely that we will define two terms for the same concept or give two meanings to the same term. The special bracketing symbols make it easy to institute mechanical checks for terms that have been introduced but not defined or defined but never used.

VII. NOW, HOW DO WE FAKE THE IDEAL PROCESS?

The preceding describes the ideal process that we would like to follow and the documentation that would be produced during that process. We fake the process by producing the documents that we would have produced if we had done things the ideal way. We attempt to produce the documents in the order that we have described. If we cannot get a piece of information, we note that in the part of the document where the information should go and proceed to design as if that information were expected to change. If we find errors we change them and make the consequential changes in subsequent documents. We make the documentation our medium of design and no design decisions are considered to be made until their incorporation into the documents has been approved at all levels. No matter how often we stumble on our way, the final documentation will be easier to understand and accurate. We do not show the way things actually happened, we show the way we wish they had happened and the way things are.

Even mathematics, the discipline that many of us regard as the most rational of all, follows this procedure. Mathematicians diligently polish their proofs, usually presenting a proof very different from the first one that they discovered. A first proof is often the result of a tortured discovery process. As mathematicians work on proofs, understanding grows and simplifications are found. Eventually, some mathematician finds a simpler proof that makes the truth of the theorem more apparent. The simpler proofs are published because the readers are interested in the truth of the theorem, not the process of discovering it.

We believe that analogous reasoning applies to software. Those who read the software documentation want to understand the programs, not to relive their discovery. By presenting rationalised documentation we provide what they need.

Our documentation differs from the idealised documentation in one important way. We make a policy of recording all of the alternatives that we considered and rejected, including decisions that were recorded in the earlier versions of a document. For each, we explain why it was considered and why it was finally rejected. Months, weeks, or even hours later when we wonder why we did what we did, we can go back and find out why. Twenty years from now the maintainer will have many of the same questions and will find his answers in our documents.

An illustration that this process pays off is provided by a software requirements document that we wrote some years ago as part of a demonstration of the ideal process [9]. Normally, one assumes that a requirements document is produced before coding starts and is never used again. However, that has not proven to be the case. The original version of the software, which satisfies our requirements document, is still undergoing revision. The organisation that has to test the software after each change uses our document extensively to choose the tests that they do. When new changes are needed, the requirements document is used in describing what must be changed and what cannot be changed. The first document produced in the process is being used many years after the software went into service. The clear message is that if the documentation is produced with care, it will be useful for a long time. Conversely, if it is going to be extensively used, it is worth doing right.

It is very hard to be a rational designer and we will probably never achieve it. In our attempts to follow this process, we have often found places where we inherit a design decision that was made for unknown reasons. An example is the value of a constant in an equation that we would like to use. When we ask for a derivation of the constant, we find that there is none or that the derivation is not valid. When we press further, we are told that the decision was made "because it works". In such situations the designer can either open a research project to find out why it works or simply "Get On With It". Those who are paying for our work have made "GOWI" a standard response to many such problems, and we do not expect that real work will ever be different. However, wherever we have made decisions "because they work", we will record the honest reason for our decision rather than mislead the future maintainers into thinking that we had a deep and philosophic reason for what we did.

VIII. ACKNOWLEDGEMENTS

Stuart Faulk and John Shore of NRL provided thoughtful reviews of this paper.

Funding for this research was supplied by the U.S. Navy and by the National Science and Engineering Research Council (NSERC) of Canada.

REFERENCES

1. Britton, K.H., Clements, P., Parnas, D.L., Weiss, D. Interface Specifications for the A-7E (SCR) Extended Computer Module; NRL Memorandum Report 4843, Jan. 1983.

2. Britton, K.H., Parker, R.A. and Parnas, D.L. "A Procedure for Designing Abstract Interfaces for Device-Interface Modules", Proceedings of the Fifth International Conference on Software Engineering, 1981.

3. Britton, K.H. and Parnas, D.L. A-7E Software Module Guide, NRL Memorandum Report 4702, December 1981.

4. Brooks, F.P. Jr. The Mythical Man-Month: Essays on Software Engineering. Addison-Wesley Publishing Company, 1975.

5. Clements, P., Parker, A., Parnas, D.L., Shore, J. and Britton, K. A Standard Organization for Specifying Abstract Interfaces, NRL Report 8815, 14 June 1984.

6. Clements, P., Parnas, D. and Weiss, D. "Enhancing Reusability with Information Hiding", Proceedings of a Workshop on Reusability in Programming, pp. 240-247, Sept. 1983

7. Elovitz, Honey S. "An Experiment in Software Engineering: The Architecture Research Facility as a Case Study", Proceedings of the Fourth International Conference on Software Engineering, Sept. 1979.

8. Heninger, K.L. "Specifying Software Requirements for Complex Systems: New Techniques and their Application", IEEE Transactions on Software Engineering, vol. SE-6, pp. 2-13, Jan. 1980.

9. Heninger, K., Kallander, J., Parnas, D.L. and Shore, J. Software Requirements for the A-7E Aircraft, NRL Memorandum Report 3876, 27 November, 1978.

10. Linger, R.C., Mills, H.D., Witt, B.I. Structure Programming: Theory and Practice, Addison-Wesley Publishing Company, 1979.

11. Parker, A., Heninger, K., Parnas, D. and Shore, J. Abstract Interface Specifications for the A-7E Device Interface Module, NRL Memorandum Report 4385, 20 November, 1980.

12. Parnas, D.L. "On the Design and Development of Program Families", IEEE Transactions on Software Engineering, Vol. SE-2, No. 1, March, 1976.

13. Parnas, D.L. "Designing Software for Extension and Contraction", Proceedings of the Third International Conference on Software Engineering, pp. 264-277, 10-12 May, 1978.

14. Parnas, D.L. An Alternative Control Structure and its Formal Definition, Technical Report FSD-81-0012, Federal Systems Division, IBM Corporation, Bethesda, MD, 1981.

15. Parnas, D.L., Clements, P. and Weiss, D. "The Modular Structure of Complex Systems", Proceedings of the Seventh International Conference on Software Engineering pp. 408-417, March 1984.

FORMALIZATION IN SYSTEMS DEVELOPMENT

Lars Mathiassen and Andreas Munk-Madsen
Computer Science Department
University of Aarhus
Denmark

Abstract

Formalizations are related both to types of expression and
to types of behaviour. The limits to applying formalizations
in these two senses are discussed and illustrated by examples from practical systems development. It will be established that formalizations are valuable in some situations,
but insufficient in others. The alternative to uncritically
using formalizations is that system developers analyse the
situations in which they find themselves, and from there
choose a combination of a formal and an informal approach.

1. Introduction

For several years computer scientists have engaged in discussions on methods for program development. These discussions have not always left
practitioners with clear advice on and guidelines for programming. On
the contrary, a major aspect like the significance of formalizations
has provoked clearly conflicting viewpoints.

Our interest lies with methods for developing computer based systems in
organizations. Program development is thus only a sub-activity in the
wide spectrum of activities with which we are concerned. These activities are analysis, design, coding, testing, conversion; and not to forget, the very important activities of systems development management.

We experience a wide gap between the discussion in scientific literature
and practical systems development. In spite of the intensity of the discussions formalizations are only used to a limited extent. It is natural
to pose the question: Why? - What are formalizations after all? What are
the limits to using formalizations in systems development? Which alternatives to formalizations can be proposed?. In this paper these questions
are discussed. Examples of situations in practical systems development

are used as illustrations.

2. Methods for Formalization

In our terminology, a *method* consists of prescriptions for carrying out
a certain type of work process (Mathiassen 81). In addition to these prescriptions, a method is characterized by its *application area* - i.e. the
type of work processes in which the method may be applied - and its *perspective* (i.e. some assuptions) on the nature of these work processes and
their environment.

The prescriptions of a method are given in terms of: techniques, tools,
and principles of organization. A *technique* is a way of carrying
out a work process with regard to the nature of the task and product. A
systems development method may, for instance, include stepwise refinement as a programming technique. A *tool* enters into the work process as
an aid. Usually at least one technique is attached to each tool. Structure diagrams (Jackson 83) is an example of a description tool prescribed
in a systems development method. *Principles of organization* prescribe
how the work should be carried out under given conditions. Conditions
include the fact that resources are limited, and the fact that several
people have to cooperate. Dividing a project into phases with built-in
checkpoints is an example of applying a principle of organizing a system development process. This principle serves to improve the control
of the process.

In our context - systems development - the term formal may be connected
to types of *expression* (descriptions, specifications, programs), and to
types of *behaviour* (when carrying out systems development and when programming). According to Oxford Advanced Learner's Dictionary of Current
English, *formal* denotes "in accordance with rules, customs, and convention". In the more restricted context of program development, Naur understands the term formal in the specific sense of: expressed purely by
means of symbols given a specialized meaning. Furthermore he stresses
that the formal mode of expression merely is an extension of the informal
one, not a replacement of it (Naur 82). We agree with this view, and
consequently talk about degrees of formalization.

Seen from the point of view of formalization a method for systems development can provide at least two interesting types of prescriptions.
First it can prescribe the use of description tools and related techni-

ques which imply a certain degree of *formalized expression*. Secondly it can prescribe the use of principles for organizing the work which imply a certain degree of *formalized behaviour*. Many discussions can be traced back to the fact that this distinction has not been made clear. Method designers usually create the first type of guidelines and call these methods; software managers think they buy the second type and are badly disappointed.

In the following we will discuss the limits and alternatives to formalization. Regarding limits we are primarily concerned with *when* formalizations are useful (application area). We give less attention to the question of the degree of formalization. Section 3 will discuss formalizations in relation to the use of description tools and the techniques attached to them. Here we address the issue of description. Section 4 will discuss prescriptions for formalized behaviour, especially principles for organizing development activities. Here we address the issue of management.

3. Description

Descriptions - of any degree of formalization - play an important rôle in the system development process. One of the most important sub-products - the program code - is a formalized description. Descriptions of computer systems and the users' work and organization appear in all activities which directly aim at manufacturing the product: analysis, design, coding, test, and conversion. Important intermediate products include: descriptions of the users' current work and organization, functional requirement specification, overall technical design, overall functional design, detailed technical design, detailed functional design, code, technical conversion plan, and functional conversion plan.

3.1. Possibilities and Problems

Example 1:

A system development project aimed at developing an interactive budget system. The overall design of the new system had been reviewed and accepted. One of the next steps was to design a module which would accept statements of amounts in various currencies from a character string. This module should recognize valid inputs and transform them into an internal representation, and it should give appropriate error messages.

In this case formalization of the set of valid inputs was helpful. The programmer chose to specify a table, describing a finite state machine accepting valid inputs. By doing so the programmer obtained several advantages. The correctness of the specification was in this case intuitively clear, and the program structure could be derived almost directly from the input description.

Naur mentions tabular descriptions as an example of profitable application of formalization (Naur 82). Tabular descriptions are, as he puts it, the obvious means for helping to assure that in a certain situation all cases, or all combination of cases, are considered and treated properly. More generally Naur argues that simple formalizations are of great practical value. Any of the various descriptions which are created during a system development effort may in fact employ any number of different formal notations side by side without contradictions. Using simple formalizations can both be practical and efficient.

Regarding descriptions in general we see at least four motivations for formalizations.

1. Formalized descriptions are imperative in the man-machine dialogue, because machines so far only can interpret and execute formalized descriptions.

2. A formalized description can be an effective means to avoid ambiguity and obtain conciseness in the communication between people.

3. A required use of formalizations can support the system developer's understanding because they force him to think.

4. In systems development several types of descriptions occur, including requirements and designs. If the problem can be described in a formalized way, the solutions may be more easily deduced, or it may be easier to verify the solution.

In example 1 the third and fourth of these points are met. In our experience this is the case in many system development situations. We find that practitioners are too poorly acquainted with the various tools for formalizing descriptions. Michael Jackson's structure diagrams (Jackson 75) are commonly known, but only a minority know of the existence of an equivalent notation: regular expressions, which are linear and therefore

Example 2:

During the development of a computer based production planning system much time was spent trying to specify the computation of throughput time. Everyone involved knew the meaning of this quantity - throughput time was in this context a well-known term. However, every suggestion for a formalized specification of a calculation procedure was met with the same critisism by the production planners: the suggested calculation was too simple. Finally it became clear that it was not a case of specifying an existing computation procedure. The production planners had never before computed *the throughput time - the values were* estimated *on the basis of personal experience, simple individual principles, and knowledge of the given situation.*

Example 2 indicates that the system developers chose the wrong approach because they wished to employ a specific tool. It would certainly be nice if the computation of the throughput time could have been specified in a formalized way - because then the assignment would have been more or less completed. But the formalized approach was not suitable in this situation. The problem was not to specify the computation of througnput time, but rather to analyse and design how reasonable estimates of throug put time could be determined with the aid of computer based tools. The alternative would be to start analysing the production planners' work, and how the throughput time occured in their work.

Part of the literature sees program development as an activity which takes its starting point in a well-defined problem, and the objective of the activity is to develop a program which solves the problem in question. In reality the problem is seldom well-defined from the start. As Polya puts it in terms of practical problem solving in general: "unknowns data and conditions are more complex and less sharply defined in a practical problem than in a mathematical problem" (Polya 57). As implied in example 2, one of the fundamental issues in systems development is in fact to set the problem, i.e. to determine what the system should be able to do, and how it should interact with the organization's work processes.

Example 3:

During the development of an accounting system a problem surfaced as the design activities expanded. The system developers designed one solution after the other, but all solutions were rejected by the users, either on the grounds that the proposed system did not integrate the accounts of the hitherto separated company divisions, or on the grounds that the proposed system would radically change the way of working in one of the accounting departments.

The basic problem in this situation was that the system developers were faced with inconsistent requirements: on one hand their assignment was to develop a system which was common for all the departments, on the other each department wished to maintain their individuality. A naive suggestion would be that a formalized description of the requirements would have surfaced this problem earlier. But in the actual case the project group did realize that they faced inconsistent requirements. They just hoped that they could provoke a decision by working out and presenting various suggestions for the design of the system. They did not, however, succeed in this, and many efforts were wasted.

Example 3 illustrates one of the difficult problems in systems development. Inconsistent requirements appear frequently, and sometimes they are solved through open discussions. What really makes this case difficult is that the users in the different departments do not want to face the underlying conflict.

Any description tool would be of little help in this situation. The problem *appears* to be that the users are dissatisfied with a given design proposal; they want a more sophisticated design. Accepting this interpretation the system developers are left with going back home to specify a more refined solution. In principle the situation could be handled in this way, i.e. by making two systems in one. This solution would, however, neither be economical nor practical (it would involve account numbers with 40 digits). The point is that the situation *appears* to be a description or a design problem, but in *reality* it involves a latent conflict in the organization. This suggests that the system developers should force the organization to take a stance.

3.2. Limits to Formalization

We think that ideally the following conditions should be met before a tool for formalizing descriptions is applicable in a given situation:

1. The syntax and semantics of the tool should be well-defined.

2. The tool should be tested in practical situations.

3. A phenomenon which is suitable for formalized description must be identified.

4. The tool should fit the task. I.e., the tool should capture the properties of what is to be described.

5. System developers should be trained in using the tool.

Let us relate the examples to conditions 3 and 4. In example 1 both conditions were met, and the application of formalizations proved useful. In example 2 condition 3 was apparently met: the system developers found a phenomenon, i.e. computation of throughput time which was suitable for formalized description. However, focusing on this phenomenon represented a misinterpretation of the assignment. Here the application of a specific tool misled the system developers. In example 3 the system developers attempted to design several solutions in a situation where they faced conflicting requirements. What appeared to be a description problem was in reality an organizational problem. Here conditions 3 and 4 were in a way met, but no description tool would do in the situation.

More generally the state-of-the-art and the nature of systems development can be related to the above-mentioned conditions as follows:

1. There are many well-defined tools.

2. The simple tools have been tested. Method makers often promote the more advanced tools without drawing attention to the fact that the tools are still on the experimental stage.

3. Descriptions of computer systems can be formalized. Descriptions of organizations can only partly be formalized due to their social nature.

4. The application area and the perspective of description tools are seldom properly defined.

5. System developers in general know too little about tools for formalizing descriptions.

3.3. Alternatives to Formalization

The quality of the existing tools, seen in relation to the nature of the system development process, indicates that the system developers should have the possibility to *choose their own tool in any given situation.*

Formalizations are of great practical value as a possible extension of
a basically informal means of expression. Today practical systems development is very much based on informal means of expression. The quality of the specifications may be improved through a *more disciplined application of informal means of expression*, and through an *increased partial application of formalizations* (Naur 82).

When attention is drawn to formalizations there is a tendency to neglect
the activities in the system development process for which formalizations
are unsuitable, especially the analysis of the users' work and organization. *Tools and techniques for analysing and designing the users' work
and organization* ought to play a more dominant rôle in the discussions
and the research.

Relating description issues to organizational problems and conflicts
can be achieved through an *experimental strategy* (Floyd 84). An experimental strategy can be advantageously employed to clarify situations
characterized by ambiguity and uncertainty (Davis 82).

4. Management

We now turn to the second interpretation of formalizations. This section
will discuss formalizations - especially principles of organization -
in connection with system development management. The term management
denotes all the activities in a system development project which are
necessary because the project is carried out by more than one person,
and which do not directly contribute to the production of the system.
These management activities include planning and evaluation of resources, activities, and products; regulation of conditions; configuration
management; and general management activities like marketing and motivation. Depending on the organization, some of these activities are performed by the system developers themselves, and others by managers.

The central question is: in which situations does system development
management benefit from formalizations as prescribed in the rules and
procedures of a method?

4.1. Possibilities and Problems

Example 4:

In a project the amount of work was estimated when the overall design was almost completed. The project was broken down into tasks which had an estimated size of 100 to 400 man hours each. The estimates were based on the system developers' rather extensive experience with the application and the development environment. However, system test and conversion were estimated to only 6% of the total development time. It actually took 20%, which is close to the textbook recommendations (Boehm 81) But neither textbooks nor company statistics were consulted.

Here formalization could have helped to improve an important intermediate product - the estimate. The rule: "Compare the allocation of resources for activities with statistics" is easy to implement, and the advantages of doing so are self-evident.

Regarding formalization of behaviour in general we see at least two motivations:

1. Formalization is a means to increase the quality and efficiency of work processes.

2. Formalization is a means to improve the efficiency of external control of work processes through reports and directives.

In example 4 the first of these points is met.

Example 5:

A project was heavily up-staffed after one man-year had been spent on overall design. The design was, however, not completed at this stage. A further 15 man years were spent in a rather chaotic programming activity.

The existence of a procedure for product acceptance, e.g. a "formal technical review" (Freedman and Weinberg 82) might have given management a warning not to up-staff. In this situation it is, however, more doubtful whether such a procedure would have been of any use. The first risk of failure is that the review offers an incorrect assessment. The second risk is that it might be decided that there is no time for a review because the project is behind schedule. And the third risk is that management might choose to ignore the review report. In the actual case management already acts at variance with general experience by violating Brooks' law: "Adding manpower to a late software project makes it later" (Brooks 82).

Example 6:

*A project worked in an organization where procedures required that a
steering committee accepted the overall design. The steering committee,
however, accepted an overall design which had many defects. Confronted
with critisism the project leader admitted the defects, but did nothing
to improve the product, arguing that the product had been accepted. Later the introduction of the new system had to be postponed because of
serious defects in the system.*

Here a procedure is applied which is based in the second motivation mentioned above - but only ostensibly. This results in a wrong picture of
the situation - which is really worse that a blurred one. The point is
that rules and procedures can be used to place responsibilities formally. However, as we have seen in this example, rules and procedures may
also work as pretexts for doing nothing, and they can support opportu-
nistic adjustment of behaviour. They may thus - directly contrary to the
intention - counteract genuine problem solving. This phenomenon is generally known as the dysfunctional effects of bureaucracies (March and
Simon 58).

Example 7:

*The method section of a data service organization was responsible for
improving the working practices in systems development. The section saw
its main task in producing guidelines which were adapted to the organization. Thus the activities mainly consisted of looking for solutions
in the available literature, in participating in courses and meetings,
and in writing. The results of these activities were mainly reports containing guidelines which were only observed to a modest degree in the
organization.*

The immediate problem is that the section is primarily concerned with
producing guidelines, while it ignores the follow-up activities which
should ensure that these guidelines are observed in practice. In relation to the chosen strategy for changing working practices, the section
only solves one part of the task. The heavy problems related to bringing
new methods into practical use are left to random initiatives. Why then
is it carried out in this way? A simple answer would be that the method
section is staffed with system developers, and that they think that programmers are programmable (Weinberg 82).

There is, however, an underlying problem connected to the chosen strategy. Changing working practices is separated as an independent function,
and no attention is paid to the actual problems related to systems development. The fundamental assumption seems to be that systems development can be carried out in a standardized manner; independent of the qualifications and characteristics of the involved participants, and independent of the situation in which a given project finds itself (Kraft 77).

4.2. Limits to Formalization

Examples 4 to 7 are illustrations of the use of rules and procedures for management purposes. What are the limits to formalization?

To answer this we will have to look at the general *mechanism* which makes formalization work as a means for regulating behaviour: In a given situation there will be a rule or a procedure according to which an activity must be carried out. The idea is that the rules or procedures ensure the necessary coordination between various activities. At the same time they replace the involved peoples' reflections and save time, or they replace the involved peoples' lack of reflection and improve quality. To make this mechanism work, a number of conditions must be met:

1. The system development process must be well understood so that typical situations can be identified and related to available rules and procedures.

2. Rules and procedures must be applicable in practice. Generally this requires that the course of a project is highly predictable.

3. Rules and procedures must be thoroughly tested to ensure quality.

4. Rules and procedures must be adapted frequently in accordance with changing environments.

5. System developers must be well trained in using the available rules and procedures.

Let us relate the examples to these conditions. In example 4 the conditions are met, but the rule is not implemented. In example 5 condition 1 is not met. The reason for the unsuccessful course of events is that management fails to understand the situation. In example 6 the problems relate to condition 3 and 5: Management does not take the procedure seriously; instead of undertaking an actual evaluation of the project group's work, management merely accepts it automatically. The project group, on the other hand, takes the procedure seriously and uses it to evade responsibility. In example 7 the method developers never succeed in training the system developers in new methods; condition 5 is not met

In relation to these conditions the state-of-the-art and the nature of the system development activities may be seen as follows:

1. The system development process is only partly understood. Situations can only be described reasonably unambiguously on a general level. Moreover, systems development projects are carried out in environments which often are characterized by bounded rationality, ambiguities, and conflicts (Mathiassen 81).

2. The individual activities can only be described on a general level. System developers deal with analysis as well as with design; and they deal with problem setting as well as with problem solving. System developers do not deal with routine production.

3. Most methods are not thoroughly tested before they are put into use. how many independent test reports for systems development methods are available?

4. In most organizations very little effort is spent on adjusting and changing methods. Moreover, most methods claim general applicability. To be adaptable to changing environments the conditions for applying a method must be made explicit. This is not the case today.

5. Training is typically ignored. Reading the rules and procedures is in most cases assumed to be enough.

4.3. Alternatives

The alternative to formalizations for management purposes is better insight and understanding. The alternative to rules and procedures is concepts. The alternative to telling people *what* they should do, is to make them understand *why* they should do it.

In practice system developers often find themselves in unknown and unpredictable situations. There is only one way out of it: *they must choose their own method*. The point is fundamentally the same as in the relation between formalizations and descriptions. Basically system developers have to rely on informal and situation-determined behaviour (Davis 82). Formalized behaviour should be seen as a possible supplement, which in certain situations may improve quality and efficiency. However, it is just as important to establish a disciplined regulation of the informal behaviour.

To achieve this it is necessary, during the course of a project, to be able to describe situations a project might find itself in and compare it with other situations (Lanzara and Mathiassen 84). Furthermore it is necessary to know the causal relations between the characteristics of a situation and the conditions that created it (Munk-Madsen 84). And it is especially necessary to know possible ways of acting in different types of situations - including to know in which situations formalizations may be advantageously applied.

Finally there is the question of how working practices are actually changed. Some organizations completely ignore this problem. But the typical ways today are courses and manuals presenting guidelines without giving the participants the opportunity to try them out. An alternative would be to go through illustrative cases and examples instead of just presenting guidelines, and to establish practical experiments with new working practices in selected projects.

5. Summary

Part of the literature on program development is based on a number of assumptions according to which a programming process has the following characteristics:

1. It is based on a well-defined problem.

2. Exactly one programmer is involved.

3. The result is a running program.

4. The program is to be used by the programmer himself.

These assumptions are practically never valid in system development projects - and it is probably only a minority of practical programming processes which fit into this picture. Typical system development processes have the following characteristics:

1. They are based on complex situations which may be characterized by ambiguity as well as conflict. At the same time problems continually shift during the course of the process.

2. There are several people with different qualifications and experience involved.

3. The result is new working processes and new forms of organization which entail new computer based systems and tools. A major problem is to design the interplay between these elements.

4. The so-called users rarely participate in the project, and different groups of users have different expectations and requirements to the results of the process.

This article has discussed the application of formalization in relation to the latter type of situation. One objective of the article has been to extend the discussion of formalizations from a narrow programming context to a broader systems development context. This part of the discussion has confirmed, and on some points strengthened, Naur's fundamental statement: Formalizations are of great practical value as a possible extension of a basically informal means of expression. Today practical systems development is based on informal means of expression, and the quality of the specifications need to be improved. This can be achieved through a more disciplined application of informal means of expression, and through an increased partial application of formalizations.

The other objective of this article has been to extend and clarify our concept of method and formalization. We see methods as prescriptions for regulating both the means of expression employed in descriptions and design, as well as the individual and collective forms of behaviour in practical systems development. There is almost always a considerable difference between what people say they do, and what they actually do. It is our ambition to understand and change what we actually do when we program or develop systems. From this perspective it is important to see formalizations not only in relation to means of expression, but also in relation to types of action.

Concerning the application of formalizations for managing systems development, our summarizing statement is fundamentally the same as in the relation between formalizations and means of expression: System developers basically have to rely on informal and situation-determined behaviour, because they often find themselves in unknown and unpredictable situations. Formalized behaviour is just a feasible way of improving efficiency and quality in certain situations. The important thing is to establish a disciplined regulation of the basically informal behaviour.

In practice we can nevertheless observe endeavours toward formalization of systems development both on a theoretical, and on a practical level.

Why? Is our analysis wrong? From our viewpoint the answer is simple: In practice programming and systems development are carried out within financial and organizational settings, and formalizations are not only applicable as professional tools for executing the work process in a more efficient and qualified manner. They are also often efficiently employed by external managers to exercise control over the work process.

> "To make the production of programs independent of individual programmers - in much the same way as cars are produced independently of individual automobile workers - various schemes have been proposed from time to time to standardize what programmers do ... structured programming offered an entirely new way of writing programs ... if managers could not yet have machines which wrote programs, at least they could have programmers who worked like machines." (Kraft 77).

There are, however, limits to regulating organizational behaviour by rules and procedures - even though this may run counter to the beliefs of the true bureaucrat. In many situations - especially when programming or developing systems - people have to go by intuition, bypass rules, or find new ways to solve the problems facing them.

References

Boehm, B.W. (1981). Software Engineering Economics. Prentice-Hall.

Brooks, F.P. jr. (1982). The Mythical Man-Month. Addison-Wesley.

Davis, G.B. (1982). Strategies for Information Requirements Determination. IBM Systems Journal, 21. pp. 4-30.

Floyd, C. (1984). A Systematic Look at Prototyping. In Budde,R. et al (Eds.) Approaches to Prototyping. Springer-Verlag.

Freedman, D.P., Weinberg, G.M. (1982). Handbook of Walkthroughs, Inspections, and Technical Reviews. Little, Brown and Co.

Jackson, M.A. (1975). Principles of Program Design. Academic Press.

Jackson, M.A. (1983). System Development. Prentice-Hall.

Kraft, P. (1977). Programmers and Managers. Springer-Verlag.

Lanzara, G.F., Mathiassen, L. (1984). Mapping Situations within a System Development Project. University of Aarhus, DAIMI PB-179.

March, J.G., Simon, H.A. (1958). Organizations. Wiley.

Mathiassen, L. (1981). Systems Development and Systems Development Method. University of Aarhus, DAIMI PB-136 (in Danish).

Munk-Madsen, A. (1984). Practical Problems of System Development Projects. In Sääksjärvi, M. (Eds.). Proceedings of the Seventh Scandinavian Research Seminar on Systemeering. (To appear).

Naur, P., (1982). Formalization in Program Development. BIT, 22, pp. 437-453.

Polya, G. (1957). How to Solve It. Doubleday and Company.

Weinberg, G.M. (1982). Overstructured Management of Software Engineering. Course notes for Problem Solving Leadership Workshop.

SPECIFYING AND PROTOTYPING:
SOME THOUGHTS ON WHY THEY ARE SUCCESSFUL

{Daniel M. Berry[1] , Jeannette M. Wing[2]}

Computer Science Department   Computer Science Department
University of California   University of Southern California
Los Angeles, CA 90024   Los Angeles, CA 90089
U. S. A.

Abstract

Two methods that have been successful in producing good software are 1) specifying and then implementing and 2) prototyping and then implementing. This paper identifies what the two methods have in common, namely that the implementation is the second time through carefully thinking about the problem. It proposes that perhaps this common aspect is more important to the successes of the methods than other aspects of the methods.

1.   Introduction

1.1.   Our Background

We both work actively in the fields of specification and verification. In addition to doing research in these fields, we both consult for a company, SDC, which specializes in implementing secure systems by first formally specifying them, then verifying that the specifications meet some of the desired properties, and then finally implementing the systems. We both also have implemented software by first prototyping it and then implementing it a second time.

1.2.   Purpose of this Paper

The purpose of this paper is to promote some needed discussion of the reasons why projects are successful when they are successful*. Since it is difficult to conduct controlled experiments on such projects, our conclusions are at best conjectures. We hope that we can provoke sufficient debate so that more accurate conclusions can be reached by a consensus of the actual workers in such projects. Regardless of what the ultimate conclusions, the thoughts presented in this paper impact the choice of methods for software development, project management, and tool development. In this paper, we are thinking in print with hopes that the community joins us.

1.3.   Our Claim

We have observed a number of successful software development projects. Some were developed by a method that we call *specifying*, some others were developed by a method that we call *prototyping*, and still others were developed by other methods which are not discussed here. These terms are defined in more detail in the next section. For now, it suffices to say that in each method, the method is named by what is done in the first stage. In this first stage the product of the method, either a specification or a prototype, is thoroughly checked with the help

---

[1] This work was supported in part by the University of California MICRO Program, SDC, A Burroughs Company, and NCR Corporation.

[2] This work was supported in part by the National Science Foundation under Grant No. ECS-8403905.

* Note that we are not attempting to determine why projects fail. We hope that in determining why successful projects succeed, the ideas can be applied to increase the probability of success in all projects. Examination of the reasons for project failure is also necessary, but space simply does not permit it.

of automated tools and possibly even executed. The second stage in both is the implementation stage, in which what is learned in the first stage is applied to produce a suitable production version of the software. What is common to the two methods is what we call the *second time phenomenon*. That is, the delivered, production quality software is a second pass through the problem which follows a formally stated and machine-checked first pass. In the specifying case, the specification is formal and it can be checked by verifying, with the aid of a verification program, that it meets desired properties and that it is consistent. In the prototyping case, the prototype, i.e., the program, is formal, and it can be checked by a compiler or interpreter, the run-time environment, and the users when running the program.

We wonder if the most important factor in the success of these projects is the fact that the delivered software is a second pass after a formal, machine-checked first pass. That is, we wonder if this second time phenomenon is more critical to the successes than any other factors arising from the particulars of specifying and prototyping *per se*.

1.4. Outline of Rest of Paper

In Section 2, we clarify what we mean by the terms "specifying" and "prototyping." In Section 3, we elaborate on our claim by focusing on the similarities between the two methods and enumerating some successful applications of both methods. In Section 4, we explore the implications of our claim as it impacts on software methods, languages, tools, and project management. In Section 5, we present arguments that favor one method over the other by focusing on some differences between the two. Finally, in Section 6, we briefly state our conclusions.

2. Clarification of Terms

The two methods, *specifying* and *prototyping*, both start with informal requirements and have two major development stages. They have the same second stage, which is the implementation stage, and differ only in their respective first stages. In this section, we define what we mean by the terms "specifying" and "prototyping" by describing what happens in their first stages. These definitions are important because if any ingredient is left out, then the implementation cannot rightfully be called a second formal and machine-checked pass through the problem.

By *specifying*, we mean the following process:

1. writing a formal specification of the proposed software using some precisely defined and machine-processable specification language such as Affirm [Aff81], Gypsy [Gyp78], Ina Jo® [Ina80], Larch [GH83], and SPECIAL [Hdm79], and
2. checking this specification with the aid of its language processor and other tools. This checking includes as much of the following as possible

   a. syntax checking,
   b. type checking,
   c. verifying that the specification is formally consistent,
   d. verifying that the specification meets stated correctness criteria such as invariants, and
   e. (possibly) exercising the specification on actual or symbolic data with the help of a symbolic evaluator, such as UNISEX for the Ina Jo language [KE83] and the symbolic evaluator of McMullin and Gannon [McG83].

   Typically, the first two of these checks are done by the language's processor. The conjectures for the two verification checks are generated by this processor, and the conjectures are proved to be theorems with the aid of an associated, possibly interactive, theorem prover.

By *prototyping*, we mean the following process:

1. writing a first version of the software and bringing this version to a running state using an implemented pro-

---

® Ina Jo is a trademark of SDC, A Burroughs Company.

gramming language, which may be different from that used to write the production version,

2. checking this first version with the language's processors and tools, and

3. subjecting this first version to the end-users' acceptance tests.

By *first version*, we include also possibly incomplete versions written for exploration and experimentation by the programmers and clients [Flo84].

The checks done during the second and third steps of this process include syntax checking, type checking, and interface checking, and run-time checking. The first three checks are typically done by a compiler of the language and the fourth done with the code generated by this compiler perhaps in conjunction with a special debugging run-time system. Alternatively, these checks may be done by an interpreter of the language.

Observe that a programming language is a formal language; it has precise syntax and semantics just as any other language more traditionally considered to be a specification language. In the same light, it is clear that a program is just as much a formal statement of an algorithm as is a more traditional first-order predicate calculus specification of the algorithm.

3. Elaboration of Our Claim

3.1. Similarities Between Specifying and Prototyping

Close examination of the two methods shows that they have much in common and one wonders if what they have in common is the major reason for their success. In both cases, one must write a complete formal description of the system before beginning to code the system in its deliverable, production form. In the specifying case, the formal description is written typically in a first-order predicate calculus language, in a set theoretic language, or in an algebraic framework. In the prototyping case, the formal description is the first implementation, possibly in a language other than the production version language, i.e., in a so-called very high level language. Thus, in either case, one crucial result is a formal description of the software.

In both cases, the formal description is then subjected to a thorough battery of machine checks. These include syntax and type checking. These include interface consistency checks. In addition, in the specifying case, these may include the generation and subsequent verification of theorems that assert the consistency of the specification and that it meets stated requirements. These checks may also include execution with test data with the aid of a symbolic evaluator. In the prototyping case, the program is run with test data. Besides this testing against the data, given a suitable language implementation, the run-time system also performs a number of run-time semantic tests such as checking that variables are initialized before use, subranges and array bounds are observed, nil pointers are not dereferenced, etc. In addition, there may be symbolic evaluators, execution tracers, snapshot generators, etc. that allow the testers to observe the details of the program's execution. In either case, by the time the specification or prototype is accepted as done, the writers have had to eliminate many, many bugs and to iron out many, many wrinkles.

These machine-aided tests are crucial. They help to eliminate conceptual errors in the understanding of the problem that lead to serious design flaws. Anyone who has written a specification or prototype to completion knows how picky the machine tests are. Anyone who has written one of these without the benefit of machine processing knows how easy it is to handwave one's way into overlooking major design flaws and major processing errors. Machine-processing and checking help prevent cheating.

Furthermore, formality of the language used in specifying or prototyping is critical. If the language were not formal, then it could not be machine-processed and checked. The language's semantics would remain sufficiently fuzzy to permit human ambiguity. This ambiguity is useful for human-to-human contact, but is potentially disastrous to the completion of a software project.

Therefore, with either method, the writing of the production version of the software, i.e., what is done in the second stage of each method, constitutes a second pass through the problem, in which the first pass has had the purpose of finding many, if not all, of the tricky corners of the problem. We believe that *the fact that this is the second pass through the problem* is more important to the success of software projects than in what language the first pass was written and whether the machine processing involved proving theorems or executing the program on test data.

3.2.   In Support of Our Claim

To substantiate our claim, we list in this section some successful examples of specifying and prototyping. In addition to these examples of successful projects, some documented "folklore" also lend support to our observation of the *second time phenomenon* and the commonality between specifying and prototyping. Many books on software engineering, e.g., [CL76, LHN79, KP74], admonish the programmer not to be afraid to throw programs out and start all over. Brooks [Bro75] even suggests *planning* to throw early versions away.

3.2.1.   Some Successful Applications of Specifying

The successful projects that have used specifying as its method include the LSI Guard done at I.P. Sharp [Sta81], the COS/NFE project done at Compion [SW82], the SCOMP project done at Honeywell [Fra83], the SIFT project done at SRI [MS82], the Message Flow Modulator done at Austin [GSS82], the Secure Release Terminal done at SDC [HAK83], and the signalling system done at the General Electric Company [CCI81]. In each case the system was formally specified and the resulting specification was verified to meet its requirements with the help of an automatic or interactive theorem prover. The system was then implemented and is now running. Landwehr has a longer list of all such projects, successful and not so successful [Lan83].

3.2.2.   Some Successful Applications of Prototyping

The successful prototyping projects are too numerous to list completely and include the following well-known (at least to the authors) examples: the UNIX™ operating system done at Bell Labs and at UC Berkeley [Unix], the Device Independent TROFF done at Bell Labs [Ker82], the Cedar system at done at Xerox Parc [Tei84], the REVE term rewriting system generator done at MIT and the University of Nancy [Les83, FG83], the Affirm specification and verification system done at USC's Information Sciences Institute [Aff81], the EMAS operating system done at the University of Edinburgh [SRSY77, SYRS80, RS82], and the S-port portable version of SIMULA done at the Norwegian Computing Center [NCC??]. In each case the current delivered version of the software is at least the second, or is built based on experiences with at least one other, earlier system.

Further discussions of prototyping may be found in the *Software Engineering Notes* issue containing the working papers submitted to the ACM SIGSOFT Rapid Prototyping Workshop [Pro82]. Of relevant interest is the healthy dosage of papers relating prototyping with specifying, including those on executable specifications which are therefore prototypes [Smo82, GM82, Dav82, Fea82, BGW82] and the process of prototyping specifications [Mac82, KK82, HH82]. Also, the recent proceedings, *Approaches to Prototyping* [BKMZ84], thoroughly explores many aspects of prototyping. Of relevant interest, the first article by Floyd [Flo84] attempts to reconcile the wide variety of views as to what is prototyping; in all of these views of prototyping, the prototype is a first version of at least a two-version progression.

3.3.   Qualifications to Our Claim

We do not mean to imply that two times is necessary or even sufficient for success. There are and will be first-time projects done well and there are and will be second-time projects done poorly even if the first pass is done well. All we are doing is trying to identify the major reason for success in the two methods and the cited projects.

We acknowledge that the perception of success via either specifying or prototyping may be more psychological and attributable to learning than anything else. For instance, some successful applications of prototyping may not even have started off as attempts to prototype. They may have been projects in which the software was done twice because the first effort, though satisfactory, was not perfect and because other desired enhancements were

---

™UNIX is a trademark of AT&T Bell Laboratories.

discovered or requested. Similarly, in [GHW82], the authors state that the process of specifying, i.e., understanding and learning about the problem to be specified, is at least as or often more beneficial than having the resulting specification.

4. Implications of Our Claim

This section describes some implications of accepting the validity of our claim. These are offered to explain the methodological impact of the claim.

4.1. What Should Not Work

The reader should correctly infer that we do not believe that a first pass that is done without the benefit of machine-processing is likely to lead to as successful an end-product. Thus, for example, the use of non-processed specifications or specifications involving second-order logic (which is not processable) should be discouraged. Likewise, we discourage prototyping that is too rapid or haphazard. More specifically, the following two activities are less useful than the activities of specifying and prototyping as defined in Section 2.

1. Using non-machine checked formal specifications. A non-machine checked formal specification is as good as an informal specification. Although both may be useful pieces of documentation, to prevent the specifier from "cheating" and to ensure at least the consistency of the specification, it is more valuable to use and rely on machine-checked specifications. We maintain that the process of specifying is still valuable, whether or not the product is eventually checked. With the proper social processes [DLP79], i.e., many people carefully poring over such specifications, these too can lead to successful projects, e.g., the Ada® compiler done with the help of the Vienna Definition Method [CO84]. A specification, however, must be written at least with the intention that it be checked, and ideally with tools that help perform the checks.
2. Rapid prototyping when done too haphazardly or with the intention of throwing out versions. Probably no one would advocate non-systematic approaches to software development. A prototype should be written with as much attention paid to good planning and design as that paid in any implementation effort, even if it is not intended to be the final version. Making modifications made to a well-designed prototype should go faster than making them to a poorly-designed one. Also, systematic planning and recording of what modifications are made at each stage can speed up the entire process itself.

4.2. What Should Work: Combining Specifying and Prototyping

4.2.1. Methods

The traditional software life cycle method includes one or more specification phases in which specifications in varying degrees of formality are written. In practice, however, rapid prototyping is a method often used to get a working system up quickly. According to our claim these two methods are not incompatible since one can view writing a formal specification as writing a first prototype. Instead of choosing one method over another, it may prove beneficial either to follow both in parallel or to interleave the two activities and to compare intermediate results at their intersecting formal specification/first prototype step.

4.2.2. Languages

In order to support specifying and prototyping as compatible activities, the problem of which languages to use arises. There are three languages for which choices must be made: the specification language, the prototyping language, and the (eventual) implementation language. One must choose which particular language to use for each and whether any should be the same. These decisions can greatly influence the speed and cost of software development.

® Ada is a trademark of the U. S. Department of Defense (AJPO).

Traditionally, specification and implementation languages were different, but currently the distinction between the two is blurring. Executable specification languages, such as OBJ [GT79] and GIST [BGW82], can be used as high-level programming languages. Very high level programming languages, such as SETL [KS84], and applicative programming languages, such as Prolog [CM81] and FP [Bac78], can be used as specification languages. More consistent with our claim, however, is to use an executable specification language as a prototyping language, though not necessarily as the eventual implementation language. Thus, specifications must be executable, a viewpoint which many designers of specification languages currently advocate [GM82, Zav84, Orl84], or at least be subject to machine-aided semantic checks [GH83]. Furthermore, if the specification and prototyping languages are chosen to be the same, but different from the implementation language, the transition from the specification/prototyping language to the implementation language must still be made.

4.2.3. Project Organization

Given that methods and languages overlap, one needs to rethink how to organize a project to obtain reliable and correct software as efficiently and economically as possible. Most software projects are organized along a traditional life cycle approach. If prototyping is to be accepted as a viable parallel activity or otherwise somehow integrated into the life cycle approach, then guidelines for managing, controlling, and budgeting for prototyping need to be made with the same concern as for the other activities in the life cycle. In any project in which reliability, security, safety, correctness, or user-friendliness is important, i.e., all but the most trivial or private programs, the project must be organized and budgeted to allow for the two times through the problem.

5. Differences Between Specifying and Prototyping

So far, we have focused on the commonality between the two activities of specifying and prototyping as ways of systematically developing software. Now, in order discharge our duty to attempt to find an *absurdum* of an unverifiable hypothesis, we will discuss some of their differences. We have made the distinctions between specifying (the activity) and a specification (the product of specifying), and between prototyping and a prototype. The important differences between specifying and prototyping are not differences between performing the two different activities, but are differences between the products of having performed them, i.e., specifications and prototypes, and their intended uses.

As stated in Section 1.2, we wish to promote some needed discussion on why specifying and prototyping are both successful methods. To provide grounds for further discussion, in this section we examine arguments first in favor of specifying and then in favor of prototyping. The arguments for specifying are the traditional ones propounded by the specification community; those for prototyping are taken from conclusions from documented experiments, which were conducted to compare specifying and prototyping. For each of the arguments, we propose counterarguments to show how the argument either does not hold in practice or presumes definitions of specifying or prototyping different from those we gave in Section 2.

5.1. In Favor of Specifying

5.1.1. Main Argument

5.1.1.1. Specifications are Independent of Implementations

A specification is written independently of any of its implementations. Consequently, specifications serve more easily than prototypes do for the following two uses. First, a specification is a contract between a user and an implementor. On one side of the contract, a user need be concerned with only the specification and not with any of its possible implementations. In principle, to understand the behavior of an implementation, the user need look only at its specification and neither look at the implementation nor execute it. On the other side of the contract, the implementor need be concerned with only satisfying a specification without any knowledge about any of the users of the implementation. This argument holds for whether a user is a person or another piece of software.

The second use is that a specification is a common reference point among the several implementors on the same project. This use is especially important for large software projects where implementation work is divided among a team of programmers and a specification is composed of specifications of pieces of the software. Each member of the team is thus concerned only with implementing and maintaining a piece of the software and making sure that it satisfies a piece of the entire specification.

5.1.1.2. A Counterargument

On the other hand, the above advantages can be ascribed to a well-written program that is taken to be a specification. The point is that the above main argument presumes the following three beliefs:

1. It is better to understand the behavior of a system by reading a specification of its behavior than by running the system.
2. It is easier to understand the behavior of a system by reading a specification than by reading an implementation, i.e., the program text.
3. Specifications are written in a more abstract manner than are implementations.

The first belief is always true under circumstances in which running the system is either dangerous or prohibitively expensive. Examples of such systems are real-time systems with potential consequences of loss or destruction of life. It is also true under circumstances where the user of a system is concerned with the properties a system guarantees and not with the operational details of the system. Examples of such properties are security [HAK83], reliability [MS82], and performance [Zav82]. This first belief, however, is not necessarily true in other circumstances. There may be problem domains in which it is better to run the system than to read its specification because it would be easier for the user to understand the system by observing its behavior than by reading about it. For example, users may rather run a series of acceptance tests over systems that are heavily dependent on human interaction, e.g., interfaces to text editors, database query systems, or CAD/CAM systems, instead of (or in addition to) reading their specifications.

The second belief is not always true. Many specifications are hard to read because of the language they are written in, their size, or lack of machine support to aid in understanding them. Conversely, many implementations are easy to read because of the language they are written in, their design (their modular decomposition and proper choice of data types), and richness of machine support (structured editors, libraries).

Similarly, the third belief is not always true. An unskilled specifier may expose implementation details or make premature design decisions in his or her specification. Conversely, a highly skilled programmer who makes use of the abstraction power of the implementation language may hide implementation details in order to make the resulting software more easily modified [Par72, Mye79].

5.1.2. Three Other Arguments

One: One can deduce properties of a system from a specification without running the system. As argued previously, there are some circumstances in which one cannot or should not run a system. Also, one may want to check for desired (or undesired) properties of a system even before implementation has begun in order to see how design decisions interact. In both cases, a specification can be used to derive properties that may or may not have been originally desired by the user. Such feedback can be used to accept or reject the system, or it may induce a change to the system or to the specification itself [Win84]. In practice, however, only a few experiments have been performed on non-trivial examples where non-trivial properties were derived [Hen79, MS79, GH80]. In some cases, it is even difficult to know what properties one might want to deduce [Win80]. Finally, this difference between specifications and prototypes can be counted as an advantage only if the specification is small enough to do proofs by hand or if there is sufficient software support to do proofs by machine.

Two: A specification is intended to be a consistent and complete description of a system whereas a prototype is intended to be an approximation of the eventual system. This difference points out that a prototype is typically written with intentional incompletenesses in mind and even with intentional inconsistencies. A prototype may leave the implementation of certain features of the desired system for future versions; it may even differ in contradictory ways from the final system. This difference between a specification and a prototype counts as an advantage for specifications if one views a specification as system documentation. A prototype that is incomplete or inconsistent cannot be used as a reliable piece of system documentation. However, at least for the reason of consistency, we exclude this sort of prototype as a basis for the method we described. Furthermore, a specification can easily be written, perhaps intentionally, with the same incomplete coverage as the above described prototype. Thus again, the argument boils down to how the specification or prototype is actually written.

Three: Specifications can be written in a language that is more abstract than any programming language and that is possibly non-executable. Not bound to traditional programming languages, a specifier is free to write specifications with assertions that take full advantage of the power of set operations or that quantify over infinite sets. The properties of expressibility and understandability should guide the choice of a specification language. The various branches of mathematics provide their own languages for expressing properties of their systems. Hence, mathematics provide a rich set of languages from which to base specification languages. On the other hand, mathematical languages are not easily understood, especially by those not trained in mathematics. Educating non-mathematicians* in specification languages remains an important practical problem. In addition, a skillful prototyper can modularize an implementation using the same high level abstractions with well-named functions so that its structure is identical to that of a highly abstract mathematical specification.

5.2. In Favor of Prototyping

In order to argue in favor of prototyping and to present counterarguments, we begin by summarizing the main results of two experiments documented in the literature.

Experiment 1: Gray, Boehm, and Seewaldt [BGS84] describe an experiment comparing prototyping to the more traditional life cycle approach, which includes specifying the software; this specifying, however, may be only informal. The purpose of their experiment is to determine which method produces the best software. They had several student groups apply the two methods to the same software product development. They found that prototyping, as opposed to specifying,

1. tends to produce a smaller product with roughly equivalent performance with less effort,
2. tends to produce higher equivalent user satisfaction per person-hour but lower delivered source instructions per person-hour,
3. tends to produce better human-machine interface, continual availability of a running version, and reduced deadline effects,
4. tends to produce software that is perceived to be easier to maintain, but
5. tends to lead to less planning and more testing and fixing, and to more difficult integration.

Experiment 2: Alavi [Ala84] describes the results of interviewing groups of users and systems analysts to determine which method was more satisfying. She finds that prototyping, as opposed to the more traditional life cycle methods, is perceived to facilitate better communication between users and designers during the design and implementation of the system and thus to facilitate better utilization of the system by the users. The users appeared more satisfied with the accuracy and the helpfulness of the output of a prototyped system than of one developed by life cycle methods. She concludes, however, that in designing innovative systems with fuzzy, not well-understood requirements, prototyping should be done by skilled people. She also concludes that in some cases prototyping may not be useful.

Boehm reaches this last conclusion on economic grounds [Boe81]. He argues that for well-understood problems, it is wasteful to prototype.

---

* Even mathematicians trained in one branch, e.g, numerical analysis, require additional training to understand languages used in other branches, e.g., number theory.

While the above described experiments clearly show the benefits of prototyping§ the results are strictly speaking not applicable to our definitions of the terms. First, the specifying or traditional life cycle method tested does not necessarily include machine-checkable formal specifications. Second, neither experiment is carried out through the second stage of the prototyping, i.e., when a production version is produced. It would be interesting to follow up these experiments up with this consideration.

Finally, Brooks points out one advantage of prototyping that may not be obtainable if specifying is done: when something gets running, the morale of the workers goes sky high. We have observed, however, the same jump in morale when an arduous effort in specifying finally results in a verified and consistent specification.

6. Conclusions

To do a good job on any large complicated project, one must understand the problem – a lack of understanding can lead to catastrophic failures. One is more likely to obtain this requisite understanding when building a "complete" model of the intended system, e.g., a formal specification or a prototype, than when simply handwaving through an incomplete design. The importance of machine-checking in this process is that it helps to ensure that one's model is complete and to prevent overlooking or ignoring tricky details. Thus, when going through a problem the second time, one can take advantage of the knowledge gained from having already gone through a formal understanding of the problem once.

We have attempted to expose the issues while suggesting our own favored conclusions. Of course, until some controlled experimentation can be done to test our hypotheses, the conclusions can only be conjectures. We hope that the conjectures are convincing and that this discussion has promoted useful debate.

Acknowledgements

The authors have benefited from discussions with Orna Berry, Myron Hecht, Tom Hinke, Nancy Leveson, and Ben Livson.

Bibliography

[Ala84]   Alavi, M., "An Assessment of the Prototyping Approach to Information Systems Development," *CACM* 27:6, June, 1984.

[Bac78]   Backus, J., "Can Programming Be Liberated from the von Neumann Style? A Functional Style and Its Algebra of Programs," *CACM*, 21:8, Aug., 1978.

[BGW82]   Balzer, R.M., Goldman, N.M., and Wile, D.S., "Operational Specification as the Basis for Rapid Prototyping," "Special Issue on Rapid Prototyping, Working Papers from the ACM SIGSOFT Rapid Prototyping Workshop," *SOFTWARE ENGINEERING NOTES* 7:5, Dec., 1982.

[BGS84]   Boehm, B.W., Gray, T.E., and Seewaldt, T., "Prototyping vs. Specifying: A Multi-Project Experiment," *Proceedings of the Seventh International Conference on Software Engineering*, Orlando, FL, May, 1984.

[Boe81]   Boehm, B.W., *Software Engineering Economics*, Prentice-Hall, Englewood Cliffs, NJ, 1981.

[Bro75]   Brooks, F.P., Jr., *The Mythical Man Month, Essays on Software Engineering*, Addison-Wesley, Reading, MA, 1975.

[BKMZ84] Budde, R., Kuhlenkamp, K., Mathiassen, L., and Züllighoven, H. (Eds.), *Approaches to Prototyping*, Springer-Verlag, Berlin, 1984.

[CCI81]   CCITT, "Specifications of Signalling System No. 7," *Yellow Book, VI*, Fascicle VI-6, Recommendations Q.701-Q.741, 1981. Referenced in [Orl84] by J. Woodcock.

---

§ In some cases the benefits are only perceived, but the perception is the benefit.

[CL76] Chmura, L.J. and Ledgard, H.F., *COBOL with Style, Programming Proverbs*, Heyden, Rochelle Pk., NJ, 1976.

[CO84] Clemmensen, G.B. and Oest, O.N. "Formal Specification and Development of an Ada Compiler — A VDM Case Study," *Proceedings of the Seventh International Conference on Software Engineering*, Orlando, FL, May, 1984.

[CM81] Clocksin, W.F., and Mellish, C.S., *Programming in Prolog*, Springer-Verlag, Berlin, 1981.

[Dav82] Davis, A.M. "Rapid Prototyping Using Executable Requirements Specification," "Special Issue on Rapid Prototyping, Working Papers from the ACM SIGSOFT Rapid Prototyping Workshop," *SOFTWARE ENGINEERING NOTES* 7:5, Dec., 1982.

[DLP79] De Millo, R.A., Lipton, R.J., and Perlis, A., "Social Processes and Proofs of Theorems and Programs," *CACM*, 22:5, pp. 271-280, 1979.

[Fea82] Feather, M. "Mappings for Rapid Prototyping," "Special Issue on Rapid Prototyping, Working Papers from the ACM SIGSOFT Rapid Prototyping Workshop," *SOFTWARE ENGINEERING NOTES* 7:5, Dec., 1982.

[Flo84] Floyd, C., "A Systematic Look at Prototyping," in [BKMZ84], pp. 1-18, 1984.

[Fra83] Fraim, L.J. "SCOMP: A Solution to the MLS Problem," *Computer* 16:7, July, 1983.

[FG83] Forgaard, R., and Guttag, J.V., "REVE: A Term Rewriting System Generator with Failure-Resistant Knuth-Bendix," in *Procceedings of an NSF Workshop on the Rewrite Rule Laboratory*, September, 1983, J.V. Guttag, D. Kapur, and D.R. Musser, (editors), available as a General Electric Technical Report No. 84GEN008, April, 1984.

[GM82] Goguen, J.A. and Meseguer, J., "Rapid Prototyping in the OBJ Executable Specification Language," "Special Issue on Rapid Prototyping, Working Papers from the ACM SIGSOFT Rapid Prototyping Workshop," *SOFTWARE ENGINEERING NOTES* 7:5, Dec., 1982.

[GT79] Goguen, J.A., and Tardo, J., "An Introduction to OBJ: A Language for Writing and Testing Formal Algebraic Program Specifications," *Proceedings Conference on Specifications of Reliable Software*, Boston, 1979.

[Gyp78] Good, D.I., Cohen, R.M., Hoch, C.G., Hunter, L.W., and Hare, D.F., "Report on the Language Gypsy, Version 2.0," Tech. Report ICSCA-CMP-10, University of Texas, Austin, Sept., 1978.

[GSS82] Good, D.I., Siebert, A.E., and Smith, L.M., "Message Flow Modulator," Final Report, Institute for Computing Science TR-34, University of Texas, Austin, Dec., 1982.

[GHW82] Guttag, J.V., Horning, J.J., and Wing, J.M., "Some Notes on Putting Formal Specifications to Productive Use," *Science of Computer Programming*, 2:1, Oct., 1982.

[GH83] Guttag, J.V., and Horning, J.J., "An Introduction to the Larch Shared Language," *Proceedings IFIP Congress 1983*, Paris, 1983.

[GH80] Guttag, J.V., and Horning, J.J., "Formal Specification as a Design Tool," *Proceedings Principles of Programming Languages Conference*, Las Vegas, 1980.

[Hen79] Heninger, K.L. "Specifying Software Requirements for Complex Systems: New Techniques and Their Application," *Proceedings Conference on Specifications of Reliable Software*, Boston, 1979.

[HAK83] Hinke, T., Althouse, J., and Kemmerer, R.A., "SDC Secure Release Terminal Project," *Proceedings of the 1983 Symposium on Security and Privacy*, Oakland, CA, April, 1983.

[HH82] Hooper, J.W. and Hsia, P., "Scenario-Based Prototyping for Requirements Identification," "Special Issue on Rapid Prototyping, Working Papers from the ACM SIGSOFT Rapid Prototyping Workshop," *SOFTWARE ENGINEERING NOTES* 7:5, Dec., 1982.

[Orl84] *International Workshop on Models and Languages for Software Specification and Design*, Orlando, Florida, Workshop Notes, R.G. Babb and A. Mili, editors, Département d'Informatique, Université Laval, Québec, DIUL-RR-8408, March, 1984.

[KE83]   Kemmerer, R.A. and Eckmann, S.T., "A User's Manual for the UNISEX System," Department of Computer Science, UCSB, Santa Barbara, CA, Dec., 1983.

[Ker82]   Kernighan, B.W., "A Typesetter-independent TROFF," Computing Science Technical Report No. 97, Bell Laboratories, Murray Hill, NJ, 1982.

[KP74]   Kernighan, B.W. and Plauger, P.J., *The Elements of Programming Style*, McGraw-Hill, New York, 1974.

[KK82]   Klausner, A. and Konchan, T.E., "Rapid Prototyping and Requirements Specification Using PDS," "Special Issue on Rapid Prototyping, Working Papers from the ACM SIGSOFT Rapid Prototyping Workshop," *SOFTWARE ENGINEERING NOTES* 7:5, Dec., 1982.

[KS84]   Kruchten, P., and Schonberg, E., "The Ada/Ed System: A Large-Scale Experiment in Software Prototyping Using SETL," in [BKMZ84], pp. 398-415, 1984.

[Lan83]   Landwehr, C.E., "The Best Available Technologies for Computer Security," *Computer* 16:7, July, 1983.

[LHN79]   Ledgard, H.F., Hueras, J.F., and Nagin, P.A., *Pascal with Style, Programming Proverbs*, Heyden, Rochelle Pk., NJ, 1979.

[Les83]   Lescanne, P., "Computer Experiments with the REVE Term Rewriting system Generator," *Proceedings of Tenth Symposium on Principles of Programming Languages*, Austin, TX, Jan., 1983.

[Hdm79]   Levitt, K.N., Robinson, L., and Silverberg, B.A., "The HDM Handbook," Vols. 1-3, SRI International, Menlo Pk., CA, 1979.

[Ina80]   Locasso, R., Scheid, J., Schorre, D.V., and Eggert, P.R., "The Ina Jo Reference Manual," TM-(L)-6021/001/000, System Development Corporation, 1980.

[Mac82]   MacEwan, G.H., "Specification Prototyping," "Special Issue on Rapid Prototyping, Working Papers from the ACM SIGSOFT Rapid Prototyping Workshop," *SOFTWARE ENGINEERING NOTES* 7:5, Dec., 1982.

[MG83]   McMullin, P.R., and Gannon, J.D., "Combining Testing with Formal Specifications: A Case Study," *IEEE-TSE*, SE-9:3, May, 1983.

[MS82]   Melliar-Smith, P.M., and Schwartz, R.L., "Formal Specification and Mechanical Verification of SIFT: A Fault-Tolerant Flight Control System," *IEEE Transactions on Computers*, C-31:7, July, 1982.

[Mye78]   Myers, G.J., *Composite/Structured Design*, Van Nostrand Reinhold, New York, 1979.

[NCC??]   "Programmer's Reference Manual for S-PORT SIMULA 67 System, Norwegian Computing Center, (date cannot be determined from document).

[Par72]   Parnas, D.L., "On the Criteria to be Used in Decomposing Systems into Modules," *CACM*, 15:2, Dec., 1972.

[RS82]   Rees, D.J., "The Kernel of the EMAS 2900 Operating System," *Software—Practice and Experience* 12, 655-667, 1982.

[SRSY77]   Shelness, N.H., Rees, D.J., Stephens, P.D., and Yarwood, J.K., "An Experiment in Doing it Again, *But Very Well This Time*," CSR-18-77 Department of Computer Science, University of Edinburgh, December, 1977.

[SYRS80]   Stephens, P.D., Yarwood, J.K., Rees, D.J., and Shelness, N.H., "The Evolution f the Operating System EMAS 2900", *Software—Practice and Experience* 10, 993-1008, 1980.

[Smo82]   Smoliar, S.W., "Approaches to Executable Specifications," "Special Issue on Rapid Prototyping, Working Papers from the ACM SIGSOFT Rapid Prototyping Workshop," *SOFTWARE ENGINEERING NOTES* 7:5, Dec., 1982.

[Pro82]   "Special Issue on Rapid Prototyping, Working Papers from the ACM SIGSOFT Rapid Prototyping Workshop," *SOFTWARE ENGINEERING NOTES* 7:5, Dec., 1982.

[Sta81]   Stahl, S., "LSI GUARD System Specification (Type A)," MTR-8452, MITRE Corp., Bedford, MA, Oct., 1981.

[SW82]   Sutton, S.A. and Wilut, C.K., "COS/NFE Functional Description," DTI Document 389, Compion Corp., Champaign, IL, Nov., 1982.

[Tei84]   Teitelman, W., "A Tour Through Cedar," *Proceedings of the Seventh International Conference on Software Engineering*, Orlando, FL, May, 1984.

[Uni81]   "The UNIX Programmer's Manual," Bell Telephone Laboratories, Murray Hill, NJ, June, 1981.

[Aff81]   Thompson, D.H. and Erickson, R.W. (Eds.), "AFFIRM Reference Manual," USC Information Sciences Institute, Marina Del Rey, CA, Feb., 1981.

[Win80]   Wing, J.M., "Experience with Two Examples: A Household Budget and Graphs," USC/ISI Affirm Memo-30-JMW, Aug., 1980.

[Win84]   Wing, J.M., "Helping Specifiers Evaluate Their Specifications," *Proceedings Second International Conference on Software Engineering*, AFCET, Nice, France, June, 1984.

[Zav82]   Zave, P., "An Operational Approach to Requirements Specification for Embedded Systems," *IEEE-TSE*, SE-8:3, May, 1982.

[Zav84]   Zave, P., "The Operational Versus the Conventional Approach to Software Development," *CACM*, 27:2, Feb., 1984.

A Formal Specification of Line Representations on Graphics Devices

Lynn S. Marshall

Department of Computer Science

University of Manchester

Manchester, UK

M13 9PL

Abstract

To show that a computer graphics system functions properly it is necessary to prove that the images it produces are correct. Most graphical devices are unable to exactly represent an image, or even just a straight line. Thus each device must display an approximation to the ideal. This paper presents a formal specification of the properties any reasonable approximation to a straight line should have. Bresenham's algorithm is shown to satisfy this specification and extensions to the specification are discussed.

1 Introduction

Formal specification is a useful tool in many areas of computer science since it allows the aims of a computer system to be clearly and unambiguously expressed, and statements concerning the system to be formally proven [17]. Formal specification of computer graphics systems is in its infancy. Research in this field has been pioneered by Carson [7], Gnatz [14], and Mallgren [19]. Formal specification is of great potential help in computer graphics.

Graphical data is usually in the form of images composed of various drawing primitives such as points, lines, and text. Most graphical devices are unable to represent drawing primitives exactly and thus must produce an approximation to the ideal. This makes the use of conventional program verification tools, such as a test driver, very difficult. Graphical Kernel System (GKS) is the new draft international standard for two-dimensional interactive computer graphics [13]. Designing test suites for GKS implementations is certainly not straightforward [5], and work on formal specification of GKS is underway [8,21].

A formal description of the approximation to an image that a given computer graphics device should display will be useful in proving that the various devices in a computer graphics system function correctly. The idea of specifying what comprises a valid approximation to some ideal picture on a given graphics device has been deliberately ignored in previous research in the formal specification of graphics area. Mallgren [19] says, "the display system is assumed to provide a recognizable approximation to this representative picture," while Carson [7] admits, "of course, someone must eventually describe how a line should look but we could treat this as a binding issue, not a specification issue." However, it seems meaningless to maintain that a graphics program is functioning correctly unless it produces recognizable output. Carson [7] notes the following:

> "At one extreme, nothing at all is said about the actual effects on a display surface when an output primitive is drawn. This would enable any vendor to claim that almost any implementation conformed to the standard, since it would be impossible to test implementations. At the other extreme, the ... specification could completely describe the effects of output primitives in terms of parameters such as addressability, color, hardware, text fonts, etc. that apply to typical display devices. Unfortunately, any parameter set considered by the specifiers placed unfair restrictions on manufacturers of certain classes of display devices. Furthermore, fixed parameters would inhibit the degree of technological flexibility available to implementors."

Thus, it is necessary to devise a specification that will permit the display of any one of a range of approximations to a picture so allowing any reasonable output, but only reasonable output.

Section 2 of this paper discusses graphics devices and their capabilities, and section 3 describes lines and their attributes. In section 4 a formal specification of thin solid lines is given, while section 5 describes various line drawing algorithms, and section 6 is a proof that Bresenham's line drawing algorithm satisfies the specification. Section 7 suggests some extensions to the specification, and a discussion of ideas for further research and conclusions follow in sections 8 and 9. Appendix A shows a sample line plotted by various line drawing algorithms. A thick line specification can be found in an extended version of this paper [20].

2 Graphics Devices

The two major graphical display device types are the vector device and the raster device [11]. A picture on a vector device is composed of straight line segments, while on a raster device the picture is made up of picture elements, or pixels, at fixed positions. Vector drawing displays and pen plotters are examples of vector devices. Raster devices include raster displays, laser printers and electrostatic plotters [29]. The graphics device model used is that of a raster device since drawing lines on vector devices is simpler.

A graphics device displays images in a number of colours. It may be capable of depicting thousands of colours, a range from black to white, or possibly just two colours (binary). For simplicity the model of a raster device is limited to two colours: a background colour (OFF) and a foreground colour (ON). The display surface is composed of pixels, each one unit square with its centre having integer coordinates. Each pixel on the screen of the device may be either ON or OFF, and the pixels approximating the line are those to which the foreground colour is assigned.

3 Lines

A straight line to be displayed on a graphical device usually has a number of associated parameters. It must have a start point, an end point, a width, a linetype, and a colour. The line can be any length, have any slope, be thick or thin, and solid or broken. Since the pixels of the raster device lie in a grid formation, the device must produce an approximation to the line to be displayed. Thus, the representation of a line on a raster device is non-trivial. The following specification is for thin solid lines having integral endpoints.

4 Straight Solid Thin Lines with Integral Endpoints on a Two-Colour Raster Device

What properties should the approximation to a line on a raster device have? As stated earlier, the properties given should be specific enough to allow only reasonable approximations but general enough to allow any reasonable approximation. Thus it is inappropriate to specify an exact algorithm since a range of approximations is permitted. Neither is it appropriate for the representation to be entirely implementation dependent as the role of the specification is to limit the implementor.

4.1 Properties

The following are some intuitive ideas concerning the approximation to a straight line on a raster device:

1. If a pixel is ON it must be "close" to the line.
   (i.e., No pixels that are very far from the line should be ON.)

2. If a pixel is "very close" to the line it must be ON.
   (i.e., No pixels very close to the line should be OFF.)

3. If two pixels are adjacent, on the same side of the line and the further of the two from the line is ON then the closer of the two to the line must also be ON.

4. The pixels which are ON form a connected region with no holes or bends.

4.2 Notation

The notation used is adapted from the Vienna Development Method (VDM) [18].

4.2.1 Data Types and Instances

A data type is defined in one of three ways. It may be a basic data type a, a composite data type, or a data type having multiple components. A basic data type is defined as follows:

        Data-type$_1$ = English description of the data type

A composite data type is a collection of another data type. For example:

        Data-type$_2$ = set of Data-type$_1$

If the data type has multiple components it is defined as follows:

$$\text{Data-type}_3 ::$$
$$\quad\quad \text{PART}_1 : \text{Data-type}_1$$
$$\quad\quad \text{PART}_2 : \text{Data-type}_2$$
$$\quad\quad\quad\quad \vdots$$
$$\quad\quad \text{PART}_n : \text{Data-type}_n$$

A data type name is made up of the underscore (−), alphabetic, and numeric characters. The name normally begins with a capital, with the remainder being lower case. Special names using bold letters and special symbols may be used for the basic data types (e.g. $\mathbf{R}^* = \text{reals} \geqslant 0$). The components of a data type are given names in upper case, possibly with a subscript. If there are any special restrictions to a data type these are expressed using the **require** keyword. For example:

$$\text{Data-type}_4 : \text{set of Data-type}_1 \quad [\; \text{require set of Data-type}_1 \neq \{\} \;]$$

4.2.2 Function Definitions

A function is defined as follows:

$$\text{Function} : \text{Data-type}_1 \times \text{Data-type}_2 \times \dots \times \text{Data-type}_n \rightarrow \text{Data-type}$$
$$\text{Function}(\; d_1, d_2, \dots, d_n \;) \triangleq \text{mathematical function description}$$

The name of the function is the word preceding the colon (:). The function name usually starts with a letter but may begin with a greek character. The input data type is described as the Cartesian product followed by the type of the function. The function is then described in postfix format, using instances of the input data types. Infix format is used for some two-parameter functions. The only unusual constructs used in the function descriptions are the **require** and **where** keywords; **require** is used to restrict the input to a function, similar to restricting a data type as described above, and **where** is used to allow an abbreviation to be used in the function description. For example:

$$\text{Setfunc} : \text{set of } R \rightarrow R \quad [\; \text{require set of } R \neq \{\} \;]$$
$$\text{Setfunc}(\; \text{elements} \;) \triangleq \; \dots N \dots$$
$$\quad\quad \text{where } N = \text{Max}(\; \{\; \text{elements} \;\} \;)$$

4.3 Specification

The above mentioned concepts are now formalized.

4.3.1 Data Types

A *line on the screen with integral endpoints:*
$$\text{Line} :: \quad [\; \text{require } P_1 \neq P_2 \;]$$
$$\quad P_1 : \text{Pixel}$$
$$\quad P_2 : \text{Pixel}$$

A *pixel on the screen:*
$$\text{Pixel} ::$$
$$\quad X : Z_x$$
$$\quad Y : Z_y$$

Z_x : integral x-range of screen $\subset Z$
Z_y : integral y-range of screen $\subset Z$

The set of pixels turned on when approximating a line:
Pixel-set : set of Pixel

A line ∈ R²:
Realline :: [**require** $P_1 \neq P_2$]
  P_1 : Point
  P_2 : Point

A point ∈ R²:
Point ::
  X : R
  Y : R

R : reals
R* : reals $\geqslant 0$
R² : Cartesian plane
Z : integers
B : Booleans

Note that Pixel is treated as a subset of Point. Thus any function accepting a Point as a parameter will also accept a Pixel (but not vice versa).

4.3.2 Make-Functions

Make-functions are used to form instances of a multiple component data type. A compound type written in the form (x, y) is always assumed to be of type Point (or Pixel). To form an instance of any other compound data type a make-function is used. Assume we have a type as follows:

     Data-type ::
        D_1 : $Type_1$
        D_2 : $Type_2$
        ⋮
        D_n : $Type_n$

Then to form an instance of this data type the following function would be used:
      mk-Data-type : $Type_1 \times Type_2 \times \ldots \times Type_n \to$ Data-type
      mk-Data-type($d_1, d_2, \ldots, d_n$) $\triangleq \iota$ d ∈ Data-type.
       ($D_1(d) = d_1 \wedge D_2(d) = d_2 \wedge \ldots \wedge D_n(d) = d_n$)

4.3.3 Point Operations

Addition:
  $+_p$: Point $\times$ Point $\to$ Point
  $P_1 +_p P_2 \triangleq (X(P_1) + X(P_2), Y(P_1) + Y(P_2))$

Subtraction:
  $-_p$: Point $\times$ Point $\to$ Point
  $P_1 -_p P_2 \triangleq (X(P_1) - X(P_2), Y(P_1) - Y(P_2))$

Multiplication:
  $\cdot_p$: R $\times$ Point $\to$ Point
  $c \cdot_p p \triangleq (c \cdot X(p), c \cdot Y(p))$

  x_p : Point $\times$ Point $\to$ Point
  $P_1 x_p P_2 \triangleq (X(P_1) \cdot X(P_2), Y(P_1) \cdot Y(P_2))$

Division:

    /p : Point × Point → Point

    P_1 /p P_2 ≙ (X(P_1) / X(P_2), Y(P_1) / Y(P_2))

Less Than:

    <p : Point × Point → B

    P_1 <p P_2 ≙ (X(P_1) < X(P_2)) ∧ (Y(P_1) < Y(P_2))

Less Than or Equal to:

    ≤p : Point × Point → B

    P_1 ≤p P_2 ≙ (X(P_1) ≤ X(P_2)) ∧ (Y(P_1) ≤ Y(P_2))

Summation:

$$\sum_{i=1}^{n} {}_p : \text{Point} \times \text{Point} \times \ldots \times \text{Point} \to \text{Point}$$

$$\sum_{i=1}^{n} {}_p \, P_i ≙ (\sum_{i=1}^{n} X(P_i), \sum_{i=1}^{n} Y(P_i))$$

4.3.4 Line Operation

Equality:

    $=_1$: Realline × Realline → B

    $l_1 =_1 l_2$ ≙ ($P_1(l_1) = P_1(l_2) ∧ P_2(l_1) = P_2(l_2)$) ∨

                ($P_1(l_1) = P_2(l_2) ∧ P_2(l_1) = P_1(l_2)$)

4.3.5 Function Specification

Is the approximation to the given line valid and within a tolerance of δ?

    Validapprox : Pixel—set × Line × R^* → B

    Validapprox(pixset, line, δ) ≙

        (∀ pix ∈ pixset. Withintol(pix, line, δ))

        if a pixel is ON it is "close" to the line

        ∧ (∀ pix ∈ Pixel. (Nearline(pix, line) → pix ∈ pixset))

        if a pixel is "very near" the line it is ON

        ∧ Closrptson(pixset, line)

        any pixel closer to the line than a pixel that is ON is ON

        ∧ Validpic(pixset)

        the pixel formation is valid

Is the pixel within the given tolerance of the line?

    Withintol : Pixel × Line × R^* → B

    Withintol(pix, line, δ) ≙ ∃ p ∈ Point.

      (Onlineseg(p, line) ∧ Maxdist(pix, p) ≤ δ)

Is the point on the line segment?

    Onlineseg : Point × Line → B

    Onlineseg(p, line) ≙ ∃ δ ∈ [0,1]. (p = P_1(line) +p (δ ·p Δ(line)))

What is the difference between the endpoints of the line?

    Δ : Line → Point

    Δ(line) ≙ P_2(line) -p P_1(line)

What is the maximum horizontal or vertical distance between the two points?

    Maxdist : Point × Point → R^*

    Maxdist(P_1, P_2) ≙ Max({ |X(P_1) - X(P_2)|, |Y(P_1) - Y(P_2)| })

What is the maximum of the set?
    Max : set of R → R [require set of R ≠ {}]
    Max(s) ≙ ι a ∈ s. (∀ b ∈ s. (a ⩾ b))

Is the pixel very close to the line?
    Nearline : Pixel × Line → B
    Nearline(pix, line) ≙ Endpt(pix, line) ∨ Linethru(pix, line)

Is the pixel an endpoint of the line?
    Endpt : Pixel × Line → B
    Endpt(pix, line) ≙ pix = P_1(line) ∨ pix = P_2(line)

Does the line run right through the pixel?
    Linethru : Pixel × Line → B
    Linethru(pix, line) ≙ ∃ p_1, p_2 ∈ Point.
    (Onlineseg(p_1, line) ∧ Onlineseg(p_2, line)
    ∧ ¬Adjcorn(p_1, p_2, pix) ∧
    ∧ ((Onreallineseg(p_1, Leftbord(pix))
        ∧ Onreallineseg(p_2, Rightbord(pix)))
    ∨ (Onreallineseg(p_1, Botbord(pix))
        ∧ Onreallineseg(p_2, Topbord(pix))))

Are the two points adjacent corners of the pixel?
    Adjcorn : Point × Point × Pixel → B
    Adjcorn(p_1, p_2, pix) ≙ p_1 ≠ p_2 ∧ let rline = mk−Realline(p_1, p_2) in
    (rline $=_1$ Leftbord(pix) ∨ rline $=_1$ Rightbord(pix)
    ∨ rline $=_1$ Botbord(pix) ∨ rline $=_1$ Topbord(pix))

What is the left border of the pixel?
    Leftbord : Pixel → Realline
    Leftbord(pix) ≙ mk−Realline(pix $+_p$ (−1/2,−1/2), pix $+_p$ (−1/2,1/2))

What is the right border of the pixel?
    Rightbord : Pixel → Realline
    Rightbord(pix) ≙ mk−Realline(pix $+_p$ (1/2,−1/2), pix $+_p$ (1/2,1/2))

What is the bottom border of the pixel?
    Botbord : Pixel → Realline
    Botbord(pix) ≙ mk−Realline(pix $+_p$ (−1/2,−1/2), pix $+_p$ (1/2,−1/2))

What is the top border of the pixel?
    Topbord : Pixel → Realline
    Topbord(pix) ≙ mk−Realline(pix $+_p$ (−1/2,1/2), pix $+_p$ (1/2,1/2))

Is the point on the given real line segment?
    Onreallineseg : Point × Realline → B
    Onreallineseg(p, rline) ≙ ∃ δ ∈ [0,1]. p = P_1(rline) $+_p$ (δ $·_p$ $Δ_r$(rline))

What is the difference between the endpoints of the real line?
    $Δ_r$: Realline → Point
    $Δ_r$(rline) ≙ P_2(rline) $-_p$ P_1(rline)

Are all pixels closer to the line than an ON pixel ON?
    Closrptson : Pixel−set × Line → B
    Closrptson(pixset, line) ≙ ∀ pix_1, pix_2 ∈ Pixel.
    ((Adjacent(pix_1, pix_2) ∧ ¬Oppsides(pix_1, pix_2, line)
    ∧ Closrl(pix_1, pix_2, line) ∧ pix_2 ∈ pixset) ⇒ pix_1 ∈ pixset)

Are the two pixels adjacent?
    Adjacent : Pixel × Pixel → B
    Adjacent(pix_1, pix_2) ≙ (Mindist(pix_1, pix_2) = 0)

What is the minimum horizontal or vertical distance between the two points?
      Mindist : Point × Point → R*
      Mindist(p₁, p₂) ≜ Min({ |X(p₁) - X(p₂)|, |Y(p₁) - Y(p₂)| })

What is the minimum of the set?
      Min : set of R → R [require set of R ≠ {}]
      Min(s) ≜ ι a ∈ s. (∀ b ∈ s. (a ≤ b))

Are the pixels on opposite sides of the line?
      Oppsides : Pixel × Pixel × Line → B
      Oppsides(pix₁, pix₂, line) ≜ pix₁ ≠ pix₂ ∧ ∃ p ∈ Point.
        (Inlineseg(p, mk-Line(pix₁, pix₂)) ∧ Online(p, line))

Is the point a non-endpoint of the line segment?
      Inlineseg : Point × Line → B
      Inlineseg(p, line) ≜ ∃ δ ∈ (0,1). (p = P₁(line) +ₚ (δ ·ₚ Δ(line)))

Is the point on the line?
      Online : Point × Line → B
      Online(p, line) ≜ ∃ δ ∈ R. (p = P₁(line) +ₚ (δ ·ₚ Δ(line)))

Is the first pixel closer to the line than the second?
      Closrl : Pixel × Pixel × Line → B
      Closrl(pix₁, pix₂, line) ≜ ∃ δ ∈ R*.
        (Withintol(pix₁, line, δ) ∧ ~Withintol(pix₂, line, δ))

Is the pixel formation valid?
      Validpic : Pixel-set → B
      Validpic(pixset) ≜ Validrows(pixset) ∧ Validcols(pixset)

*Are the rows of the display valid? (i.e. Do only rows in a continuous range
contain ON pixels and is each of these rows valid?)*
      Validrows : Pixel-set → B
      Validrows(pixset) ≜ ∃ y₁, y₂ ∈ Z_y. (y₁ ≤ y₂ ∧
        ∀ y ∈ (Z_y - { y₁,...,y₂ }). (∀ x ∈ Z_x. (x,y) ∉ pixset)
        ∧ ∀ y ∈ { y₁,...,y₂ }. Validrow(pixset, y))

*Is this row of the display valid? (i.e. Does this row have only one continuous
range of pixels ON?)*
      Validrow : Pixel-set × Z_y → B
      Validrow(On, y) ≜ ∃ x₁, x₂ ∈ Z_x. (x₁ ≤ x₂ ∧
        ∀ x ∈ (Z_x - { x₁,...,x₂ }). (x,y) ∉ pixset ∧
        ∀ x ∈ { x₁,...,x₂ }. (x,y) ∈ pixset)

*Are the columns of the display valid? (i.e. Do only columns in a continuous range
contain ON pixels and is each of these columns valid?)*
      Validcols : Pixel-set → B
      Validcols(pixset) ≜ ∃ x₁, x₂ ∈ Z_x. (x₁ ≤ x₂ ∧
        ∀ x ∈ (Z_x - { x₁,...,x₂ }). (∀ y ∈ Z_y. (x,y) ∉ pixset)
        ∧ ∀ x ∈ { x₁,...,x₂ }. Validcol(pixset, x))

*Is this column of the display valid? (i.e. Does this column have only one
continuous range of pixels ON?)*
      Validcol : Pixel-set × Z_x → B
      Validcol(pixset, x) ≜ ∃ y₁, y₂ ∈ Z_y. (y₁ ≤ y₂ ∧
        ∀ y ∈ (Z_y - { y₁,...,y₂ }). (x,y) ∉ pixset ∧
        ∀ y ∈ { y₁,...,y₂ }. (x,y) ∈ pixset)

5 Thin Line Drawing Algorithms

If the specification is reasonable any of the common line drawing algorithms will satisfy it. Also, it should be easily extendable. A summary of line drawing algorithm references has been compiled by Earnshaw [9]. Sproull also discusses line drawing algorithms [27]. An outline of a variety of thin line drawing algorithms follows. Each of these algorithms satisfies the above specification. The pixel set for each algorithm and the appropriate tolerance are given.

5.1 Bresenham's, Simple Digital Differential Analysis (DDA), and Chain Code Algorithms

For any given line these three algorithms produce the same approximation by sampling the line once per row or column and turning on the closest pixel to the sampled point. Whether the line is sampled by row or by column is based on the slope of the line and selected so that the maximum number of points will be sampled. The Simple DDA algorithm [23], is the most straightforward. Bresenham's algorithm [4] is optimized to use only integer arithmetic, and the Chain Code algorithm [26] stores the resulting line as a series of integers modulo 7, representing the eight different directions one can proceed to an adjacent pixel.

The line is related to the pixel set by:

pix ϵ pixset ↦
    $\exists$ n ϵ {0,...,N}. (pix = P_1(line) $+_p$ Round$_p$(n/N $\cdot_p$ Δ(line)))
    where N = Maxdist(P_1(line), P_2(line))

Round$_p$: Point → Pixel
Round$_p$(p) $\triangleq$ (Round(X(p)), Round(Y(p)))

Round : R → Z
Round(r) $\triangleq$ ι i ϵ Z. (r − 1/2 < i ⩽ r + 1/2)

These algorithms always turn on pixels which the line at least touches, and thus have a tolerance of 1/2.

5.2 Symmetric DDA Algorithm

The Symmetric DDA algorithm [23] is similar to the Simple DDA algorithm, but samples the line more frequently. The length of the line determines the number of times the line is sampled. To make the notation simpler the following abbreviations are used:

      Δx for X(Δ(line)), and

      Δy for Y(Δ(line)).

The length of the line is usually approximated by:

      Max({ $|\Delta x|$, $|\Delta y|$ }) + 1/2 $\cdot$ Min({ $|\Delta x|$, $|\Delta y|$ })

since $\sqrt{(\Delta x^2 + \Delta y^2)}$ is expensive to compute. Also, for efficiency reasons, the number of steps is chosen to be a power of two. Thus the number of sampled points is $2^n + 1$, where n is the smallest n such that 2^n > Max({ $|\Delta x|$, $|\Delta y|$ }) + 1/2 $\cdot$

Min({ |Δx|, |Δy| }). The Symmetric DDA algorithm gives a more equal density to approximations to lines of different slopes than the Simple DDA.

The line is related to the pixel set by:

pix $\in$ pixset $\Leftrightarrow$
   $\exists$ n $\in$ {0,...,N}. (pix = P_1(line) $+_p$ $Round_p$(n/N $\cdot_p$ Δ(line)))
   where N = Minvalidn(line)

Minvalidn : Line $\to$ N
Minvalidn(line) $\triangleq$ n $\in$ N. (Validn(n, line) $\wedge$
   $\forall$ m $\in$ N. (Validn(m, line) $\to$ n $\leqslant$ m))

Validn : N x Line $\to$ B
Validn(n, line) $\triangleq$ $\exists$ k $\in$ N. (n = 2^k) $\wedge$ n >
   Maxdist(P_1(line), P_2(line)) + 1/2 $\cdot$ Mindist(P_1(line), P_2(line))

The symmetric DDA algorithm always turns on pixels touched by the line and thus has a tolerance of 1/2.

5.3 All Pixels Touched Algorithm

It is easy, theoretically, to imagine a line drawing algorithm which samples the line "everywhere" thus turning on all pixels touched by the line. Of course, this could only be implemented approximately and would be inefficient.

The line is related to the pixel set by:

pix $\in$ pixset $\Leftrightarrow$
   $\exists$ p $\in$ Point. (Onlineseg(p, line) $\wedge$ pix = $Round_p$(p))

This algorithm also has a tolerance of 1/2.

5.4 Brons' Chain Code Algorithm

The Chain Code algorithm presented by Brons [6] produces a line similar, but not identical to the Chain Code algorithm discussed earlier. The chain code is produced in a recursive manner, giving successive approximations to the line until the "best" approximation is achieved.

It has not been possible to find a simple non-recursive description of this algorithm! Brons' Chain Code algorithm is often identical to the standard Chain Code Algorithm. However, in cases with |Δx| = n, and |Δy| = 1, it gives approximations with a tolerance approaching 1.

5.5 Binary Rate Multiplier (BRM) Algorithm

The BRM Algorithm [22] was once a popular line drawing algorithm due to its speed. However, it tends to produce rather inaccurate approximations and, with the advent of more accurate quick algorithms, it is rarely used. It is based on binary arithmetic. Both |Δx| and |Δy| are expressed in binary notation using n bits. The point (x_1,y_1) is turned on and a binary clock then counts from 0 to $2^n - 1$. At each stage, x is incremented if and only if the bit changing from 0 to 1 in the counter is 1 in the binary representation of |Δx|. The same applies to y.

The line is related to the pixel set by:

pix ∈ pixset ↔
  ∃ d ∈ {0,...,2ⁿ - 1}. pix = P_1(line) $+_p$

$$\text{Sign}_p(\text{ line }) \; x_p \; \sum_{i=1}^{n} \left(\text{Round}_p(\; d \; / \; 2^{n+1-i} \; \cdot_p \; c_i \;) \right)$$

  where n = Minvalidn(line),
    ∀ i ∈ {1,...,n}. c_i ∈ {(0,0),(0,1),(1,0),(1,1)}.

$$(\; | \; \Delta(\text{ line }) \; | \; = \sum_{i=1}^{n} 2^{i-1} \cdot_p c_i \;)$$

Validn : ℕ x Line → B
Validn(n, line) ≙ 2^n > Maxdist(P_1(line), P_2(line))

Sign_p : Line → Point
Sign_p(line) ≙ (Sign(X(Δ(line)), Sign(Y(Δ(line)))

Sign : Z → Z
Sign(a) ≙ if a = |a| then 1 else -1

The BRM algorithm can be very inaccurate, especially for lines with |Δx| equal to the reflection of |Δy|, in binary notation. The tolerance for this algorithm is approximately 2.

See appendix A for a sample line and the approximations produced by these line drawing algorithms.

6 Proof for Bresenham's Algorithm

Throughout this section the following abbreviations are used:
  P_1 for P_1(line)
  X_1 for X(P_1(line))
  Y_1 for Y(P_1(line))
  Δ for Δ(line)
  Δx for X(Δ(line))
  Δy for Y(Δ(line))
  R for Round
  R_p for Round_p

6.1 ∀ pix ∈ pixset. Withintol(pix, line, 1/2)

pix ∈ pixset ↔ pix = P_1 $+_p$ R_p(n/N $\cdot_p$ Δ).
Now, p = P_1 $+_p$ (n/N $\cdot_p$ Δ) is on the line segment, since 0 ≤ n/N ≤ 1. And, either Δx/N, or Δy/N is an integer, as N = |Δx| or |Δy|. Thus, Maxdist(pix, p) = |R(X(p)) - X(p)| or |R(Y(p)) - Y(p)|, and so Maxdist(pix, p) ≤ 1/2, and the ON pixel is within 1/2 of the line as desired.

6.2 ∀ pix ∈ Pixel. (Nearline(pix, line) → pix ∈ pixset)

Nearline(pix, line) ↔ Endpt(pix, line) ∨ Linethru(pix, line).
Now if the pixel is an endpoint of the line, it will be ON (cases n = 0 and n = N).
If the line runs right through the pixel, there are two cases:

Case 1: If $N = |\Delta x|$ then the line runs through the pixel in a horizontal direction, and we have that the point ($X(pix)$, $Y(pix) + \delta$), for $\delta \in (-1/2, 1/2)$, is on the line. Since $N = |\Delta x|$ this column will be sampled, and this pixel will be turned ON since $R(Y(pix) + \delta) = Y(pix) + R(\delta) = Y(pix)$.

Case 2: On the other hand, if $N = |\Delta y|$ then the line runs through the pixel in a vertical direction, and the point ($X(pix) + \delta$, $Y(pix)$), for $\delta \in (-1/2, 1/2)$, is on the line. This row will be sampled, and since $R(X(pix) + \delta) = X(pix)$, this pixel will be turned ON.

6.3 Closrptson(pixset, line)

Closrptson(pixset, line) ↦ ∄ pix_1, $pix_2 \in$ Pixel.
(Adjacent(pix_1, pix_2) ∧ ⌐Oppsides(pix_1, pix_2, line) ∧
Closrl(pix_1, pix_2, line) ∧ $pix_2 \in$ pixset ∧ $pix_1 \notin$ pixset).

Case 1: $N = |\Delta x|$, pix_1 and pix_2 are horizontally adjacent
Without loss of generality, assume Δx is positive. Then since pix_2 is ON, $X(pix_2)$ = $X_1 + n$ and $Y(pix_2) = Y_1 + R(n \cdot \Delta y / \Delta x)$. And thus, $X(pix_1) = X_1 + n + 1$ and $Y(pix_1) = Y_1 + R(n \cdot \Delta y / \Delta x)$. Now, pix_1 and pix_2 are on the same side of the line, and pix_1 is closer to the line than pix_2. So, the line must cross the line $x = X(pix_1)$ between $Y(pix_1)$ and $Y(pix_1) - 1/2$, or $Y(pix_1)$ and $Y(pix_1) - 1/2$. Thus $R((n+1) \cdot \Delta y / \Delta x) = R(n \cdot \Delta y / \Delta x)$ and thus pix_1 will be ON. Thus it is true that no such pix_1 and pix_2 exist, and the above is satisfied.

Case 2: $N = |\Delta x|$, pix_1 and pix_2 are vertically adjacent
Since pix_2 is ON, it is within 1/2 of the line. However, pix_1 is closer to the line so the points must be on opposite sides of the line, so again the above is satisfied.

Case 3: $N = |\Delta y|$, pix_1 and pix_2 are horizontally adjacent
Similar to case 2.

Case 4: $N = |\Delta y|$, pix_1 and pix_2 are vertically adjacent
Similar to case 1.

6.4 Validpic(pixset)

Validpic(pixset) ↦ Validrows(pixset) ∧ Validcols(pixset). Bresenham's algorithm only turns on pixels in rows and columns between p_1 and p_2, and it turns on at least one pixel in each of these, due to the choice of N. Thus, it is necessary only to check that each of these rows and columns is valid.

Case 1: $N = |\Delta x|$
Only one pixel will be turned on in each column, so the columns are valid. Assume we have an invalid row, ie. two pixels in a row are ON, but one in between them is

off. So $\exists$ n,m $\in$ **N**. $p_1 = P_1 +_p R_p(\ n/|\Delta x| \cdot_p \Delta line\ )$, and $p_2 = P_1 +_p R_p(\ (n+m)/|\Delta x|$ $\cdot_p \Delta line\ )$. Since p_1 and p_2 are in the same row $R(\ n \cdot \Delta y/|\Delta x|\ ) = R(\ (n+m) \cdot \Delta y/|\Delta x|\ )$, and thus $R(\ (n+i) \cdot \Delta y/|\Delta x|\ )$, for $i \in \{0,\ldots,m\} = R(\ n \cdot \Delta y/|\Delta x|\ )$. So all pixels in the row between p_1 and p_2 will be ON, and the row must be valid.

<u>Case 2</u>: $N = |\Delta y|$

The argument is the same as in Case 1, with the roles of the rows and columns reversed.

Thus Bresenham's algorithm satisfies the thin solid line specification.

7 Extensions to the Specification

7.1 Vector Devices

Although the drawing primitive on a vector device is a line, a vector device is still not able to reproduce all lines exactly. The limitation is the addressing resolution of the device. Thus, if the pixel size is set equal to the resolution of the vector device the model presented will also be appropriate for vector devices. There may be some parts of the specification that are redundant for a vector device. For example, Closrptson should always be true. But the specification will still suffice.

7.2 Lines With Non-Integral Endpoints

The specification can easily be changed to allow for lines with non-integral endpoints by using Realline everywhere instead of Line. It might be desirable to impose an additional condition on Validapprox to ensure that the pixels containing the endpoints are turned on under certain conditions, but this is probably unnecessary.

7.3 Thick Lines

It is quite easy to extend the thin solid line specification to one for solid lines of thickness "t." One question that arises is how the endpoints of the thick line should be treated, as both round-end and square-end models for thick lines exist. Another requirement that should be added to the specification is that any pixel entirely covered by the thick line should be on.

A specification including these extensions is included in the extended version of this paper [20].

8 Ideas for Further Research

8.1 Related Research

Although none of the recent formal specification of computer graphics systems research has discussed the properties of the approximation to a line on a graphics device, work was carried out in the 1960's and 1970's concerning the representation of solid thin lines on raster or incremental plotter devices [1,2,12,25]. The model used to describe a line is to number the eight pixels adjacent to a given pixel from 0 to 7 in a counter-clockwise direction starting with the pixel on the right. An approximation to a thin line, called the chain code, is then given by a sequence of numbers indicating the direction to proceed from each pixel of the approximation.

Freeman [12] notes:
All chains of straight lines must possess the following three specific properties:
1. the code is made up of at most 2 elements differing by 1 modulo 8
2. one of the two elements always appears singly
3. the occurrences of the singly occuring element are as uniformly spaced as possible

Rosenfeld [25] proves that the above is satisfied if and only if the chain code has the chord property. That is, if and only if for every point, p, of a line segment between two pixels which are ON, there is an ON pixel, pix, such that Maxdist(p, pix) < 1. No extensions are given for thick lines.

While this area has been ignored for some time, raster displays and operations on them are again being researched. Guibas and Stolfi [15] explain that it has been believed that "the graphics programmer should be spared the pain" of dealing with raster images, but it is now being realized that raster images "should be given full citizenship in the world of computer science." They discuss a function, LINE[p_1, p_2, w], which draws a line of thickness w from p_1 to p_2, but note that, "the exact definition of this shape, particularly at the two endpoints, is ... application-dependent."

8.2 Alternate Approaches

The work presented is all based on the model introduced in Section 2. If a different model to that of the square pixel is used new insight into the properties of output primitives on graphics devices might be obtained. One idea is to look at different tesselations of the Cartesian plane. What would the specification look like if hexagonal pixels, for example, were used? The concepts of rows, columns and adjacent pixels would need to be examined.

Another approach might involve the splitting of the specification into two parts: the local and global properties of the line. Local and global properties are discussed by Guibas and Stolfi [15]. A local property is one that can be checked for each pixel or small piece of the approximation. Such as:

If a pixel is ON it is "close" to the line.
On the other hand, a global property is one requiring the entire approximation to be considered as a whole. For example:

The line "looks" straight.

Examining the specification in this way may present new ideas.

The choice of distance function can also influence the specification. Although the maximum horizontal or vertical distance between two points conforms to the square pixel model, the Euclidean distance function is introduced when thick lines are discussed [20]. A different choice of distance function may simplify the specification or suggest a new model.

8.3 Further Properties of Solid Straight Lines

There are many additional properties of a solid straight line that could supplement or replace some of those given in the specification. It is desirable to come up with a simple specification and, at the same time, keep it both specific and general enough to encompass all reasonable approximations. One property the approximation should have is that the line "looks straight." This idea is incorporated in the Validpic portion of the specification. However, perhaps a better formulation of this notion can be given. For example, for a device with a very high precision, it may not be necessary to require that there are no "holes" in the approximation, as a small hole would be undetectable.

Other properties which are desirable in line drawing algorithms are:

1. A line produced has constant density.
2. All lines produced have the same density.
3. The line from p_1 to p_2 is identical to the line from p_2 to p_1.

However, these properties are not possessed by some of the commonly used algorithms. A line produced by the BRM algorithm may not be of constant density. For Bresenham's algorithm, the density of the line depends on its slope [11], and, unless the algorithm is adjusted slightly [3], lines drawn in opposite directions may differ. It may be desirable to try to incorporate relaxations of these conditions into the specification. For example:

1. A line produced has "nearly" constant density.
2. All lines produced have "approximately" the same density.
3. The line from p_1 to p_2 is "close to" the line from p_2 to p_1.

8.4 Further Extensions to the Specification

It would be interesting to give a specification for dashed lines. Dashed lines are usually defined as sections of ink and space [28]. One approach would be to split the line up into a collection of short lines, each specified as a solid line. However, as the point within the ink-space pattern to start with may be implementation dependent, this becomes quite complicated.

Another extension would include the specification of grey-scale lines on a grey-scale or multicolour device. In a grey-scale algorithm [24], each pixel is set to an appropriate shade depending on the portion of it covered by the line. Anti-aliasing [16] is even more complicated as a filtering pattern is used, along with a selection of colours, to smooth the edges of the line preventing them from appearing to be jagged.

Once the specification of a line on a graphics device is complete there are many other drawing primitives to consider, including marker, filled area, and text. And since a picture is rarely composed of a single primitive it is necessary to look at all the primitives within a picture, and decide how to deal with those that overlap, especially on a device with many colours. This problem is discussed by Carson [7], Fiume and Fournier [10], and Mallgren [19]. These so called combining functions should be specified in a formal description of the properties of a graphics device, thus giving an allowable range for the appearance of the final picture, as well as for each primitive within the picture.

Another area for research is the formal specification of the behaviour of graphics input devices.

9 Conclusions

When a new graphics device is produced, it is necessary to be certain that it functions correctly. Although the formal specification presented here is only the tip of the iceberg with regards to the specification of a complete graphics device, it is encouraging that such specifications can be produced, and actually used to prove that algorithms for drawing graphical primitives produce reasonable results.

Acknowlegements

Many thanks to Professor Cliff Jones for his assistance and encouragement, and to Steve Carson, David Duce, Elizabeth Fielding, and my colleagues at the University of Manchester for their valuable ideas and suggestions.

Appendix A — Sample Line

The following diagrams show how the various thin line drawing algorithms discussed in section 5 approximate the line from (0,0) to (21,10). This line was chosen as it illustrates the differences between the line drawing algorithms.

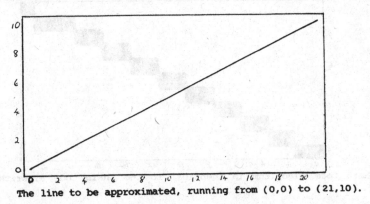

The line to be approximated, running from (0,0) to (21,10).

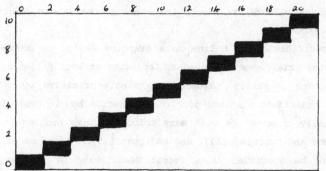

The shaded pixels indicate the approximation produced by Bresenham's, the Simple DDA, and Chain Code algorithms.

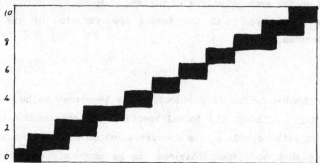

The Symmetric DDA turns on all the pixels turned on by the Simple DDA algorithm, and some additional ones.

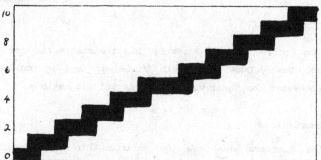

The All Pixels Touched algorithm turns on all the pixels turned on by the Symmetric DDA algorithm, and more.

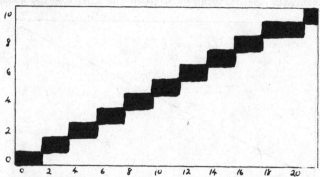

Brons' Chain Code algorithm is identical to the Chain Code algorithm except in column 20.

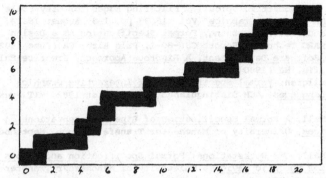

The BRM algorithm is quite inaccurate when approximating this line, since in binary form Δx is the reflection of Δy.

References

1. C. Arcelli and A. Massarotti, "Regular Arcs in Digital Contours," Computer Graphics and Image Processing Vol. 4 pp. 339—360 (1975).
2. G. Bongiovanni, F. Luccio, and A. Zorat, "The Discrete Equation of a Straight Line," IEEE Transactions on Computers Vol. C-24(3) pp. 310—313 (March 1975).
3. J. Boothroyd and P. A. Hamilton, "Exactly Reversible Plotter Paths," Australian Computer Journal Vol. 2(1) pp. 20—21 (1970).
4. J. E. Bresenham, "Algorithm for Computer Control of a Digital Plotter," IBM Systems Journal Vol. 4(1) pp. 25—30 (1965).
5. K. W. Brodlie, M. C. Maguire, and G. E. Pfaff, "A Practical Strategy for Certifying GKS Implementations," in EUROGRAPHICS 82 International Conference and Exhibition UMIST 8-10 Sept 1982, eds. D. S. Greenaway and E. A. Warman, North-Holland (1982).
6. R. Brons, "Linguistic Methods for the Description of a Straight Line on a Grid," Computer Graphics and Image Processing Vol. 3 pp. 48—62 (1974).
7. George S. Carson, "The Specification of Computer Graphics Systems," IEEE Computer Graphics and Applications Vol. 3(6) pp. 27—41 (1974).
8. D. A. Duce, E. V. C. Fielding, and L. S. Marshall, Formal Specifiation and Graphics Software, Rutherford Appleton Laboratory Report RAL-84-068, August 1984.
9. R. A. Earnshaw, Display Algorithms — History, Developments and Applications, University Computing Service, University of Leeds.
10. Eugene Fiume and Alain Fournier, A Programme for the Development of a Mathematical Theory of Computer Graphics, Computer Systems Research Group, Department of Computer Science, University of Toronto, Toronto, Ontario (1984).
11. J. D. Foley and A. van Dam, Fundamentals of Interactive Computer Graphics, Addison-Wesley Publishing Company (1982).
12. Herbert Freeman, "Boundary Encoding and Processing," pp. 241—266 in Picture Processing and Psychopictorics, eds. Bernice Sacks Lipkin and Azriel Rosenfeld, Academic Press, New York-London (1970).
13. Graphical Kernel System (GKS) 7.2 Functional Description, Draft International Standard ISO/DIS 7942 (November 14th, 1982).
14. R. Gnatz, Approaching a Formal Framework for Graphics Software Standards, Technical University of Munich.
15. Leo J. Guibas and Jorge Stolfi, "A Language for Bitmap Manipulation," ACM Transactions on Graphics Vol. 1(3) pp. 191—214 (July 1982).

16. Satish Gupta and Robert F. Sproull, "Filtering Edges for Grey-Scale Displays," ACM Computer Graphics Vol. 15(3) pp. 1-5 (August 1981).

17. John Guttag and James J. Horning, Formal Specification as a Design Tool, XEROX PARC Technical Report CSL-80-1, Palo Alto, CA (June 1982).

18. C. B. Jones, Software Development: A Rigorous Approach, Prentice-Hall, Englewood Cliffs, NJ (1980).

19. William R. Mallgren, Formal Specification of Interactive Graphics Programming Languages, ACM Distinguished Dissertation 1982, MIT Press (1983).

20. Lynn S. Marshall, A Formal Specification of Line Representations on Graphics Devices, University of Manchester Transfer Report, September 1984.

21. Lynn S. Marshall, GKS Workstations: Formal Specification and Proofs of Correctness for Specific Devices, University of Manchester Transfer Report, September 1984.

22. William M. Newman and Robert F. Sproull, Principles of Interactive Computer Graphics, McGraw Hill Kogakuska Limited (1973).

23. William M. Newman and Robert F. Sproull, Principles of Interactive Computer Graphics, Second Edition, McGraw Hill International Book Company (1981).

24. M. L. V. Pitteway and D. J. Watkinson, "Bresenham's Algorithm with Grey Scale," Communications of the ACM Vol. 23(11) pp. 625-626 (1980).

25. Azriel Rosenfeld, "Digital Straight Line Segments," IEEE Transactions on Computers Vol. C-23(12) pp. 1264-1269 (December 1974).

26. Jerome Rothstein and Carl Weiman, "Parallel and Sequential Specification of a Context Sensitive Language for Straight Lines on Grids," Computer Graphics and Image Processing Vol. 5 pp. 106-124 (1976).

27. Robert F. Sproull, "Using Program Transformations to Derive Line Drawing Algorithms," ACM Transactions on Graphics Vol. 1(4) pp. 259-273 (October 1982).

28. University of Manchester Computer Graphics Unit, Interactive Computer Graphics Course Notes (March 1984).

29. John Warnock and Douglas K. Wyatt, "A Device Independent Graphics Imaging Model for Use with Raster Devices," ACM Computer Graphics Vol. 16(3) pp. 313-319 (July 1982).

Experiences with the PSG - Programming System Generator

G. Snelting[*]

Institut für Systemarchitektur

Technische Hochschule Darmstadt

Magdalenenstr. 11

D-61 Darmstadt

Abstract The programming system generator developed at the Technical University of Darmstadt generates sophisticated interactive programming environments from formal language definitions. From a formal, entirely nonprocedural definition of the language's syntax, context conditions and denotational semantics, it produces a hybrid editor, an interpreter and a library system. The editor allows both structure editing and text editing, guaranteeing immediate recognition of syntax and semantic errors. The generator has been used to generate environments for PASCAL, MODULA-2 and the formal language definition language itself. A brief description of the generated environments and the definition language is given, and our experiences with formal language definitions are discussed from the language definer's point of view as well as from the programmer's point of view using the generated environments.

1. Introduction

The Programming System Generator PSG developed at the Technical University of Darmstadt generates language-dependent interactive programming environments from formal language definitions. From a formal definition of a language's syntax, context conditions and denotational semantics it produces an integrated software development environment. One of the major components of a PSG environment is a powerful hybrid editor which allows structure oriented editing as well as text editing. In structure mode, the editor guarantees prevention of both, syntactic and semantic errors, whereas in textual mode it guarantees their immediate recognition. The editor is generated from the language's syntax and context conditions. Furthermore, a PSG environment includes an interpreter which is generated from the language's denotational semantics. A language-independent library system is part

---

[*] Work of this author was supported by the "Deutsche Forschungsgemeinschaft", grant He 1170/2-2

of a PSG environment.

The basic units for editing and interpreting are called fragments. A fragment is an arbitrary part of a program, for example a statement, a procedure declaration or a whole program. Fragments are internally stored as abstract syntax trees. Fragments may be incomplete, that is, subcomponents may be missing. Missing subcomponents are called templates. Bottom-up system development is provided by combining fragments, while the fragments themselves are constructed top-down.

The editor supports two input modes, which may be mixed freely by the user. In textual mode, the editor behaves like a normal screen-oriented text editor with the usual capabilities to enter, modify, delete, search etc. text. By keystroke, incremental syntactic and semantic analysis are invoked. If the input was error-free, the text will be pretty-printed and editing may proceed. If any syntactic or semantic errors are detected, an error message will be displayed by a menu-driven error recovery routine. Earliest possible detection of both syntactic and semantic errors is guaranteed: As soon as a fragment cannot be embedded into a syntactically and semantically correct program, it will be classified as erroneous. For semantic errors, this works even if declarations of e.g. variable types are still missing or incomplete. In structured mode, programs are developed in menu-driven refinement or modification steps. The menus are generated according to the abstract syntax of the language. The usual structure oriented commands are offered to the user, such as refinement of a structure, selection from alternatives of a syntactic class, modification, insertion, and deletion of substructures, zooming of substructures, copying of substructures etc. However, the menus are filtered dynamically by the context analysis, such that only those menu-items producing syntactically and semantically correct refinements after selection will be offered to the user. Thus, in structural input mode, neither syntactic nor semantic errors can occur. In addition the user may retreive the context information which has been derived so far. For example, he might ask the system which variables are already declared, which variables are still undeclared, what possible types the undeclared variables may possess etc[*].

Like the other system components, the interpreter is able to handle arbitrary incomplete fragments. As long as control flow in the interpreted fragment

---

[*] According to our philosophy, declaration before use is not required. An undeclared variable is considered a semantic error as soon as the last template offering the possibility of declaring that variable has been deleted

does not touch any syntactically incomplete structure, the fragment can be
interpreted without difficulties. If flow of control encounters a template,
the editor will be invoked asking the user to enter the missing parts of the
hrlhment. Alternatively, the language definer may force the interpreter
to ask the user for e.g. values of uninitialized variables or missing
expressions.

A language-independent fragment library sytem where fragments are stored as
abstract syntax trees is also part of a generated environment. Reading,
writing and rewriting of fragments is automatically performed by the editor
if required. Deletion of fragments requires an explicit user command. PSG
environments offer the facility of redirecting input to external text files.
Furthermore, fragments may be written in pretty-printed style onto external
files.

PSG is implemented in PASCAL and runs on SIEMENS BS2000 machines. The editor
part of the system has recently been transported onto a PERQ personal
workstation. As this machine offers a high-resolution bit map display and a
pointing device (a mouse), we have been able to implement an improved user
interface.

2. What the language definer has to do

One of the most important goals during the development of PSG has been the
definition of a formal language definition language covering the whole
spectrum of a language's syntax, context conditions and dynamic semantics as
well as all of the additional information required by an interactive
environment e.g. menu texts or pretty-printing information. Thus, the
language definer working with PSG is offered a formal, nonprocedural
definition language. This is in striking contrast to most existing environment generators, which frequently support only the formal definition of the
syntactic aspects of a language. For example, the language definer working
with GANDALF [Hab82]· has to write so-called action routines in an ordinary
programming language; these action routines will perform tasks such as type
checking, code generation etc. Using the Cornell Program Synthesizer (CPS)
[Tei81], which is based on attributed grammars, the language definer has to
code certain attribute functions in the language C (recently, a more formal
specification language has been developed [Rep84]).

A PSG language definition consists of three major parts: the definition of
the syntax, the context conditions, and the denotational semantics of the
language. The first part is mandatory, the others are optional. Syntax and
semantics definition rely on well-known concepts. However, new concepts

based on AI technology had to be developed for defining and checking context conditions, due to the specific requirements of interactive environments where programs are usually incomplete containing e.g. pending variable declarations.

Definition of the syntax

The syntax definition part starts with the definition of the lexical structure of the language, which is used to generate a scanner. The language definer has to specify all reserved words and all delimiters (special symbols). Each lexical entity is given a name. For PASCAL, this looks as follows * :

```
if -> 'IF';
then -> 'THEN';
else -> 'ELSE';
becomes ->' := ';
equal ->' = ';
sem ->';';
```

etc.

The abstract syntax, which forms the second part of the syntax definition, is the core of any language definition. All other parts of a language definition refer to the abstract syntax. Abstract syntax rules look like this:

```
CLASS statement = assignment, forstatement, compound, ifstatement, call, ...
NODE assignment :: variable expression;
NODE forstatement :: Id expression to_or_downto expression statement;
NODE compound :: statementlist;
LIST statementlist = statement+;
NODE ifstatement :: expression statement [statement];
NODE call :: Id [parameterlist];
LIST parameterlist = expression+;
CLASS variable = Id, record_ref, array_ref, pointer_ref;
CLASS expression = variable, constant, addition, subtraction, ... ;
NODE addition :: expression expression;
```

etc.

CLASS rules describe syntactic alternatives. NODE rules define substructures of a syntactic entity. Substructures which are optional are enclosed in

square brackets. The number of a node's substructures is fixed, although
they may be of different syntactic type. LIST rules define syntactic
entities with a variable number of substructures of the same syntactic type.

In a PSG environment, fragments are internally represented by abstract
syntax trees. Missing substructures of a node are represented by tree
templates; they serve as placeholders for pending refinements. Missing
sublists of a list are called list templates, they may be moved, deleted and
inserted freely within a list.

The structure oriented commands and menus offered to the user are generated
according to the abstract syntax. For example, each template is associated
with a menu of refinement possibilities. However, this menu is dynamically
filtered with respect to context conditions (see below).

The concrete syntax, which is the third part of the syntax definition, is
used to generate an incremental parser. The concrete syntax is restricted to
full LL(1) grammars. It includes transformation rules which specify how to
build abstract trees from textual input. Thus the concrete syntax is
actually a string-to-tree transformation grammar. Concrete syntax rules look
like this:

```
statement ::= ...
                | NODE for, Id, becomes, expression, to_or_downto, expression,
                       do, statement => forstatement
                | NODE begin, statementlist, end => compound
                | NODE Id, optparameterlist => call;
statementlist ::= LIST statement+-sem;
optparameterlist ::= [lp,parameterlist,rp];
to_or_downto ::= TERMINAL to | TERMINAL downto;
```

etc.

The NODE, LIST and TERMINAL keywords and the '[', ']', and '=>' delimiters
specify how to build the abstract tree during the parsing process. However,
the situation is not always that simple. Frequently, a concrete syntax does
not merely reflect the rules of the abstract syntax, due to operator
precedences or left-factorization used to avoid LL(1)-conflicts. For
example,

```
expression ::= simple_expression, simplexpr_tail;
simple_expression ::= factor, ...;
simpleexpr_tail ::= UPDATENODE equal, simple_expression => equal_expr
                  | EMPTY;
```

Here, the UPDATENODE and EMPTY rules will construct a correct equal_expr

node, although the rules reflect operator precedence and are left-factori-
zed.

The parser will parse any input entered in textual mode. It accepts arbitrary valid prefixes of any input conforming to the syntactical category of a
given template. If any syntax errors are detected, a recovery routine will
compute a menu comprising all local correction possibilities, which is
presented to the user. The user may then correct his input either in textual
mode or by selection among the menu items.

Being the fourth part of the syntax definition, the format definition is a
tree-to-string transformation grammar which is used to construct the
external textual representation of an abstract tree. Prettyprinting information is part of the format definition:

forstatement => | for Id becomes expression to expression do statement [2];
ifstatement => | if expression then statement[2] (statement[2] -> | else,);

In the example, '|' means start of a new line, and indentation factors may
be specified inside square brackets. Parentheses are used to specify
conditional formatting: the keyword 'ELSE' will be displayed only if the
optional else-part of an 'ifstatement' is indeed present. Conditional
formatting is used also to re-insert parentheses into expressions if
neccessary due to operator precedence (note that parentheses are discarded
during parsing and that operator precedences are reflected by the abstract
tree's structure). A string-to-tree-to-string transformation which is
performed by parsing textual input, building the abstract tree and pretty-
-printing the abstract tree must yield the original input text exactly
except for spaces, newlines and redundant parentheses.

In the last part of the syntax definition, headers and menu texts have to be
specified which are used to generate the textual representation of templates
and menus. For each name occuring in the abstract syntax an external name
has to be specified:

statement -> 'Anweisung';
ifstatement ->'Bedingte Anweisung';

For each syntactic class, menu texts have to be specified:

statement -> 'Zuweisung', 'FOR-Anweisung', 'Verbundanweisung', ... ;

For purposes of generality, syntactic entities may posses different external
names, depending on their occurence in templates or in menus.

The definition of context conditions

The context analysis of PSG has been of special interest, since the classical methods like attributed grammars [Knu68] turned out to be inadequate even if attribute evaluation is performed incrementally [Rep83]. Consider the following situation: In a PASCAL program-fragment, the variables 'a' and 'i' have not yet been declared or used, and a declaration-template is still present. Now the user enters an incomplete assignment:

    a[a[i+1]]:=

Although 'a' and 'i' are still undeclared, the context analysis must derive immediately that 'i' has type integer (or a subrange thereof), that 'a' is a one-dimensional array with index and component type integer, and that the still missing right-hand side of the assignment must also be compatible with integer. If a user types 'TRUE' as the right side, a semantic error must immediately be reported. In addition, the menu for the right-hand side template should be filtered in such a way that the menu item for the constant 'TRUE' will not be displayed, as well as all other non-integer expression items.

The classical methods follow the scheme: first inspect the declarations and collect information about e.g. types of variables, then use this information to check type incompatibilities in expressions etc. This scheme does not work in the above example.

The concept of context relations [Hen84] has been developed to overcome these difficulties with the classical methods. The basic idea is to compute a set of still possible attributes for each node of an incomplete fragment. A collection of still possible attribute assignments to the nodes of a fragment is called a context relation. If such a relation consists of exactly one tuple, the context information is unambiguous. If a relation is empty, a semantic error has been detected. It can be shown that the context relation of a composite fragment is just the natural join of the relations of its subfragments. Therefore context conditions may be computed incrementally during editing. As context relations are in general of infinite size, they are represented in a finite way using so-called term form relations with variables. The basic idea is to describe the set of possible attributes by a grammar, the so-called data attribute grammar. Infinite sets of attributes are then represented by incomplete derivation trees according to the data attribute grammar; in addition these derivation trees may contain arbitrary functional dependencies between (sub)trees.

To specify context conditions, the language definer first has to define the scope and visibility rules of the language. This information is used to determine whether all the different occurences of an identifier in a fragment actually denote the same "abstract" identifier. If so, their corresponding sets of still possible attribute values may be intersected. The second part of the context conditions definition is the specification of the data attribute grammar. Here, the structure of the attributes of the language is defined. Typical rules look like this:

```
NODE attribute :: type class;
CLASS type = simple_type, array_type, set_type, ... ;
CLASS simple_type = arithmetic, ordinal;
CLASS arithmetic = integer, real;
CLASS ordinal = integer, boolean, subrange, enumeration, ... ;
NODE settype :: ordinal;
NODE arraytype :: index_types type;
LIST index_types = ordinal+;
CLASS class = variable, ctype, constant, procedure, function, ... ;
```

etc.

The attribute format definition forms the third part of the context conditions definition. Similar to the format definition of the context-free part of the language definition, it specifies how attributes shall be displayed to the user if he looks at the symbol table.

The last and most important part of the context condition definition is the specification of the so-called basic relations, which must be specified for all terminals and each node rule of the abstract syntax. As the context relation of a fragment is the join of the relations of its components, specification of the basic relations provides enough information to analyse each fragment incrementally. A basic relation consists of a set of tuples which define a (possibly infinite) set of attribute assignments to the components of a node rule resp. a terminal. For instance, the basic relation of a syntactic integer number consisting of a single tuple might be:

```
Int: MK-attribute(integer, constant);
```

which specifies that an integer number has type integer and is a constant. More sophisticated specifications can be obtained by using variables, which specify that certain subattributes must be identical. The basic relation for an assignment

```
assignment :: variable expression
```

contains three tupels, which use the variable TYPE:

assignment: NIL MK-attribute(TYPE, variable) MK-attribute(TYPE, computational)
　　　　　| NIL MK-attribute(real, Variable) MK-attribute(integer, computational)
　　　　　| NIL Mk-attribute(TYPE, function) MK-attribute(TYPE, computational);

which says that in an assignment either

- the left-hand side is a variable of a certain TYPE, and the right-hand
  side is an expression of the same TYPE, or
- the left-hand side is a real variable, and the right-hand side is an
  integer expression, or
- the left-hand side is a function identifier with a certain result TYPE,
  and the right-hand side is an expression of the same TYPE. [*]

During editing, an inference engine is used to derive context information
from the basic relations as demonstrated in the above example. Note the
similarity to the AI-paradigma of inference-rule-based deduction systems.

The definition of semantics

Within the PSG system, the dynamic semantics of a language is defined in
denotational style [Gor79]. The denotational semantics is used to generate
an interpreter. The semantic functions are defined in a META-IV-like [Bjo78]
extension of type-free lambda calculus. This metalanguage supports high-
-level conceps like lists and maps and allows the definition of higher-
-order-functionals of arbitrary rank. The terms of the metalanguage are used
as an universal intermediate language. If a fragment is to be executed, it
will be translated into a term of the metalanguage, using the definitions of
the semantic functions. This term will be interpreted, that is, reduced to
normal form. The resulting term is the result of program execution.

In contrast to systems like SIS [Mos79] our interpreter allows interaction
with the user during program execution in order to supply input data, to
enter values of uninitialised variables etc.

The definition of the semantics consists of three parts. First of all, a
set of auxiliary functions to be used elsewhere in the semantics definition
may be defined. For example, the definition of a "distributed concatenation"
function for a list of lists (which is supposed to be used in several
distinct semantic functions for different types of lists) looks as follows:

```
disconc = LAM list_of_lists. IF NULL list_of_lists THEN <>
                ELSE CONC HEAD list_of_lists, (disconc TAIL list_of_lists);
```

Here, LAM denotes functional abstraction, parentheses denote functional

---

[*] For the sake of readability, this specification does not exactly
reflect the ISO-standard "assignment compatibility"

application. NULL is a test for the empty list, CONC, HEAD and TAIL have their usual meanings, and '<>' denotes the empty list.

The main part of the semantics definition comprises the semantic functions for each syntactic entity. In a PASCAL-subset without GOTOs and side effects of functions, the meaning of a statement may be defined as a functional which maps environments onto functions which map states to states. The meaning of an expression is a functional which maps environments onto functions from states to values. An environment is a map which maps identifiers to <location, descriptor> pairs. A state is a map which maps locations to values. Thus, the semantic function for a conditional statement might look as follows:

```
ifstatement: LAM env. LAM state. IF (( |[ expression ]| env) state)
             THEN (( |[ statement 1 ]| env) state)
             ELSE (( |statement 2:LAM env.LAM state.state| env) state);
```

The '|[' and ']|' brackets are the "meta-brackets" which denote the meaning functions of the subcomponents of a node. The special form '|' ... '|' is used for subcomponents which are optional (as the ELSE-part in our example). If the optional subcomponent is missing, the function following the colon will be used.

The third part of the semantics definition describes the meanings of the executable fragments. Typical examples are

```
procedure_declaration: '', ERROR 'Procedure declaration is not executable';
statement: 'Result of statement execution with no variables declared
           or initialized:', (( |[ statement ]| []) []);
```

where '[]' denotes the empty map. Note the difference between the result of a 'statement' execution specified here and the semantic function for the syntactic class 'statement', to which the above definition refers.

3. Experiences with the generator and the generated environments

Until now, environments have been generated for Algol60, PASCAL, MODULA-2, the language definition language itself, and some experimental specification languages. The language definition environment has been used intensively not only by the members of the project team, but also by lots of students, as PSG has been used along with other systems (GAG [Kas80] and GANDALF) in student projects for the implementation of a PASCAL-subset. The PASCAL--environment was used to implement other parts of the PSG system. Since feel that by now we have gathered enough experience to compare our approach to others.

The benefits of a formal language definition language

We think that by now state of the art has reached a point where all of the language specific parts of an environment can be formally described and automatically generated, at least for languages of a complexity not greater than that of e. g. PASCAL.

The use of a formal language definition language has many advantages:

- In view of the power and complexity of the generated environments, PSG language definitions are very short. Typically, they vary in size between 240 lines for an Algol60 environment without context conditions and semantics and 3600 lines for a MODULA-2 environment including full specification of context conditions and denotational semantics.
- The expressive power of the language definition language allows concentration on the relevant aspects of a language definition. The language definer does not have to concern himself with minor details such as the organization of symbol tables etc.
- PSG language definitions are safe, since all inconsistencies in a definition are detected at generation time.[*]
- The modular design of the language definition language improves readability and reliability. It allows the independent definition of the syntactic, context dependent, and semantic aspects of a language, once the abstract syntax has been defined.
- a formal language definition language is an ideal tool during the development of new languages. In a "language design lab", language definitions are easily modified and tested.

As a consequence, the amount of manpower to generate an environment is small: A moderately awake graduate student with some background in programming languages and some initial knowledge of the PSG user interface will specify and debug an Algol60 definition without context conditions and semantics within ten days. The MODULA-2 environment including full specification of context conditions and denotational semantics was defined as part of a diploma thesis within eight months [Klu84].

---

[*] At the moment, this is not true for the semantics definition, as it is based on type free lambda calculus. However, the implementation of a type inference algorithm allowing handling of polymorphism, overloading and coercions is about to be completed (see [Let84]).

The benefits of the hybrid editor approach

In [Fei84], Kaiser and Feiler state for structure oriented editors that
"in order to modify an expression, ... , the user must understand the underlying tree representation and enter a tedious serious of tree oriented clip,
delete and insert commands. Unfortunately, complete parsing of all expressions is also nonoptimal". This is true not only for expressions, but also
for arbitrary structured statements as well as for any syntactic entity
including complete programs. In [Rep81], Teitelbaum and Reps state that
"(the change of a while loop into a repeat loop) must be accomplished by
moving the constituents of the existing WHILE-template into a newly inserted
UNTIL-template. Although such modifications can be made rapidly ..., they
are admittedly awkward". Within a PSG environment, problems of this kind
do not exist, since users may switch freely between textual mode and
structure mode. Furthermore, our experience indicates that experienced
programmers prefer textual mode not only for modifications, but also to
enter e.g. a sequence of statements or even a whole procedure. Since the
parser accepts arbitrary incomplete input and, in case of syntax errors,
generates a menu of all possible local recovery actions, textual input mode
seems to be quite attractive for users who know the concrete syntax of their
language. Furthermore, arbitrary parts of a fragment may be read in from an
external textfile. On the other hand, unexperienced users tend to prefer
structured mode. By simply selecting menu items, they need not bother about
syntactic details which they do not know. Thus, the possibility to mix
textual mode and structure mode freely seems to be the most flexible,
general, and user friendly solution to the dichotomy of viewing programs
either as text or as structure.

The benefits of dynamic context sensitive menu filtering

We believe that preventing mistakes is far superior to making the user fix
them. Within a PSG environment, structured mode prevents syntactical and
semantical errors due to the dynamic context-sensitive menu filtering. This
feature is not provided by any other environment known to us. In textual
mode, the user may always type arbitrary nonsense, but syntactical and
semantical errors will be detected immediately. This guarantees that
programs are correct at every stage of their development.
There is, however, one problem in connection with certain modifications: if
a user modifies e.g. a procedure declaration by adding an extra parameter,
context incompatibilities will occur at each place where the procedure is
called. If the calls are modified first, they will become incompatible with
the procedure declaration. At the moment, the user can circumvent such

situations by temporarily deactivating the context analysis. It is planned to modify the context analysis in a way that enables it to tolerate faulty subtrees temporarely.

Drawbacks in generality and performance

PSG is not the ultimate system, as there remain several unsatisfying points. The current implementation of the definition language imposes some restrictions on the class of languages which may be defined with PSG.

First of all, if the concrete syntax of a language cannot be made LL(1), the language cannot be defined within PSG. It should be possible, however, to incorporate a more powerful parsing technique such as LALR(1) (which is used also in MENTOR [Kah83]). Note that any parser must fullfil the requirement that arbitrary valid prefixes of arbitrary sentential forms must be parseable, and that syntax recovery menus must be computable.

Certain languages have context conditions which are not definable within the current definition language. The scope and visibility analysis cannot handle features like elliptical record references in PL/1 or FORWARD procedure declarations in PASCAL (which will lead to a 'double declaration' error). Within our framework - no declarations required before use - FORWARD declarations do not make sense anyway. The context analysis phase is unable to handle user-defined polymorphic or overloaded objects such as overloaded functions in ADA. We are currently working on a more powerful specification language for context conditions which will overcome these shortcomings. Finally, the semantics definition language is unable to handle any form of parallelism.

The performance of PSG environments has not yet reached production quality, as far as context analysis and program execution are concerned. For the context analysis, this is primarily a problem of the current implementation, which is merely a prototype. However, the intrinsic complexity of the method is greater than that of e.g. attributed grammars: For an abstract syntax tree containing n nodes the Reps/Teitelbaum algorithm will perform with $O(n)$, wheras our method requires $O(n \ln(n))$.

The performance difficulties concerning program execution are of a slightly different nature, as we have difficulties to see how to speed up the interpreter simply by improving its implementation. The interpreter is much faster than that of SIS. However, it is not fast enough for production programs, as is also noted by Pleban for PSP ([Ple84]). We hope that these shortcomings may be overcome by compilation of the metalanguage terms [Bah84b], utilizing techniques like data flow analysis , elimination of unneccesary call-by-name and delayed evaluation, and elimination of tail recursion and linear recursion.

4. Conclusion

We presented the PSG programming system generator, which generates interactive programming environments from formal language definitions. The pros
and cons of using a formal, entirely nonprocedural language definition
language have been discussed. It turned out that use of a formal definition
language allows very simple and rapid generation of reliable and powerful
environments. On the other hand, certain complicated features of certain
languages are not definable with the currently implemented definition
language, and the performance of the generated environments has not yet
reached production quality. Nevertheless, we believe that the use of formal
language definitions is an appropriate tool, and that the shortcomings in
performance will be captured by more sophisticated implementations, which
are still under way.

5. Acknowledgements

I thank the other members of the project team, namely R. Bahlke, W. Henhapl,
M. Hunkel, M. Jäger and T. Letschert for their valuable comments during
the development of this paper.
I also wish to thank the referees for their pertinent remarks.

6. References

[Bah84a] Bahlke, R. and Snelting, G.: Programmiersystemgenerator. Arbeits-
bericht 1984. Bericht PU2R2/84, Fachgebiet Programmiersprachen
und Übersetzer II, Technische Hochschule Darmstadt, Februar 1984.

[Bah84b] Bahlke, R. and Letschert, T.: Ausführbare denotationale Semantik.
Proc. 4. GI-Fachgespräch Implementierung von Programmiersprachen,
Zürich, März 1984.

[Bjo78] Bjørner, D. and Jones, C.B. (eds.): The Vienna Development Method:
The metalanguage. LNCS 61, Springer Verlag 1978.

[Fei84] Kaiser, G.E. and Feiler, P.: Generation of language-oriented editors.
Proc. Programmierumgebungen und Compiler, Berichte des German Chapter
of the ACM 18, Teubner 1984.

[Gor79] Gordon, M.J.C.: The denotational description of programming languages,
an introduction. Springer 1979.

[Hab82] Habermann, N. et al.: The second compendium of GANDALF documentation. Carnegie-Mellon-University, May 1982.

[Hen84] Henhapl, W. and Snelting, G.: Context relations - a concept for incremental context analysis in program fragments. Proc. 8. GI-Fachtagung Programmiersprachen und Programmentwicklung, Informatik Fachberichte 77, Springer Verlag 1984.

[Kah83] Kahn, G. et al: Metal: A Formalism to specify formalisms. Science of Computer Programming 3 (1983) 151-188.

[Kas80] Kastens, U. and Zimmermann, E.: GAG - A generator based on attributed Grammars. Universität Karlsruhe, Institut für Informatik, Bericht Nr 14/80, 1980.

[Klu84] Klug, M.: Implementation of MODULA-2 with the PSG-System. Diploma Thesis, TH Darmstadt, 1984 (In German).

[Knu68] Knuth, D.E.: Semantics of context-free languages, Mathematical Systems Theory 2, 127-145, June 1968.

[Let84] Letschert,T.: Type inference in the presence of overloading, polymorphism, and type coercions. Proc 8. GI-Fachtagung Programmiersprachen und Programmentwicklung, Informatik Fachberichte 77, Springer 1984.

[Mos79] Mosses, P.: SIS - Semantics implementation system, Reference Manual and user guide, Report DAIMI DC-30, Aarhus University 1979.

[Pau82] Paulson, L.: A semantics-directed compiler generator. Proc. 9th ACM POPL conference, Albuquerque 1982, 224-239.

[Ple84] Pleban, U.: Formal Semantics and Compiler Generation. Proc. Programmiersprachen und Compiler, Berichte des German Chapter of the ACM 18, Teubner 1984.

[Rep83] Reps, T., Teitelbaum, T. and Demers, A.: Incremental context-dependent analysis for language-based editors. ACM TOPLAS 5, No. 3 (1983), 449-477.

[Rep84] Reps, T. and Teitelbaum, T.: The Synthesizer Generator. SIGPLAN Notices Vol. 19, No. 5, 1984.

[Tei81] Teitelbaum, T. and Reps, T.: The Cornell Programm Synthesizer: a syntax-directed programming environment. CACM 24, No. 9 (1981).

SOFTWARE CONSTRUCTION USING TYPED FRAGMENTS

Nazim H. Madhavji
Nikos Leoutsarakos
Dimitri Vouliouris

School of Computer Science
McGill University
805 Sherbrooke Street West
Montreal, PQ,
CANADA H3A 2K6

ABSTRACT

Recent research in the field of programming environments has resulted in integrated systems which demonstrate their use in the development of small programs. It is argued here that such systems are not suitable for non-trivial software development, as they support programming-in-the-small only. This paper introduces a new concept of a typed fragment called *fragtype*, which makes the notion of a software building block concrete. With the help of the underlying fragtype driven structured editor, and a fragment library, such building blocks can be used to construct a well-formed large software edifice.

1. Introduction

The concept of integration has recently precipitated widespread research efforts in combining programming tools, such as an editor, compiler, linker and debugger into coherent programming environments. Examples of such systems include the Cornell Program Synthesizer [TeiRe81], ALOE [MedNo81], MENTOR [DHKL84], Magpie [DelMS84], POE [FJMPS84], PECAN [Reiss84] and COPE [ArcCo81]. While such systems have clearly demonstrated their use in the development of syntactically, and in some cases, static-semantically correct *small* programs, their viability is still to be tested in the development of *reasonably large* programs.

It is argued here that currently available program synthesizers are not suitable for non-trivial software development, primarily because they support programming-in-the-small only. For the development of reasonably large programs, a highly integrated scratch pad facility based on a new concept of a fragment type, called *fragtype*, is proposed here.

Fragtypes have a formal basis, similar to data types in Pascal-like programming languages, and therefore they provide protection during the construction of software. A fragment of a certain fragtype can contain objects which are compatible with that fragtype only. Such objects can be of small granularity, such as an expression or they can be of large granularity, such as a subsystem of a program. Thus, a fragment is a formal structure of variable granularity.

In order to manipulate fragments, the scratch pad provides a structured editor which can be used to create a new fragment. The editor also has the capability to develop, refine and assemble existing fragments into a new one, possibly of a different fragtype, in an integrated and well-defined manner. Thus, the editor is a machine for fabricating software from fragments of various fragtypes.

One striking difference between this editor and other structured editors is that the former is driven by fragtypes. Hence, it automatically adjusts itself according to the fragtype of the fragment being operated upon. This is a dynamic feature of the editor, as a fragtype can change at any time depending on the user action. It is this feature of the editor, combined with the concept of fragtypes, which makes the scratch pad flexible enough to suit wide varieties of software development methodologies and yet provide protection during software construction.

Seven major software engineering notions considered in the design of the scratch pad are:
- Software building blocks.
- Rigorous construction.
- Top-down and bottom-up methodologies.
- Repository for building blocks.
- Integration of activities.
- Testing of building blocks.
- Development tool.

The above mentioned points are a subject of current research in the context of the MUPE-2 project at McGill University. This paper focuses on the scratch pad facility which is an important component of the project. Before considering the scratch pad in more detail, the next section puts it into perspective.

2. The MUPE-2 Environment: An Overview

The McGill University Programming Environment (MUPE-2), is an integrated environment for the design, development and use of Modula-2 [Wirth82] programs. The level of MUPE-2 (see Figure 1) can be viewed as above that of program synthesizers, but beneath that of full software engineering environments, such as CADES [Snowd81], PWB/UNIX [Ivie77], SDS [Alfor81] and others.

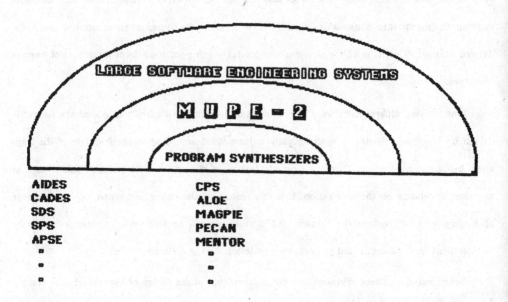

AIDES   CPS
CADES   ALOE
SDS   MAGPIE
SPS   PECAN
APSE   MENTOR

Figure 1 - The level of MUPE-2

MUPE-2 has a characteristic coloured user interface, which is divided into what are termed the module screen, the procedure screen and the scratch pad, as shown in Figure 2. The module screen is used for programming-in-the-large on a chosen implementation module. Here, with the use of its context-sensitive structured editor, a number of operations can be performed on the internal nodes of the module tree. Besides, the module screen can communicate with the scratch pad by transferring subsystem fragments to/from the personal fragment library called FRAGLIB.

The procedure screen is used for programming-in-the-small on a chosen procedure/module (e.g. T) from the current module on the module screen, thus maintaining the complete

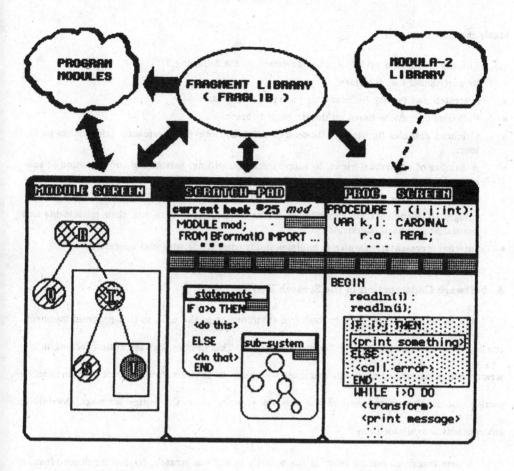

Figure 2 - MUPE-2 screen layout.

environment of the procedure. Operations of the editor permit manipulation of language and meta-language templates and English phrases. Besides, similar to the module screen, the procedure screen can communicate with the scratch pad by transferring procedure fragments to/from FRAGLIB.

The scratch pad is a context-free multi-purpose workbench of the system, where subsystem and procedure fragments may be developed, assembled and tested for inclusion in the main program or in FRAGLIB. Together, the three screens serve the widely known activities of software engineering: programming in-the-large and in-the-small, design, experimentation and testing in a highly integrated manner.

The key features of MUPE-2 are summarised by the following :

- Its partitioned user interface.
- A scratch pad facility for operating on typed fragments.
- Universal operations based on the structured cursor.
- Coloured graphics for visually (instead of textually) conveying semantic information to the user.
- A number of contextual views, to support display, editing, assembling and execution of sub-system and program fragments.
- Call-tree and user selected walk-through mechanisms.
- Integrated documentation capability based on programming decisions, their refinements and textual or graphical comments.
- Internal representation which is minimal and is compatible with user operations.

3. Software Construction in the Scratch Pad

The scratch pad provides a context-free environment to the user, so that program fragments can be developed independent of the main program. This implies that semantic checking in the scratch pad is performed up to the fragment boundary. In contrast, full semantic checking can be carried out in the procedure and the module screens, since the entire language (Modula-2) environment is available there.

A new fragment can be built in the scratch pad, from scratch, by jotting down ideas as English phrases or by constructing an expression, statements, declarations, a procedure, a module, a system-layer (described later) or a subsystem. This construction is facilitated by the underlying structured editor. For identification purposes, a fragment may be given a name with its description. By default, the system issues an unique fragment number.

If desired, an existing fragment can be selected from a set of working fragments, or it can be unhooked from FRAGLIB, the fragment library. The library is a collection of fragments designed in the scratch pad, hooked fragments of a procedure from the procedure screen and hooked fragments of a subsystem from the module screen.

The underlying editor has the capability to manipulate fragments of different fragtypes, so that they can be developed, refined and assembled into new fragments in an integrated but orderly manner. A new fragment can be hooked into FRAGLIB for later use on any of the three screens or it can be retained in the scratch pad as one of the working fragments.

3.1. Software Building Blocks

Construction of a reasonably large program generally involves programming in-the-large and in-the-small. During this activity, many utilise both top-down and bottom-up methods of development. However, a system can take a long period to complete, and therefore, rapid prototyping is often desirable to quickly determine the nature of the eventual system. In addition, during the design of such a system, one may experience mundane tasks of re-inventing program structures that are already in use in other projects, and often, one may need to search for efficient and well-written algorithms.

Well-defined software building blocks are a step towards solving the above mentioned problems in software engineering, as they provide formal structures for assembling and re-using software. In MUPE-2, a fragment is a building block, and it is well-defined because it is a fragtyped structure which can be identified through its attributes. A fragtype indicates how the associated fragment can be combined with other structures.

The following list describes the basic form of fragtypes.

Expression: This fragtype contains one expression only.

Declarations: This fragtype contains a sequence of declarations only.

Statements: This fragtype contains a sequence of statements only.

Procedure: This fragtype contains one procedure only.

Module: This fragtype contains one module only.

System-layer: This fragtype contains a combination of procedures, modules and subsystems which have the same parent. For example, in Figure 3, (B, C, D) is a system-layer of node A; whereas, (P, A) is a system-layer for node X.

Subsystem: This fragtype contains a combination of procedures and modules which have a hierarchical relationship. This relationship is structural, shown by the tree arcs, and is according to the target language rules. In addition, the *uses-relationship* is based on procedure calls within a given node, and is dealt with by the incremental semantic analyser. Figure 3 shows that A(B, C, D) and X(P, A) are subsystems, where leaf nodes are treated as procedures or modules as the case may be.

Abstract: This fragtype contains a sequence of English-like phrases only. Each phrase is an abstract representation, at a user chosen conceptual level, of a programming solution. For example, a list of phrases may represent a layer of system modules, a set of declarations, a set of statements, etc. This choice of target objects is a user's decision. MUPE-2 does not *understand* a phrase, as it is not knowledge based. Hence, onus is upon the user to make certain that the phrase is written with intent.

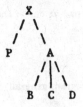

Figure 3 - Subsystem and System-layer relationships

The breakdown of fragtypes above is generalised, in order to avoid specific details of Modula-2. In this language, for example, there can be several kinds of subsystems, such as Implementation-Module-Subsystem, Unit-Subsystem, Procedure-Subsystem and Program-Module-Subsystem. Also, there is richness in fragtypes for data declarations and module interface. In contrast, fragtypes for Pascal are much simpler. This simplicity is reflected in the homogeneity of subsystem and system structures described above. In essence, the concept of fragtypes is powerful enough to be applicable to a class of programming languages.

A parallel can be drawn between fragtypes and Pascal-like data types. Whereas fragments of various fragtypes can be used to construct larger structures such as procedures, modules and subsystems, data items of various types can be used to construct smaller structures such as lists, trees and arrays. In contrast, however, a fragtype is subject to transitions from one fragtype to another.

Figure 4 illustrates the flexibility together with the protection provided by fragtypes and their operations during system construction. For example, it shows that a fragment of fragtype Abstract can be refined into a fragment of another fragtype. This is useful for both programming in-the-small and in-the-large. It also shows that statement and declaration fragments can be turned into procedure and module fragments, say, in bottom-up design. Similarly, procedures and modules can form a system-layer which can then be turned into a proper subsystem. Notice that

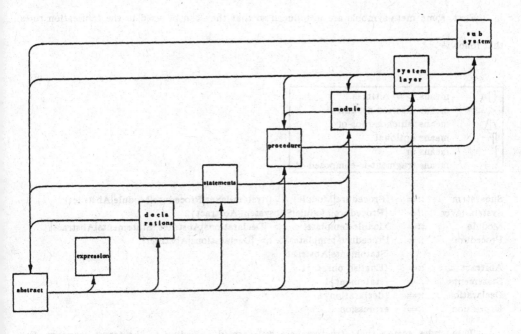

Figure 4 - Fragtype transition diagram

it is also possible to arrive at smaller structures from larger ones, and to transform procedures and modules.

These transitions of fragtypes are achieved by using various commands, such as Copy/Insert, Delete, Transform, Replace/Refine, and their variants. However, before illustrating specific examples of usage, the next section introduces semantic rules which are applied during the fabrication of software.

3.2. Rigorous Construction

Because fragtypes are formal, similar to data types in Pascal-like languages, it is possible to formulate semantic rules to ensure correct fragtype transitions, and fragtype compatibility rules to ensure well-formed fragments.

First, some meta-symbols are introduced so that they can be used in the fabrication rules that follow:

{}n	means >= n times
<...>	means inserted-around
/\	means which-is-root-of
[]	means optional
|	means or
::=	means fragment-is-composed-of

Subsystem	::=	(Procedure|Module) /|\ (System-layer|Procedure|Module|Abstract)
System-layer	::=	{Procedure|Module|Subsystem|Abstract}2
Module	::=	Module-template <...> [Declarations|Abstract][Statements|Abstract]
Procedure	::=	Procedure-template <...> [Declarations|Abstract] [Statements|Abstract]
Abstract	::=	{English phrase}1
Statements	::=	{statement}1
Declaration	::=	{declaration}1
Expression	::=	expression

These rules ensure that structures are well-formed according to the target language. For example, inserting a fragment of fragtype Declarations in the midst of a fragment of fragtype Statements is not possible. This principle is similar to the data type compatibility rules in strongly typed languages. The benefit here is that a system constructed from basic building blocks is completely well-formed.

It is worth mentioning here that the fabrication rules do not restrict shared use of a component by other components. This is a semantic issue which is resolved by the semantic analyser. In MUPE-2, the user is informed about legal calls to procedures from a given component in a subsystem, with the help of colour coding.

Besides fragment-level semantics, there can be semantic checking within a fragment. For example, in the following fragment of declarations, 'elementtype' is not defined.

Declarations
TYPE
range = 1 .. 10;
a = ARRAY [range] OF elementtype;

This could have been deliberate, as it may already have been defined in the procedure in which this fragment is to be inserted. Therefore, 'elementtype' is highlighted with a colour which means *semantic caution* rather than semantic error. Such checking for a fragment is possible by retaining a local symbol table.

An important point to note is that semantic checking terminates at the boundary of a fragment. This is because the fragment is context-free. All semantic failures in a fragment, which would normally be flagged as semantic errors on the procedure and the module screens, are flagged as semantic cautions on the scratch pad.

Notice that in the case of a newly created fragment of fragtype Statements, all variables are semantic cautions. In the case of a fragment of fragtype Subsystem, checking can be more extensive because simple operations such as insert and delete can have major effects on the rest of the subsystem, in terms of non-local accesses and procedure calls.

At the point of insertion of a fragment in an environment (i.e. another fragment, current procedure or module), incremental semantic checking takes place. If the environment is on the scratch pad then semantic cautions, if any, are highlighted. Otherwise, semantic errors are highlighted.

3.3. Top-down and Bottom-up Methodologies

While the fragtype compatibility rules described in the previous section are rigorous, they do not support any particular development methodology. In particular, providing flexibility of top-down and bottom-up methodologies at any stage of software development is an important asset of a development tool.

The scratch pad provides this flexibility by automatically changing the fragtype of a particular fragment, depending on a user action. Figure 5 shows the operations which can trigger off a fragtype change, and Figure 6 is an example sequence of top-down and bottom-up actions. From this, it is clear that the scratch pad facilitates programming in-the-large and in-the-small, and top-down and bottom-up methods, in an integrated and orderly manner.

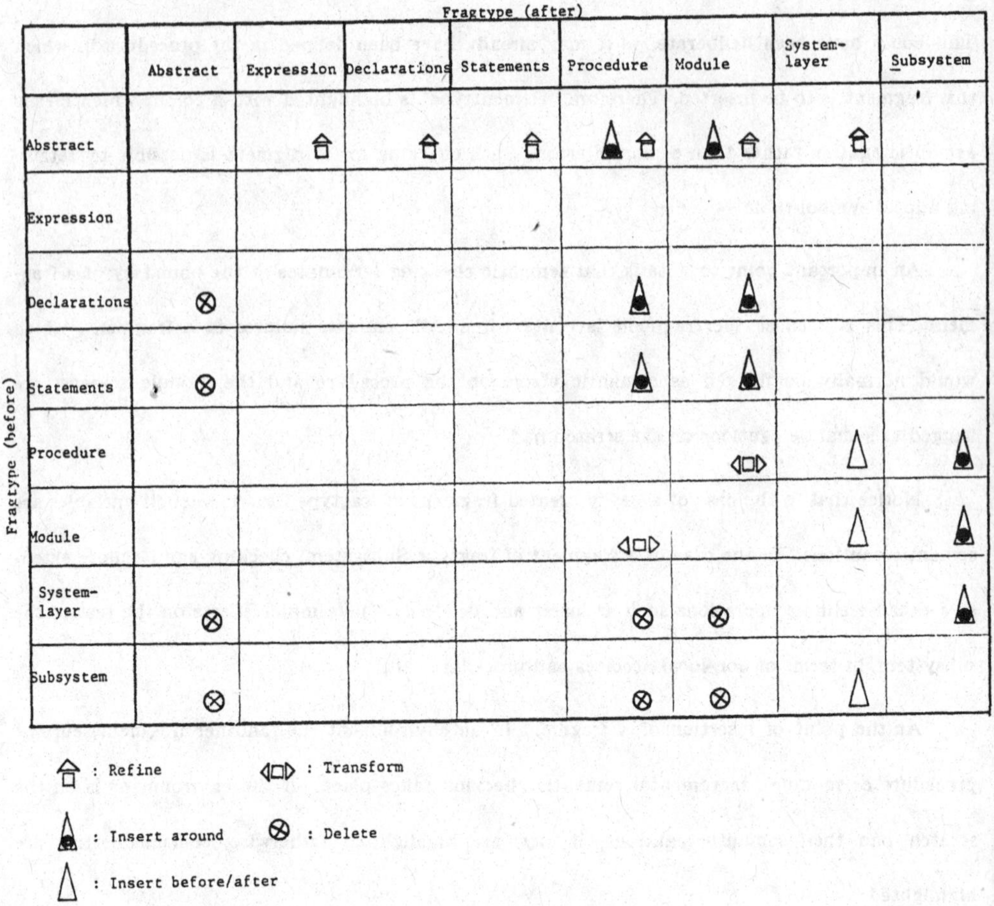

	Fragtype (after)							
	Abstract	Expression	Declarations	Statements	Procedure	Module	System-layer	Subsystem
Abstract		Refine	Refine	Refine	Insert around + Refine	Insert around + Refine	Refine	
Expression								
Declarations	Delete				Insert around	Insert around		
Statements	Delete				Insert around	Insert around		
Procedure						Transform	Insert before/after	Insert around
Module					Transform		Insert before/after	Insert around
System-layer	Delete				Delete	Delete		Insert around
Subsystem	Delete				Delete	Delete	Insert before/after	

(left axis label: Fragtype (before))

⇧ : Refine ◁□▷ : Transform

🔺 : Insert around ⊗ : Delete

△ : Insert before/after

Figure 5 - Operations that trigger off a fragtype change

The *basic form* of the actions that change one fragtype into another are precisely those which are available on the procedure screen and the module screen. In fact, one uses the same editor on the scratch pad, and thus, uniformity is maintained by the system.

3.4. Repository for Building Blocks

The scratch pad derives its power from the formal concepts introduced thus far and the tools that support these concepts. One such tool is the fragment library (FRAGLIB).

FRAGLIB saves, and makes available, fragments of various fragtypes. These fragments are

174

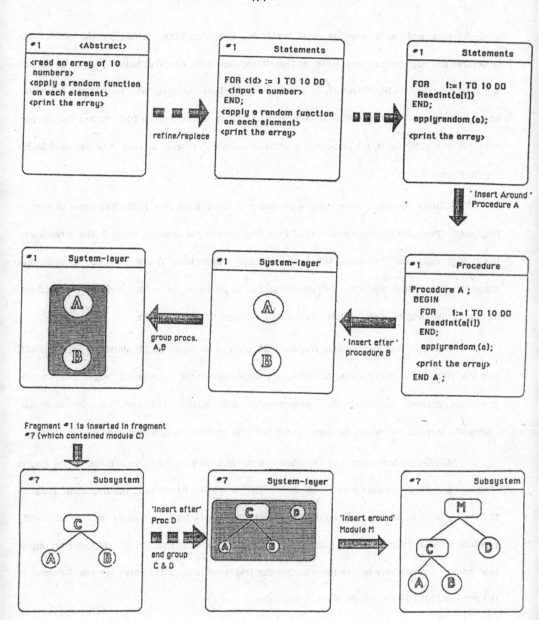

Figure 6 - An example of integrated operations

normally commonly used routines, data structures and algorithms; intra-program usable data structures and algorithmic fragments, and partially completed new fragments, system-layers and sub-systems. FRAGLIB, therefore, is a repository for both complete and incomplete fragments and sub-systems. Together with the other tools provided in the scratch pad, such a facility permits one to rapidly construct prototype, partial or complete systems, as they may not need building from scratch.

The library structure is basically a hierarchy of rings. Each ring holds fragments of various fragtypes. The internal representation of each fragment is the same as those in the scratch pad itself, and those on the other two screens. Thus transporting fragments can be somewhat simplified. In addition, while the current design has no provision for version control of a fragment, such a facility may be included later on top of the kernel library structure.

Parallel work to the idea of a fragment library can be found in TI [Balze81], PSI [Brots81] and PA [Water82]. These three, however, are knowledge-based approaches, which rely on programming clichés, and deal with programming-in-the-small. The last one, in particular, represents program structures as plans, and it provides an editor which operates on such plans.

In MUPE-2, a fragment may be referenced to, from any of the three screens, by its system allocated number or its user given name or description if any. By default, the fragment 'hung' on the current hook is accessed. In addition, a descriptive search facility (such as 'man -k' on UNIX) provides a list of fragments that might be of interest. It is clear that FRAGLIB forms an important and an unavoidable bridge for transporting fragments among the three screens. Without it, the power of MUPE-2 would be severely curtailed.

3.5. Development Tool

Underlying the concept of a fragtype is a single fragtype driven editor which handles both programming in-the-large and in-the-small, and top-down and bottom-up methodologies. This same editor is available in varying strengths on the three screens.

For example, on the procedure screen, the editor will function only on one procedure or a module at a time (i.e. Procedure or Module fragtype). On the module screen, it will function on the module tree skeleton (i.e. Subsystem fragtype). Yet in the scratch pad, it will vary according to the fragtype of the fragment being edited.

Fragtype changes in the scratch pad (see Figure 5) trigger off dynamic changes in the editing capabilities. This implies that, the editor is context-sensitive [MadVL84]. Thus, when editing a fragment of fragtype Statements, only those features of the editor are active that permit syntactically correct construction of the statements. In addition, by, say, inserting a procedure template around all the statements, the editing capabilities now automatically switch to that which are valid for a whole procedure. Based on the same principle, when the fragtype of a fragment changes from Procedure into System-layer for example, the editing capabilities change from programming-in-the-small to programming-in-the-large.

The uniformity in this *all in one* structured editor is achieved primarily because of its following two main characteristics:
(i)   The editor always operates on a fragment of some fragtype, and
(ii) It integrates programming in-the-large and in-the-small, and top-down and bottom-up methodologies.

To the user, this approach results in the following three principal benefits:
(i)   The notion of a software building block is concrete.
(ii) The building blocks can be used to construct a well-formed software edifice, and
(iii) The engineering process is versatile.

4. Conclusion

A novel approach to programming is proposed in this paper, to overcome some of the difficulties apparent in programming environments, such as those mentioned in [TeiRe81, DelMS84, FJMPS84] and others. The authors believe that for engineering non-trivial piece of software in an integrated manner, a programming environment should be more than just a structured editor and a run-time system with debugging aids.

In particular, a scratch pad facility which is based on the concept of a fragtype, together with its fragment library, would achieve for reasonably large programs what Pascal has achieved for small programs. That is, formalisation of a fragment and flexibility in its utilisation.

The work described in here is ongoing, but an area of immediate concern is the testing of fragments in the scratch pad. This problem is being approached in two ways. One is the system generated environment for a fragment, and another is a user *hard-wired* environment. While both schemes may be desirable, the latter appears to be a non-trivial task for dynamic data structures [MadWi81, Madha84].

Finally, MUPE-2 owes much to the recent and current research in programming environments, which has pointed out the need for a scratch pad facility.

ACKNOWLEDGEMENT

The work described in this paper was in part supported by FCAC, Quebec, Canada under Grant 290-19.

5. References

[Alfor81] Alford, M.W.: *SDS: Experience with the Software Development System*. In Software Engineering Environments, (ed) Hünke, H., North Holland Pub. Co., Amsterdam, 1981.

[ArcCo81] Archer, J.E., Conway, Jr and R.: *COPE: A Cooperative Programming Environment*. Technical Report 81-459, Cornell University, June 1981.

[Balze81] Balzer, R.: *Transformational Implementation: An Example*. IEEE Trans. Soft. Eng., Vol. SE-7, Jan. 1981, pp. 3-14.

[Brots81] Brotsky, D.C.: *Program understanding through cliché recognition*. M.S. thesis proposal, MIT, Cambridge, MA., 1981.

[DHKL84] Donzeau-Gouge, V., Houet, G., Kahn, G., Lang, B.: *Programming Environments Based on Structured Editors: The MENTOR Experience*. In Interactive Programming Environments (eds.) Barstow,D.R., et al., McGraw-Hill, 1984.

[DelMS84] Delisle, N.M., Menicosy, D.E., Schwartz, M.D.: *Viewing a Programming Environment as a Single Tool*. Proc. ACM SIGSOFT/SIGPLAN Soft. Eng. Symposium on Practical Software Development Environments, ACM Sigplan Notices, Vol. 19, No. 5, May 1984, pp. 49-56.

[FJMPS84] Fischer, C.N., et al.: *The Poe Language-Based Editor Project* Proc. ACM SIGSOFT/SIGPLAN Soft. Eng. Symposium on Practical Software Development Environments, ACM Sigplan Notices, Vol. 19, No. 5, May 1984, pp. 21-29.

[Ivie77] Ivie, E.L.: *The Programmer's Workbench - A machine for Software Development*. Comm. ACM, Vol. 20, No. 10, Oct. 1977, pp. 746-753.

[Madha84] Madhavji, N.H.: *Visibility Aspects of Programmed Dynamic Data Structures*. Comm. ACM, Vol. 27, No. 8, Aug. 1984, pp. 764-776.

[MadVL84] Madhavji, N.H., Vouliouris, D. and Leoutsarakos, N.: *The Importance of Context in an Integrated Programming Environment*. To appear in the Proc. 18th Annual Hawaii Int. Conf. on System Sciences, Hawaii, Jan. 1985.

[MadWi81] Madhavji, N.H., and Wilson, I.R.: *Dynamically Structured Data*. Software-Practice and Experience, Vol. 11, No. 12, Dec. 1981, pp. 1235-1260.

[MedNo81] Medina-Mora, R., Notkin, D.S.: *ALOE users' and implementors' guide.* Tech. Rep. CMU-CS-81-145, Dept. of Comp. Science, Carnegie-Mellon Univ., Pittsburgh, Pa., Nov. 1981.

[Reiss84] Reiss, S.P.: *Graphical Program Development with PECAN Program Development Systems.* Proc. ACM SIGSOFT/SIGPLAN Soft. Eng. Symposium on Practical Software Development Environments, ACM Sigplan Notices, Vol. 19, No. 5, May 1984, pp. 30-41.

[Snowd81] Snowdon, R. A.: *CADES and Software System Development.* In Software Engineering Environments, (ed) Hünke, H., North Holland Pub. Co., Amsterdam, 1981.

[TeiRe81] Teitelbaum, T., Reps, T.: *The Cornell Program Synthesizer: A syntax directed programming environment.* Comm. ACM, Vol. 24, No. 9, Sept. 1981, pp. 563-573.

[Water82] Waters, R. C.: *The Programmer's Apprentice: Knowledge Based Program Editing.* IEEE Trans. Soft. Eng., Vol. SE-8, No. 1, Jan. 1982, pp. 1-12.

[Wilan80] Wilander, J.: *An Interactive Programming System for Pascal.* In Interactive Programming Environments, (eds.) Barstow, D.R., et al., McGraw-Hill, 1984.

[Wirth82] Wirth, N.: *Programming in Modula-2.* Springer Verlag, 1982.

Graph Grammar Engineering: A Method Used for the Development of an Integrated Programming Support Environment

G. Engels, W. Schäfer

Angewandte Informatik, FB 6, Universität Osnabrück

Postfach 4469, D-4500 Osnabrück

Abstract

We introduce a method to specify the functional behaviour of software tools in an incremental and integrated software development environment. This specification method is based on graph grammars. It is an adequate method to specify the behaviour of all software systems using graphs as internal data structures. We show that a specification can be developed systematically by which the adaptability of the environment is increased towards modification of tools or extension by new tools. Furthermore, guidelines for the implementation can directly be derived from this specification.

Key Words: integrated tools, graph grammars, programming support environments, programming-in-the-small, software engineering, specification

1. Introduction

The systematic development of large software systems requires a precise description of its desired behaviour. Depending on the used method such a **specification** of the behaviour is a more or less formal description on a conceptual level (cf. /SF 76/). In this paper we introduce a specification method based on graph grammars. This method is shown to be adequate if graphs are the underlying data structures on the conceptual level. This means that the behaviour of the software system can be described by graph transformations.

The method is applied to the specification of the tools of an Incremental Programming Support Environment (**IPSEN**) (cf. /Na 84/). The task of such an environment is to facilitate the development and maintenance of software documents. Software documents are for example (a piece of) a description of the modularization of a software system, the source code of a module, a technical documentation, etc.

Furthermore, we show that such an operational specification on a conceptual level also leads to a specification in a second sense denoting the result of the design phase in a software life cycle model. This specification determines the **decomposition** of the software system **into modules** and serves as the guideline for the implementation phase. So, the reader may be aware that we talk about two levels of the term 'specification'.

IPSEN in particular has some external characteristics which influence the design of the user interface.

(1) Input and output of software documents is always **syntax-directed** and **incremental**, i.e. it is done in logical portions of an underlying syntax definition of a class of software documents. Incrementality means that syntax-analysis, evaluation, or execution is even possible for partial programs, specifications, etc.

(2) The tools in IPSEN are **integrated** in different senses: (a) Most of the technical activities of the software life cycle are supported, (b) the tools are combining activities which nowadays are regarded to belong to different activities in life cycle models, (c) all tools have a uniform user interface, i.e. the user is not aware of an internal change between different tools.

This incremental and integrated mode implies that the sequential organisation of activities in usual life cycle models can no longer be sustained. For example, whenever an increment of the specification is put in (design phase), checks for the intermodular connections may immediately start (integration phase). Furthermore, this part of the specification may now be changed (usually in maintenance phase). Therefore, we have grouped the activities in the following task areas: **programming in the large** (any activities directed to the level above single modules), **programming in the small** (any activities directed to the level of single modules), and, finally, **project organisation and project management.**

The incremental and integrated mode yields the following main characteristic of IPSEN. All information contained in an external representation of a module, specification, etc. is represented in and can be accessed from a high-level intermediate data structure. As the conceptual model for this data structure we use graphs. The reason is that graphs are a uniform model which can be applied to any task area. In particular, we have a **system graph** as intermediate representation of a module decomposition, a **module graph** for a single module, a **documentation graph** for technical documentation, etc. Structural information is expressed by labeled nodes and labeled edges whereas only nonstructural information is expressed by additional attributes. Aspects of editing, evaluating and execution of software documents can be treated by this model as further information for any purpose can be expressed by graphs without leaving the class of graphs. The uniform model heavily facilitates the development of integrated tools. Any kind of modification of these graphs by any tool can be specified by graph grammars.

By listing the internal characterisic we have also mentioned the main difference between IPSEN and other programming environments. These environments rather independently developed similar integrated concepts (cf. Gandalf /Ha 82/, Mentor /DG 80/, Cornell Program Synthesizer /TR 81/, Pecan /RE 84/). However, using graphs and not trees as intermediate data structures and graph grammars as specification instrument is specific to IPSEN. In all other approaches trees are regarded as the main conceptual model for the intermediate data structure which yields a lot of problems. A big part of the structural information has to be expressed in attributes as it cannot be expressed in trees. This yields partially complex attribute evaluation algorithms (cf. /RT 83/). Furthermore, additional and quite different complex internal data structures are introduced, when extending the environment to new tools (e.g. Pecan /Re 84/).

Please note that this is not an argument for avoiding attributes at all. Attributes are necessary for expressing values. We pledge for using the same graph model for all structural information.

In this paper we mainly deal with the specification of the **integrated tool set** for **programming in the small** by **graph grammars.** Such a tool set (cf. /Na 84/) consists of e.g. a syntax-aided editor, a tool for static analysis of the data flow in a module, and a tool for static instrumentation by e.g. the insertion of breakpoints. A module is executed by interpreting the corresponding module graph. This execution is supported by e.g. tools for runtime data inspection resp. for establishing specific environments for the test of procedures.

Since all tools use the module graph as internal data structure, such a graph has to represent a lot of different tool-specific information. Thus, it yields a complex problem to specify the behaviour of all tools by one graph grammar. We show that this **complexity** can be **decreased** by developing an independent graph grammar specification for each tool in a first step, and by combining these graph grammars in a second step. Thereby, this also serves as a **guideline** for the **efficient** implementation of the different tools. Such a **specification engineering** using graph grammars is the crucial point of this paper. It was applied to all tools for the task area programming in the small. So, the composition of these specifications is our main concern here, whereas the systematic development of a single graph grammar specification, namely the syntax-aided editor, was described in /EG 83/.
The proceeding presented here can be analogously transferred to other tools and task areas in IPSEN. For a specification editor this is documented in /LN 84/. The specification engineering is one result of the IPSEN project: It is more the development of new concepts for the specification and implementation of a programming support environment which is our main goal than an industrial implementation.

. The **organisation** of the **paper** is as follows: The next section describes the systematic development of the module graph based on the syntax of the programming language Modula-2. (Modula-2 is chosen as the programming language to be supported as well as implementation language, because it offers adequate concepts for programming in the small and programming in the large.) In section 3 the modification of this module graph by different tools is specified using graph grammars. Section 4 gives an idea, how this specification has to be changed to get more efficient module graph modifications. In section 5 it is shown how this formal specification of the functional behaviour directly leads to different implementation techniques of the tools. Section 6 summarizes the main ideas of this paper.

2. The Module Graph

As mentioned in the introduction the module graph serves as the common, high-level data structure for all tools of the area programming in the small. It is an abstract representation which contains all tool-specific informations. In a module graph all structural information is expressed by different labeled nodes and edges, while all non-structural information is expressed by additional tool-specific attributes.

Because of the incremental mode in IPSEN the module graph itself is a composition of **graph increments.** Since module graphs have to represent modules written in Modula-2, the graph increments heavily depend on the underlying programming language grammar. Such a grammar is usually designed with respect to certain properties, e.g. an efficient deterministic context free syntax analysis. This causes the grammar to contain a lot of technical nonterminals, which do not reflect logical portions of the language. In order to get reasonable graph increments these technical nonterminals have to be eliminated. We introduce a normal form for such a string grammar respecting the logical portions of the syntax corresponding to the increments.

2.1 Normalized Backus-Naur Form (BNF)

Such a string grammar **normal form** is characterized by a disjoint decomposition of the set of nonterminal symbols into three groups. (We use the BNF-notation to describe the productions of a context free string grammar.)

The first group contains the so-called **alternative nonterminals** and **optional nonterminals.** The right-hand side of all productions with an alternative nonterminal as left-hand side consists of a series of alternatives all of which are nonterminal or terminal symbols (cf. fig. 2.1). The right-hand side of the productions corresponding to optional nonterminals consists of two alternatives, the empty word and a nonterminal describing the optional part.

The second group is built by so-called **compound nonterminals** describing a part of the 'structure' of a module. The right-hand side of the corresponding productions is one sequence of nonterminal and terminal symbols (cf. fig. 2.1). The third group contains **list nonterminals** describing non-empty lists of elements of a certain kind (e.g. statement_list).

> alternative nonterminal:
> <statement> ::= <assignment_statement> | <while_statement> | <for_statement> | ...
>
> structure nonterminal:
> <while_statement> ::= while <expression> do <opt_statement_list> end

Fig. 2.1: Nonterminals and productions of a normalized Modula-2 BNF

It is the task of the IPSEN designer to transform a given programming language grammar into such a normal form. Since the resulting grammar is not uniquely determined, the grammar designer indirectly also determines the form of a module graph. It is to be seen in the next section, how this grammar influences the module graph increments.

2.2 Graph Increment Classification

Graph increments are associated with each compound or list nonterminal and its corresponding production, respectively. These **compound** and **list graph increments** consist of a root node (labeled by an indication for the corresponding increment) and as many compound graph increments the edges between the root node and its sons are labeled additionally according to their semantics (cf. fig. 2.2). In list graph increments the order of the list elements is expressed by additional edges labeled by 'ord' (cf. fig. 2.3).

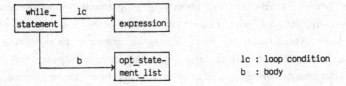

lc : loop condition
b : body

Fig. 2.2: compound graph increment

Since the lexical structure of identifiers or literals is not interesting for any IPSEN tool it will not be represented in a module graph. Therefore, identifiers and literals are represented by so-called **simple graph increments.** These increments consist only of a single node attributed with a string representing a concrete identifier or literal (cf. fig. 2.3).

```
procedure EXAMPLE;
var X : INTEGER;
begin
    ...
    while X < 0 do
    ...
    X := ...
    end
end EXAMPLE;
```

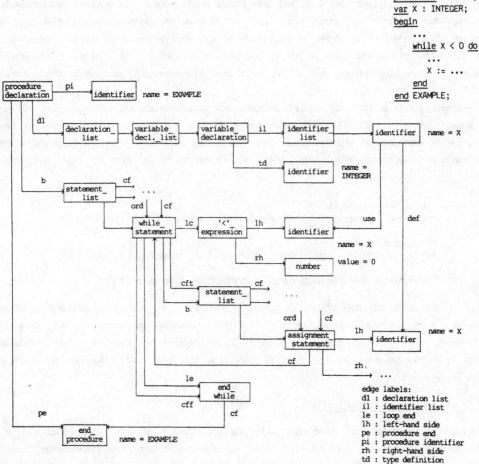

edge labels:
dl : declaration list
il : identifier list
le : loop end
lh : left-hand side
pe : procedure end
pi : procedure identifier
rh : right-hand side
td : type definition

Fig. 2.3: module graph example

Neglecting the ord-edges between list elements the composition of this graph increments yields a tree which is well-known as the abstract syntax tree in literature (cf. e.g. /DG 80/). It forms the spanning tree of the module graph and reflects the structural information of a module given by the context free syntax. Concrete syntax is not represented in the graph as it expresses no structural information. It will be the task of an unparser to generate source text including the concrete syntax from this abstract representation. Figure 2.3 presents the module graph representation of an incomplete Modula-2 procedure.

2.3. Module Graph Supplements

Besides the relations expressed by the spanning tree further relations between the graph increments are expressed by additional edges. For example, to ease and speed up **context sensitive** checks after an incremental modification of a module we introduce edges between the declaration of a variable and its defining (the variable is getting a new value) and using occurrencies (the value is read) in the statement part. The defining occurrencies are connected by a 'def'-edge with the declaration, whereas the using occurrencies are connected by a 'use'-edge with the declaration (cf. fig. 2.3).

By the composition of graph increments all allowed control flows in a module are determined. This information is expressed in a module graph by three different labeled edges, the cf-edge for unconditional control flow, and the cft- (control flow true) or cff- (control flow false) edge if the control flow depends on a condition (cf. fig. 2.3).

Of course, these additional edges in a module graph can be read by all tools working on the module graph. Besides that, all tools may introduce further edges and nodes to express their **tool-specific** structural informations. Examples are edges to express the data flow in a module (set-use edges), or the textual order of a corresponding source text (unparsing edges).

In the other projects mentioned in the introduction the internal data structure is a tree so that all these relations have to be expressed by additional attributes. The lack of those approaches is that the inherent structure of a software document is described in different notions, namely trees and attributes. In IPSEN only one formal notion, namely graphs, is used to denote structure. Only non-structural information is expressed by attributes. Examples are values of literals, unparsing information as concrete syntax, storage addresses of data objects, etc..

3. Specification of Programming Support Tools

The commands of the area programming in the small allow a user to edit a module, to analyze it, to execute it, to instrument it by different test facilities, etc. These commands are part of an integrated tool set, i.e. the user is not aware of an internal change e.g. between the editor and the interpreter.

The execution of such a user command internally implies the activation of one tool action or for more comfortable user commands a sequence of tool actions. Since all tools work on the same internal data structure, the module graph, each tool action implies a sequence of module graph modifications. These modifications are done incrementally. This means that after a modification of a graph increment in the module graph by one tool, all other tool-specific informations of this graph increment are immediately updated, too. So, the term 'incremental' occurs in two senses: the incremental behaviour of all tools at the user interface on one side and the incremental updating of the module graph on the other side.

In this section we show that an operational specification of such an integrated and incrementally working tool set can be developed by graph grammars in several steps. At first, the modification of graph increments and the incremental updating of other tool-specific informations has to be specified. Afterwards each tool can be specified independently by combining these modifications of the common internal data structure. At the end, the specification of all tools can be combined in one common graph grammar. This graph grammar is the operational specification of the integrated tool set.

Such a systematic proceeding reduces the complexity of specifying a large integrated tool set and, furthermore, increases the adaptability towards the modification of a tool or the extension by new tools.

Each execution of a tool action may be considered as a module graph transformation together with a corresponding evaluation of tool-specific attributes. Therefore, **attributed graph grammars** are a formal method to specify the behaviour of tools. Such attributed graph grammars consist of a set of attributed graph rewriting rules, called productions, containing an embedding rule and attribute evaluation instructions. The application of productions is defined by replacing one occurrence of the left-hand side in the host graph by the right-hand side. The embedding rule defines how the replacing graph has to be connected to the host graph. Attribute evaluation instructions are short Modula-2 code pieces, here usually simple assignments. They have to be executed as part of the application of an attributed graph grammar production. For a more formal introduction of graph grammars the reader is referred to /Na 79/ and /Bu 81/.

The position in a module actually handled by the user is marked by a special cursor node in the module graph. This implies that each production contains this cursor node on both sides, and that the occurrence of the left-hand side in the host graph is determined uniquely and can be found efficiently.

The combination of tools resp. the execution of one tool action often implies a determined order of different tool actions resp. of different graph modifications. Such a determined order of graph grammar production applications can be specified by so-called **control procedures** written like Modula-2 procedures the bodies of which contain the activation of other control procedures or productions. Therefore, we are using programmed sequential and attributed graph grammars.

Let us show now that these graph grammars are an adequate method for specifying the internal behaviour of programming support tools and their integration in a programming support environment.

The specification consists of three **layers,** a data structure oriented lowest layer and two functional layers upon that.

The **lowest layer** provides all control procedures and productions specifying all elementary modifications of the module graph. This includes the insertion and deletion of graph increments, and the modification of additional, tool-specific edges, nodes, and attributes. The control procedures and productions are gathered up in different graph grammars, for example Graph_Increment_Productions, Control_Structure_Supplements, Source_Text_Supplements. Examples of such productions are given in the following figures. The embedding rule will be omitted because it is the identity.

<u>production</u> insert_while_statement_graph_increment;

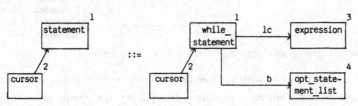

Fig. 3.1: production of graph grammar Graph_Increment_Productions

We add an 'end'-node to each graph increment representing a control structure, where the control flow of that control structure flows together:

<u>production</u> insert_while_statement_control_flow;

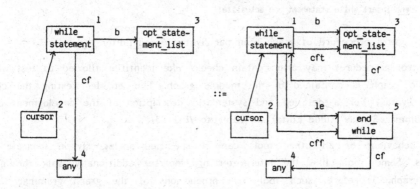

Fig. 3.2: production of graph grammar Control_Structure_Supplements

As an example for the graph grammar Source_Text_Supplements we consider the information needed by an unparser to generate source text from the module graph. Therefore, the graph increments have to be connected by further edges labeled by 'u' reflecting the textual order, and node attributes have to be added containing unparsing schemes describing the missing concrete syntax and the layout of the corresponding source text.

<u>production</u> insert_while_statement_unparsing_supplements;

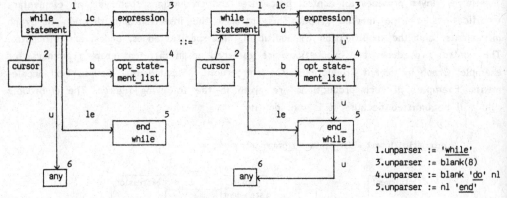

1.unparser := 'while'
3.unparser := blank(8)
4.unparser := blank 'do' nl
5.unparser := nl 'end'

Fig. 3.3: production of the graph grammar Source_Text_Supplements

In the **second layer** all tools will be specified by independent graph grammars. These graph grammars consist of control procedures determining the order of applications of control procedures and productions of graph grammars of the lowest layer.

As an example we specify the insertion of a while-statement and the actualisations of other tool-specific informations by a control procedure of the tool Syntax_Aided_Editor.

```
procedure insert_while_statement_and_actualize;
begin
    insert_while_statement_graph_increment;
    insert_while_statement_control_flow_supplements;
    insert_while_statement_unparsing_supplements;
end insert_while_statement_and_actualize;
```

Fig. 3.4: control procedure of graph grammar Syntax_Aided_Editor

Such control procedures may also contain checks like identifier_allowed to test whether a specific graph is contained in the module graph. This enables testing the context sensitive syntax. For a detailed and systematic description of the development of the graph grammar Syntax_Aided_Editor we refer to /EG 83/.

The behaviour of all other tools can be specified analogously in separate graph grammars. Some tools like the Interpreter or Unparser additionally walk through the module graph. Therefore, such tools use productions of the graph grammar Cursor_ Movements to move the cursor node in the module graph.

Since each tool was specified in a separate graph grammar a **third layer** is needed for specifying their combination. This means to specify functional dependencies which can be done by control procedures adequately. As an example we indicate the control procedure that specifies the execution of a while-statement using a loop-counter. In control procedures a simple user interface behaviour can be specified, too.

```
      procedure execute_while_loop_with_loop_counter;
      var number: integer;
      begin
         insert_loop_counter; (* control procedure of static_instrumentation *)
         interprete_loop_with_loop_counter( number );
         user_message( 'number of loop executions:', number );
      end execute_while_loop_with_loop_counter;
```

Fig. 3.5: control procedure of the graph grammar Tool_Handler

The whole functional composition / decomposition of graph grammars and the distinction between these three layers is illustrated in figure 3.6.

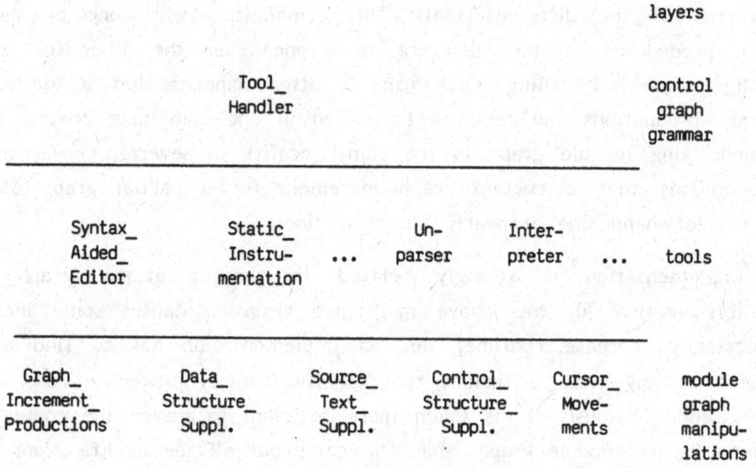

					layers
	Tool_ Handler				control graph grammar
Syntax_ Aided_ Editor	Static_ Instru- mentation	...	Un- parser	Inter- preter ...	tools
Graph_ Increment_ Productions	Data_ Structure_ Suppl.	Source_ Text_ Suppl.	Control_ Structure_ Suppl.	Cursor_ Move- ments	module graph manipu- lations

Fig. 3.6: the composition of the control graph grammar Tool_Handler

Such a layered approach of a graph grammar specification enforces a slightly modification of the usual definition of applicability of graph productions (cf. /Na 79/). That definition requires that a production or test is only applicable to a host graph iff the left-hand side is a **subgraph** of the host graph. But, to enable the sequential application of the productions of fig. 3.1 - 3.3 in the control procedure of fig. 3.4, we require that the left-hand side is contained as a **partial graph** in the host graph. Such a modification allows each tool a restricted, tool-specific view of the graph increments and the independent construction of the control procedures in the two functional layers.

Summarizing the approach we can say that the graph grammar Tool_Handler contains all control procedures and productions of the first and second layer and combines the control procedures of the second layer such that each command given by a user corresponds to a control procedure.
This formal composition / decomposition of graph grammars reflects the composition / decomposition of tools of an integrated tool set. Each command given by a user corresponds to a control procedure of this graph grammar Tool_Handler.

Besides this functional composition / decomposition we also have a data-structure oriented composition / decomposition, namely the composition / decomposition of a module graph of / into graph increments and tool-specific informations. The reader should be aware that this composition /decomposition is described by the graph grammar Tool_Handler, too.

4. Condensation of Graph Grammar Productions

The concept of an independent graph grammar specification for each tool, as explained in section 3, sometimes yields some inefficiences in the following sense.
Each control procedure of the graph grammar Tool_Handler was formed by combining the control procedures of the different tools. This combination was done by sequentially calling control procedures of the different tools one after the other (cf. fig. 3.5.). Because of this sequential calling mechanism it often happens that a lot of control procedures resp. productions and tests to be called in one combining control procedure change the underlying module graph in the same locality in several, consecutive steps. Same locality means that a certain graph increment (or a partial graph of this) is contained in the left-hand side of nearly all productions.

As the implementation is strongly related to the operational graph grammar specification (cf. section 5), the above mentioned situation causes some inefficiences which unneccessarily increase runtime, i.e. an implementation has to find a (partial) graph increment at any time a further tool specific control procedure resp. a further production is called. Obviously, it is much more efficient to search the common partial graph only once in the module graph, and then carry out all the modifications described by the according control procedure.

To realize this idea, we change our graph grammar specification. This modification is to 'summarize' as many productions as possible of one control procedure. It is done in two systematic steps which will be shown now.

In the **first step** we summarize a sequence of partial graph replacements into one partial graph replacement. This implies that the independent specification of each tool can no longer be sustained.

As an example we summarize the two productions 'insert_while_statement_control_ flow' (cf. fig.3.2) and 'insert_while_statement_unparsing_supplements' (cf. fig.3.3) called by the control procedure 'insert_while_statement_and_actualize' (cf. fig.3.4).

The embedding rule informally says that all incoming edges of node 1 are identically transferred to node 1 on the right-hand side. All outgoing edges labeled with 'u' or 'cf' of node 1 become outgoing edges of node 5 of the right-hand side. The formalism for the notation of the embedding rules is borrowed from /NA 79/.

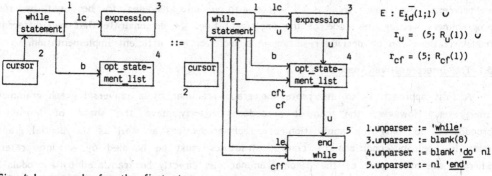

Fig. 4.1: example for the first step

The **second step** is based on the observation that the right-hand side of one production is identical to the left-hand side of other productions. In this case, the consecutive application of two productions can again be summarized. This situation often appears, when an increment is inserted in the module graph. As an example we regard the production 'insert_while_statement_graph_increment' (cf. fig. 3.1) and the above mentioned production (cf. fig. 4.1). By this step here, the right-hand side of the production in fig. 3.1 is replaced by the right-hand side of the production in fig. 4.1. The embedding rule and attribute transformation still hold.

After these two steps, the control procedure insert_while_statement_and_actualize now consists of only one production. The same steps can be done analogously for each such control procedure.

Unfortunately, the approach has two disadvantages. If you want to change the actions of one tool, or extend the programming environment by a new tool you will have to repeat these steps. (After a single graph grammar for the modified or new tool was developed.)
Furthermore, it has to be done by hand. The reason is that the condensation of productions heavily depends on their special shape, i.e. it is difficult to determine which edges are inserted by an embedding rule (cf. fig. 4.1), or which edges or nodes have to be added or omitted when mixing two productions (cf. fig. 4.1 the nodes marked with 'end-while' and 'expression').

Nevertheless, it is not useless to do these steps, as the advantage of this approach is that one can derive directly a more efficient implementation by using the same formalism as when specifying the different tools (cf. section 5).

5. Implementation Issues

The graph grammar Tool_Handler is an operational specification of all tools for programming in the small. In this chapter we show how such a specification directly leads to a guideline for the implementation of the tools. This guideline, i.e. a specification in the second sense, yields a further decomposition of the programming environment. But now, this is a decomposition into modules to be used by the programmers writing the code of the implementation. We demonstrate that two different modularizations can be derived resulting in a more or less efficient implementation.

5.1 The Interpretative Approach

A first approach is to interpret the graph grammar by a universal graph grammar interpreter. However, the control procedures already have the shape of Modula-2 procedures. So, only the application of graph productions as well as the partial graph tests in boolean conditions of control structures must be handled by an interpreter, whereas the other part of the graph grammar can directly be translated by a Modula-2 compiler. (This, of course, was one of the reasons to choose the special notion of control procedures for programming in graph grammars.)

A rough overview on this part of the IPSEN-specification is given now in terms of a module concept developed in the IPSEN-project, too. Other parts, as e.g. the auxiliary components to realize the sophisticated and hardware independent I/O-handling, are described in /ES 84/ in more detail.

In this module concept we distinguish different types of modules. **Data type** modules encapsulate a data structure together with its operations, whereas **function** modules summarize a class of complex algorithms. These algorithms are based on operations of one or more data type modules as well as other function modules. We say, module A is usable in module B, if module B imports explicitly resources of the export interface of A. For further details of this concept we refer to /LN 85/.

The data structure 'graph' together with its operations is encapsulated in the data type module Graph. It exports resources like 'Insert node with label x and attribute y', 'Replace edge a by edge b', etc.. In reality this module is a rather big subsystem containing a graph storage, i.e. a system to store, retrieve and modify arbitrary graphs (cf. /BL 84/).

A second data type module GraGra_Productions provides a storage for arbitrary graph grammar productions and partial graph tests. In our case, all productions and tests of the lowest layer of the graph grammar Tool_Handler are stored.

A function module GraGra_Production_Interpreter exports resources to apply graph grammar productions and tests. To implement these resources this function module uses the two data types modules to read a certain production or test and to find the occurrence of a partial graph as well as to replace it.

The control procedures are implemented by a further function module Graph_Modification. Its implementation is given by the Modula-2 part of the control procedures. Interpretation of graph grammar productions and tests is done by use of resources of the module GraGra_Production_Interpreter.
According to the division in different graph grammars for each tool and a corresponding graph grammar in the highest layer this function module can be subdivided in different function modules for each tool and a coordinating function module upon them.

Analogously to the decreased complexity in the graph grammar specification this division yields a more elucid modularization.

Furthermore, all these function modules use a subsystem called User_Interface to realize the I/O-operations contained in the control procedures.

By this model of a graph grammar interpreter we get two main advantages: After having specified the different tools, one has the possibility of quickly testing these tools by using the interpreter (rapid prototyping). Furthermore, this specification can easily be changed by only changing one graph grammar. So, in this realization strategy the stress is layed upon adaptability and not on efficiency on a certain machine.

5.2 The Compilative Approach

Now we renounce the concept of interpreting the productions in order to get a more efficient implementation. Of course, it is a step towards inflexibility. So this step should only be done when the test phase is finished and the environment has to be tuned up.

What we do now is to **implement** any **application of a production** or **graph test** directly as a (Modula-2) program. Here, we do not search the left-hand side in the host graph by a partial graph test and then replace it by a right-hand side (both done by the interpreter). Instead, we directly 'implement' a graph rewriting step by inserting /deleting the nodes and edges which are the result of the application of a rule. Here, we also introduce the knowledge of the underlying class of graphs (in our case the module graph). Please note that the actual position of modification is internally indicated by the cursor node.

Such a procedure implementing the application of a special production or test uses the resources of the module Graph. Furthermore, the one to one correspondence between a production and a procedure need not to be sustained. Graph algorithms, namely special partial graph tests or replacements which are used for the application of many rules of the given graph grammar can be written as procedures and can be called in any application of the different rules.

Of course, this approach changes the design of IPSEN. The two modules GraGra_Productions and GraGra_Production_Interpreter are replaced by a function module. Its resources are procedure calls for the different productions of the given graph grammar which is again in our case the lowest layer of Tool_Handler. The application of different productions is implemented directly using the elementary graph operations of the module Graph.

6. Conclusions

We have indicated that graphs grammars are a well-suited specification method to describe the internal behaviour of an integrated set of programming support tools working on graphs as high-level data structures. As the resulting graph grammar is an operational specification which means programming on an 'abstract level', we can use software engineering methods like modularization and integration to decrease the complexity of such an 'abstract' program. So, the specification of the tools can be done rather independently which makes the specification elucid and flexible both needed for modifying or adding tools. The complex problem of specifying a lot of tools on a quite complicated graph structure is decreased by a layered approach to the definition of such a graph grammar. The specification is also a guideline for the implementation of such an environment, i.e. it directly leads to a main part of the result of the design phase (also called specification).

The main topics of IPSEN are the development of such conceptual ideas as well as the implementation of a programming support environment on a minicomputer. Up to now, the graph storage (/BL 84/) and parts of the user interface (especially a window manager) are implemented. The graph grammar specification for the syntax-aided editor and most parts of the other tools for programming in the small (Interpreter, Static_Instrumentation, Unparser) are under elaboration and will be implemented soon in a prototype version of IPSEN.

Acknowledgements.

The authors are very indebted to M. Nagl and C. Lewerentz for many fruitful discussions.

References

/BL 84/ Brandes, Th./Lewerentz, C.: GRAS: A Non-standard Data Base System within a Software Development Environment, Tech. Rep. OSM - I18, Univ. of Osnabrueck

/Bu 81/ Bunke, H.: Attributed Programmed Graph Grammars as a Tool for Image Interpretation, Purdue University, Techn. Report TR-EE-81-22

/DG 80/ Donzeau-Gouge, M. et.al.: Programming Environments Based on Structured Editors - The MENTOR Experience, Techn. Report 26, INRIA, France

/EG 83/ Engels, G./Gall, R./Nagl, M./Schäfer, W. : Software Specification using Graph Grammars, Computing 31, 317-346

/ES 84/ Engels, G./ Schäfer, W.: The Design of an Adaptive and Portable Programming Support Environment, submitted for publication

/Ha 82/ Habermann, N. et.al.: The Second Compendium of GANDALF Documentation, Techn. Report, May 1982, Dept. of Computer Science, Carnegie-Mellon University, Pittsburgh

/LN 84/ Lewerentz, C./ Nagl, M.: A Formal Specification Language for Software Systems Defined by Graph Grammars, in U. Pape (Ed.): Proceedings WG'84 on 'Graphtheoretic Concepts in Computer Science', Linz: Trauner Verlag

/LN 85/ Lewerentz, C./Nagl, M.: Incremental Programming in the Large: Syntax-aided Specification Editing, Integration and Maintenance, to appear Proc. 18th Hawaii International Conference on System Sciences

/Na 79/ Nagl, M.: Graph-Grammatiken - Theorie, Anwendungen, Implementierung, Wiesbaden: Vieweg-Verlag

/Na 84/ Nagl, M.: An Incremental Programming Support Environment, to appear in Computer Physics Communications, North-Holland

/Re 84/ Reiss, St.: PECAN: Program Development Systems That Support Multiple Views, in Proc. of the ACM SIGSOFT/SIGPLAN Software Engineering Symposium on Practical Software Development Environments, Pittsburgh

/RT 83/ Reps, T./ Teitelbaum, T.: Incremental Context-Dependent Analysis for Language-Based Editors, ACM TOPLAS, Vol. 5, No. 3, 449-477

/SF 76/ Schnupp, P./ Floyd, Ch.: Software - Programmentwicklung und Projektorganisation, Berlin: Walter de Gruyter

/TR 81/ Teitelbaum, T./Reps, T.: The Cornell Programm Synthesizer - A syntax-directed Programming Environment, CACM 24 , 9 , 563-573

Multidimensional
Tree-Structured File Spaces

Douglas N. Kimelman
Department of Computer Science
University of Manitoba
Winnipeg Manitoba Canada

ABSTRACT

Development projects are often based on large collections of information.   This information is typically maintained in a set of files.
Current file system and database structures are inadequate for storing
and manipulating this information.

This paper defines a new class of high-level data structures called
"m-dimensional n-ary tree-structured spaces" (also called "md-nt spaces"), and discusses their use in the organization of the files of development project file systems.

The md-nt space organization allows the primary file system structure to represent relationships between files which are difficult or
impossible to represent with conventional structures.   A fundamental
aspect of this organization is that arbitrary semantics, such as implications in terms of a software module's nesting, or in terms of its
position within a sequence of revisions, may dynamically be associated
with this structure.   This enables the primary file system structure
to become the basis for automatic system functions such as the recom-
pilation of source code, the propagation of sets of changes to all appropriate files,   or the storage and regeneration of revisions of a
file.   With conventional systems, such operations are accomplished in
a manual, ad-hoc, and error-prone fashion, or via mechanisms which are
external to the primary file system structure, and hence contrary to
the goal of an integrated environment.

This paper also discusses some of the considerations in the design and implementation of such a file system. A prototype implementation is described, and an evaluation of the effectiveness of md-nt spaces in a software development environment is presented.

INTRODUCTION

Computer systems are often the primary facilities underlying development projects in a number of different areas. Such areas include software development, document preparation, image processing, graphics generation, circuit board layout, VLSI chip design, and many other areas of design and manufacturing.

These projects are often based on large collections of information. This information is typically maintained in a set of files.

For software development, the information which is to be managed for the programming and maintenance stages ranges from very high-level definitions, to high-level textual "source code" from which the "end product" is automatically generated, to intermediate representations, to the target machine code.

Document preparation may require source text containing formatting control words, displayable formatted output which may be marked up by reviewers, and phototypesetter data streams.

VLSI design may require that logic diagrams, circuit schematics, and geometry layouts all coexist, along with block diagrams, high level specifications, and the results of various analyses of a circuit.

In addition, for projects in any of these areas, this variety of information is often accompanied by information relating to project planning and scheduling, directions and procedures for processing files, characteristics and attributes of various files, relationships between files, and logs and histories of activities related to various files.

Further, there are typically numerous evolutionary versions of the various files. Some are archived and maintained only for the sake of posterity. Others are still active. For software systems, there might be three or four different releases and sub-releases in production, others being tested, and yet others in early development. Often, a progression of revisions for a given file exists within a given release of a system. For documents, a number of drafts may exist for each edition of a document.

As well as evolutionary versions of a file, numerous alternative variations of a file may exist. For a software development system, these may depend on which machine and system will eventually act as host to the resulting code. Variations may also exist according to which set of selectable features have been chosen.

Throughout this paper, software development projects will be used as an example of projects which have relatively demanding and reasonably well formalized information organization requirements.

INADEQUACIES OF CURRENT STRUCTURES

Current file system structures are inadequate for storing and manipulating development project information.

The UNIX file system [Ritchie and Thompson 1974] (UNIX is a Trademark of Bell Laboratories) exhibits a number of the inadequacies which are common to contemporary file systems. UNIX attempts to represent many different properties of a collection of files with a single hierarchical structure. Pathnames such as '/ u / smith / mydbms / cmds / source / 68k / newversion / util.c' are not uncommon. With systems such as UNIX, the file hierarchy becomes extremely cluttered, the manipulation of files becomes quite cumbersome, and the maintenance of large programs becomes quite complex and error-prone. In some cases, UNIX utilities such as RCS [Tichy 1982] or SCCS [Rochkind 1975] are used to maintain all of the versions of a particular source file in a single space-efficient archive (incorporating a differential base+delta storage scheme). In these cases, maintenance procedures are further complicated by the fact that these versions must be accessed via special-purpose commands. The versions can not be manipulated by the standard UNIX utilities. UNIX also makes use of "makefiles" [Feldman 1975] which describe dependencies between files, and procedures for processing and updating files. Such dependency information is external to the primary file system structure, and thus is potentially redundant. As well, the standard utilities are not aware of such information. Thus this information is not applied in many situations where it might be of further use.

Current database systems are better able to represent various relationships between a number of files in a uniform fashion, but are too cumbersome to be effective in a development project environment.

A number of authors have addressed the inadequacies of current file and database systems. Thall's KAPSE for the Ada Language System [Thall 1982] (Ada is a trademark of the Department of Defense, Ada Joint Program Office) formalizes a UNIX-like hierarchy by explicitly specifying directories as being either groupings of subordinate files, or groupings of revisions of a file, or groupings of variations of a file due to such factors as additional features or different target machines. As well, Thall formalizes the notions of file attributes and secondary associations between files. He provides automatic selection of file variations based on a desired set of attribute values.

The TRW "Software Productivity System" [Boehm et al. 1982] incorporates a hybrid "master database" which consists of a relational database coupled with a hierarchical file system and a version control system.

Cheatham's "Program Development System" [Cheatham 1981] for the ECL Programming System uses a relational database with a fixed set of attributes to store the modules of a software development project.

Goldstein and Bobrow's "Personal Information Environment" [Goldstein and Bobrow 1980] for the SMALLTALK system is based on "layered networks", in which each element of an unordered set of contexts is a linear array of partial module networks.

In general, none of these systems fully combines a powerful generally applicable structure, with high level operations, and with formal
semantics for automating various file oriented procedures.

Many language-directed systems such as CADES [McGuffin et al.
1979], Mentor [Donzeau et al. 1980], and "The GANDALF Software Development Environment" [Habermann and Notkin 1982] concentrate on the use
of a hierarchy, possibly with labelled edges, to represent (with very
fine granularity) the abstract structure and some of the semantics of
a particular item such as a program, or a module, or a document.
These systems devote little attention to the more global organization
of these trees within a development project environment.

This paper provides a brief overview of a file system structure
which is currently being developed by the author. The major contributions of this research are: a formal high-level organization for previously ad-hoc collections of files, a powerful means of viewing and
manipulating these files, the formal association of semantics and consequences with file system structures, and the integration of traditionally distinct areas such as the primary file system structure,
version control, and configuration management. These advances will
also be applicable in areas outside of software development, such as
document preparation, VLSI design, graphics, and others.

PROPOSED FILE SYSTEM STRUCTURE

The structure developed as a result of this research is one in
which each file of a file system is regarded as a point in a "multidimensional n-ary tree-structured space" (also called an "m-dimensional n-ary tree-structured space", or an "md-nt space").

Each point in an md-nt space has m coordinates, one for each dimension. Where the axes of a conventional space are linear, each axis of
a tree-structured space is a tree (or, in fact, a singly-rooted network). Each coordinate of a point, then, is a pathname derived from
the axis tree for the corresponding dimension. As an example, a point
in a four dimensional space, with the pathname 'compiler . parser .

treemgr . addnode' as its coordinate in the 'function' dimension, and
with the pathname 'vax . 11_750' as its coordinate in the 'host' dimension might be identified by

        [function : compiler . parser . treemgr . addnode ;
          version : release1 . subrelease2 ;
          host : vax . 11_750 ;
          phase : source . definitions].

Such a space may be regarded as a cartesian product of the m n-ary
trees which are its axes.

   For a particular software development project, a space could be defined to have a dimension in which a point's coordinate reflects the
function of the corresponding file, and a dimension in which a point's
coordinate reflects the version of the file.   The axis for the function dimension might be

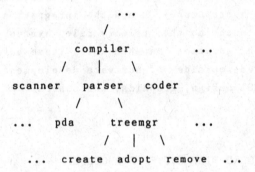

and the axis for the version dimension might be

                0
              /   \
            1   2
          /   \
        1.1   1.2   .

(Note that the values of the version axis which are below the second
level of the tree, e.g. 1.2, are automatically qualified relative to
the second level of the tree, e.g. 1, when they are displayed).   A
point (or file) in such a space would be

```
[ function : compiler . parser . treemgr . create ;
  version : 1.2 ]  .
```

Although the space considered in this section has a single axis for each dimension, this need not always be the case.   It is possible, in general, for one subspace to have a different axis in a given dimension than another subspace.   Thus it is possible, for example, for different functions to have different versions. The issues of varying axes and orthogonality are discussed in another paper currently being prepared by the author.

The points of an md-nt space may be connected.   Each point would have a set of links in each dimension, which would connect it to its children in that dimension.   For the space being considered here, children of the point

```
[ compiler ; 1 ]
```

in the 'function' dimension would be

```
[ compiler . scanner ; 1 ]
[ compiler . parser  ; 1 ]
[ compiler . coder   ; 1 ] .
```

In the 'version' dimension, children would be

```
[ compiler ; 1.1 ]
[ compiler ; 1.2 ] .
```

Such a structure may be traversed in the conventional fashion, by moving from one point to the next, along one of the links from a parent to a child. Each such move can be taken along any one of the dimensions of the space. For example, in order to get from the point

```
[ compiler ; 1 ]
```

to the point

```
[ compiler . parser . treemgr ; 1.2 ]
```

one could move, in the 'function' dimension, from

    [compiler ; 1]

to

    [compiler . parser ; 1]

to

    [compiler . parser . treemgr ; 1]

and then, in the 'version' dimension, to

    [compiler . parser . treemgr ; 1.2] .

Alternatively, one could move, in the 'function' dimension, from

    [compiler ; 1]

to

    [compiler . parser ; 1]

and then, in the 'version' dimension, to

    [compiler . parser ; 1.2]

and then, in the 'function' dimension, to

    [compiler . parser . treemgr ; 1.2] .

Thus, an md-nt space may also be regarded as a colored directed
graph, in which an edge is colored according to the dimension in which
it links its initial and terminal vertices.

The points of an md-nt space can be projected in various ways, in
order to provide a number of different views of the entire space.
When performed in the context of a suitable view, tasks such as ex-

tracting all of the source files for a particular release of a software system, or extracting all of the releases for a particular source file, which can be quite complicated with conventional file systems, become straightforward.

For the space being considered here, the projection of the points onto a single hierarchy, by version within function, could be displayed textually as

```
    . . .
  compiler
          ; 0
          ;      1
          ;          1.1
          ;          1.2
          ;      2
      scanner
          ; 0
          ;      1
          ;          1.1
          ;          1.2
          ;      2
      parser
          ; 0
    . . .
```

An alternative projection, by function within version, could be displayed textually as

```
0
          ; 1 . . .
          ; compiler
          ;     scanner
          ;     parser
          ;          pda
          ;          treemgr
          ;          . . .
          ;
     1
               ; . . .
               ; compiler
               ; . . .
     . . .                    .
```

An md-nt space can be sliced across various dimensions, along various coordinates in other dimensions, in order to yield a multidimensional subset of its points. Projections and slices allow the suppression of file system detail which is extraneous in a given situation. Thus, tasks such as the manipulation of the source files for one release of a software system in isolation from the source for all of the other releases, or the manipulation of all of the releases of a particular source file as a group, are greatly simplified.

For the space being considered, a slice across the version dimension, along the function coordinate 'parser', would be

```
          parser;0
          /      \
   parser;1    parser;2
    /      \
parser;1.1  parser;1.2      .
```

The projection of this slice onto the version axis would appear simply as

A particular meaning, or "semantic", which a user intuitively associates with a certain kind of link between the files of an md-nt
space, may be made known to the system. For the example being considered here, the "revision-of" semantic could be associated with the
version axis by a command such as

    C: attach rev-of to version

in order to inform the system that the kind of link which exists between

    [parser ; 1]   (call it 'P')

and

    [parser ; 1.1]   (call it 'CV')

means that "'CV' is a revision of 'P'".

As a result, certain kinds of actions, or "consequences", could be
performed automatically by the system on files connected by such
links. For example, any changes made to 'P' could automatically be
applied by the system to 'CV' as well. As another example, for economy of storage space, the system might elect to store only the differences between the contents of 'P' and the contents of 'CV', rather
than storing the entire contents of 'CV' as a separate file.

PROTOTYPE

A preliminary prototype for the structural aspects of the md-nt file space organization has been implemented as a user-mode layer above the UNIX file system. Each point of an md-nt file space is stored as a single UNIX file. All information concerning the structure of the space is stored in another UNIX file. The "structure file" and the "point files" are kept in a single UNIX directory.

A formalized extension of the UNIX command language is provided by an interpreter which has been implemented as a layer above the UNIX shell, using LEX and YACC [Johnson and Lesk 1978]. The language includes commands for manipulating the points of an md-nt space, and will include a powerful regular-expression sub-language for identifying the points of a space. Commands concerning the structure of the space are processed directly by the interpreter, and their actions are reflected in the underlying UNIX files. Ordinary UNIX commands, including those which deal with files of the multidimensional space, are simply passed on to the shell, after any point references are expanded and translated into UNIX file names.

Currently, the representation for the structure of the space, which is stored in the structure file, is a simple set of multi-linked nodes. Each point of the space is represented by a single node. Each node has a set of links which identify its parent, its first child, and its next sibling, in each dimension. Other representations being considered include: a simple hashed table of nodes, which contains no structural information, but which is augmented by a set of linked nodes representing the various axes; or, a representation which is based on an extended relational database.

In order to allow more effective experimentation with the semantic aspects of md-nt spaces, a more complete integration with the UNIX environment must be undertaken. This integration could be achieved by an interface implemented as a layer above the standard file access library. This would present md-nt spaces at a more fundamental level within the system.

CONCLUSION

Initial experience suggests that the md-nt file space organization can be a powerful and effective component of an integrated development project environment. This organization capitalizes on the considerable degree of orthogonality which is present in the file spaces of most large development projects. However, most such file spaces also include some dependencies. More work is required on handling these dependencies in a uniform fashion within the framework of md-nt spaces.

REFERENCES

[Boehm et al. 1982]
   Boehm, B.W., Elwell, J.F., Pyster, A.B., Stuckle, E.D., and Williams, R.D. "The TRW Software Productivity System," Proc. 6th International Conf. on Software Engineering, September 1982.

[Cheatham 1981]
   Cheatham, T.E. "An Overview of the Harvard Program Development System," in [Hunke 1981].

[Donzeau et al. 1980]
   Donzeau-Gouge, V., Huet, G., Kahn, G., and Lang, B. "Programming environment based on structured editors: The Mentor Experience," INRIA Research Report No. 26, July 1980.

[Feldman 1979]
   Feldman, S.I. "Make - A Program for Maintaining Computer Programs," Software Practice and Experience 9(3), March 1979.

[Ferch et al. 1978]
   Ferch, H.J., Neufeld, G.W., and Zarnke, C.R. "MANTES User Manual," University of Manitoba, August 1982.

[Goldstein and Bobrow 1980]
Goldstein, I.P., and Bobrow, D.G. "A Layered Approach to Software
Design," Xerox Palo Alto Research Center CSL-80-5, December 1980.

[Habermann and Notkin 1982]
Habermann, A.N., and Notkin, D.S. "The GANDALF Software Development Environment," Carnegie-Mellon University, January 1982.

[Hunke 1981]
Hunke, H., ed. "Software Engineering Environments," North Holland, 1981.

[Johnson and Lesk 1978]
Johnson, S.C., and Lesk, M.E. "UNIX Time-Sharing System: Language
Development Tools," The Bell System Technical Journal 57(6), July
1978.

[McGuffin et al. 1979]
McGuffin, R.W., Elliston, A.E., Tranter, B.R., and Westmacott,
P.N. "CADES - Software Engineering in Practice," Proc. 4th Inter-
national Conf. on Software Engineering, 1979.

[Ritchie and Thompson 1974]
Ritchie, D.M., and Thompson, K. "The UNIX Time-Sharing System,"
Communications of the ACM 17(7), July 1974.

[Rochkind 1975]
Rochkind, M.J. "The Source Code Control System," IEEE Transactions on Software Engineering SE-1(4), December 1975.

[Thall 1982]
Thall, R.M. "The KAPSE for the Ada Language System," Proc. of the
AdaTEC Conference on Ada, October 1982.

[Tichy 1982]
Tichy, W.F. "Design, Implementation, and Evaluation of a Revision
Control System," Proc. 6th International Conf. on Software Engi-
neering, September 1982.

APPENDIX: A SAMPLE FILE MANIPULATION SESSION

This appendix briefly illustrates a way in which the points of an md-nt space might be manipulated in a MANTES-like [Ferch et al. 1982] environment.

Note: '*' is used as a "wildcard" pattern rather than as a symbolic reference to the current file or record, ';' is used as a delimiter of coordinates in point identifiers rather than as a command separator, '--' is used to introduce comments, and '. . .' is used to mean "et cetera". Text entered by the user is in lowercase.

```
C:  . . .
C: display_axis dim=module

    COMPILER
        SCANNER
        PARSER
            SYMMGR
            TREEMGR
        CODER

C: display_axis dim=version

    TOP
        1
        2
                2.1
                2.2
                2.3
        3

C: use projection=module,version
                -- causes version within module for display, and module before
                -- coordinate before version coordinate for file identifiers
C: display f=[compiler;top]

    COMPILER
            ; TOP
            ;       1
            ;       2
            ;               2.1
            ;               2.2
            ;               2.3
            ;       3
        SCANNER
            ; TOP
            ;       1
            ;       2
            ;               2.1
            ;               2.2
            ;               2.3
            ;       3
        PARSER
            ; TOP
            ;       1
            ;       2
            ;               2.1
            ;               2.2
            ;               2.3
            ;       3
        . . .
```

```
C: use projection=version,module
C: display top;compiler

    TOP
            ; COMPILER
            ;       SCANNER
            ;       PARSER
            ;           SYMMGR
            ;           TREEMGR
            ;       CODER
        1
            ; COMPILER
            ;       SCANNER
            ;       PARSER
            ;           SYMMGR
            ;           TREEMGR
            ;       CODER
        2
            ;  . . .
        2.1
                ;  . . .
        2.2
                ;  . . .
        2.3
                ;  . . .
        3
            ;  . . .

C: use projection=module
C: use f=[module:current; version:*]
                    -- note: each coordinate of a file
                    -- designator is defaulted or
                    -- overridden separately
C: display compiler

    COMPILER
        SCANNER
        PARSER
            SYMMGR
            TREEMGR
        CODER

C: transfer symmgr under scanner
                -- moves the file for module symmgr
                -- under the file for module scanner
                -- (rather than the file for module
                -- parser) FOR EACH version
C: use f=version:3
                -- restrict operations to the slice
                -- with version coordinate '3'
                -- (rather than all versions)
C: create optimizer after coder
                -- just for version 3
                -- (see the display below)
C: use f=version:*
                -- back to dealing with all versions
                -- by default
C: create parser;version:2.1.1 under parser;version:2.1
```

```
C: use projection=module,version
C: display compiler;top
   COMPILER
               ; TOP
               ;       1
               ;       2
               ;               2.1
               ;               2.2
               ;               2.3
               ;       3
        SCANNER
                  ; TOP
                  ;       1
                  ;       2
                  ;               2.1
                  ;               2.2
                  ;               2.3
                  ;       3
            SYMMGR
                      ; TOP
                      ;       1
                      ;       2
                      ;               2.1
                      ;               2.2
                      ;               2.3
                      ;       3
          PARSER
                    ; TOP
                    ;       1
                    ;       2
                    ;               2.1
                    ;                       2.1.1
                    ;               2.2
                    ;               2.3
                    ;       3
            TREEMGR
                      ; TOP
                      ;       1
                      ;       2
                      ;               2.1
                      ;               2.2
                      ;               2.3
                      ;       3
        CODER
                  ; TOP
                  ;       1
                  ;       2
                  ;               2.1
                  ;               2.2
                  ;               2.3
                  ;       3
      OPTIMIZER
                  ;       3
```

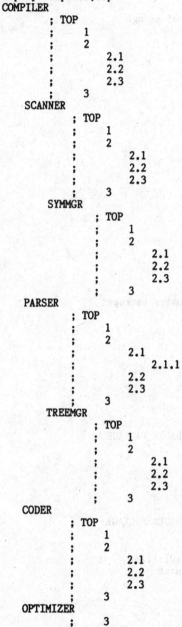

```
C: use f=[module:symmgr; version:current]
C: use projection=version
C: display top
                    -- i.e. the versions of symmgr


    TOP
         1
         2
              2.1
              2.2
              2.3
         3


C: list version:3 first/2

    1.    *PROCESS;
    2.     SYMMGR: PROC OPTIONS(MAIN);

C: list version:1 first/2

    1.    *PROCESS;
    2.     SYMMGR: PROC OPTIONS(MAIN);

C: after version:1 first by=.01

    1.    *PROCESS;
    1.01  /* symmgr - symbol table manager package
    1.02  *
    1.03  * routines exported:
    1.04  *    addsym( . . .
    1.05  *    delsym( . . .
     . . .
    1.28  */

C: list version:1 first/4

    1.    *PROCESS;
    1.01  /* SYMMGR - SYMBOL TABLE MANAGER PACKAGE
    1.02  *
    1.03  * ROUTINES EXPORTED:

C: list version:3 first/4

    1.    *PROCESS;
    1.01  /* SYMMGR - SYMBOL TABLE MANAGER PACKAGE
    1.02  *
    1.03  * ROUTINES EXPORTED:
    -- (the changes which inserted 1.01:1.28
    -- were propagated to all subsequent
    -- versions as a result of the
    -- "revision-of" semantic being
    -- associated with axes of the
    -- version dimension)
```

```
C:  . . .
C:   -- now, assuming a somewhat larger space
C: display_axis dim=phase

    TOP
        SPECS
            DFD
        SRC
            DCLS
            BODY
        INTERM
            SYMTAB
            OBJCODE
        TARGET
            LOAD
        DOCN
            PGM_GUIDE
            USER_REF


C: display_axis dim=host

    TOP
        MOTOROLA
        8
                6800
                6801
                6809
        32
                68000
                68010
                68020
        INTEL
        8
                8080
                8085
        16
                8088
                8086
        32
                432
        ZILOG
        8
                Z80
        32
                Z8000

C: use projection=module,host,phase
C: display f=[module:symmgr;
              host:(motorola,zilog).8.*;
              phase:src.*] depth=0

    SYMMGR; MOTOROLA.8.6800; SRC.DCLS
                                    BODY
                         6801; SRC.DCLS
                                    BODY
                         6809; SRC.DCLS
                                    BODY
             ZILOG.8.Z80; SRC.DCLS
                                BODY
```

```
C: use f=[phase:src.*;host:68000]
C: use projection=module,phase
C: display f=[parser.*]

    PARSER
            ; SRC
            ;        DCLS
            ;        BODY
        TREEMGR
            ; SRC
            ;        DCLS
            ;        BODY

C: scan [parser;dcls] f:1 'fixed bin'

    . . .

C: off
```

A THEORY OF ABSTRACT DATA TYPES FOR PROGRAM DEVELOPMENT:
BRIDGING THE GAP?

T.S.E. Maibaum
Department of Computing
Imperial College of
Science and Technology
London
UK.

Paulo A.S. Veloso
Depto. de Informatica
PUC/RJ, Rio de Janeiro
Brasil.

M.R. Sadler
Department of Computing
Imperial College of
Science and Technology
London
UK.

Abstract: This paper outlines a logical approach to abstract data types, which is motivated by, and more adequate for (than algebraic approaches), the practice of programming. Abstract data types are specified as axiomatic theories and notions concerning the former are captured by syntactical concepts concerning the latter. The basic concepts of namability, conservative extensions and interpretations of theories explain implementation, refinement and parameterisation. Being simple, natural and flexible, this approach is quite appropriate for program development.

Key Words: abstract data types, axiomatic theories, incomplete specifications, program development, stepwise refinement, implementation, parameterisation, interpretation, conservative extension, namability.

1.   Introduction

This paper outlines and illustrates a logical approach to the specification and implementation of abstract data types (ADT's) and software, which is directly motivated by, and more adequate for the practice of software engineering. There is still, we feel, a large gap between existing formal methods work on theories of ADT's and the actual practice of programming. The most important aspects of this gap concern the lack of a clear relationship between formal specification and actual programs and the technical inadequacies of formal theories of specification and implementation.

Let us look more closely at this gap with reference to examples from the current literature. Theories of specification and implementation usually do not give an adequate account of how programs are actually produced to realise the presented specification and implementation. For example, in [GHM] an implementation is defined equationally with claims that their equational definitions can be translated easily into programs in some programming language. This may be reasonably seen to be the case for functional (applicative) languages [He'80] and easy examples, but is certainly not the case for other kinds of languages and more complicated examples. In any case, what criteria can we use to decide whether this allegedly easy step is actually correct? This is not discussed. In the algebraic theories [GTW'78, Eh'81, EKP'79, WPPDB'80, WB'82, SW'82, Ga'83, BG'81], development is kept totally within the same formalism with no interface defined other than inadequate statements such as: At the end of the development process, the primitive data types of a programming language can be used. How they can be used and how programs are actually produced is never adequately discussed or is left as an open problem [BG'81].

In [L'79] we can see an informal approach to program specification and development in the ADT framework which interfaces well with a given programming language. In fact, descriptions of behaviour are given in a form which is very close to the language. However, the specifications and development are highly informal and so it is difficult to see how to verify correctness of any of the steps.

Another aspect of the gap is the difference between what software

---

*Research partly sponsored by CNPq, FINEP and SERC (UK).

engineers feel is required at the specification stage and what formal theories require one to state. The algebraic theories require details to be specified which might more often be left as details of implementation (or as we will point out, may not need to be dealt with at all!). One example is an operation like choosing an arbitrary element of a set. We would like to say just this (i.e. have an underdetermined operation) but, for example, the algebraic theories based on initiality force us to define at the specification level, which element of the set we will choose. Errors present a similar situation. Often (when fault tolerance is not an important consideration, for example), we wish to specify the behaviour under normal conditions of the system we are developing and do not require anything about error situations. This is what is expressed by conventional input/output specifications. Algebraic theories generally require us to give complete specifications and require us to deal with these abnormal situations at the specification level, either by using error specifications whose theory is quite complex ([Go'77,Go'83,P'84]) or partial algebras and definedness predicates which again tend to be complex and difficult ([BW'82, WPPDB'83]) or else by being somewhat informal [G'77].

Finally, let us turn to the process of implementation/development. This process is generally seen in terms of the following diagram:

$$S1 \text{-------} > S2'$$
$$\uparrow$$
$$S2 \text{------} > S3'$$
$$\uparrow$$
$$S3 \dots$$

$$SN\text{-}1 \text{----} > SN'$$
$$\uparrow$$
$$SN$$

We wish to implement specification S0 and we decide that we wish to use S1 as a basis for a first step in this process. We then enrich (extend) S1 by adding new symbols and properties so that we can realise the operations of S0 in terms of those of S1. This realisation is effected by a translation from S0 to S1' (the extension of S1); for example, theory morphisms in algebraic theories. The software engineer would mimic this process by writing a cluster of procedures C01 to implement the operations of S0 assuming those of S1 as primitive. It is not clear how he would prove the correctness of his procedures with respect to the original specification, even if he were interested, as he has no obvious interface between this implementation step (S0 in S1 via S1') and the programming language and its associated logic.

Supposing that this first implementation step is done, the software engineer might then wish to proceed by implementing S1 in S2 (via the extension/enrichment S2'). Having then written the corresponding cluster of procedures C12, he would then have a collection of procedures (C01 and C12) which he would say together implemented S0 in S2. Moreover, he would expect that the modularised reasoning he had done (in justifying the steps from S0 to S1 via S', the writing of the cluster C01, the step from S1 to S2 via S2' and the development of the cluster C12) to justify the correctness of the composed implementation of S0 in S2 and use the set of procedures in C01 and C12 as the programming language realisation of this composition. Unfortunately, most theories would not allow him to make this assumption! For example, in [Eh'82], in order to compose S0 in S1 via S1' with S1 in S2 via S2', one is obliged to "reprogram" S0 in S2 via a further extension. So one would have two extensions of S2:S2' to implement S1 and S2" to implement S0. Thus no cluster C01 could have been written before the compostion as its proof of correctness can only be supplied at the end of the process of implementation when we have finally reprogrammed S0 in SN. So it would seem that we have to keep redoing work we have already done - proving the correctness of the implementation of S0. Moreover, in [Eh'82] translations (implementations) do not preserve all properties of the specification S0 - only so-called ground properties (formulae in which no variables appear). Thus, any reasoning about a program P using S0 would bot be valid once an implementation step is taken as invariably this involves non-ground properties and these may not be preserved. (Actually algebraic methods are also deficient in another sense with respect to verifying program properties since reasoning about programs generally requires something equational logic does not provide - the use of quantifiers. This is particularly true, for example, in the case of loop invariants in imperative language programs).

Again, in [SW'82], implementations do not in general compose. Again, property preservation is the problem (see counter example on page 485 of [SW'82]). A technical way of putting this is that the categories of specifications as objects and translations as arrows/morphisms have too many such arrows.

To bridge the gap, it is our intention to outline a theory which makes a better approximation to the objects (specifications) and arrows (translations) which should be present in order to support the practices of software engineering, in particular stepwise development and certification.

Among the methodological advantages of this method are:

(i) Specifications need say only as much as is thought desirable. There is an allowance for underdetermined operations and partially defined operations (if popping the empty stack is never used in a program, then there is no need to specify what happens in this situation), thereby simplifying the treatment of errors.

(i) The language of first order logic is a powerful and succinct formalism compared to the more restrictive formalisms used elsewhere.

(iii) The theory is closer to the usual logics of programs (usually extensions of first order logic).

(iv) The restrictive notion of sufficient completeness ([Gu'77, Ga'83, WPPDB'83, WB'82]) is replaced by a more permissive concept, thus contributing to the ease of use and expressiveness of the formalism.

Among the technical advantages of this method are:

(i) There is a powerful proof theory which, for example, allows the use of general formulae including quantifiers, justifies the use of structural induction and the development of canonical forms and provides a natural basis for proofs of termination for programs using ADT's.

(ii) There is a natural interface between implementation steps and input/output specifications for programs to realise these steps.

(iii) Implementations always compose and the composition is constructed directly and automatically from the components. Moreover, the correctness of the composition is guaranteed by the correctness of the components. Compostion of implementations is associative and implementations "commute" with instantiation of parameters in a parameterised type.

(iv) Implementations preserve all provable properties. Thus, proofs of correctness of programs remain valid after implementation.

(v) Equality is dealt with as any other predicate (i.e. it is not interpreted as identity). Thus there is no need as in the algebraic theories, to introduce a "semantic" equality different from the "=" used in equations. This reflects the reality that abstract objects are often represented by more than one concrete object. These concrete objects are equivalent but <u>not</u> identical.

The technical justification of these claims is provided elsewhere ([MV'81, MSV'83, MSV'83a, SM'84]). Here we hope to present our case for the methodological benefits of the theory.

2. <u>Namability and Incomplete Specifications</u>

For a very simple example consider the ADT with one sort (<u>Nat</u>), one constant symbol (<u>zero</u>) and one unary operation symbol (<u>succ</u>) specified by the following two sentences (with leading universal quantifiers implicit, as usual):

(1) ~ <u>zero</u> = <u>succ</u>(n)

(2) <u>succ</u>(m) = <u>succ</u>(n) -> m = n

Notice the occurrence of the binary predicate symbol =. We shall consider = to be present in every specification together with the usual axioms stating that the realisation of = is a congruence [E'72]. Also assumed present in every specification is the following <u>namability axiom</u>

(N) ($\forall$ n:<u>Nat</u>) [n = <u>zero</u> v n = <u>succ</u> (<u>zero</u>) v ...

... v n = <u>succ</u>(...<u>succ</u>(<u>zero</u> ...) v ...]

This is an infinitary sentence (in $L_{\omega_1 \omega}$), stating that every element of the domain of <u>Nat</u> must be the value of a ground (variable-free) term.

It is well-known, and easy to see, that every model of (1), (2) and (N) in which = is realised as identity is isomorphic to the standard model N of the natural numbers. In fact, any model A of the above axioms is such that the quotient A/=A (where =A is the realisation of = in A) is isomorphic to N. (We shall not require that = be realised always as identity for reasons to be clarified in the sequel). One very important consequence of the namability axiom will be an induction axiom

($\forall$ n:<u>Nat</u>)[n = zero v($\exists$ m:<u>Nat</u>)[n = suc(m)]]

Now consider the result of enriching the above ADT with a binary predicate intended to mean "less than". Call it <u>NAT</u>; its language is

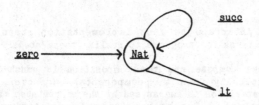

We can specify <u>Nat</u> by adding to the above specification, for instance, the following sentences (which amount to a recursive definition of <u>lt</u>)

(3) <u>lt</u>(<u>succ</u>(m),<u>succ</u>(n)) <-> <u>lt</u>(m,n)

(4) <u>lt</u>(<u>zero</u>,<u>succ</u>(n))

(5) ~lt(zero,zero)

(6) ~lt(succ(m),zero)

We remark that this theory is a _conservative extension_ [Sh'67] of the preceding one, for the addition of the new axioms (3)-(6) does not enable the derivation of any new theorem in the old language, i.e. without _lt_.

A more interesting example is the ADT _SET of NAT_, intended to mean finite sets of naturals. Its language is

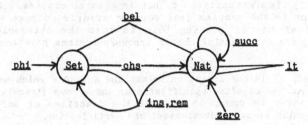

Consider the following axioms (where the sorts of the variables are m,n:_Nat_; s,t:_Set_)

(7) [(∀ n:_Nat_) _bel_(n,s) <-> _bel_(n,t)] -> s = t

(8) ~ _bel_(n,_phi_)

(9) _bel_(m,_ins_(s,n)) <-> m = n v _bel_(m,s)

(10) _bel_(m,_rem_(s,n)) <->~ m = n & _bel_(m,s)

(11) ~ s = _phi_ -> _bel_(_chs_(s),s)

Axiom (7) can be regarded (as its converse is a consequence of the underlying axioms for =) as defining = (short for = $_{Set}$)in terms of _bel_ (onging). That is part of the reason why we do not require = to be realised as identity. Namely, in a complex data type equality among objects of a (structured) sort will in general depend upon its component objects, having to be programmed (cf. equality among arrays), rather than being simple logical identity.

Axioms (8), (9), (10) define, in the same spirit, _phi_, _ins_ and _rem_ in terms of _bel_. But, in contrast, we give no similar complete definition for _chs_. For, we want _chs_ to be an underdetermined operation to choose an element from a non-empty set. And axiom (11) states just that! Notice in particular, that it says nothing about _chs_(_phi_) because at this point we have decided not to be interested in this particular error situation.

In order to clarify this let us consider a specific ground term

t = _ins_(_ins_(_phi_,_succ_(zero)),zero)

(which denotes the set {0,1}). From the preceding axioms we are able to deduce (as expected) sentences like

bel(_succ_(zero),t)
~ t = _phi_
t = _ins_(_ins_(_phi_,zero),_succ_(zero))
rem(t,_succ_(zero)) = _ins_(_phi_,zero)

properties of the specification SO - only so-called ground properties (formulae in which no variables appear). Thus, any reasoning about a program P using SO would bot be valid once an implementation step is taken as invariably this involves non-ground properties and these may not be preserved. (Actually algebraic methods are also deficient in another sense with respect to verifying program properties since reasoning about programs generally requires something equational logic does not provide - the use of quantifiers. This is particularly true, for example, in the case of loop invariants in imperative language programs).

Again, in [SW'82], implementations do not in general compose. Again, property preservation is the problem (see counter example on page 485 of [SW'82]). A technical way of putting this is that the categories of specifications as objects and translations as arrows/morphisms have too many such arrows.

To bridge the gap, it is our intention to outline a theory which makes a better approximation to the objects (specifications) and arrows (translations) which should be present in order to support the practices of software engineering, in particular stepwise development and certification.

Among the methodological advantages of this method are:

(i) Specifications need say only as much as is thought desirable. There is an allowance for underdetermined operations and partially defined operations (if popping the empty stack is never used in a program, then there is no need to specify what happens in this situation), thereby simplifying the treatment of errors.

(i) The language of first order logic is a powerful and succinct formalism compared to the more restrictive formalisms used elsewhere.

(iii) The theory is closer to the usual logics of programs (usually extensions of first order logic).

(iv) The restrictive notion of sufficient completeness ([Gu'77, Ga'83, WPPDB'83, WB'82]) is(replaced by a more permissive concept, thus contributing to the ease of use and expressiveness of the formalism.

Among the technical advantages of this method are:

(i) There is a powerful proof theory which, for example, allows the use of general formulae including quantifiers, justifies the use of structural induction and the development of canonical forms and provides a natural basis for proofs of termination for programs using ADT's.

(ii) There is a natural interface between implementation steps and input/output specifications for programs to realise these steps.

(iii) Implementations always compose and the composition is constructed directly and automatically from the components. Moreover, the correctness of the composition is guaranteed by the correctness of the components. Compostion of implementations is associative and implementations "commute" with instantiation of parameters in a parameterised type.

(iv) Implementations preserve all provable properties. Thus, proofs of correctness of programs remain valid after implementation.

(v) Equality is dealt with as any other predicate (i.e. it is not interpreted as identity). Thus there is no need as in the algebraic

We can also deduce, of course, bel(chs(t),t) and even

chs(t) = zero v chs(t) = succ(zero)

But we cannot deduce either equation of the above disjunction! In other words, the above axioms do not enable us to compute a specific natural number as the value of chs(t). And they should not! If they did we would have overspecified chs, which is still regarded as arbitrary choice. It would be premature at this level of specification to describe exactly how such an element is to be picked. This should be left to a future refinement, or perhaps to the implementation phase, when the consequences of such a decision can be better evaluated.

But how do we guarantee that chs(t) is indeed a natural number? Notice that, by syntax, chs(t) is of sort Nat. And our namability axiom (N) guarantees that any object of a domain of sort Nat (in particular the object denoted by chs(t)) is a standard natural number, thus preventing chs(t) from becoming a non-standard natural number. Compare this with the more conceptually complicated notions of data and hierarchy constraints in [BG'79,BG'81, WPPDB'83] and the semantic constraints of [MV'81].

As we have a new sort, we also have the corresponding namability axiom

$$(\forall \, s{:}\underline{\text{Set}}) \; V \; (s = t)$$
$$t \; \text{in} \; T$$

where T is an enumeration of all ground terms of sort Set and V represents infinite disjunction. As a consequence we again have a schema of induction. More important is the fact that every object of sort Set has a "normal form" involving only phi and ins, which are then the constructor operations [GH'78]. This is again a consequence of the above namability axiom.

In general, a specification for an ADT consists of a many-sorted first-order theory presented by a language L and a set of axioms G. For each sort s in S we assume a binary predicate symbol $=_s$ in L. The machinery of the logic of namability has for each sort s in S

- the usual equality axioms
- a namability axiom $(\forall \, x{:}s) \; V \; (x = {}_st)$
  $$t \; \text{in} \; T$$

where T is an enumeration of the ground terms of sort s (in addition to the usual logic axioms). The logic of namability also has an infinitary rule of inference (a ω-rule) which allows us to manipulate the namability axiom to derive induction schema, normal forms, etc. See [B'77] for details of ω-rules.

3. Program Development and Verification

The proposed approach aims at being partucularly appropriate for program construction by means of ADT's. As a simple example to illustrate this we shall consider sorting. We can formulate it as the construction of a program P that receives as input a set t of natural numbers and outputs a sequence q of natural numbers such that is-sort(q,t), where is-sort is defined by

(12) is-sort(q,t) <-> ordered(q) & same(q,t)

Here the language consists of the following sorts and predicates

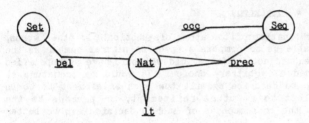

(the intended realisation of <u>occ</u> is occurrence of a number in a sequence and that of <u>prec</u>(m,n,q) is that m occurs in q before n) so that <u>ordered</u> and <u>same</u> are defined by

(13) <u>ordered</u>(q) <-> ($\forall$ m,n:<u>Nat</u>) [<u>lt</u>(m,n)

                & <u>occ</u>(m,q) & <u>occ</u>(n,q) -> <u>prec</u> (m,n,q)]

(14) <u>same</u>(q,t) <-> ($\forall$ n:<u>Nat</u>) [<u>occ</u>(n,q) <-> <u>bel</u>(n,t)]

We now have a natural interface to our programming language as the input output specification of our sort porgram P is: {<u>true</u>} P {is_sort(q,S_o)} where S_o is the input set.

For operations we have all those of <u>SET of NAT</u> plus a constant symbol <u>lmbd</u> of sort <u>Seq</u> such that

(15) ~ <u>occ</u>(n,<u>lmbd</u>)

and an operation symbol <u>ordins</u>: (<u>Seq,Nat</u>) -> <u>Seq</u> partly specified by

(16) <u>ordered</u>(q) -> <u>ordered</u>(<u>ordins</u>(q,n))

(17) <u>occ</u>(m,<u>ordins</u>(q,n)) <-> m = n & <u>occ</u>(m,q)

Given this ADT <u>SORT of NAT</u> it is quite natural to conceive our program P first as an abstract program that repeatedly removes elements from the input set and inserts them (respecting their relative order) into an initially empty sequence. In order to formalise this intuition it is useful to extend the specification of our ADT by the following definition

(18) <u>is-transf</u>(q,t,s_o) <-> ($\forall$ n:<u>Nat</u>)[<u>bel</u>(n,s_o)
                               <-> <u>bel</u>(n,t) v <u>occ</u>(n,q)]

We are thus led to the following abstract program

```
t:=s_o; q:=lmbd;
  {ordered(q) & is-transf(q,t,s_o)}
while ~t = phi do
  n:=chs(t)      {bel(n,t)};
  q:=ordins(q,n);
  t:=rem(t,n)    {~ bel(n,t)}
end
```

We have already annotated the program with the loop invariant

      <u>ordered</u>(q) & <u>is-transf</u>(q,t,s_o)

and some assertions following immediately from axioms (10) and (11).

In view of (12), the verification conditions [Ma'74] (for partial correctness) include for instance,

(19) $\underline{is\text{-}transf}(q, t, s_o) \dashrightarrow [\underline{bel}(n, t) \dashrightarrow \underline{is\text{-}transf}(\underline{ordins}(q, n),$
$$\underline{rem}(t, n), s_o)]$$

This (and the other verification conditions) follow easily from the preceding axioms.

A usual method to prove termination is that of the well founded set [Ma'74]. Here we can employ the set of ground terms with the well founded relation of "being a subterm". Indeed we can show, using the normal form of section 2,

$\underline{bel}(n, t) \rightarrow \underline{rem}(t, n) < t$

which suffices to guarantee termination.

An advantage of the proposed approach is exactly this: we generally can employ the syntactical well-founded relation of being a subterm in order to prove termination, rather than having to create a special well founded set for almost every program.

Notice that we have proved the total correctness of our program based only on the ADT specification, thus without needing complete definitions for $\underline{chs}$ or $\underline{ordins}$.

In fact, in line with the methodology of program construction by means of ADT's, we employed an ADT close to the problem. That is why we use $\underline{ordins}$ and $\underline{prec}$, not usually thought of as available to manipulate sequences. We shall take care of this in the next section by implementing the ADT $\underline{SORT\ of\ NAT}$ in terms of more "concrete" ADT's.

4.   Implementations (and Refinements) As Interpretations

The ADT used in the program for sorting is $\underline{SORT\ of\ NAT}$. We are now going to implement it in terms of the list of naturals. We will use the ADT $\underline{LIST\ of\ NAT}$ with the following language

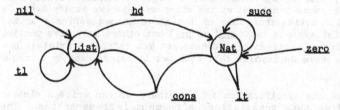

Its specification consists of that for $\underline{NAT}$ plus the following axioms

(20) $\underline{cons}(m, x) = \underline{cons}(n, y) \rightarrow x = y \ \& \ m = n$

(21) $\underline{hd}(\underline{cons}(m, x)) = m$

(22) $\underline{tl}(\underline{cons}(m, x)) = x$

(23) $\underline{tl}(\underline{nil}) = \underline{nil}$

(Recall that we also have namability and $=_{List}$ as a congruence). Notice in particular that we cannot deduce a value for $\underline{hd(nil)}$. All we know from (N) is that $\underline{hd(nil)}$ is some natural.

We can implement <u>SORT of NAT</u> into <u>LIST of NAT</u>, sort by sort. Consider first the sort <u>Set</u>.

The first thing to do is decide which lists will represent sets. Our intuition tells us we need only those lists with nonrepeated occurrences of elements. So, we extend <u>LIST of NAT</u> with the

(24) <u>set-rep</u>(x) <-> ($\forall$ n:<u>Nat</u>) [<u>is-in</u>(n,x) -> <u>once</u>(n,x)]

where

(25) <u>is-in</u>(n,x) <-> ~ x = <u>nil</u> & [<u>hd</u>(x) = n v <u>is-in</u>(n,<u>tl</u> (x))]

(26) <u>once</u>(n,x) <-> ~ x = <u>nil</u> & [<u>hd</u>(x) = n & ~ <u>is-in</u>(n,<u>tl</u>(x))]
$\qquad$ v [~ <u>hd</u>(x) = n & <u>once</u>(n,<u>tl</u>(x))])

<u>set-rep</u> is called a <u>relativisation predicate</u> and it is used to delineate those lists which actually represent a set from those that do not. (It sorts the wheat from the chaff!).

We now have to extend <u>LIST of NAT</u> by concepts corresponding to those of <u>SET of NAT</u>: for each symbol phi, <u>bel</u>, etc., we introduce in <u>LIST of NAT</u> the corresponding primed one <u>phi</u>', <u>bel</u>', etc. For instance

(27) <u>phi</u>' = <u>nil</u>

(28) <u>ins</u>'(x,m) = y <-> [<u>is-in</u>(m,x) & y = x] v[~ <u>is-in</u>(m,x) & y = <u>cons</u>(m,x)]

(29) <u>rem</u>'(x,m) = y <-> [~ <u>is-in</u>(m,x) & y = x]
$\qquad\qquad\qquad\qquad\qquad\qquad$ v [<u>is-in</u>(m,x) & y = <u>tl</u>(x)]

(30) <u>chs</u>'(x) = m -> <u>is-in</u>(m,x)

(31) <u>bel</u>'(m,x) <-> <u>is-in</u>(m,x)

(32) x = '<u>Set</u> y <->:($\forall$ n <u>Nat</u>) [<u>is-in</u>(n,x) <-> <u>is-in</u>(n,y)]

Notice that = , not being considered a logical symbol realised as identity, undergoes the same treatment as the other symbols (we employ here = '<u>Set</u> for clarity). Also notice that some of the above axioms define a primed symbol in terms of list symbols (e.g. <u>phi</u>' as <u>nil</u>) but others only give partial definitions. In particular, notice that we have not yet defined completely how <u>chs</u> is to operate, nor have we imposed that each set be represented by a unique list.

Having translated one specification into another, we can write a cluster of procedures to realise this translation/refinement/implementation. The procedures correspond in a one to one fashion to the operations and predicates of the abstract specification being implemented. Thus, in the example above, we have procedures defining <u>phi</u>', <u>ins</u>', <u>rem</u>', <u>chs</u>', <u>bel</u>' and = '<u>Set</u> (as well as the operations of NAT). We can define the input/output specifications for these procedures by using (24), ..., (32). For example, the function (procedure) INS (corresponding to <u>ins</u> and <u>ins</u>') takes arguments m_0 of sort <u>Nat</u> and x_0 of sort <u>List</u> and has the specification

{<u>set-rep</u>(x_0) & <u>nat-rep</u>(m_0)}

$\qquad$ INS(x_0,m_0)

{(<u>is-in</u>(m_0,x_0) & INS = x_0)
v (~ <u>is-in</u>(m_0,x_0) & INS = <u>cons</u>(m_0,x_0)}

So the input specification indicates that the function is guaranteed or expected to work only for concrete representatives of abstract objects while the output specification is the definiens of the definition of _ins'_ in terms of list operations. Developing and proving such a program correct can of course use the logic of the programming language and assume the properties of lists.

Now for the sort _Seq_ it is natural to use a list as representing a sequence. So the corresponding representation predicate is trivial, and similarly for equality between sequences.

For the constant, operation and predicate symbols of sort _Seq_, we introduce, for instance

(33) _ordins'_(x,m) = y -> _ordered'_ (y)
          & ($\forall$ n:_Nat_) (_is-in_(n,y) <-> n = m v _is-in_(n,x))

(34) _prec'_(m,n,x) <-> ~ x = _nil_ & [(_hd_(x) = m & _is-in_(n,_tl_(x)))
                     v _prec'_(m,n,_tl_(x))]

Notice that we do not have to worry about symbols like _same_, etc., that were introduced by definition. As we will see later, such definitions can be "carried forward" in implementations in an automatic fashion.

Finally, we can naturally represent the sort _Nat_ of _SORT of NAT_ identically by the sort _Nat_ of _LIST of NAT_. So this part is trivial.

By adding axioms (24) through (34) to _LIST of NAT_ we have built a conservative extension of the latter. Call this extension _LIST of NAT by SORT of NAT_. Now, each sentence of the language of _SORT of NAT_ can be translated into a corresponding one, its primed and relativised version. For instance consider axiom (10), which after being written with explicit leading universal quantifiers is translated to

(35) ($\forall$ x:_List_) ($\forall$ i,j:_Nat_) {_set-rep_(x) & _nat-rep_(i) & _nat-rep_(j)
       ->[_bel'_ (i,_rem'_(x,j)) <-> i =$'_{Nat}$ j v _bel'_(i,x)]}

The use of relativisation predicates with the translation of quantified formulae reflects the idea that properties of sets, when translated, are meant to hold only for lists which really represent sets.

Now, in order to guarantee the correctness of the implementation (and of our program for sorting) we have to verify that each realisation of _LIST of NAT_ induces a realisation of _SORT of NAT_. This can be done as follows. Firstly for each axiom of _SORT of NAT_ we verify that its translation is a theorem of _LIST of NAT by SORT of NAT_. For instance, (35) follows from _LIST of NAT_ plus (25), (28) and (32) together with the definition of =$'_{Nat}$. Secondly, we verify closure of the relativisation predicates under the corresponding primed operations. For instance,

($\forall$ x:_List_) ($\forall$ i:_Nat_) [_set-rep_(x) & _nat-rep_(i) -> _set-rep_(_ins'_(x,i))]

follows from _LIST of NAT_ plus (24), (25), (26) and (28), together with the definition of =$'_{Nat}$. Thirdly, we have to verify the translation of the underlying equality and namability axioms. For instance, we have to verify that

($\forall$ x,y:_List_) ($\forall$ i:_Nat_) {_set-rep_(x) & _set-rep_(y) & _nat-rep_(i)
       ->[x =$'_{Set}$ y -> _ins'_(x,i) =$'_{Set}$ _ins'_(y,i)]}

(which states the substitutivity of =$'_{Set}$ with respect to _ins'_) and

$$(\forall\ x{:}\underline{\text{List}})\ [\underline{\text{set-rep}}(x)\ \rightarrow\ V\ (x\ =\text{'}\underline{\text{Set}}\ t\text{'})]$$
$$t\ \text{in}\ T$$

where t' denotes the translation of t in an enumeration T as before (which states the namability of $\underline{\text{set-rep}}$ by primed $\underline{\text{Set}}$ operations).

After these verifications we have a correct implemenation of $\underline{\text{SORT of NAT by LIST of NAT}}$.

In general, our notion of $\underline{\text{implementation}}$ is a slight generalisation of the familiar logical concept of $\underline{\text{interpretation between theories}}$ [E'72,Sh'67,VP'78]. A (correct) implementation of an ADT $\underline{A}$ presented by $(L_A,\ G_A)$ by an ADT $\underline{C}$ presented by $(L_C,\ G_C)$ consists of a conservative extension $\underline{A}$ by $\underline{C}$, obtained by adding to $(L_A,\ G_A)$ partial specifications for the primed symbols of $\underline{A}$ and the relativisation predicates for the sorts of L_A, together with an interpretation of the theory $\underline{A}$ into the theory of $\underline{A}$ by $\underline{C}$.

This notion appears to capture what a programmer does when implementing $\underline{A}$ by $\underline{C}$: the partial specifications for the primed symbols correspond to the input-ouput specifications for the procedures he writes to realise the corresponding symbols of $\underline{A}$ in terms of the symbols of $\underline{C}$. (Notice, in particular, that the test for equality in $\underline{A}$ is now realised by a procedure in $\underline{C}$). Also, the relativisation predicates correspond to the representation invariants of [G'77]. The abstraction mapping or representation function is implicitly given by the interpretation, which is both a conceptual and technical advantage.

One should notice that with this implementation we have a proven correct sorting program receiving sets of naturals represented by lists of naturals and outputting the corresponding sorted lists. But we have $\underline{\text{not}}$ yet completely committed ourselves to a particular sorting algorithm, because $\underline{\text{chs}}$' and $\underline{\text{ordins}}$' are still only partly specified. (We are committed only to the families of algorithms of sorting by selection or by insertion [Kn'75,D'77]).

In order to illustrate refinements as interpretations let us consider refining $\underline{\text{chs}}$' and $\underline{\text{ordins}}$'. The former is partly specified by (30) only to pick an element of a list, whereas the latter is partly specified by (33) only to insert an element into a list preserving the relative order. Suppose we decide to refine $\underline{\text{chs}}$' to pick the least element occuring in a list and accordingly $\underline{\text{ordins}}$' to insert an element at the head of a list.

This refinement step can be described as the (non-conservative) extension of $\underline{\text{LIST of NAT by SORT of NAT}}$ by means of the following axioms

(36) $\underline{\text{chs}}\text{'}(x)\ =\text{'}i\ \rightarrow\ {\sim}x\ =\text{'}\underline{\text{nil}}\text{'}\ \&\ \underline{\text{occ}}\text{'}(i,x)\ \&\ (\forall\ j{:}\underline{\text{Nat}})\ (\underline{\text{occ}}\text{'}(j,x)$
$\rightarrow\ i\ =\text{'}\ j\ v\ \underline{\text{lt}}\text{'}(i,j))]$

(37) $\underline{\text{ordins}}\text{'}(x,i)\ =\text{'}\ \underline{\text{cons}}(i,x)$

(Notice that this still does not assign a value to $\underline{\text{chs}}(\underline{\text{phi}})$, which we do not need for our program).

Alternatively this refinement can be regarded as a simple implementation of $\underline{\text{LIST of NAT by SORT of NAT}}$ contensions into $\underline{\text{LIST of NAT by SORT of NAT}}$ (conservatively) extended by (36) with $\underline{\text{chs}}$" in lieu of $\underline{\text{chs}}$' and (37) with $\underline{\text{ordins}}$" in lieu of $\underline{\text{ordins}}$', where the interpretation is the identity but for

$\underline{\text{chs}}\text{'}\ \rightarrow\ \underline{\text{chs}}$" and $\underline{\text{ordins}}\ \rightarrow\ \underline{\text{ordins}}$"

We can now illustrate how such implementations compose. Suppose we have the ADT $\underline{A}$ implemented in the ADT $\underline{B}$ by means of the conservative extension $\underline{C}$ of $\underline{B}$ and the interpretation of $\underline{A}$ into $\underline{C}$. Similarly for $\underline{B}$ interpreted in $\underline{E}$

which is a conservative extension of $\underline{D}$. Diagrammatically,

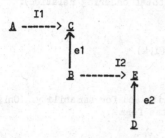

where I1 and I2 are interpretations and e1 and e2, conservative extensions.
Then there exists $\underline{F}$ such that

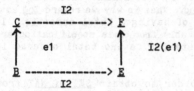

is a pushout (i.e. there is a least $\underline{F}$). $\underline{F}$ is essentially $\underline{E}$ with the translations of the formulae defining e1 by I2 (extended as identity to the symbols introduced in e1). So the extension e1 is just carried forward (in translation) and all its consequences are still (translated) consequences). Then the composition is represented by composing the conservative extensions e2 and I2(e2) and composing the interpretations I2 and I1. The methodological point to note is that $\underline{F}$, I2, and I2(e1) are automatically constructable and the software engineer need not actually worry himself about it!

5.   Parameterisation As Interpretation

If we look back at our abstract program P for sorting we see that it does not depend heavily on the exact nature of the elements. In fact, we used more properties of sets and sequences (and, in the implementation, lists) than properties of the natural numbers, the usage of the latter being confined to a small corner. Of course, we have a case of parameterisation.

In order to illustrate the main ideas of our approach to parameterisation let us consider the simple case of SET of NAT. The idea is that SET of NAT can be obtained from the parameterised ADT SET of TOD by substituting NAT for the parameter TOD. Now, what is SET of TOD? Well, SET of TOD should be the same as SET of NAT but with the nature of the elements left completely open (except for the fact that it has a "less than" ordering, since we intend to use it for sorting). So, as far as sets are concerned, we should have the same specification as before.

To be more precise, the language of SET of TOD is

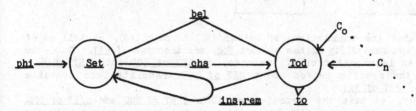

The axioms are those concerning the set symbols i.e. (7) through (11) plus the following (stating that <u>to</u> is to be realised as a total ordering relation).

(38) ($\forall$ i:<u>Tod</u>) ~ <u>to</u> (i,i)

(39) ($\forall$ i,j,k:<u>Tod</u>) <u>to</u> (i,j) & <u>to</u> (j,k) -> <u>to</u> (i,k)

(40) ($\forall$ i,j:<u>Tod</u>) <u>to</u> (i,j) v i = j v <u>to</u> (j,i)

We still have the underlying axioms for equality and for namability. Only notice that the namability axiom for sort <u>Tod</u> has the form

($\forall$ i:<u>Any</u>) (i = C_0 v i = C_1 v ... v i = C_n v ...)

This is the only axiom mentioning the constant symbols C_0, ..., C_n, ... As there are no axioms jointly mentioning some C_n with some other symbol, the C_n's are not constrained to any particular value in a realisation. Their only role is naming the elements of a domain of sort <u>Tod</u>. That is why we regard <u>Tod</u> as a parameter, subject to the only constraint of having a total order <u>to</u>. In particular the only interesting results derivable from this specification are those one might call results concerning sets per se and total orders, in general.

Now, how do we pass parameters in order to obtain <u>SET of NAT</u> from <u>SET of TOD</u>? This is performed by the assignment p, of sorts

<u>Tod</u> |-> <u>Nat</u>

and of symbols

<u>to</u> |-> <u>lt</u>
C_0 |-> <u>zero</u>
C_1 |-> <u>succ(zero)</u>
....

We extend this assignment p to be the identity on the remaining symbols, so that it builds a copy of this part of the language of <u>SET of TOD</u> on top of that of <u>NAT</u>. Thus, this mapping will translate identically axioms (7) through (11). These axioms together with those of <u>NAT</u>, (1) through (6), will give the specification of <u>SET of NAT</u>. Pictorially

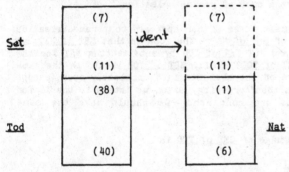

Notice that the translations of axioms (38) through (40), as well as of the equality and namability axioms of sort <u>Tod</u>, are theorems of <u>NAT</u>. Thus, the outcome is an interpretation of theories, of <u>SET of TOD</u> into <u>SET of NAT</u>. Hence, all the results proved about <u>SET of TOD</u> translate into provable properties of <u>SET of NAT</u>.

Similarly, we have the parameterised ADT's <u>SORT of TOD</u> and <u>LIST of TOD</u>. Application of assignment p will build the expected ADT's together with the corresponding interpretations

  S[p] of <u>SORT of TOD</u> into <u>SORT of NAT</u>

and

  L[p] of <u>LIST of TOD</u> into <u>LIST of NAT</u>

  In the previous section we gave an implementation of <u>SORT of NAT</u> into <u>LIST of NAT</u>. Now, we consider the implementation I[-], which is the same except that it is the identity on sort <u>Tod</u> and its symbols <u>to</u>, $C_0, C_1 \ldots$. This is a "parameterised" implementation of <u>SORT of TOD</u> into <u>LIST of TOD</u>.

  In a natural way, the parameter assignment p coupled with this "parameterised" implementation I[-] defines the original implementation I[p] of <u>SORT of NAT</u> into <u>LIST of NAT</u>. Furthermore, the following diagram (where the horizontal interpretations come from parameter passing and the vertical ones correspond to implementations) commutes.

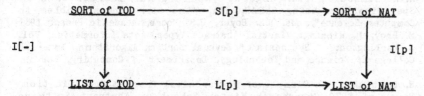

  The nice practical consequence is that we have the freedom to develop our program for sorting in a parameterised fashion and specialise the parameters to <u>NAT</u> (or any other suitable data type) when we please.

6. <u>Conclusion</u>

  We have outlined an approach to ADT's, based on logic which is a natural formalisation of what programmers (should) do.

  The key idea is that an ADT is (specified by) a (many-sorted) logical theory presented by axioms. Thus, notions concerning ADT's are captured by syntactical concepts concerning their theories. In particular,

-   the properties of an ADT are (formalised as) the theorems deduced from its axioms

-   an implementation of an ADT by another ADT is an interpretation of the theory of the former into a conservative extension of the theory of the latter

-   a refinement is an extension, which is a simple implementation

-   parameterisation is also an interpretation.

  Thus we need only the familiar logical concepts of (conservative) extension and interpretation. In general, the formulas of an extension are input-output specifications of procedures.

  As an illustration of the technical simplicity of our theory, we have the fact that parameter passing commutes with implementations. In most approaches this result has a somewhat elaborate proof. Here it is an immediate consequence of a simple but important result, namely the composability of implementations.

  Flexibility is another important asset. We are free to specify just as much as we want or need. In particular our specifications can be incomplete, sufficiently complete or even complete in the algebraic sense [G'77, GH'78, GTW'78]. This flexibility is very convenient in dealing with errors or undefined values. For instance, consider the case of hd(nil). We can decide to leave it unspecified but defined. Or we can decide to have an error constant to be the value of hd(nil) with the further choice of either specifying error propogation or leaving it open. In any case we have the well-founded relation of "being a subterm" at hand to use in proofs of termination.

Finally, the usage of simple logical concepts together with the flexibility and naturalness of this approach make it quite adequate for program development.

References

[B'77]   J. Barwise,ed: Handbook of Mathematical Logic, Studies in Logic and the Foundations of Mathematics, Vol.90, North Holland, 1977.

[BG'79]   R.M. Burstall, J.A. Goguen: The Semantics of CLEAR, A Specification Language, (as in D'79)

[BG'81]   R.M. Burstall, J.A. Goguen: An Informal Introduction to Specifications using CLEAR, in: "The Correctness Problem in Computer Science", eds. R.S. Boyer, J.S. Moore, Academic Press, 1981

[BW'82]   M. Broy, M. Wirsing: Partial Abstract Types, Acta Informatica, Vol.

[D'77]   J. Darlington: A Synthesis of Several Sorting Algorithms, Imperial College of Science and Technology, Department of Computing, London, 1977

[D'79]   B. Domolski: An Example of Hierarchical Program Specification, Proc. of 1979 Copenhagen Winter School on Abstract Software Specifications, LNCS86, Springer-Verlag

[E'72]   H.B. Enderton: A Mathematical Introduction to Logic, Academic Press, New York, 1972

[Eh'82]   H-D. Ehrich: On the Theory of Specification, Implementation and Parameterisation of Abstract Data Types, JACM, Vol. 29, No. 1, 1982

[EK'82]   H. Ehrig, H-J. Kreowski: Parameter Passing Commutes with Implementation of Parameterised Data Types, 9th ICALP, LNCS 140, Springer-Verlag

[EKMP'80]   H. Ehrig, H-J. Kreowski, B. Mahr, P. Padawitz: Compound Algebraic Implementations: an Approach to Stepwise Refinement of Software Systems, 9th MFCS, LNCS88, Springer-Verlag, 1980

[G'77]   J.V. Guttag: Abstract Data Types and the Development of Data Structures, Comm. ACM, Vol. 20, No. 6, pp. 396-404, June 1977

[G'80]   J.V. Guttag: Notes on Type Abstraction (Version 2), IEEE TSE, Vol. 6, No. 1, 1980

[Go'83]   M. Gogolla: Algebraic Specifications with Partially Ordered Sorts, Tech.Report 169, Abt. Informatik, U. of Dortmund, 1983.

[Ga'83]   H. Ganzinger: Parameterised Specifications: Parameter Passing and Implementation, ACM, TOPLAS, Vol. 5, No. 3, 1983

[GH'78]   J.V. Guttag and J.J. Horning: The Algebraic Specification of Abstract Data Types, Acta Informatica, Vol. 10, No. 1, pp. 27-52, 1978

[GHM'78]   J.V. Guttag, E. Horowitz, D.R. Musser: The Design of Data Type Specifications, in "Current Trends in Programming Methodology, Vol. IV", Ed. R.T. Yeh, Prentice Hall, 1978

[GTW'78]   J.A. Goguen, J.W. Thatcher, E.G. Wagner: An Initial Algebra Approach to the Specification, Correctness and Implementation of Abstract Data Types, in "Current Trends in Programming Methodology, Vol. IV", Ed. R.T. Yeh, Prentice Hall, Englewood Cliffs, 1978

[H'80]   U.L. Hupbach: Abstract Implementation of Abstract Data Types, 9th MFCS, LNCS88, Springer-Verlag, 1980

[He'80]   P. Henderson: Functional Programming: Application and Implementation, Prentice-Hall, 1980

[H'72]   C.A.R. Hoare: Proof of Correctness of Data Representations, Acta Informatica, Vol. 4, pp. 271-281, 1972

[J'80]   C.B. Jones: Software Development: a Rigorous Approach, Prentice-
              Hall, London, 1980
[Kn'75]   D.E. Knuth: The Art of Computer Programming, Vol. 3, Addison
              Wesley, Reading, 1975
[L'79]   B. Liskov: Modular Program Construction Using Abstractions, (as in
              D'79]
[LZ'77]   B. Liskov, S. Zilles: An Introduction to Formal Specifications of
              Data Abstractions, in "Current Trends in Programming Methodology,
              Vol. I", Ed. R.T. Yeh, Prentice-Hall, Englewood Cliffs, 1977
[Ma'74]   Z. Manna: The Mathematical Theory of Computation, McGraw-Hill, New
              York, 1974
[MV'81]   T.S.E. Maibaum, P.A.S. Veloso: A Logical Approach to Abstract Data
              Types, Technical Report, Department of Computing, Imperial College,
              and Departamento de Informatica, PUC/RJ, 1981
[MSV'83]   T.S.E. Maibaum, M.R. Sadler, P.A.S. Veloso: Logical Specification
              and Implementation, Technical Report, Department of Computing,
              Imperial College, 1983
[MSV'83a]   T.S.E. Maibaum, M.R. Sadler, P.A.S. Veloso: A Straightforward
              Approach to Parameterised Specifications, Technical Report,
              Department of Computing, Imperial College, 1983
[P,84]   A. Poigne: Another Look at Parameterisation Using Suborts, MFCS84,
              LNCS176,1984.
[SM'84]   M.R. Sadler, T.S.E. Maibaum: The Logic of Namability, In
              preparation
[SW'82]   D. Sanella, M. Wirsing: Implementation of Parameterised
              Specifications, 9th ICALP, LNCS140, Springer-Verlag, 1982
[Sh'67]   J.R. Schoenfield: Mathematical Logic, Addison Wesley, Reading, 1967
[T'78]   W.M. Turski: Computer Programming Methodology, Heyden, London, 1978
[VP'78]   P.A.S. Veloso, T.H.C. Pequeno: Interpretations between Many-Sorted
              Theories, 2nd Brasilian Colloquium on Logic, Campinas, 1978
[WB'82]   M. Wirsing, M. Broy: An Analysis of Semantic Models for Algebraic
              Specifications, in "Theoretical Foundations of Programming
              Methodology", eds. M. Broy, G. Schmidt, Reidel, Dordrecht, 1982
[WPPDB'80]   M. Wirsing, P. Pepper, H. Partsch, W. Dosch, M. Broy: On
              Hierarchies of Abstract Data Types, Technische Univ., Munchen, Inst.
              Informatik, 1980
[WPPDB'83]   M. Wirsing, P. Pepper, H. Partsch, W. Dosch, M. Broy: On
              Hierarchies of Abstract Data Types, Acta Informatica, Vol. 20, Fasc.
              1, pp. 1-33, 1983

PROGRAM DEVELOPMENT AND DOCUMENTATION
BY INFORMAL TRANSFORMATIONS AND DERIVATIONS

Giovanna Petrone   Luigi Petrone
Dipartimento di Informatica
Università di Torino, Italy

1. INTRODUCTION

The content of this paper[*] is the outcome of some teaching experience and a research effort in programming methodology. However, part of the terminology has been changed and some insight has been gained as an effect of the wider perspective set out by Scherlis and Scott in their quite recent IFIP 83 paper. Their overall analysis is assumed in this paper with some limitations of objectives; in fact we are principally interested in informal, but possibly rigorous, derivations of programs and in designing adequate supporting tools. Formal derivation of programs as well as formal correctness proofs are relevant to this paper, conceptually, in that they provide an insight, a deep insight indeed, into the correctness problem. In other words, by asserting the possibility of deriving a formal correctness proof we get the assurance that the informal, but nevertheless rigorous, proofs of program derivations are not without foundations and that they can become, anytime, formal and detailed if needed.

This lack of formalism can sometime induce a lack of precision and may not always be capable of preventing the introduction of programming errors. It is however difficult to guarantee a level of absolute precision within a methodology where the human contribution is substantial. But we dare confess that our primary objective is not absolute and foolproof program correctness, but

---

(*) Preparation of this paper supported in part by NSF grant MCS -81-03718 and by project ESPRIT 125, funded by EEC.

rather a methodology for program development, documentation and understanding, and we want to privilege an intuitive deep understanding of a program from the designer point of view rather than to wait for a distant, and yet to come, automatic support for the derivation process. We are aware that some confusion exists today in the field of programming methodology between formal treatment and rigorous treatment of programs. We devote an entire section to try to clarify this issue.

2. PROGRAMMING AS AN EVOLUTIONARY PROCESS

Programming, even real word programming, is an evolutionary process |Bauer 76, Balzer 81|. The final results of the programming process, the program texts, deprived of the insight that went into their conception, are too complex to be understandable and should not be used for the maintenance process. One might even say that the program texts are as relevant to the programming process as one accidental result of the addition process, say 26, is relevant to the understanding of the concept of the integer sum. In fact, programs do not stay immobile, they evolve and modify in synchronism with the social context in which they are exploited. Therefore, we are interested in the derivation process of a program more than in the program itself |Bauer 76, Scherlis and Scott 83 and also Petrone 83|.

The first known examples of program derivation techniques were the step-wise refinements of Dijkstra |72| and Wirth |71| and the program transformations of Burstall and Darlington |77|, Manna and Waldinger |79|. However, the general framework of the latter authors, perhaps biased by their cultural background of research in mechanical theorem proving, has been that of setting up a theory and a set of tools to provide an automated environment for deriving correct programs. This latter enterprise should not exclude the need to explore and experiment derivations of programs carried out by humans but no significant effort has been made in this direction. Certainly, a lack of convenient tools makes the job more difficult. But, probably, this is also a signal that the evolutionary nature of the programming process is generally seen, in the computing community, more as an evil than as a feature that can be of great help in explaining and documenting the design of a system.

3. FORMAL SPECIFICATIONS VERSUS RIGOROUS SPECIFICATIONS

It is claimed that software implementation should start from a formal specification language. The request for formality is based upon the statement that only a formal expression would allow a correctness proof to be carried over. This statement seems to imply a framework that happens to be too restrictive specially in view of the even stronger statement that only a formal treatment would allow a sound mathematical treatment of the programming process. It has been explicitly pointed out that this may not be true (see |P. Naur 82| and |De Millo 79|). The usual presentation of mathematical proofs appearing in technical journals even if often referred to as rigorous proofs (or sometimes, perhaps improperly, as formal proofs) is never carried using a formal predefined language provided of nonambiguous formal syntax. No mathematician would accept such a constraint in his everyday work.

Problems do arise because of the already mentioned confusion between formality and rigor . In classical mathematics formality and rigor are synonyms. Rigor only means that each concept is operationally defined according to sound rules accepted in a given discipline and notations are always defined in a way that excludes ambiguity of any sort. In Logic and even more so in Computer Science formality usually indicates that a language is defined with a precise syntax , given in BNF, and a precise semantics is given that makes mechanical treatment possible for instance by allowing a mechanical proof or an automatic checking . But to request that all reasoning about programs and in particular all derivations of programs be made in a formal language is probably an useless if not harmful approach.

Formality is a price we are willing to pay only if a substantial benefit from some advantageous mechanical processing is obtained, in return. In fact, the possibility of rigorous but not formal treatment allows for greater freedom in selecting the proper framework which happens to be the most convenient for each application field or each problem at hand. Moreover, it is doubtful that one might be able to define a unique specification language suitable for the many different application fields of the real world. The argument that since a programming language like Pascal is "Universal" we should be able to define a universal specification language seems not to apply completely. In fact, the universality of a programming language is achieved in each application by means of many layered levels of abstractions, each one level requiring what cannot be considered but as a heavy effort of implementation and coding.

4. SPECIFICATION: THE FIRST IMPLEMENTATION PHASE

Obviously, software problems do not have a unique specification. Moreover, as we will show on the example of the sorting problems, certain specifications make easy to derive certain implementations and prevent, or make it difficult to derive others.

In a certain sense, the specification language is a sort of programming language and the specification phase is the first, and not the least important, implementation phase. This viewpoint is shared by some authors. Bauer and Woessner |82| speak of some specifications as pre-algorithmic formulations of problems and Scherlis and Scott |83| say that the difference between specification and implementation is not qualitative but quantitative. To support the previous view we point out the following facts:

i) Specifications can often be interpreted as trivial algorithms, the so called British Museum algorithms. For instance the specification:

$$\forall x \; \exists n \mid x \geqq 0 \implies n^2 \leqq x < (n+1)^2$$

can be interpreted as:

$$\text{given any } x \geq 0 \text{ find } n \mid n^2 \leqslant x < (n+1)^2$$

or more explicity if we know that such an n exists and $n \leq x$ it can be found by the trivial (descending) search program:

```
i := x;
while not i²≤x<(i+1)² do
    i := i - 1;
```

ii) static specifications in the Hoare style can often be transformed into recursive definitions. See program synthesis by Darlington and Manna and their folding-unfolding techniques.

iii) specifications are often expressed in terms of concrete representations of the data structures of the problem and this requires a first implementation effort, a first level of commitment.

iv) specifications are often given in terms of notions that are defined constructively, i.e. recursively.

For instance, the summation sign definition: $a = a+a+...+a$ looks certainly more esoteric than the simple constructive definition:

$$\sum_n^{m \leq n} a = 0 \qquad \sum^n = \sum^{n-1} + a_n$$

a But the latter recursive definition immediately leads to the corresponding recursive program and is fundamental to any iterative program such as

```
i := 0; s := 0;
while i  n do
    s := s + a|i|
    i := i+1
```

This appears more clearly for the usual $\underline{gcd}$ algorithm of two integers x, y. The specification is:

$$\forall x \, y \, \exists z \mid z/x \text{ and } z/y \text{ and } \forall w \mid w/x \text{ and } w/y \Longrightarrow z \geq w$$

A trivial interpretation would imply an exhaustive search. The usual algorithm can be derived only if the following two recursive equations are known:

$$gcd(x,y) = gcd(x-y,y) \text{ if } x \geq y$$
$$gcd(x,y) = x \qquad \qquad \text{ if } x=y$$

More enlightening is the example of the sort programs. To derive
a sort program one should first know what sorted sequence means.
The usual definition is given in terms of a concrete representation
of a sequence as an array:

(1) $$\forall i \; j \mid i < j \Rightarrow a[i] \leq a[j]$$

This definition, intended as a program specification, interpreted
as a prescription leads to

```
for i := 1 to n
    for j := 1 to n
        if a[i] > a[j] then exchange(a[i],a[j])
```

or, after a slight modification, to

```
for i := 1 to n
    for j := i+1 to n
        if a[i] > a[j] then exchange(a[i],a[j])
```
$$\forall i \; j \mid i < j \Rightarrow a[i] \leq a[j]$$

An alternative definition might be given recursively. A sequence
of cardinality one is ordered by definition. In formula:

$$cardinality(A) = 1 \Rightarrow ordered(A).$$

If cardinality $(A) > 1$, let us suppose that a subsequence B of A
of cardinality n-1, is ordered. In order to infer that the sequence A
is ordered one has to distinguish three cases depending on the
relative position of the left over element which can be less than
any element of the subsequence B or greater than or intermediate.
In the first two cases we have that a recursive definition of ordered
(A) might look like

(2) $$ordered(A) \Leftrightarrow ordered(B) \text{ and } B \leq C$$
$$\text{and } cardinality(C) = 1 \text{ and } A = B \text{ cat } C$$

(3) $$ordered(A) \Leftrightarrow ordered(B) \text{ and } C \leq B$$
$$\text{and } cardinality(C) = 1 \text{ and } A = C \text{ cat } B$$

where $B \leq C$ means that every element of B is less or equal than
every element of C and cat is the operation that applied to two

ordered sequences B and C such that B ≤ C gives a sequence A that happens to be ordered. In the third case we define a merge operation as an operation that, applied to two ordered sequences, gives a third sequence which happens to be ordered. In formulas:

(4)   ordered(A) $\iff$ ordered(B) and cardinality(C)=1
                              and A=merge(B,C)

A similar analysis shows that the splitting of A into B and C can be more general or that the condition cardinality(C)=1 can be released replacing it with ordered(C). We have

(5)   ordered(A) $\iff$ ordered(B) and ordered(C)
                              and B ≤ C and A=B cat C

(6)   ordered(A) $\iff$ ordered(B) and ordered(C)
                              and A=merge(B,C)

The formulas (2), (3) and (4) are in essence the guidelines for the sorting methods known as bubble-sort by minimum or by maximum or by insertion. Formulas (5) and (6) are the base for quicksort and mergesort. Even formula (1) can be used as a guideline for some methods, in particular the method comparing each element with all the others, counting the elements which are less than it and using such counters as indexes for their relative positions.

Obviously, one can easily show that the six formulas are equivalent. For instance formula 1 is equivalent to

$$\forall \, p.q \mid p < q \leq n-1 \quad a[p] \leq a[q] \quad \text{and} \quad \forall \, r \mid r \leq n-1 \quad a[r] \leq a[n]$$

i.e. to formula (2). One could certainly start from one formula, say (1) taken as the unique problem specification, and try to derive all the sorting programs from it (see Darlington |76|) but that process seems to suffer from an excess of formality, useful only if used by some automatic derivation system.

Alternatively, one could start from one specification, derive a specific program and then perform a set of program transformations to derive from it all the other sorting methods. In fact programs can be derived in a variety of ways according to different styles of derivations. We think that one should try to keep the program derivations at the highest level of abstraction for the greatest number of steps. This tactic implies using a variety of equivalent formulations of the problem to be solved or in other words implies to start the optimization job right from the beginning at the specification level, as we have done for the sorting methods.

5. DERIVATIONS OF PROGRAMS

We shall illustrate and comment on two single derivations of programs. These will be examples of what we intend by _rigorous but informal_ derivations. The first is the trivial example of the integer square root program, the second is the minimal spanning tree of a graph. Since the latter is a little longer it will be given in the Appendix. The derivations will be given as successive photographs of the program plus comment describing the modifications or transformations.

Of course the first form of the square root program is the following program, directly obtained from the specification:

$$
\begin{aligned}
&i := 0; \\
&\text{while not } i^2 \le x < (i+1)^2 \text{ do} \\
&\quad i := i+1 \\
&\{ i^2 \le x < (i+1)^2 \}
\end{aligned}
$$

The first optimization consists in noting that the while test is redundant because if $i^2 \le x$ before the loop then, after the assignment $i := i+1$, one still has $i^2 \le x$. In other words $i^2 \le x$ is a program invariant.

$$
\begin{aligned}
&i := 0; \\
&\{ i^2 \le x \} \\
&\text{while not } x < (i+1)^2 \text{ do} \\
&\quad i := i + 1 \\
&\{ i^2 \le x < (i+1)^2 \}
\end{aligned}
$$

Since $(i+1)^2 = i^2 + 2i + 1$ we need not to compute each time $(i+1)^2$ anew, but we may profit of the previous value stored into a variable, called i-plus-one-square, adding each time $2i+1$ to it. Again, instead of computing $2i+1$ anew each time, we introduce a second variable two-i-plus-one. We have:

```
i := 0;
two-i-plus-one := 1;
i-plusone-square := 1;
```

$$\left|\begin{array}{l} i^2 \leq x \text{ and two-i-plus-one} = 2i + 1 \\ \quad \text{and i-plus-one-square} = (i + 1)^2 \end{array}\right|$$

```
while not x < i-plus-one-square do
  [ i := i + 1;
  | two-i-plus-one := two-i-plus-one + 2;
  | i-plus-one-square := i-plus-one-square + two-i-plus-one
```

$$\left| \; i^2 \leq x < (i+1)^2 \; \right|$$

which is our final square-root program. It is more natural to communicate the "meaning" of the square-root program by saying that it is a linear axhaustive search optimized by simplification of the loop-test and by introducing two state variables (to use the relation $(i+1)^2 = i^2+2i+1$), than by any other way, which, using correctness proofs or hand simulation, tries to express a meaning in terms of the final program. In other words, the derivation process is a practical way to transmit the meaning of this program to a person: programmer or developer. We might even reverse the usual attitude towards program correctness. No longer do we care whether the written presentation of the previous algorithm contains bugs or typing error if the given derivation method makes us feel secure and confident to be able to reproduce the derivation process with the requested degree of precision. Absolute precision is needed in fact only for those programs which we do not know how to derive. Absolute precision is of fundamental importance only if we ignore all about an algorithm; we only know that "it works and therefore we must not touch it". For the same reasons absolute and detailed program correctness is fundamental for machine execution. A treatment analogous to the square root derivation can be easily given for other elementary programs.

Incidentaly if anyone tried to remember final programs and correctness proofs of the simple examples reported in the classical text-book of Manna |76| one would probably fail 90% of the time while it is just too trivial to derive them through a series of derivation steps.

Now a few more comments. First, if the programmer of the previous algorithm does not see immediately that $i^2 \leqslant x$ is a cycle invariant, he will come out with a little less optimized program having one more program variable (i-square) and a slightly longer cycle test, but still a reliable program properly annotated with a correctness proof. In other words, a tree of derivations is a stable process whose intermediate results are still of pratical value; it is not an all-or-nothing process.

Second, the previous derivation steps not only easily allow you to derive the square root-program, but immediately lead you to generalyze it into a similar program, say, for the cubic root, since $(i + 1)^3 = i^3 + 3i^2 + 3i + 1$, and more generally, induce you to exploit recurrence relations in order to optimize programs defined by specifications like: $\forall x \; y \; P(x,y)$.

Third, a final comment on a taxonomy of programs. Derivations of programs naturally induce a relationship of programs that are derived through the same derivation pattern and it will be natural and interesting to study programs from this point of view. But then, similarity of derivations may be quite unexpected. For instance, the sum of two symbolic polinomials, represented say by linked lists, and the program for merging two ordered sets do share the same derivation.

Can we delimit or describe the concept of derivation of a program? Certainly, such a concept will include program derivations by step-wise refinements, by transformations, by modifications and by applications of program schemata |Gerhart 76|. Step-wise refinements are well known and will not be discussed here. Transformations usually denote a program modification that leaves invariant the computed result. Transformations techniques have been widely studied: they include elimination of recursion in certain cases and generic source optimizazions. A class of transformations, better called program synthesis, deserves to be mentioned: it studies the transformation of static specifications into recursive definitions (by folding and unfolding). Program modification slightly changes a program keeping invariant only some objectives in order to solve a slightly different problem. Of course once a derivation pattern has been secured one should try to generalize it into a derivation of a schematic program or of an abstract program and, for the moment, leave to the ingenuity of the designer which schema or schematic pattern to apply in each concrete case. However, more than on abstractly studying classes of program derivations our emphasis in this research program is on concretely applying derivations of programs to specific cases as an everyday working tool of a teacher when he/she tries to "present" a program to his student or of a designer when he/she tries to document an implementation.

6. A TOOL FOR DERIVATIONS OF PROGRAMS

Programs are derived from specifications in steps and the initial phases of the derivation require the ability to express abstract algorithms. One example of abstract algorithm is the minimal spanning tree algorithm of the appendix; abstract algorithms are being currently used in the literature (see books by Aho, Hopcroft and Ullman or S. Baase). Not surprisingly abstract algorithms are expressed in an informal language, but nevertheless they can be considered to be unambiguos and rigorous (to adopt "our" terminology). Such a program design language is a sort of documentation language whose purpose is to convey ideas and not to instruct machines.

An important objective to be obtained is the derivation of the initial program design into the final implementation. The derivation must allow an easy link of each piece of program code to the design ideas that originated it in the first place. A research program on tools for program derivation has given origin to the system DUAL, described in |Petrone 82,83|.

Briefly, DUAL is an intelligent editor/incremental compiler designed to cope with the evolutionary nature of the design process as embodied by the techniques of program transformations and stepwise refinements. DUAL takes special advantage of the screen-keyboard interface to provide a natural access to the tree-structured design data base where design informations and program texts are strictly correlated.

The various steps of the design process are "photographed" by DUAL and the "movie" showing the derivation phases can be dinamically "replayed" on the screen at the visitor's (designer or maintenance-developer) will. A clear distinction between design, implementation and documentation no longer exists in DUAL. The description of a design is a description of the implementation at a higher level of abstraction and is expressed in an informal design language which, by successive modifications, will derive into the program text.

REFERENCES

Baase S. |1978| Computer Algorithms: introduction to Design and Analysis. Addison-Wesley.

Balzer R. |1981| Transformational Implementation: an example. IEEE Trans. on Soft. Eng., Vol SE-7, 3-14.

Bauer F.L. |1976| Programming as an evolutionary process. Proc. 2-nd Int. Conf. on Soft. Eng., San Francisco, 223-234.

Bauer F.L. and Wössner H. |1982| Algorithmic Language and Program Development. Springer Verlag.

Burstall R.M. and Darlington J.A. |1977| A transformation system for developing recursive programs. J. ACM 24, 44-67.

Darlington J.A. |1976| A synthesis of several sorting algorithms. Res. Rep. N.23, Dpt. of A.I., Un. of Edinburgh.

De Millo R.A., Lipton R.J. and Perlis A.J. |1979| Social processes and proofs of theorems and programs. Comm.s ACM, Vol 22-5, 271-280.

Dijkstra E.W. |1972| Notes on structured programming in Structured Programming, Academic Press.

Gerhart S.L. and Yelowitz L. |1976| Control Structure abstractions of the Backtracking Programming Technique. IEEE Trans. on Soft Eng.

Manna Z. |1976| Mathematical Theory of Computation. MC Graw-Hill.

Manna Z. and Waldinger R. |1979| Synthesis: dreams = programs. IEEE Trans. Soft. Eng., SE-5.

Naur P. |1982| Formalization in program development. Bit, 22, 437-453.

Petrone L. et alii |1982| DUAL: an interactive tool for developing documented programs by step-wise refinements. Proc. 6-th Int. Conf. Soft. Eng., Tokyo, 350-357.

Petrone L. et alii |1983| Program development and documentation by step-wise transformations: an interactive tool. Proc. Int. Comp. Symp. Nürnberg.

Scherlis W.L. and Scott D.S. |1983| First steps towards inferential programming. IFIP Congress, 199-212.

Waters R.C. |1979| A Method for analyzing loop programs. IEEE Trans. Soft. Eng., 5.

Wirth N. |1971| Program development by step-wise refinements. Comm. ACM, 14, 221-227.

APPENDIX

An example of derivation of programs: minimal spanning tree of a graph. (We reformulate in terms of derivations an example taken from the book of S. Baase).

Given an undirected graph $G=(V,E,W)$ where V, E, W are the sets of nodes, edges and associated weights, let us represent a spanning tree T of G as a subset of E.

The first important step of the derivation is to reformulate a theorem in a recursive form so that the algorithm is but a trivial implementation of the recursion.

Let us first introduce the following notations. Given a graph $G=(V,E,W)$, we want to consider the "complete" subgraphs $G_i=(V_i, E_i, W_i)$ of G which are unguely obtained in correspondence with subsets V_i of V by assuming that G is made of all the edges E_i of E whose vertices belong both to V_i. If $G_i=(V_i, E_i, W_i)$ is a subgraph of G then adjacent(V_i) is the set of all vertices of G which are not in V_i but are adjacent to same vertex of V_i and incident(V_i) is the set of all edges of E which are not in E_i but which are incident to vertices of G_i. Let P and Q denote the predicates "V_2 = adjacent(V_1)" and "E_2 = incident(E_1)" respectively.

Definition. The subgraph consisting of any vertex x of $G=(V,E,W)$ is minimal. If a subgraph $G_i =(V_i)$ is minimal and xy is the edge of minimal weight belonging to incident(V_i) then $G_{i+1}= (V_i \cup \{y\})$ is minimal. Note that if G is connected G is trivially a minimal subgraph of itself. Now we can state the recursion theorem:

Theorem. The subgraph G_1 consisting of any vertex of $G=(V,E,W)$ is minimal and its minimal spanning tree is the empty set. If $G_i =(V_i)$ is a minimal subgraph of G, and T is its MST, then if we denote with xy the edge of minimal weight belonging to incident(V_i) we have that $G_{i+1} =(V_i \cup \{x\})$ is minimal and $T_{i+1} =T_i \cup \{xy\}$ is the MST of G_{i+1}

A first high level description of the algorithm is a straighforward transliteration of the recursion theorem and is the application of the well-known schema of building a program "around" a cycle invariant

```
    V_1 <- any vertex of G
    E_1 <- empty set
    V_3 <- V - x
```

{assert: the subgraph denoted by the set V is minimal}
{assert: E is a MST for the subgraph denoted by V }

"make the predicate P true"
"make the predicate Q true"

{assert P, assert Q}

```
while E_2 not empty  do
    find an edge e in E_2 of minimum weight;
    set x to be the vertex in V_2 incident with e
    V_1 <- V_1 u {x};
    V_2 <- V_2 - {x};

    E_1 <- E_1 u {e};
    E_2 <- E_2 - {e};
```

{assert: the subgraph G_i, denoted by V_i, is minimal }
{assert: E_i is a MST for the subgraph denoted by V_i }

"restore predicates P";   "restore predicates Q"

```
    {assert P, assert Q }
    end
```

Note that when E_2 becomes empty, E_1 has grown to include all vertices belonging to one connected component of G.

The operations restoring predicates P and Q are simple, they are omitted. A first optimization is to make the set E_2 containing one edge (the one with minimal weight) for each vertex in V_2. This effects the definition of Q and the operation restoring that predicate which now becomes

```
    for each y in V₂ adjacent to x do
        if weight(xy) < weight(the edge e in E₂ incident with y)
            then E₂ <- E₂ - {e} u {xy}
```

The operation restoring predicate P becomes

```
    for each y in V₃ adjacent to x do
    V₂   - V₂ u {y};
    V₃   - V₃ - {y};
    E₂   - E₂ u {xy}
```

A second optimization is a space/time optimization. The operations restoring P and Q occur twice in the program. They can be moved from outside into the loop, their order can be inverted and the final program becomes similar to the abstract algorithm reported in Baase which is an unstructured program.

Incidentally, unstructured programs could be allowed in a derivation tree. After all, the final program texts of derivations are no longer used to convey the meaning of a design. If we revisit all the phases of this derivation we see that are simple and natural. The only points where some ingenuity is required are the initial recursion theorem and the restrictions of the sets where the search of minimum cost edge must be performed.

ASSPEGIQUE : An integrated environment for algebraic specifications

Michel BIDOIT & Christine CHOPPY

Laboratoire de Recherche en Informatique
Université de Paris-Sud
Bâtiment 490
91405 Orsay - Cedex, FRANCE

ABSTRACT

In this paper, we describe ASSPEGIQUE, an integrated environment for the development of large algebraic specifications. We first describe the underlying specification language, PLUSS-E, based on the specification-building primitives of ASL and E,R-algebras, a formal framework for exception handling. We then describe the design and organization of the specification environment. This environment allows the user to introduce specifications in a hierarchized library, to edit them through a special purpose editor (with a graphical interface), to compile them and to debug them. A symbolic evaluator and theorem proving tools completes ASSPEGIQUE into an environment suitable for rapid prototyping.

I - INTRODUCTION

It is generally agreed on the fact that algebraic specifications provide a powerful tool for writing hierarchical, modular and implementation-independent specifications. Moreover, algebraic specifications are especially suitable for rapid prototyping and are an appropriate framework for verification and validation tool development.

However, some problems have been identified when specifying realistic software using algebraic data types [BBGGG 84]. These problems are the design and management of *large specifications*, *error handling* and *error recovery* policy specification, and the lack of *computer environment* and *tools* supporting the specification stage.

The size of a specification clearly varies in accordance with the complexity of the system being specified. Therefore, specifications of large software systems cannot be managed as a whole. It is necessary to split them into smaller, hierarchized elementary units. Besides, a better modularity promotes the reusability of existing specification parts. Consequently, the design and management of large specifications require tools to structure and modularize the specifications, while the problem of the reusability and integration of existing specification parts must also be addressed. Obviously, structuration, modularization and reusability issues must be taken into account from the first stage of design of the *specification language*. Therefore, specification-building primitives as well as visibility handling primitives should be included into the specification language.

A classical difficulty in the development of large systems is that the error handling specification and the error recovery policy is done too late, very often after the specification of the normal behaviour of the system is completed. This results in expensive modifications of early design decisions. Moreover, the exception handling part of the system is often the less carefully specified. A reason of this sorry state of affair may be that very few methodological and linguistic tools are available to specify and develop software with exception handling. The programming languages which are currently in use in industrial contexts do not provide specific features for raising and handling exceptions. Fortunately, new programming languages, such as Ada [DOD 83, BGG 84], will provide such tools. It is therefore necessary to complete the algebraic specification framework in order to be able to specify error cases and error recovery.

Specific tools must also be provided that support the use of algebraic specifications. First of all, it is now widely agreed on the fact that specification languages and methods without supporting tools are not practicable. Secondly, it is especially important that specific tools with user-friendly interfaces are designed in order to bridge the gap between underlying mathematical formalisms and the user. Such tools should at least comprise intelligent (syntax directed) editors and data base facilities. It is also stressed that graphic interfaces are particularly well-suited for these purposes.

In the remaining of this paper we first give a description of PLUSS-E, a specification language with exception handling and error recovery features, we then describe the design and organization of the ASSPEGIQUE specification environment.

II - THE SPECIFICATION LANGUAGE PLUSS-E

The aim of the family of specification languages **PLUSS** is to provide a tool to express structured algebraic data type specifications. The specification languages of the PLUSS family are based upon a set of specification-building operations derived from the primitive operators suggested by *Martin Wirsing* in **ASL** [WIR 82, S&W 83, WIR 83]. The original design of PLUSS was made by *Marie-Claude Gaudel* [GAU 83].

Roughly speaking, the semantics of the PLUSS specification languages is parameterized by the class of algebras taken into account. More precisely, the semantics of each specification language of the PLUSS family follows some basic, fixed rules in what concerns the specification-building primitives but depends on the class of algebras that are allowed for this specific language. For instance, PLUSS-P will denote the specification language where *partial algebras* are chosen as models [BW 82], while PLUSS-0 denotes the specification language where the standard, usual algebras are chosen as models.

Here, we describe **PLUSS-E**, a specification language where exception handling and error recovery can be specified with a precise and formal semantics. PLUSS-E is based upon two formal approaches, the specification-building primitives of ASL and the concept of **E,R-algebras** which allows all forms of error handling (error introduction, error propagation and error recovery) [BID 84].

II.1 - E,R-algebras

Since 1976 [ADJ 76], the classical approach to algebraic data types has been shown to be incompatible with the use of operations that return error messages for some values of their arguments. In this section we describe a new formalism where all forms of error handling can be specified. Our formalism is very closed to the *error-algebras* introduced by Goguen [GOG 77] or to the work described in [GDLE 83], that is, the carrier sets of the algebras are split into okay values and error values. However, we have shown how an implicit error propagation rule may be encoded into the models without losing the possibility of error recovery. Thus all the axioms necessary to specify error propagation may be avoided, and the specifications remain well-structured and easily understandable.

The algebraic specification of error cases, error propagation and error recovery is a difficult problem [ADJ 76, GOG 77, GOG 78, PLA 82, B&W 82, EHR 83]. Our claim is that neither exception cases nor error recovery cases should be specified by means of equations, but rather by means of *declarations*. The axioms of a specification will be divided into four parts:
 - Declarations of exception cases and of recovery cases. Declarations are just terms or positive conditional terms (i.e. terms conditioned by equations).
 - Ok-axioms.
 - Error-axioms.
Ok-axioms or error-axioms are just equations or positive conditional equations.

Thus some terms will be declared to be okay, others will be declared to be erroneous. Ok-axioms and error-axioms will be used to identify ok-values and error-values respectively, no more. This will lead to more structured specifications, since the specification of the error policy (error introduction and error recovery) will be made apart from the axioms. Moreover, our framework will implement the following natural propagation rule:
errors propagate unless their recoveries are specified.
In order to allow a careful recovery policy and the use of non-strict functions, we shall use three distinct kinds of variables: ordinary variables may range over the whole carrier set, ok-variables may only range over the ok-part of the corresponding carrier set, error-variables may only range over the error part of the corresponding carrier set. As a syntactical convenience, ok-variables will always be suffixed by "+", while error-variables will always be suffixed by "-" (e.g. x+, y-, ...).

The necessary underlying theoretical material is described in [BID 84], as well as the study of sufficient conditions for initial models. Here we focus on the feasability of such specifications and their impact. As a first example of a PLUSS-E specification we describe a stack of integers which will allow one underflow, no more:

```
SPEC : STACK
    WITH : INTEGER
    SORTS : Stack

    OPERATIONS :
        empty :                          -> Stack
        underflow :                      -> Stack
        crash :                          -> Stack
        push :      Integer Stack        -> Stack
        pop :       Stack                -> Stack
        top :       Stack                -> Integer
```

VARIABLES :

    x :   Integer
    p :   Stack

EXCEPTION CASES :

    e1 :   underflow
    e2 :   crash
    e3 :   pop empty
    e4 :   top empty

RECOVERY CASES :

    r1 :   push x+ underflow

OK-AXIOMS :

    ok1 :   pop (push x p) = p
    ok2 :   top (push x p) = x
    ok3 :   push x underflow = push x empty

ERROR-AXIOMS :

    err1 :   pop empty = underflow
    err2 :   pop underflow = crash
    err3 :   push x- p = crash

END STACK.

In this stack, we shall have an infinite number of error elements, with two specific values: *underflow*, which will be obtained (as the result) when popping the empty stack; and *crash*, which will be obtained when popping *underflow*. Stack terms obtained from the *crash* stack are definitively erroneous. *Underflow* is an erroneous stack, but one can recover from this state by pushing an okay integer onto it. In all cases pushing an erroneous integer onto a stack leads to the *crash* stack.

Note also that nothing more is required than "*top empty* is an exception case"; however, if one wants to identify *top empty* with an erroneous integer, say *bottom*, an error-equation "*top empty = bottom*" may be added. Furthermore, if one wants to identify all erroneous integers with *bottom*, this can be achieved by adding the following error-equation: "$x = bottom$".

In the same way, the equation ok3 is not absolutely necessary; however, in our case we do not want to just specify that pushing an okay integer onto the *underflow* stack is a recovery case, but also that the stack obtained is equal to pushing the same element onto the *empty* stack. One explication is also needed for the error-equation err3: note that we have not (explicitely) specified that *push x- p* is an error value; this is simply a consequence of the natural error propagation rule, since *x-* denotes an error value.

II.2 - Basic specifications

In PLUSS-E, a basic specification is a *signature* together with *axioms*. Axioms are preceded by the declaration of the *variables* they use.

A *signature* begins with the key-word SORTS followed by a list of sorts. By default an empty list is equivalent to the declaration of a unique sort, which is equal to the specification name. If no new sort is required, the key-word SORT may be omitted or be replaced by the key-word NO-NEW-SORT.

The second part of the *signature* is a list of operation names together with their arity. This list begins with the key-word OPERATIONS. For instance:

$$\_[\,\_\,] : \text{Array Index} \rightarrow \text{Elem}$$

As it appears in the above example, mixfix operators with a syntax à la OBJ [GOG 83] are allowed, and the underscore is used to indicate where the operation arguments should be placed. Thus the above operation may be used to access an array element with the usual notation t[i]. Underscores may be omitted if the operation will be used in the standard prefix order. Overloading of operation names and coercions are also allowed, for instance:

$$\_ : \text{Integer} \rightarrow \text{Real}$$

The declaration of the *variables* used in the axiom part is preceded by the key-word VARI-ABLES. All the variables are implicitly universally quantified. As well as for operation names, variable names can be overloaded; this is especially useful for dealing with structured specifications. According to the syntactical convenience described in Section II.1, the declaration of a variable x implicitly contains the declaration of x+ and x-.

Declarations and *axioms* are named, and positive conditional equations (or declarations) are allowed. They are preceded by the key-words EXCEPTION CASES, RECOVERY CASES, OK-AXIOMS and ERROR-AXIOMS. An example of one of the conditional axioms that define *less or equal* on the integers is given below:

$$\text{LE5} : 0 \text{ LE } x = \text{true} \Rightarrow 0 \text{ LE s } x = \text{true}$$

Since the = sign is used to connect both terms of an equation, it can not be used as a name for the equality operation. We suggest to use $\_is\_$ to this end, as well as $\_isnot\_$ for the inequality operation.

As a last remark on basic specifications, one should note that an implicit **reachable** is embedded in such a specification. That means that only finitely generated models are taken into consideration.

II.3 - Specification construction tools

The simplest feature to build specifications from simpler ones is the **sum**, which is denoted by +. By definition, the signature of SPEC + SPEC' is the union of the signatures of SPEC and SPEC'. There is no implicit renaming as in *CLEAR* [B&G 79]. So it is possible to share subspecifications without duplicating them: for instance, if there is a sort Bool in SPEC and in SPEC', there is only a sort Bool in SPEC + SPEC'. The same rule applies for operation names. The meaning of such a specification is a class of algebras w.r.t. this signature. The algebras of this class must be models of SPEC (resp. SPEC') when they are restricted to the signature of SPEC (resp. SPEC'). Note that the concept of restriction must be suitably refined w.r.t. E,R-algebras.

A by-product of the sum is the **enrichment**, denoted by WITH, which allows to add new sorts and/or new operations and/or new axioms to a specification. An example of this construct was given.in the one-error-tolerant stack. Since specification names may also be over-loaded, one can specify the file where the specification to be enriched has to be found. This can be done using the FROM option, e.g.:

WITH : BOOL   FROM : Std-BOOL

or

WITH : BOOL   FROM : My-BOOL

Since there is no implicit renaming, **explicit renaming** is needed in the language. The syntax is straightforward:

RENAMING sort1 INTO sort2; op1 INTO op2; ... END

Sorts or operation names may be **forgotten** by writing *"name INTO "*.

A specification may be **parameterized** by another specification. The signature and the axioms of the formal parameter express the properties which are required for the argument. An argument is a couple made of a specification and a signature morphism. The signature morphism is called the *fitting morphism*. It sends sorts and operation names of the formal parameter into the relevant sorts and operations of the argument. The meaning of the application of an argument <ARG, m> to a parameterized specification SPEC(X) depends on the correctness of ARG with respect to X. The models of ARG, restricted to the signature of X w.r.t. m, must be models of X. The signature of the resulting specification is the union of the SPEC signature, where sorts and operation names coming from X are renamed by m, and of the ARG signature (i.e. the X signature disappears). The models are those of the specification w.r.t. the resulting signature.

An example of a parameterized specification, ARRAY (ELEM, INDEX), is given below. The ELEM and INDEX specifications are formal parameters. The ELEM specification does not require anything:

PAR : ELEM
    SORTS : Elem
END ELEM.

The INDEX specification is slightly richer, since the argument must provide a maximum and a minimum index, and a total ordering on the indexes. It is not given here for lack of space.

PROC : ARRAY (ELEM, INDEX)
    SORTS : Array

OPERATIONS :

init:	Index Index	-> Array
lwb:	Array	-> Index
upb:	Array	-> Index
—[—]:= —:	Array Index Elem	-> Array
—[—]:	Array Index	-> Elem

VARIABLES :

t :	Array
i, j :	Index
v, v' :	Elem

EXCEPTION CASES :

illegal-access :	$(i < lwb\ t)$ or $(i > upb\ t)$ = true	=> t[i]
illegal-modif :	$(i < lwb\ t)$ or $(i > upb\ t)$ = true	=> t[i]:=v
illegal-init :	$i > j$ = true	=> init i j

OK-AXIOMS :

bound1 :		lwb (init i j)	= i
bound2 :		upb (init i j)	= j
bound3 :		lwb (t[i]:=v)	= lwb t
bound4 :		upb (t[i]:=v)	= upb t
access1 :	i is j = true	=> (t[i]:=v) [j]	= v
access2 :	i isnot j = true	=> (t[i]:=v) [j]	= t[j]
modif1 :	i is j = true	=> (t[i]:=v) [j]:=v'	= t[i]:=v'
modif2 :	i isnot j = true	=> (t[i]:=v) [j]:=v'	= (t[j]:=v') [i]:=v

END ARRAY.

Note that there is an implicit enrichment of the formal parameters. Thus no WITH is required in the above specification. Furthermore, there is **no implicit reachable** embedded in the specification of the formal parameters, since (finitely generated) models of actual parameters may not be finitely generated models of the formal parameters.

An example of a specification built by instantiation of ARRAY is given below:

```
SPEC : STRING
    ARRAY (ELEM => CHAR, INDEX => INT25)
    RENAMING  Array  INTO String
              init   INTO emptystring
END STRING.
```

This overview of PLUSS-E is of course very incomplete. For instance, other features of this specification language deal with visibility rules and allow the user to hide some private specifications and/or sorts and/or operations.

III - THE ASSPEGIQUE ENVIRONMENT

In the previous section, we have described how exception handling and structuration features can be embedded into an algebraic specification language. Our claim is that a specification language should not only be supported by some specification method, but also by specific tools integrated into a specification environment. Parts of such environments have already been designed or described, such as OBJ, AFFIRM, the CIP Project and the LARCH Project. The main characteristics of these environments can be roughly outlined as follows:
- OBJ [GOG 81, GOG 83] has been developed in order to experiment theoretical hypothesis and specification combining tools.
- AFFIRM [AFF 81] is oriented towards proof purposes. No generic tool is provided to combine specifications. Full-sized examples were developed with this system.
- The CIP Project [CIP 81] attempts to consider in a uniform way specifications and programs.
- The LARCH Project [G&H 83] is developing tools and techniques intended to aid in the productive use of formal specifications of systems containing computer programs.

Our goal when designing the ASSPEGIQUE specification environment was to try to integrate all these characteristics. The main aspect of our specification environment is the high degree to which it allows specifications to be **modularized**. The user of ASSPEGIQUE deals with *elementary* specifications which correspond, so to speak, to *types of interest*. A major role of the specification language is to assemble these elementary specifications into more complex ones.

Modularity imposes constraints that led us to introduce sophisticated mechanisms in the specification environment. For instance, it is useful to be able to specify a type of interest without having previously specified all the *predefined* types required by this type of interest. We did in fact find ourselves obliged to abandon a wholly top-down approach in the development of elementary specifications : such an approach leaves to last those checks that the system must carry out if it is of any real value to the user. Leaving those checks to the end however means that errors may be discovered far too late. We were also obliged to abandon a wholly bottom-up approach, because such an approach does not correspond to a natural way of specifying complex data structures : the most primitive specifications are generally given last, and not first.

III.1 - Hierarchical relations within the specification library

The high degree of modularization of the library and the impossibility to follow an approach which is either strictly bottom-up or strictly top-down, mean that we have to provide the library with ordering relations : on the one hand, such relations allow to reconstitute, whenever necessary, all the *required types* (i.e. those assumed to be predefined) for a given type of interest; on the other hand, they allow to manage the consequences of a modification made on any of the elementary specifications in the library.

Two ordering relations are defined on the specification library ; before defining them formally, we shall explain their use with a simple example.

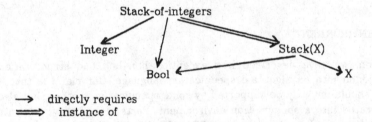

Graph of ordering relations associated with Stack-of-integers

Operations which may appear amongst the axioms of Stack-of-integers are operations on Stack(X) (instantiated), but also operations on Bool and Integer; consequently checks to be carried out on the axioms of Stack-of-integers (e.g. that all terms are well-formed) cannot be carried out before specifications Integer and Bool have been introduced into the library (since nothing prevents us from defining Integer or Stack(X) before defining Bool) : Stack-of-integers requires {Integer, Bool}.
Moreover any modification to X or Stack(X) must lead to reconsideration of Stack-of-integers : after a modification Integer may no longer be a suitable parameter.

More precisely, the ordering relations provided within the library are defined as follows :
1. The ordering relation *requires* is defined as being the transitive and reflexive closure of the relation *directly requires*, defined as follows :

a specification S2 *directly requires* a specification S1 if and only if S2 is built as an enrichment of S1 (S1 is on the list of specifications enriched by S2) or if S2 is an instance of a parameterized specification which directly requires S1 (e.g. in the example above, Stack-of-integers is an instance of Stack(X), which directly requires Bool; it is self-evident that the instantiated parameter is excluded from the definition above : Stack(X) directly requires X, but Stack-of-integers does not).

2. The ordering relation *depends on* is defined as being the transitive and reflexive closure of *directly requires or is an instance of*.

N.B. : As mentioned above, the relation *requires* will in particular allow computation of the set of all the operations that may appear in an axiom of the specification considered, while the relation *depends on* will allow to propagate modification consequences in the library.

III.2 - Overall organization of ASSPEGIQUE

The tools available in the ASSPEGIQUE environment include : a **special purpose editor**, **modification tools**, a **compiler**, a **debugger**, a **symbolic evaluator** and **theorem proving tools**. They are available to the user through a **user interface** and access the specification library through the **hierarchical library management tool** (see figure on next page).

Particular attention has been paid to the **interaction with the user** : all the tools are interfaced in a uniform way and make full use of full-screen multiwindow display and graphic facilities to provide a user-friendly interaction ; among others, this includes the use of on-screen and pop-up menus, and on-line help and documentation facilities, detailed according to the degree of expertise of the user.

The role of the **hierarchical library management tool** is to maintain the library coherence w.r.t. the ordering relations between the specifications ; in particular, the management tool updates the library information file.

The **specification editor** (cf. III.3) is syntax-directed which does not mean that the user has to deal with the internal representation of the specification : the *concrete views* available to the user are a *text representation* of the specification and a *graphic representation* of its signature. Modifications and creations are performed by the user at the level of these concrete views, the corresponding internal representation being accordingly updated.

The **specification compiler** plays two roles :
1. It computes the *grammar* associated with the specification; this grammar allows to analyse the axioms defined in the specification, to verify that they are syntactically correct and to resolve overloading conflicts. To achieve these purposes, the specification compiler uses the grammar generator and the parser described in [VOI 84].
The grammar associated with a specification S is defined as the union of grammars of all specifications required by S and of operations defined within S. Consequently, the compilation of a specification cannot take place before all specifications on which it depends have been introduced. The compilation of a specification may moreover require that specifications which are required but have not yet been compiled (or have been changed since their last compilation) are compiled first.
2. The compiler produces an internal form of the specification which will be directly usable by software accessing the library : symbolic evaluator, theorem prover, program construction assistance tool [BGG 83].

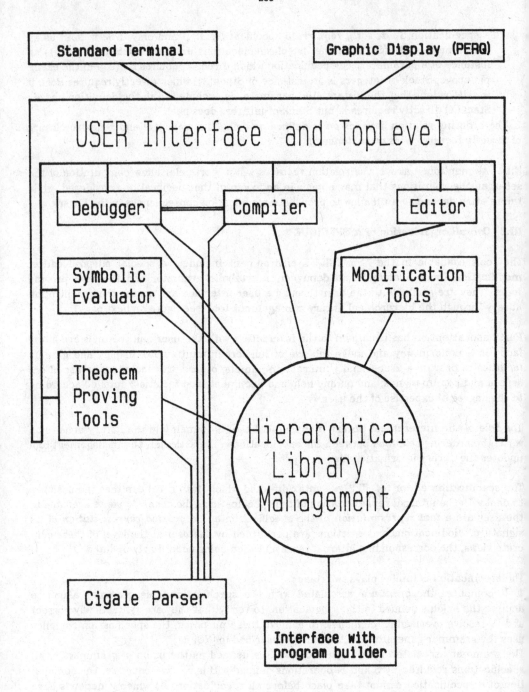

The internal form associated with a specification is made up of LISP property lists : this type of internal form is especially flexible, and has shown itself very convenient for handling problems raised when interfacing ASSPEGIQUE with external tools.

The **specification debugger** is automatically loaded by the compiler when errors are detected ; it allows interactive debugging of the specification. In particular, and this is a contrast with the editor, the debugger is not loaded unless all required specifications do in fact exist (and have been compiled). The debugger consequently allows to debug axioms interactively, which is impossible at the general editing level.

The **symbolic evaluator** computes the canonical form of any term w.r.t. the axioms. The symbolic evaluator takes into account conditional axioms and parameterization [KAP 83]. The **theorem proving tools** use the techniques described in [BID 82].

Finally, the specification environment is provided with tools whose aim is to make operations easier and to maximize the possibilities for **re-using** specifications. Consequently suitable tools allow to copy a specification, to enrich it by adding new operations or axioms, or to rename an operation or an axiom, etc.

III.3 - The ASSPEGIQUE syntax-directed full-screen editor

As outlined before, the originality of the editor is that, while offering all the flexibility in use of a full-screen editor, it establishes links between the external concrete views (text, graphics) and the internal representation, making it a syntax editor [EDS 83]. Any movement within the text or the graphic representation of the description is also a movement within the corresponding tree, and any modification is taken into account at both levels by means of a validation mechanism. The part of the editor devoted to the specification text was developed as an extension of WINNIE [AMA 83], a full-screen multi-window editor. The graphical part of the editor was derived from a graphical interactive editor for Petri-nets, PETRI-POTE [BEA 83].

The editor displays a template which depends on the construction primitive (enrichment, formal parameter, parameterized type, etc...), and on the *style* of specification (basic, with error handling, etc...). For instance, the figure on next page shows how the screen looks like at some stage of the edition of a specification *enriching* other ones, written in a *basic style*.

The template displayed may be broken down into :

1. A heading part which includes the name of the type (SPEC clause), the names of the required types (WITH clauses) and the names of the files containing their descriptions (FROM clauses), as well as the names of sorts involved in the type description (SORTS clause); the user may create as many WITH FROM clauses as there are required types.

2. An OPERATIONS part, in which the name and syntax of each operator is specified (note that the parser and incremental grammar generator [VOI 84] allow the user to indicate where the operation arguments should be placed).

3. A VARIABLES part : name and type of variables.

WELCOME IN THE "ASSPEGIQUE" SPECIFICATION ENVIRONMENT !!!

```
+------------------------------------------------------------------------+
|SPEC : STACK                                                            |
|        WITH : BOOL      FROM : Std-BOOL                                 |
|        WITH : INT       FROM : My-INT                                   |
|                                                                        |
|        SORTS :  Stack                                                   |
|------------------------------------------------------------------------|
|OPERATIONS : Use INS-* to edit operations through the PERQ interface    |
|    empty :  -> Stack                                                    |
|    push _ onto _ : Int Stack  -> Stack                                  |
|    pop _ : Stack  -> Stack                                              |
|    top _ : Stack  -> Int                                               |
|    is empty ? _ : Stack  -> Bool                                        |
|    height _ : Stack  -> Int                                            |
|*                                                                       |
|VARIABLES :                                                             |
|    x : Int                                                             |
|*   s : Stack                                                           |
|AXIOMS :                                                               |
|*   top-1 : top push x onto s = x                                       |
```

```
(ASSEDIQUE<mod>) Value : t
```

EDIT OPS
```
~~~~~~~~~~~~~~~~~
    HELP !!!
    OUT !
   Add sort
Add sort of int.
 Add operation
Delete sort/op
Rename sort/op
~~~~~~~~~~~~~~~~~
 Back to Spec.
~~~~~~~~~~~~~~~~~
```

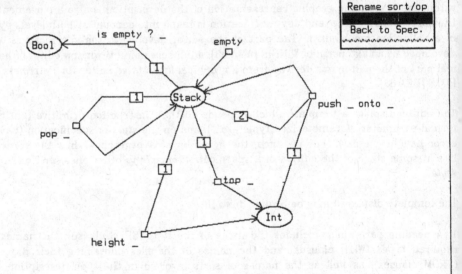

4. The AXIOMS part (which would be divided into four sub-parts, if the specification were written in the *error handling style*.)

Any declaration (name of type, name and syntax of operation, etc...) is called an entity. A star indicates that the following entity has not been validated yet. Validation consists in checking the syntax of an entity declaration, and in completing the corresponding sub-tree of the internal representation.

In what concerns the signature (sorts and operations), the user may either type in directly the text in the text view or use the PERQ graphical interface. In this case, (s)he just needs to select the appropriate command in the pop-up menu and draw, say, the operation, by pointing at the domains and codomain sorts (the operation arrows are then drawn automatically by the system).

IV - CONCLUSION

In this paper, we have shown how to systematically cope with structuration and exception handling at the specification level by providing an appropriate specification language; we also described a specification environment that supports such a language and therefore its practical use. The tools integrated in ASSPEGIQUE range from a high-level syntax-directed editor to a symbolic evaluator and theorem proving tools; therefore, PLUSS-E and ASSPE-GIQUE are especially well-suited for rapid prototyping purposes [CHO 85]. Industrial sized experimentations on ASSPEGIQUE are currently under development, and will provide a firm basis to further versions.

A kernel system of ASSPEGIQUE consisting in the top-level and user-interface, the specification editor together with its graphic interface, a specification compiler, a symbolic evaluator, the special purpose grammar generator and the parser, theorem proving tools has been implemented on VAX-UNIX and PERQ-POS. This system has been demonstrated at the 7th International Conference on Software Engineering, Orlando, USA and at the 2nd AFCET Conference on Software Engineering, Nice, France.

V - ACKNOWLEDGEMENTS

This work is partially supported by A.D.I. Contract No 639 and the C.N.R.S. (Greco de Programmation).

Special thanks are due to *Marie-Claude Gaudel* for many helpful suggestions and discussions in designing the PLUSS-E language. We also thank *Frederic Voisin, Stephane Kaplan, Marianne Choquer, Michel Beaudouin-Lafon* who respectively made the parser, the symbolic evaluator, the theorem proving tools and the graphic interface.

VI - REFERENCES

[ADJ 76] Goguen J., Thatcher J., Wagner E., "An Initial Algebra approach to the specification, correctness, and implementation of abstract data types" in Current Trends in Programming Methodology, Vol.4, Yeh Ed. Prentice Hall, 1978 (also IBM Report RC 6487, October 1976).

[AFF 81] Gerhart S.L., "AFFIRM Reference Manual", UCS-Report (Marina del Rey), 1981.

[AMA 83] Amar P., "Winnie : un éditeur de textes multifenêtres extensible", Actes des Journées BIGRE (Le Cap d'Agde), 1983.

[BBGGG 84] Bidoit M., Biebow B., Gaudel M.-C., Gresse C., Guiho G., "Exception handling : formal specification and systematic program specification", Proc. 7th I.C.S.E., Orlando, USA, 1984.

[BEA 83] Beaudouin-Lafon M., "Petripote: a graphic system for Petri-Nets design and simulation" Proc. of 4th European Workshop on Applications and Theory of Petri Nets, Toulouse, France, 1983.

[BID 82] Bidoit M., "Proofs by induction in "fairly" specified equational theories" Proc. 6th German Workshop on Artificial Intelligence, Bad Honnef, Germany, Springer-Verlag IFB 58, 1982.

[BID 84] Bidoit M., "Algebraic specification of exception handling and error recovery by means of declarations and equations", Proc. 11th ICALP, Antwerp, 1984.

[BCK 84] Bidoit M., Choppy C., Kaplan S., "ASSPEGIQUE : un environnement de spécification algébrique", Proc. 2nd AFCET Software Engineering Conference, Nice, 1984, pp357-371

[BGG 83] Bidoit M., Gresse C., Guiho G., "CATY : Un système d'aide au développement de programmes", Actes des Journées BIGRE 83 (Le Cap d'Agde), 1983.

[BGG 84] Bidoit M., Gaudel M.-C., Guiho G. "Towards a systematic and safe programming of exception handling in ADA" Proc. of Ada-Europe/Ada TEC Conf., Brussels, June 1984.

[B&W 82] Broy M., Wirsing M., "Partial Abstract Data Types" Acta Informatica, Vol.18-1, Nov 1982.

[B&G 79] Burstall R., Goguen J., "The semantics of CLEAR, a specification language", in Abstract Software Specifications, D. Bjorner Ed., LNCS 86, Springer-Verlag, 1979.

[CIP 81] CIP language group "Report on a wide spectrum language for program specification and development", Rapport TUM-I8104 (Munich), 1981.

[CHO 85] Choppy C., "Tools and techniques for building rapid prototypes", AFCET Workshop on "Prototypage, Maquettage et Génie Logiciel", Lyon, January 1985.

[DOD 83] "The programming language ADA - Reference Manual" United States Department of Defense, January 1983.

[EDS 83] "Les éditeurs dirigés par la syntaxe", Journées d'Aussois - INRIA Ed. (Rocquencourt - France), 1983.

[GAU 83] Gaudel M.-C., "Proposition pour un Langage d'Utilisation de Spécifications Structurées : PLUSS", C.G.E. Research Report, 1983.

[GDLE 83] Gogolla M., Drosten K., Lipeck U., Ehrich H., "Algebraic and operational semantics of specifications allowing exceptions and errors" Proc. 6th GI-Conference on Theoretical Computer Science, LNCS 145, 1983, Springer-Verlag.

[GOG 77] Goguen J.A., "Abstract errors for abstract data types" in Formal Description of Programming Concepts, E.J. NEUHOLD Ed., North Holland, New York 1977.

[GOG 78] Goguen J.A., "Exception and Error Sorts, Coercion and Overloading Operators" S.R.I. Research Report, 1978.

[GOG 81] Goguen J.A., Parsaye-Ghomi K., "Algebraic denotational semantics using parameterized modules", Tech. Report CSL-119, SRI International, UCLA, 1981.

[GOG 83] Goguen J.A., "Parameterized Programming", Proc. Workshop on Reusability in Programming, Stratford CT, USA, 1983.

[G&H 83] Guttag J.V., Horning J.J., "An introduction to the LARCH shared language", Proc. IFIP 83, REA. Mason ed., North Holland Publishing Company, 1983.

[KAP 83] Kaplan S., "Un langage de spécification de types abstraits algébriques", Thèse de 3ème

260

cycle, LRI (Orsay - France), 1983.

[PLA 82] Plaisted D., "An initial algebra semantics for error presentations" Unpublished Draft, 1982.

[S&W 83] Sanella D., Wirsing M., "A Kernel Language for Algebraic Specification and Implementation", to appear in Int. Conf. on Foundations of Computing Theory, Bergholm, Sweden, 1983.

[VOI 84] Voisin F., "CIGALE : un outil de construction incrémental de grammaire et d'analyse d'expression", Thèse de 3ème cycle, Orsay (France), 1984.

[WIR 82] Wirsing M., "Structured algebraic specifications", Proc. AFCET Symp. on Mathematics for Computer Science, Paris, France, 1982.

[WIR 83] Wirsing M., "Structured algebraic specifications : A kernel language", PhD. Thesis, Munchen, Germany, 1983.

APPLICATION OF PROLOG
TO TEST SETS GENERATION FROM ALGEBRAIC SPECIFICATIONS

L. Bougé (*), N. Choquet (**), L. Fribourg (**), M.C. Gaudel (***)

(*) LITP, Université Paris 7, 2 place Jussieu, 75251 Paris Cedex 05, France
(**) Laboratoires de Marcoussis-C.G.E, route de Nozay, 91460 Marcoussis, France
(***) LRI, Université Paris Sud, 91405 Orsay, France

ABSTRACT

We present a method and a tool for generating test sets from algebraic data type
specifications. We give formal definitions of the basic concepts required in our approach
of functional testing. Then we discuss the problem of testing algebraic data types implementations. This allows the introduction of additional hypotheses and thus the description
of an effective method for generating test sets. The method can be improved by using
PROLOG. Indeed, it turns out that PROLOG is a very well suited tool for generating test
sets in this context. Applicability of the method is discussed and a complete example is
given.

INTRODUCTION

Functional or "black-box" testing has been recognized for a long time as an important
aspect of software validation [Howd 80], [ABC 82]. It is especially important for large-
sized, long-lived systems for which successive versions have to be delivered. In this case,
non-regression testing may be long, difficult and expensive. It should depend only on the
functional specifications of the system [Paul 83].

However, most of the studies on test data generation have focused on program dependent
testing [Haml 75], [Clar 76], since it was possible to use the properties of a formal object:
the program. Of course such an approach is necessary but not sufficient [Gour 83]. The
emergence of formal specification methods makes it possible to found functional testing
on a rigorous basis. In this paper we present a method and a tool for generating test sets
from algebraic data type specifications. We consider hierarchical, positive conditional
specifications with preconditions. More precisely, we study how to test an
implementation of a data type against a property (an axiom) which is required by the
specification. The formal specification is used as a guideline to produce relevant test
data.

As asserted in [BA 82], it is especially dangerous, when studying testing and correctness
to use informal definitions, even if they seem obvious. For instance, it is shown in [BA 82]
that two different, but rather similar, formal definitions of what an "adequate test set" is,
lead to very dissimilar issues.

The first part of this paper is therefore devoted to formal definitions of several concepts:
first we give the fundamental properties of what we call a **collection of test sets**; then we
state the hypotheses which are assumed during the testing process and ensure the
acceptability of the considered collections of test sets. This notion of acceptability is

defined and discussed with respect to the classical properties required for test selection criteria [GG 75]: reliability, validity and lack of bias.

In the second part, we show that using algebraic data types allows the introduction of further hypotheses and enables the test sets generation.

The third part describes how to improve this method using PROLOG. It turns out that PROLOG is a very well suited tool for generating test sets in this context. In particular it automatically provides partitions of the domains of the variables. Of course, the use of PROLOG somewhat limits the kinds of specifications and properties which can be considered. However these limitations could be alleviated by extensions of PROLOG (e.g. [Komo 80], [Nais 82], [DJ 84], [GM 84], [Frib 84], etc.)

1. BASIC NOTIONS IN TESTING THEORY

It is now widely recognized that a sound theory of testing must focus not only on the question "What is a test?". Goodenough and Gerhart [GG 75] took a decisive step forward by enlarging this question to "What is a test criterion?". A criterion makes it possible to decide whether a given set of data can be validly considered as a test. [Boug 82] suggests one more step: one globally considers the whole testing process, or at least a model of it. Indeed, the properties of test data are not independent from the method used to perform testing and to handle results.

1.1. DEFINITIONS

The **Testing Process Diagram** (fig. 1) is an attempt to model the sequence of operations that take place between the problem definition ("Does this system validate this property?") and the conclusion ("Yes, as far as I can assure it" or "No, definitely not").

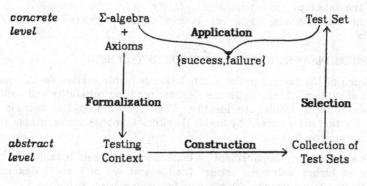

fig.1 Testing Process Diagram

Here we consider an implementation to be a Σ-algebra (i.e. a set of operations on some sets of values) and we want to test whether this algebra satisfies a set of axioms. However, the definitions we give are general.

The problem to be solved is formally stated as a **Testing Context** C. It is mainly made up of the property A to be tested (the axioms) and previous knowledge about the system under test (the given algebra). The idea of testing a partially defined/known object has recently been introduced by De Millo et al. [BDLS 80], [Budd 81], [Howd 82]. We think it is quite fundamental. One never knows the object under test perfectly. One only knows that it satisfies some properties H, which come from the context or from previous tests or proofs.

In the case of a program, one knows the semantics of its elementary components, but not its behavior over its whole domain. In the case of a Σ-algebra, one knows the behavior of lower-level type operations (Integer, Boolean...), perhaps some axioms which are a priori satisfied by this algebra (using some previous validation results), but certainly not the whole functional behavior of the algebra. Hopefully the algebra presently under test satisfies properties H.

Once a testing context C has been stated, the next step in the testing process is to build a **collection of test sets** from C. Such a collection is a family of test sets (T_n) indexed by positive integers. We require this family to be **asymptotically reliable**: it means that if T_{n+1} is successful then T_n is successful. This new notion is introduced to express the idea that increasing the size of a test set increases the quality of testing. In fact, here the classical concept of **test selection criterion** is replaced by the notion of collection: the (T_n) are all the test sets possibly selected by the given criterion. We will later show that the qualities of a criterion can be expressed as constraints on the sequence (T_n).

In this paper, testing is trying to answer a finite number of elementary questions of the form (at least in the case of an equational specification)
"Does the Σ-algebra X satisfy equation t=t' ?"
The straightforward way to do this is to consider all the possible instantiations of the variables occurring in the equation and to compute both sides of the equation in X. Each T_n is a subset of the possible instantiations of the equation. We shall note

$T_n = \{t_i = t'_i\}$.

The last step to perform in the testing process is to select a test set T_n and to compute it in the Σ-algebra. If all the equations $t_i = t'_i$ are satisfied then the result of the testing process is "success"; if not, it is "failure" and one can conclude that the Σ-algebra, i.e. the data type implementation, is faulty.

The criterion for choosing n is of course strongly related to cost/quality requirements.

1.2. FUNDAMENTAL PROPERTIES OF A COLLECTION OF TEST SETS

The significance of the testing process conclusion is highly related to the quality of the test sets collection. Goodenough and Gerhart required **reliability** and **validity** for test selection criteria, leading to **ideality**. They proved that the success of the application of a test set selected by an ideal criterion implies correctness. Here we follow a similar approach.

Reliability is a consistency requirement. A collection of test sets is said to be reliable if a test set of higher index is "better" than a test set of lower index whatever potential Σ-algebra is considered. This can be formally written as follows

$$\forall n \in \mathbf{N}, \ (H \cup T_{n+1}) \mid\text{-} T_n$$

This requirement is slightly weaker than Goodenough and Gerhart's and, is called **asymptotic reliability**. It captures the fact that testing is fundamentally an incremental process.

Validity means that any incorrect behavior will be revealed by some test data in some T_n, i.e.

$$(H \cup (\cup_n T_n)) \mid\text{-} A$$

If testing is successful using all test sets T_n then the algebra fulfills the required properties. A collection which satisfies this property is said to be **asymptotically valid**.

One more property is required for test sets collections. It is the **lack of bias**. Any correct algebra should pass any test set T_n. It is precisely the converse of validity:

$$\forall n \in \mathbf{N}, (H \cup A) \mid\text{-} T_n$$

If a test using the test set T_p selected from the collection (T_n) fails then the algebra does not satisfy the axioms. It turns out that most "natural" test selection criteria satisfy this property (for instance, see Goodenough and Gerhart's criteria). A similar property is considered in [Gour 83].

A (asymptotically) reliable, (asymptotically) valid and unbiased collection of test sets is said to be **acceptable**. These three properties ensure that the higher the index of the selected test set, the better the conclusion of the testing process. The existence of an acceptable collection of test sets is strongly related to the properties of A and H (see [Boug 82] and [Boug 83] for details). An interesting feature of algebraic data type specifications is that they do not involve any existential quantifiers. This ensures the existence of such a collection under standard extra hypotheses to be listed below.

1.3. REGULARITY AND UNIFORMITY HYPOTHESES

The problem of testing axioms for a Σ-algebra is thus reduced to seeking an acceptable collection of test sets for a testing context. It is only possible if some powerful assumptions on the Σ-algebra are available. Such assumptions are left implicit in most testing methods. For notational convenience, let us assume hereafter that we are testing an axiom of the form $t(x)=t'(x)$. Thus, in the following, test sets T_n are sets of instantiations of this equation.

1.3.1. Regularity hypotheses

Let us assume it is possible, in some way, to associate a level of complexity with each element of Σ-algebra carriers. The **regularity hypothesis** states that the axiom under test behaves regularly with respect to this measure. If it holds for any object of complexity less than k (k being a parameter), then it holds for any object.

$$\forall x \, (\text{complexity}(x) \leq k \Rightarrow t(x)=t'(x)) \Rightarrow \forall x \, (t(x)=t'(x))$$

Typically, complexity will be the length of a representative Σ-term denoting an object. In the case of program testing, it corresponds to the computation complexity. Thus regularity hypotheses reflect path analysis testing strategies [Howd 76], [WHH 80].

1.3.2. Uniformity hypotheses

If no complexity measure is available , we are faced with the well-known problem of partitioning variable domains in such a way that the axiom under test "behaves uniformly" on these subdomains. Formally speaking, it means that the following **uniformity hypothesis** is satisfied for each subdomain

$$\exists x \, (t(x)=t'(x)) \Rightarrow \forall x \, (t(x)=t'(x))$$

It is modelled by introducing a **new** constant c of suitable type, a **meta-constant**.

The value of such a constant is intuitively a random value of the subdomain. The hypothesis can thus be expressed as well by

$$(t(c)=t'(c)) => \forall x \ (t(x)=t'(x))$$

This typically leads to random testing strategies and subdomain testing strategies [WC 80], [ZW 81].

2. APPLICATION OF THE THEORY TO ALGEBRAIC DATA TYPE SPECIFICATION TESTING

We now focus on the specific kind of testing we are dealing with: testing a data type implementation against an algebraic data type specification.

2.1. THE PROBLEM

Algebraic specifications of data types are widely recognized as a useful formal specification method. See for instance [BH 85]. A specification is given by
    a many-sorted signature Σ, i.e. a list of functional symbols on a set of sorts S, and
    a set of Σ-axioms E.
The problem is: are the axioms of E satisfied by a given Σ-algebra X.

---

specif queue-of-int =
enrich bool, int *by*
sort queue;
operations

emptyq :		-> queue
append :	queue * int	-> queue
remove :	queue	-> queue
first :	queue	-> int
isempty :	queue	-> bool

variables
    Q,Q': queue
    I: int
precondition
    pre(first,Q) = (isempty(Q)=false)
axioms
    A1: isempty(emptyq)=true
    A2: isempty(append(Q,I))=false
    A3: remove(emptyq)=emptyq
    A4: isempty(Q)=true => remove(append(Q,I))=emptyq
    A5: isempty(Q)=false => remove(append(Q,I))=append(remove(Q),I)
    A6: isempty(Q)=true => first(append(Q,I))=I
    A7: isempty(Q) = false => first(append(Q,I)) = first(Q)

fig.2 Specification of Queue of Integers

Usually, one deals with hierarchical abstract data types [GH 78], [Bido 81], [BDPP 83]. A sort of interest s_i is distinguished in S, and Σ is accordingly split into signature Σ_i (i standing for interest) and Σ_p (p standing for primitive). Σ_i contains operations where at least one input or output variable is of sort s_i.
Hierarchical algebraic data types induce in a natural way a similar structure into the

testing process: lower level modules are first tested against their specification, then higher level ones. Of course, the testing of higher level modules can use the fact that lower level modules were successfully tested.

We consider only a restricted class of algebraic specifications characterized as follows:
   hierarchical specifications;
   a predefined boolean specification with two constants, **true** and **false**;
   preconditions on operators and conditional equations, with a restricted form.
Premises of preconditions and conditional equations are restricted to be **boolean equations**, i.e. equations of the form **t=true** or **t=false** where t is a term of boolean sort. The reasons for this restriction appear in part 3. An example of such a specification is given on figure 2.
Conditional axioms such as A6 or A7 of figure 2 are valid for an algebra X if for any instantiation of Q and I which satisfies the preconditions and premises, both sides of the conclusion equation yield the same value in X.

2.2. BASIC HYPOTHESES FOR TEST SETS GENERATION

The basic assumption for test construction in such a framework is the **Correlation principle**
   "There exists a narrow correlation between specification structure and implementation structure."
This is a postulate. It may definitely not be the case for our specific algebra X. In fact, because of the increasing use of construction methods guided by specifications [B2G3 84], using top-down, bottom-up, stepwise refinement, this principle is more and more valid as time goes. This principle is closed to the so-called competent programmer hypothesis [Budd 81]. It is more or less assumed by most of testing methodologies.

This principle is used to derive the following three hypotheses.

Finitely generated and non-trivial algebras

The first hypothesis restricts the considered algebras to be finitely generated with respect to hierarchy [WPP 83], [SW 83]. It means that any element of X can be denoted abstractly by application of operations of Σ_i (the operations of interest) to elements of lower sort. In the queue example of figure 2, any queue element of X can be then obtained as a sequence of remove and append operations on emptyq. This hypothesis states that the specification under test covers all parts of X. Any element of X can thus be denoted as a formal term of the specification.

It is necessary to avoid trivial algebras, i.e. algebras where any property is satisfied. We assume therefore that the implementation of predefined booleans satisfies the property **true≠false**.

Uniformity hypotheses for lower sorts

The specification under test is hierarchical. At testing time, lower level modules already exist (or can be simulated) and have been successfully tested against their specification. If the specification is hierarchically consistent then the correctness of lower types is preserved. One is therefore entitled to set uniformity hypotheses about lower level domains. For instance in the queue specification (see figure 2) the values of integer operands are not significant.

Regularity hypothesis for the sort of interest

The sort of interest is the actual subject of the testing process. Because algebras are finitely generated, the computational complexity of objects is directly connected to the syntactical complexity of their denotation. A possible complexity measure of an element x of X is then the length of the smallest Σ_i-term denoting x. Having in mind such a complexity measure, a regularity hypothesis directly arises. If the implementation works in all simpler cases, it will do so in more complex cases. The distinction between "simpler" and "more complex" cases is stated by choosing a complexity level k. We call k the level of the test set.

2.3. TEST SETS GENERATION ALGORITHM FOR EQUATIONAL SPECIFICATIONS

Consider an equational axiom of the form
$$t(x_1, ..., x_m) = t'(x_1, ..., x_m)$$
both sides being terms of the sort of interest. Under the three hypotheses above, we can describe an acceptable collection of test sets (T_n). Test set T_k is the **finite** set $\{t_i = t'_i\}$ of all the closed instantiations of the axiom under test obtained as follows.

Instanciation algorithm (equational case)
    for i = 1 **to** m **do**
    if x_i is a variable of the sort of interest
    then instantiate it by **all** the terms of size less than k
        which contain no variable of the sort of interest
    done

    for each of the resulting instanciated equations **do**
        for each variable y **do**
            instantiate y by a **new** meta-constant c, one for each uniformity
            subdomain of the sort of y
        done
    done

Running test set T_k simply consists of checking the validity of all its totally instantiated equations $t_i = t'_i$ on the Σ-algebra under test X. Because no variables are left, this is simply done by computing each side of the equation and checking that both yield the same value. When computing, random values of the corresponding subdomain are substituted for meta-constants.

Consider the case where a set of **constructors** (see section 3.2) is given together with the specification of the type of interest. Hypotheses can then be strengthened by assuming that X is actually finitely generated with respect to those constructors. Instantiation may thus be limited to those terms of size less than k which are combinations of constructors. The number of generated instantiations is then considerably decreased. This corresponds precisely to optimizing a test set by discarding redundant tests. This optimization is usually left implicit in testing methodologies.

Our specifications generally contain conditional axioms (see fig. 2). It may then happen that no term of size less than level k validates the premise of some axiom. It would thus be declared valid because it is vacuously satisfied for all those terms. Some check must therefore be added to ensure that all axioms have actually be tested (premises are satisfied in enough representative cases). However, another more efficient approach is to selectively generate terms that validate some premise. This is the subject of the next section.

3. TEST SETS GENERATION FOR CONDITIONAL AXIOMS

3.1. Use of PROLOG to satisfy relations

A PROLOG program is made up of Horn clauses. A Horn clause is a conditional formula made of a head part and a body part; the head part is a relation P over terms, and the body part is a list of conditions under which the head part is true.

A PROLOG interpreter uses automatic deduction methods (resolution) to compute the terms which satisfy a relation characterized by the clauses of the program.

When a relation P(X) is written in PROLOG, then given the goal: ?-P(X), the interpreter instantiates X with the terms satisfying P.

Example:
    What are the values of X such that X>2?
    Booleans are defined by true and false.
    Integers are built on 0 and succ, with in addition an operator le: int * int --> bool, defined in PROLOG by:
        le(0,X,true).
        le(succ(X),0,false).
        le(succ(X),succ(Y),B):- le(X,Y,B).
    Given the goal
        ?- le(X,succ(succ(0)),false).
    the interpreter provides the general solution:
        X = succ(succ(succ(Y))),
    where Y takes any value.

Theoretically, the resolution strategy underlying PROLOG provides all the solutions for a goal [Clar 77].

A solution computed by the PROLOG interpreter is either a fully instantiated term or a term containing variables; in the latter case, the computed term embodies a whole class of solutions, since any instantiation of the computed term is a particular solution of the goal. This PROLOG computation feature is used hereafter.

One advantage of PROLOG in our framework is the handling of conditional axioms. However some limitations, due to the fact that equality is not handled, still exist. But some propositions are presently being submitted to alleviate this restriction [DJ 84],[GM 84],[Frib 84].

3.2. Converting a specification into PROLOG

A specification which satisfies the syntactical restrictions we have introduced on algebraic specifications in part 2.1 can generally be translated into PROLOG, (a similar translation is developed in [HS 85]).

Axioms are viewed as definitions of function symbols. Syntactically, a function symbol f is defined by a set of axioms of the form :

$$(a(u)=true) \ \& \ (b(u')=false) => f(v)=g(w), \qquad (*)$$

where f and g are function symbols; u, u', v, w are vectors of terms, and a, b are symbols of boolean functions; a(u)=true and b(u')=false are the **constraint equations**.

Axioms are thus implicitly oriented. The symbol f appearing in the axiom above is said to be **specified**. A function symbol specified by no axiom of the specification is called a

basic symbol or **constructor**. In this paper, we assume that there is no equation between constructors.

Axioms are translated into **Horn clauses**. The first step is to modify the signature. All the function symbols of arity n specified by axioms in the original specification are replaced in the new specification by relation symbols of arity n+1. For instance, the **operator** remove(q) (see fig. 2) becomes the **relation** remove(Q1,Q2). The only remaining terms in the translation are those formed with constructors and variables only. For instance, the constructors of the queue type are emptyq and append. Terms like emptyq and append(Q,I) are preserved.

In a second step, **axioms** are turned into **Horn clauses**. For simplicity, consider an axiom such as (*), where ú, u', v are made of constructors and variables only. It becomes:

$$f(v,Z) :- a(u,true), b(u',false), R(X,Z),$$

where X is the set of variables appearing in v, and R(X,Z) expresses in a relation form the functional equation: Z=g(w). Intuitively speaking, Z is no more than an intermediate result.

When u, u', or v contain derived operators, there is a preliminary transformation in order to reduce this case to the previous one.

The last step is to plug possible **preconditions** on f into the Horn clause. If there is pre(f,x) = p(x) in the original specification, then the final clause is

$$f(v,z) :- a(u,true), b(u',false), p(v,true), R(X,Z).$$

An example is given in figure 3.

C1: isempty(emptyq,true).
C2: isempty(append(Q,I),false).
C3: remove(emptyq,emptyq).
C4: remove(append(Q,I),emptyq):-isempty(Q,true).
C5: remove(append(Q,I),append(Q',I)):- isempty(Q,false),remove(Q,Q').
C6: first(append(Q,I),I):- isempty(append(Q,I),false),isempty(Q,true).
C7: first(append(Q,I),J):- isempty(append(Q,I),false),isempty(Q,false),first(Q,J).

fig.3 Translation of the queue specification into PROLOG

3.3. Constraint-driven generation of terms

Generally speaking, each clause C derived from the specification is of the form:
f(I,O):- A(I), R(I,O), where A(I) expresses the preconditions and the premises of the original axiom. Terms satisfying A(I) are precisely those needed at the end of section 2.3 to test this original axiom in a non-trivial way. These terms are obtained by submitting the goal ?- **A(I)** to PROLOG.

Consider for instance clause C5 in fig.3 . In the queue example, the relevant terms are obtained by submitting ?- isempty(Q,false). This yields the general answer
Q = append(Q',I).

This example is a simple one. Let us consider a more interesting example - *insertion into a sorted list* -, which is completely given in appendix.
Consider the clause C6 in this new example.

C6: insert(ap(L,X),Y,ap(ap(L,X),Y)):- sorted(ap(L,X),true),le(X,Y,true).
The constraints here are : sorted(ap(L,X),true) and le(X,Y,true),
where le (≤) is described by:

    le(0,X,true).
    le(succ(X),0,false).
    le(succ(X),succ(Y),B):-le(X,Y,B).

and sorted is described by:

    sorted(el,true).
    sorted(ap(el,X),true).
    sorted(ap(ap(L,X),Y),B):- le(X,Y,true),sorted(ap(L,X),B).
    sorted(ap(ap(L,X),Y),false):- le(X,Y,false).

The constraint on C6 is solved with the goal

    ?-sorted(ap(L,X),true),le(X,Y,true). If we limit L to lists of length 1,
L=ap(el,I), the goal becomes

    ?- sorted(ap(ap(el,I),X),true),le(X,Y,true). We obtain the answers:
    $I = 0, X = 0, Y = \_$;
    $I = 0, X = succ(0), Y = succ(\_)$;
    $I = succ(0), X = succ(0), Y = succ(\_)$;
    etc ...

These answers correspond to the triples <I,X,Y> of terms of the form:

    $< succ^m(0) , succ^n(0), succ^n(\_) >$, with $0 \le m \le n$

A standard PROLOG interpreter, using a depth-first strategy, will go into an infinite
branch. It will generate a collection of solutions with increasing complexity, satisfying
the goal. Unfortunately some branches might be ignored. If we stop execution after a
finite number of steps, we do not have all the terms t such that complexity(t)≤k.
To get an acceptable test sets collection, all branches must be explored. This requires
active control of the search strategy . This control is provided in PROLOG extensions
such as MU-PROLOG and METALOG [Nais 82] [DL 84]. It is then possible to get all the
terms of length less than some bound k.
PROLOG may provide terms with variables. These terms correspond to a class of
solutions. Thus PROLOG automatically provides some uniformity hypotheses. Variables
correspond to meta-constants (see section 2.3) .

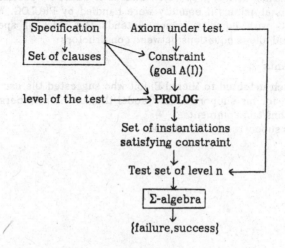

fig.4 *Diagram of test sets generation*

The method is summarized in figure 4. For each clause we generate terms satisfying the constraints of the clause: PROLOG will generate all of them, provided we can control the exploration of infinite branches. We take this set of terms as a domain on which we make regularity hypotheses. PROLOG helps us to partition it into uniformity sub-domains, from which we extract test data through the use of meta-constants. Thus, the definition domain has been partitionned into regularity and uniformity sub-domains. The generated test sets collection is "acceptable" according to the theory described in section 1.3, provided the search strategy is complete.

CONCLUSION

The idea of using PROLOG, or some extension of PROLOG, to generate test sets seems promising. In this paper we suggest a method which is based on the theory of testing presented in section 1. This method is applicable provided the hypotheses of section 1 are satisfied; the specifications can be translated into PROLOG; and it is possible to control the search strategy in the PROLOG interpreter. Algebraic specifications are especially well suited to such an application since it is possible to define some restrictions on them, such as those presented in section 2, so that the two first requirements of the method are satisfied.

This paper applies the method to positive conditional algebraic specifications using search strategy control provided by METALOG. The method was applied to test real-time software such as alternating bit protocol implementations and telephone switching modules. PROLOG provides a partition into uniformity domains. METALOG is very convenient for defining general search strategies which correspond to regularity hypotheses: when working with a new specification it is only necessary to define the complexity of the test data for the sort of interest.

However, to be generally applicable, this method must be improved in two directions. First the cost in time and space of PROLOG implementations must be decreased. The main limitations experienced using the examples were those of the computation time and memory overflows.

Second the class of considered specifications must be enlarged as far as possible in order to avoid rewriting the specifications for generating test sets. There is an inherent limitation to the method since the tested properties must ensure the existence of an acceptable test sets collection. Such is not the case if there is an existential quantifier in the property. However it would be possible to consider full positive conditional axioms if equality were handled by PROLOG. We are working on such a PROLOG with equality, which extends the class of specifications under consideration and allows equations between constructors.

Acknowledgements

We are very much indebted to Michel Bidoit who suggested the use of PROLOG and to Jan Komorowski for his support. M.C. Gaudel thanks the members of IFIP-WG2.2 for fruitful discussions and comments.
This research is supported by CIT-Alcatel.

REFERENCES

[ABC 82] W.R. Adrion, M.A. Branstad and J.C. Cherniavsky, "Validation, verification and testing of computer software", ACM Comp. Surv. 14, 2 (June 82).

[Bido 81] M. Bidoit, "Putting together fair presentations of abstract data types into structured specifications", Rept. No. 15/81, GRECO, France (1981).

[Boug 82] L. Bougé, "Modélisation de la notion de test de programme; application à la production de jeux de tests", Thèse de 3ème cycle, Université Paris 6, Paris (Oct. 1982).

[Boug 83] L. Bougé, "A proposition for a theory of testing: an abstract approach to the testing process", Rept. No. PB-160, DAIMI, Aarhus University, Denmark (may 83), to appear in Theor. Comp. Science.

[Budd 81] T.A. Budd "Mutation analysis: ideas, examples, problems and prospects", in: Computer Program Testing, B. Chandrasekran and S. Radicchi, eds. (North-Holland, 1981) 129-148.

[BA 82] T.A. Budd and D. Angluin, "Two notions of correctness and their relation to testing", Acta Informatica 18 (1982) 31-45.

[BDLS 80] T.A. Budd, R.A. De Millo, R.J. Lipton and F.G. Sayward, "Theoretical and empirical studies on using program mutation to test the functional correctness of programs", Proc. 7th Ann. ACM Symp. Princ. Prog. Lang., Las Vegas (Jan. 1980) 220-233.

[BH 85] B. Biebow and J. Hagelstein, "Algebraic specification of synchronization and errors: a telephonic example", Proc. Coll. Soft. Eng., Berlin (1985), this volume.

[B2G3 84] M. Bidoit, B. Biebow, M.C. Gaudel, D. Gresse and G. Guiho, "Exception handling: formal specification and systematic program construction", Proc. Int. Conf. Soft. Eng., Orlando, Florida (1984).

[Clar 77] K.L. Clark, "Predicate logic as a computational formalism", Research Rept., Dept. of Computing, Imperial College, London (1977).

[Clar 76] L. Clarke, "A system to generate test data and symbollicaly execute programs", IEEE Trans. Soft. Eng. SE-2, 3 (1976) 215-222.

[DJ 84] N. Dershowitz and N.A. Josephson, "Logic programming by completion", Proc. 2nd Int. Logic Programming Conf., Uppsala, Sweden (July 1984) 313-320.

[DL 84] M. Dincbas and J.P. Le Pape, "Metacontrol in logic programs in METALOG", 5th Generation Conf., Tokyo, Japan (Nov. 1984).

[Frib 84] L. Fribourg, "Oriented equational clauses as a programming language", J. Logic Programming, 2 (Oct. 1984) 165-177.

[Gour 83] J.S. Gourlay, "A mathematical framework for the investigation of testing", IEEE trans. Soft. Eng. SE-9, 6 (1983).

[GG 75] J.B. Goodenough and S.L. Gerhart, "Toward a theory of test data selection", IEEE Trans. Soft. Eng. SE-1, 2 (1975).

[GH 78] J. Guttag and J. Horning, "The algebraic specification of abstract data types", Acta Informatica 10, 1 (1978).

[GM 84] J. Goguen and J. Meseguer, "Equality, types, modules and generics for logic programming", Proc. 2nd Int. Logic Programming Conf., Uppsala, Sweden (July 1984) 115-125.

[Haml 75] R.G. Hamlet, "Testing programs with finite sets of data", Rept. No. TR-388, U. of Maryland, College Park (August 1975).

[Howd 76] W.E. Howden, "Reliability of path analysis strategies", IEEE Trans. Soft. Eng. SE-2, 3 (1976) 208-214.

[Howd 80] W.E. Howden, "Functional program testing", IEEE Trans. Soft. Eng. SE-6, 2 (1980) 162-169.

[Howd 82] W.E. Howden, "Weak mutation testing and completeness of test sets", IEEE Trans. Soft. Eng. SE-8, 4 (1982) 371-379.

[HS 85] J. Hsiang and M. Srivas, "A Prolog environment for developing and reasoning about data types", Proc. Coll. Soft. Eng., Berlin (1985), this volume.

[Komo 80] H.J. Komorowski, "Qlog - The software for prolog and logic programming", Proc. of the Logic Programming Workshop, Debrecen, Hungary (1980) 305-320.

[Nais 82] L. Naish, "An introduction to MU-PROLOG", Technical Rept., Dept. of Computer Science, U. of Melbourne (1982).

[Paul 83] J. Paul, "Approche pour une certification fonctionnelle de systèmes à partir de spécifications externes", Internal rept., CIT, Lannion, France (1983).

[SW 83] D. Sanella and M. Wirsing, "A kernel language for algebraic specification and implementation", Proc. Int. Conf. Foundations Computing Theory, Bergholm, Sweden (Aug. 1983).

[WC 80] L.J. White, E.J. Cohen, "A domain strategy for computer program testing", IEEE Trans. Soft. Eng. SE-6, 3 (1980) 247-257.

[WHH 80] M.R. Woodward, D. Hedley and M.A. Hennel, "Experience with path analysis and testing of programs", IEEE Trans. Soft. Eng. SE-6, 3 (1980) 278-285.

[WPP 83] M. Wirsing, P. Pepper, H. Partsch, W. Dosch and M. Broy, "On hierarchies of abstract data types", Acta Informatica 20, 1 (Oct. 1983).

[ZW 81] S.H. Zeil, L.J. White, "Sufficient test sets for path analysis testing strategy", Proc. 5th Int. Conf. Soft. Eng., San Diego, Calif. (March 1981) 184-191.

APPENDIX

EXAMPLE: SORTED LISTS

The sort of interest is the sort sorted-list.
The lower sorts are the integer and boolean sorts.

Specification of the type list of integer, with the operation sort:

specif sorted-list =
enrich bool, int *by*
sort list;
operations

el :		-> list	/* empty-list *constructor* */
ap :	list * int	-> list	/* append *constructor* */
sorted :	list	-> bool	
insert :	list * int	-> list	/* defined for a sorted list */

variables
L : list;
X, Y : int;
preconditions
/* The operation insert is used to insert an integer in a sorted list and to get as a result a sorted list. */
pre(insert,L,X) = (sorted(L) = true)
axioms
A1: sorted(el)=true
A2: sorted(ap(el,X))=true
A3: le(X,Y)=true => sorted(ap(ap(L,X),Y))=sorted(ap(L,X))
A4: le(X,Y)=false => sorted(ap(ap(L,X),Y))=false
A5: insert(el,X)=ap(el,X)
A6: le(X,Y)=true => insert(ap(L,X),Y)=ap(ap(L,X),Y)
A7: le(X,Y)=false => insert(ap(L,X),Y)=ap(insert(L,Y),X)

Specification of the integer type:

specif integer =
enrich bool *by*
sort int;
operations

0 :		-> int	/* *constructor* */
succ :	int	-> int	/* *constructor* */
le :	int * int	-> bool	

variables
X,Y : int;
axioms
A8: le(0,X) = true
A9: le(succ(X),0) = false
A10: le(succ(X),succ(Y)) = le(X,Y)

Translation of the specification of the integer type into PROLOG:

C8: le(0,X,true).
C9: le(succ(X),0,false).
C10: le(succ(X),succ(Y),B):- le(X,Y,B).

Translation of the specification of the sorted-list type into PROLOG:

C1: sorted(el,true).
C2: sorted(ap(el,X), true).
C3: sorted(ap(ap(L,X),Y),B):- le(X,Y,true), sorted(ap(L,X),B).
C4: sorted(ap(ap(L,X),Y),false):- le(X,Y,false).
C5: insert(el,X,ap(el,X)):- sorted(el,true).
C6: insert(ap(L,X),Y,ap(ap(L,X),Y)):- sorted(ap(L,X),true),le(X,Y,true).
C7: insert(ap(L,X),Y,ap(Z,X)):- sorted(ap(L,X),true),le(X,Y,false),insert(L,Y,Z).

Instantiation sets generated for sorted:

We suppose that integer and boolean sorts are tested.
* For A1, the instantiation sets generated are empty for any n because there is no variable in this axiom: $I_n = \{\}$, $\forall n$
Thus an acceptable test sets collection is: $T_n = \{(sorted(el)=true)\}$, $\forall n$

* For A2, there is no constraint on X. We make a uniformity hypothesis on integer and obtain the instantiation sets:
$I_n = \{<\text{meta-int}>\}$, $\forall n$
$T_n = \{(sorted(ap(el,X))=true), X \in I_n \}$, $\forall n$

* For A3, the instantiation sets are made of tuples $<L,X,Y>$. There is a constraint on X,Y: le(X,Y,true), solved in PROLOG with the goal ?-$le(X,Y,true)$.
PROLOG answers:
$$X_1 = 0, Y_1 = \_;$$
$$X_2 = succ(0), Y_2 = succ(\_);$$
...
$$X_{n+1} = succ^n(0), Y_{n+1} = succ^n(\_);$$
As there is no constraint on the variable L of list sort, we make a uniformity hypothesis and substitute a meta-constant for the variable of this sort. Thus we deduce for a level n the instantiation set:
$I_n = \{<\text{meta-list}_1,0,\text{meta-int}_1>,$
$<\text{meta-list}_2,succ(0),succ(\text{meta-int}_2>,$
...
$<\text{meta-list}_n,succ^{n-1}(0),succ^{n-1}(\text{meta-int}_n)>\}$
$T_n = \{(sorted(ap(ap(L,X),Y))=sorted(ap(L,X))), <L,X,Y> \in I_n \}$

* For A4, the instantiation sets are obtained in a similar way and we get for a level n:
$I_n = \{<\text{meta-list}_1,succ(\text{meta-int}_1),0>,$
$<\text{meta-list}_2,succ(succ(\text{meta-int}_2)), succ(0)>,$
...
$<\text{meta-list}_n,succ^n(\text{meta-int}_n), succ^{n-1}(0)>\}$
$T_n = \{(sorted(ap(ap(L,X),Y))=false), <L,X,Y> \in I_n \}$

Instantiation sets generated for insert:

• For A5, as the only variable in the axiom is X, we obtain:

$I_n = \{<\text{meta-int}>\}$, Vn

$T_n = \{(\text{insert}(\text{el},X)=\text{ap}(\text{el},X)), X \in I_n \}$, Vn

• For A6, an instantiation set is made of tuples: $<L,X,Y>$ with the constraint $\text{le}(X,Y,\text{true})$ on X and Y, and with the constraint $\text{sorted}(\text{ap}(L,X),\text{true})$ on L and X.
These constraints are solved with the goal: ?- *sorted(ap(L,X),true),le(X,Y,true)*.
PROLOG answers:

$L = \text{el}, X = 0, Y = \_;$

$L = \text{el}, X = \text{succ}(0); Y = \text{succ}(\_);$

...

These answers are infinite and L is always equal to el: we are in an infinite branch. With a standard PROLOG interpreter, we obtain the following instantiation set for level n:

$I_n = \{<\text{el},0,\text{meta-int}_1>,$

$<\text{el},\text{succ}(0), \text{succ}(\text{meta-int}_2)>,$

...

$<\text{el},\text{succ}^{n-1}(0), \text{succ}^{n-1}(\text{meta-int}_n)>\}$

$T_n = \{(\text{insert}(\text{ap}(L,X),Y) = \text{ap}(\text{ap}(L,X),Y)), <L,X,Y> \in I_n \}$

• For A7, the instantiation sets are obtained in a similar way with the goal:
?- *sorted(ap(L,X),true),le(X,Y,false)*.
We obtain the following instantiation set for level n:

$I_n = \{<\text{el},\text{succ}(\text{meta-int}_1),0>,$

$<\text{el},\text{succ}(\text{succ}(\text{meta-int}_2)),\text{succ}(0)>,$

...

$<\text{el},\text{succ}^n(\text{meta-int}_n),\text{succ}^{n-1}(0)>\}$

$T_n = \{(\text{insert}(\text{ap}(L,X),Y) = \text{ap}(\text{insert}(L,Y),X)), <L,X,Y> \in I_n \}$

A PROLOG Environment for
Developing and Reasoning about Data Types[1]

Jieh Hsiang   Mandayam K. Srivas
Department of Computer Science
State University of New York at Stony Brook
Stony Brook, NY 11794
U.S.A.

Abstract

PROLOG is a programming language based on first order logic. The feature that distinguishes PROLOG from most other programming languages is that the execution of PROLOG programs is based on subgoal reduction and unification. Unfortunately, the reliance on unification for execution has also inhibited PROLOG from utilizing some recently developed concepts in programming languages such as abstract data types. In this paper we introduce a discipline for incorporating abstract data types into PROLOG, and study the use of PROLOG as a uniform programming environment for the specification, implementation, and verification of PROLOG programs. We illustrate the application of the environment to the development of abstract data types in PROLOG.

In addition to producing executable specifications, the proposed discipline also provides automatic means of refining a specification into an implementation. We also present a PROLOG-based inductive theorem proving method for proving properties of data types and correctness of implementations.

1. Introduction

In this paper, we study the use of PROLOG as a uniform environment for the systematic development of data types in PROLOG. That is, its use for the specification, implementation and verification of data types represented and used as PROLOG programs.

The idea that PROLOG can naturally be used as a specification cum implementation language is well-known. It has been used in [Dav82] and [HaT82] for systematically developing PROLOG programs. However, none of these works address the formal development of abstract data types, nor do they provide proof facilities for verification. In order to incorporate all three aspects of data type development, our environment consists of a PROLOG interpreter augmented with three primitives - *Refine*, *Ver_Cond_Gen*, and *Ind_Prove*. *Refine* is a program transformation processor; *Ver_Cond_Gen* generates verification conditions that have to be proved to establish the correctness of a data type implementation; *Ind_Prove* is the theorem proving primitive that proves the correctness of the verification conditions and properties of PROLOG programs in general. We have implemented a system (in a version of CPROLOG for the VAX11-780 machine) that supports our methodology. The environment assists in performing the following activities in the development of data types.

[1]Research supported in part by the National Science Foundation under grants DCR-8401624 and DCR-8319066

(1) *The design and specification of abstract data types*: Our discipline requires the separation of the operations of data types ([GuH78], [GTW78]) into two categories: *constructors* - operations which uniquely define the terms in the domain of the data types, and *defined operations* - operations that are defined in terms of the constructors. Only the constructors are represented as functors while the defined operations are represented as predicates. Therefore a *specification* of a data type consists of PROLOG programs that define the defined operations as relations on the constructor terms. Such an approach not only eliminates the need for any special unification algorithm (as required by other approaches such as [Kor83] and [SuY84]), but also produces executable specifications.

(2) *Implementation of data types*: Since the specifications written using the aforementioned discipline are executable PROLOG programs, there is no need for a different implementation. However, sometimes for reasons of efficiency and convenience of representation, one would want to implement the data types (and their operations) differently. We propose methods (that are implemented by *Refine*) for mechanically deriving an implementation for a defined operation of a data type from its specification once an implementation for the constructors are given. The proposed discipline for building specification enables the transformation methods to be easily automated. The methods can also be used to transform a program that uses the specification of a data type into one that uses an implementation of the data type.

(3) *Proving Properties of Programs*: Data type verification includes mainly two aspects: (i) proving that the data types defined (as specifications) have the desired properties (such as associativity for *append*), and (ii) an implementation of the data type is correct with respect to the specification. If the implementation is derived automatically as described above, the correctness of the implementation is guaranteed as long as the implementation of the constructors is correct. If the user wishes to derive the implementation himself (manually), then to prove the correctness, the user has to specify the *representation invariant* and the *representation equivalence* that characterize the representation scheme used by the implementation. *Ver_Cond_Gen*, the verification condition generator, will then generate the verification conditions, which will, in turn, be proved with the help of *Ind_Prove*. The task of generating the verification conditions is considerably easier in PROLOG than in other program languages with verification capability since the verification conditions are representable in the same language.

In order to carry out the entire verification step in PROLOG, we introduce an new inductive theorem proving method. This method has the ability to prove universally quantified properties expressed in Horn clauses, in particular those which require structural induction. It is also tailored to utilize the existing PROLOG facilities such as backtracking, and can be easily built into the PROLOG machinery. While a detailed design of this PROLOG based inductive theorem prover is given in [HsS84a], in this paper we give an overview of the method, and use it to carry out the verification of programs in our environment.

AFFIRM [Mus80] and OBJ [GoT79] are two examples of (non-PROLOG based) systems built for the verification of abstract data types. Neither, however, has been able to unify the different phases of program development into one language framework. In AFFIRM the programs are written in Pascal while the statement of the verification conditions and their proofs are carried out in a framework based on rewrite rule theory [HuO80]. OBJ is a system for writing and testing algebraic program specifications. Although it can in principle be used as a programming language (since it allows algebraic specifications to be executed), it lacks the expressive power of a general purpose language. The important advantages of our system over the above term rewriting based systems are that (1) ours does not need a Knuth-Bendix type completion procedure, that is potentially non-terminating, for proving inductive theorems, and (2) ours can handle conditionally defined axioms more effectively.

The next section describes how abstract data types can be specified in PROLOG. Section 3 is concerned with implementation of abstract data types. It discusses several transformation techniques for transforming a specification of a data type into an implementation. Section 4 deals with the formulation and generation of the verification conditions for proving correctness of abstract data type implementations. Section 5 gives an overview of the inductive PROLOG theorem prover *Ind_Prove*. The last section has the concluding remarks.

2. Abstract Data Types and Their Specifications

2.1. Designing Data Types in PROLOG

A major issue that has to be addressed in building abstract data types into PROLOG is to determine how the operations of the data types should be specified. Two main approaches have been used for incorporating data types into PROLOG. The *predicate approach*, which is practiced commonly, represents all the operations of a data type as predicates on *List* and *Nat* (natural number) which are readily available in PROLOG. Such an approach treats all operations in a data type on a flat structure. The *functional approach* (egs., [Kor83], [SuY84]) encourages representing operations as functors. The axioms that the terms constructed using the operations satisfy are treated in the unification process by some additional mechanisms. The functional methods provide the convenience of having nested terms, but their additional unification mechanisms may become a source of inefficiency or, worse yet, they may change the semantics of the programs.

We use a hybrid approach. We partition the operation set of a data type into two groups: the *constructors* and the *defined operations* [HuH80]. The constructors are a set of operations that can generate every value of the data type *uniquely*. (Such a restriction excludes data types such as *Set* from our domain of application, since the constructors of *Set* do not construct values uniquely. However, if the constructors of the data type exhibit properties such as associativity and commutativity for which special purpose complete unification algorithms exist ([Sti81], [Fag84]), our method still applies provided such a special purpose unification algorithm is implemented in the PROLOG system.) The defined operations perform other interesting computations, and are defined in terms of the constructors. In our approach *only* the constructors are represented as functors, and the defined operations are represented as predicates. An n-ary defined operation $p(x_1, \cdots, x_n)$ is represented as the $(n+1)$-place predicate $p(x_1, \cdots, x_n, x_{n+1})$. Thus, in our system (functional) terms appearing in a PROLOG program contain only constructors of data types.

Consider the data type *List* that is commonly used in PROLOG. The constructors for *List* are the empty list [ ], and the *cons* operator denoted as $[A \mid L]$. All other operations on *List* can be specified in terms of the above constructors, and are considered as defined operations. As a second example, consider the data type *Tree* intended to model binary trees that can store arbitrary information in their nodes. *Tree* can be designed in PROLOG by choosing two new constructors *emptytree* and *mktree*: *emptytree* constructs an empty binary tree; *mktree*(L, N, R) is a ternary constructor that builds a binary tree with L and R as its left and right subtrees, and N as the label at its root. Predicates such as *ltree* and *rtree* that extract the left and the right subtree, and *isin* that checks the membership of a node in a tree, are some of the defined operations of *Tree*.

The most significant difference between our approach and functional approaches is that our method does not need a unification process different from the one in PROLOG. Most functional approaches require more elaborated unification procedures in order to unify terms which satisfy additional (functional) axioms. In paramodulation-type approaches, such as [Kor83], such a unification algorithm affects the efficiency considerably; in others, especially those that use term rewriting-based unification algorithms (such as [SuY84]), these unification algorithms may result in a change in semantics due to incomplete or infinite unification processes. (See [Hul80] for a discussion of unification algorithms for equational theories based on term rewriting.) Other significant advantages, all of which arise because of the separation of constructors from defined operations, of our approach over the other two approaches are that ours provides (1) the ability to successfully execute specifications of data types, (2) the ability to automatically transform specifications into implementations, and (3) the ability to use structural induction in a natural way while proving properties.

2.2. Specification of Data Types

The *Specification* of a data type consists of defining (as PROLOG programs) each of the defined operations as a relation on the constructor terms of the type. The specification of a data type is always executable because, firstly, it is a PROLOG program, and secondly, the constructor terms uniquely construct the values of the data type. For example, the operation *append* on *List* can be specified as follows.

Specification of append

append: List × *List* × *List*

append([ ], L, L).
append([X | $L1$], $L2$, [X | $L3$]) :- *append*($L1$, $L2$, $L3$).

As a second example, consider the data type *Tree* with a defined operation *isin* which checks the membership of a node inside a given tree. We assume that there exist data types *Node* and *Bool* (constructors *true* and *false*) specified elsewhere; *diff* is a predicate on nodes that checks syntactic inequality on nodes (egs., *diff*(X,X) fails, and *diff*(X,Y) succeeds where X and Y are unbound variables), and *or* is a *Bool* predicate. Then *isin* can be specified as a predicate relating the terms constructed out of the constructors of *Tree* as follows.

Specification of Tree

Functors	emptytree	:	$\rightarrow$	Tree
	mktree	:	Tree $\times$ Node $\times$ Tree $\rightarrow$	Tree

Predicate   isin   : Tree $\times$ Node $\times$ Boolean

isin (emptytree , E, false).
isin (mktree (L , N , R), N, true).
isin (mktree (L , N , R), E , B) :- diff(N , E), isin (L , E , B1)
                      isin (R , E , B2), or (B1, B2, B).

It is important to note that the purpose of our methodology is to help structure PROLOG programs hierarchically using the data abstraction discipline. Our environment does not perform type checking or type inference [Mis84] in PROLOG. For instance, the environment does not ensure that the arguments to an invocation of *append* are *List* objects. Another issue that we do not address is parameterized data types ([Ehr81], [Gog82], [Pad82]).

3. Implementation of Data Types

Since the specifications of data types written using our discipline are executable PROLOG programs, there is no need for a different implementation. However, sometimes for reasons of efficiency and convenience of representation, one might want to implement the data types (and their operators) differently. The user can implement a data type either manually, or automatically with the help of *Refine*.

3.1. Manual Implementation

Implementing a data type (T) consists of (i) picking a representation scheme for the objects of T in terms of the objects of a chosen *representation* type R, and (ii) implementing the constructors and defined operations of T in terms of the constructors and defined operations of R. We discuss the two approaches to implementation in the next two sections.

Suppose we want to implement *Tree* using a sequential representation scheme in which a tree T is represented as a pair (list) of lists $[L_1, L_2]$. L_1 is the in-order enumeration of the nodes of T; L_2 is a list that keeps track of the position of the root of every subtree of T in the in-order enumeration of the nodes of that subtree. In generating L_2 the subtrees of T are themselves considered in a preorder sequence. Such a representation scheme is convenient for checking membership in a tree as well as decomposing trees into and building trees from smaller ones. A few example representations are given below.

$T_1 = emptytree$	[[ ], [ ]]
$T_2 = mktree(T_1, \; C, \; T_1)$	[[C], [1]]
$T_3 = mktree(T_2, \; B, \; T_2)$	[[C B C], [2 1 1]]
$T_4 = mktree(T_3, \; A, \; mktree(T_1, \; E, \; T_1))$	[[C B C A E], [4 2 1 1 1]]

The PROLOG program shown below gives an implementation for *isin* based on the above representation scheme. Note that the implementation is more efficient than the specification of *isin*, because in the latter a given node would be searched in the right subtree even if it was already located in the left subtree. In the following the predicate that implements an operation of *Tree* uses the name of the operation in uppercase so that the correspondence between them is apparent. (We use this convention throughout the paper for convenience although PROLOG does not allow predicate names to begin with an upper case letter.) The implementation also assumes the existence of a data type *Nat* (for natural numbers) with constructors *zero* and *plus* 1.

Implementation of Tree

EMPTYTREE ([[ ], [ ]]).

MKTREE ([[ ], [ ]], N, [$R\,1$, $R\,2$], [[$N \mid R\,1$], [$1 \mid R\,2$]]).
MKTREE ([[$X\,1 \mid L\,1$], [$X\,2 \mid L\,2$]], N, [$R\,1$, $R\,2$], [[$X\,1 \mid T\,1$], [I, $X\,2 \mid T\,2$]]):-
$\qquad$ *MKTREE* ([$L\,1$, $L\,2$], N, [$R\,1$, $R\,2$], [$T\,1$, [$J \mid T\,2$]]), $I = plus\,1(J)$.

ISIN ([[ ], $R\,1$], X, *false*).
ISIN ([[$X\,1 \mid L\,1$], $R\,1$], $X\,1$, *true*).
ISIN ([[$X\,1 \mid L\,1$], $R\,1$], Y, B) :- *diff*($X\,1$, Y), *ISIN* ([$L\,1$, $R\,1$], Y, B).

3.2. Automatic Transformation of Specifications

Another way to obtain an implementation is by automatically transforming the specification. We refer to an implementation obtained in this fashion a *direct implementation* since they are obtained directly from a specification. We present two methods for transforming a specification into an implementation, both of which are incorporated into *Refine* in our environment. Both the methods assume that there exist implementations (which the user is expected to furnish) for a small subset of operations of the data type, and produce implementation for the rest of the operations. The first method assumes the existence of implementations for the constructors of the type, and produces implementation for each of the defined operations. The second method assumes the existence of implementations for the constructors as well as a (predefined) set of basic defined operations, and derives implementations for the rest of the defined operations in terms of the former. A direct implementation derived using the second method is usually more efficient than the one derived by the first one because we have a larger (and a more versatile) set of predicates that can be used as primitives in the direct implementation. The two methods are described below.

Although a direct implementation might not always be as efficient as a user defined implementation, it is still useful because it is guaranteed to be correct provided the implementation of the operations in terms of which the direct implementation is derived is correct. A direct implementation can be used to test a given representation scheme before designing an implementation that is more efficient but also more intricate than the direct implementation.

Note that the methods of transformation given below can very well be used to refine a program that uses the specification of a data type to one that uses an implementation of the data type. This is because in our method the formalism of a program that uses the specification of a data type is no different from that of the specification itself.

3.2.1. Method 1

A defined operation (predicate) p of a data type T is specified as a relation on the constructor terms of T. The clauses in the specification of p contain the constructors and the defined operations of T. An implementation of p has to define a predicate P that expresses a relation on the constructor terms of the representation type R. Thus, one way of transforming a specification of p into an implementation is the following: Replace the constructors and defined predicates of T in every clause in the specification by the predicates implementing them. For a defined operation the replacement is trivial since both the operation and its implementation take the form of predicates. For a constructor the replacement is not so obvious because a constructor, which is a functor in specification, appears as a predicate in the implementation. Also, a constructor may appear as a part of a nested term.

A constructor term has to be "flattened" before the constructors are replaced by their corresponding implementing predicate. For example, a constructor term $f(g(X), h(Y))$ is replaced by a new variable Z, and the conjunction of predicates $F(X1, Y1, Z), G(X, X1), H(Y, Y1)$ is prefixed to the body of the clause in which the constructor term appears. (F, G, and H are the predicates implementing the constructors f, g, and h, respectively.) Thus, a clause of the form

$$p(f(g(X), h(Y)), L) :- q(X, Y, L),$$

where p and q are two defined operations of T is transformed into the following clause:

$$P(Z, L) :- F(X1, Y1, Z), G(X, X1), H(Y, Y1), Q(X, Y, L).$$

There is, however, one problem with the above transformation. The execution of the transformed clause can be quite inefficient. This is especially so when the representation scheme is such that there are several different values of R representing the same value of T. In such a case there can be several different values for X and Y for a given Z such that the conjunction of the predicates F, G, and H is satisfiable in the above clause. The behavior of Q is identical on each of the possible values of X and Y because (1) these values are equivalent representations of Z, and (2) the predicates implementing the operations of T are congruent with respect to the class of equivalent representations. However, an execution of the above program in PROLOG would unnecessarily consider each of these values while backtracking. This could even cause infinite computation if the class of equivalent representations of an abstract value is infinite. The above problem can be avoided by fixing, with an appropriate use of "cut", the instantiations generated for X and Y at the end of the processing of the conjunction of predicates replacing the constructor term. One way of doing this is to substitute a new goal $newp(X, Y, Z)$, where $newp$ is a predicate symbol that does not clash with any other symbols in use, for the conjunction of predicates obtained by flattening the constructor term. $Newp$ is defined to be the conjunction of predicates followed by a "cut". Hence, we transform the clause shown above into the following two clauses.

$$P(Z, L) :- newp(X, Y, Z), Q(X, Y, L).$$
$$newp(X, Y, Z) :- F(X1, Y1, Z), G(X, X1), H(Y, Y1), !.$$

It should be noted that the introduction of "cut" as described above is completely automatic, and is not left to the discretion of the user. Although the implementation derived is not in pure PROLOG, the semantics of the program will not be changed. This is because (1) the constructors of T create the values of T uniquely, and (2) the instantiations discarded by the use of "cut" are equivalent to (with respect to a particular value of T) the first instantiations generated by *newp*. Note that condition (1) has to be satisfied for the transformation to work. The reason for this is explained at the end of the section.

A precise description of the transförmation steps to be performed on every clause in the specification is given below:

(1) *Constructor replacement*: Every constructor term of *t* that appears in the clause is subjected to the following constructor-replacement steps.

    (a) *Flatten* the term *t* into a conjunction of predicates $\overline{G}$ as informally illustrated above. Let $X_1, \cdots, X_n$ be the variables in *t*, and Z be the new variable in G that the whole term stands for.

    (b) Replace every occurrence of *t* in the clause by Z.

    (c) Add the new goal $newpred(X_1, \cdots, X_n, Z)$ to the front of the body of the clause, where *newpred* is a new predicate symbol (chosen so that it does not clash with any existing predicate symbol in the program) defined by the clause given in step (d) to follow.

    (d) Add the following new clause to the program: $newpred(X_1, \cdots, X_n, Z) :- \overline{G}, !$.

(2) *Defined operation replacement*: Every occurrence of a defined operation of the data type (such as, *isin*) is replaced by its corresponding implementing predicate (*ISIN*, in our example).

For example, an application of the above transformation steps on the specification of *isin* would result in the direct implementation shown below.

A Direct Implementation of Isin

$ISIN(T, E, false) :- newpred\,1(T)$.
$ISIN(T, N, true) :- newpred\,2(L, N, R, T)$.
$ISIN(T, E, B) :- newpred\,3(L, N, R, T), diff(N, E)$,
      $ISIN(L, E, B1), ISIN(R, E, B2), or(B1, B2, B)$.

$newpred\,1(T) :- EMPTYTREE(T), !$.
$newpred\,2(L, N, R, T) :- MKTREE(L, N, R, T), !$.
$newpred\,3(L, N, R, T) :- MKTREE(L, N, R, T), !$.

This kind of mechanical transformation cannot be applied in a system like FUNLOG ([SuY84]) for transforming FUNLOG programs into PROLOG programs without nested terms. This is because terms in FUNLOG may contain, as functors, constructors as well as defined operations of data types. Hence, the terms that are being transformed have an equivalence relation (that is not identity) defined on them by a set of axioms. This can create problems when the *semantic unification* (used in [SuY84]) of terms results in more than one unifier. In such a case the corresponding transformed PROLOG program can run into an infinite loop while trying to backtrack. For instance, consider the following clause in FUNLOG, and its corresponding translation by *Refine* into PROLOG. *f* and *g* are defined functions on *Integer* whose predicate counterparts are F and G.

$$p\left(f\left(g\left(X\right)\right)\right) :- q\left(X\right). \qquad \text{(In FUNLOG)}$$
$$p\left(Z\right) :- F\left(X1, Z\right), G\left(X, X1\right), q\left(X\right). \qquad \text{(Transformed into PROLOG)}$$

Let us suppose that $f\left(g\left(X\right)\right) = 1$ has more than one unifier, one of which satisfies q. (This can happen if f and g are many-to-one.) Then, the execution of the query $p\left(1\right)$ may run into an infinite loop in the PROLOG program while the FUNLOG program gives an answer. This can happen if the first value for $X1$ generated by PROLOG does not give the right value for X, and g maps infinitely many values to the same value. In this case PROLOG never gets an opportunity to backtrack to F to get an alternate value for $X1$ since it is busy resatisfying G infinitely many times. Note that in this case one cannot introduce "cut" as described earlier because different possible instantiations generated for X and $X1$ in this case are not equivalent.

3.2.2. Method 2

As mentioned earlier, method 2 produces an implementation assuming that there exist implementations for the constructors and a special set of basic defined operations, called the *decomposers* and *constructor-checkers*, of the type. Hence, this method can only be applied to a special class of data types, called *expressively rich* data types [KaS80], that have the decomposers and constructor-checkers as part of their operation set.

To automate this method it is necessary to identify the operations of the type that can serve as the decomposers and the constructor-checkers of the type. In general, we need a theorem prover for this purpose because it is necessary to check if an operation satisfies the properties that characterize a decomposer (or a constructor-checker). Since our environment has the required theorem proving ability (in the form of *Ind_Prove*) the method can be mechanized without much difficulty.

The decomposers and constructor-checkers of a type permit one to decompose and uniquely determine the structure of the constructor terms of the type. For example, the data type *Tree* introduced earlier would become expressively rich when augmented with the operation *components* (extracts the left subtree, the right subtree, and the root of the tree), *isempty* (checks if a tree is empty), and *isnonempty* (checks if a tree is nonempty). The operation *components*, acts as the decomposer; *isempty* and *isnonempty* can be used as constructor-checkers for the constructors *emptytree* and *mktree*, respectively. The specifications and implementations of these operations are given in Appendix I.

This method derives an implementation for a defined operation with respect to the decomposers and constructor-checkers. It is similar to the previous method except that the constructor replacement is done in terms of the decomposers and constructor-checkers. More details of the method can be found in [HsS84b].

4. Expressing Properties to be Proved

Two kinds of properties concerning data types need to be verified: (1) properties that a specification ought to satisfy, and (2) correctness of an implementation of a data type. Since our theorem prover primitive *Ind_Prove* is within the PROLOG framework, these properties should be formulated as PROLOG clauses as well. While properties in (1) have to be given by the user manually, the verification conditions in (2) can be generated with the assistance of another primitive, *Ver_Cond_Gen* of our system.

Let the property to be proved be $\forall \overline{X} \phi(\overline{X})$, where $\phi(\overline{X})$ is the Horn clause $\forall \overline{Z}(P_1(\overline{X}, \overline{Z}) \wedge \cdots \wedge P_n(\overline{X}, \overline{Z}) \supset Q(\overline{X}, \overline{Z}))$. The formula $\phi(\overline{X})$ is converted into the PROLOG clause:

$$prop(\overline{X}) :- P_1(\overline{X}, \overline{Z}), \cdots, P_n(\overline{X}, \overline{Z}), Q(\overline{X}, \overline{Z}).$$

with the consequent $Q(\overline{X}, \overline{Z})$ as the last subgoal to be satisfied. *Prop* will be used only as an input to the theorem prover *Ind_Prove*, and not for any other purposes.

Note that the logical meaning of *prop* is not tautologically equivalent to ϕ. This discrepancy does not have any deleterious effect because *prop* is only used as a means of representing the property to be proved and not as a predicate in any other clause. Moreover, our theorem prover requires the antecedents (P_i's) to be processed before the consequent (Q). The left-to-right evaluation strategy of PROLOG and the order of predicates in *prop* accomplish this ordering requirement automatically.

4.1. Correctness of Abstract Data Types

Proving the correctness of an implementation of a data type consists of first specifying the intended representation scheme, and then showing that the algebra defined by the specification is an homomorphic image of the one defined by the implementation under the intended representation scheme.

The representation scheme is specified by means of two predicates: *representation invariant*, and *representation equivalence*. The representation invariant characterizes the (sub)set of values (of the representation type) that are permitted to represent the abstract values. The representation equivalence characterizes an equivalence relation that relates all valid representation values representing the same abstract value. In the *Tree* implementation, for example, the representation invariant is expressed in two parts (for convenience) both of which have to be satisfied. *Inv* 1 expresses the constraint that "if a pair of lists $[L_1, L_2]$ is a valid representation of a tree then L_1 and L_2 have the same length". *Inv* 2 expresses the constraint necessary on the numbers in L_2: the first element in L_2 which denotes the position of the root in L_1 has to be a number between 1 and the length of L_2; the two segments of L_2 that represent the two subtrees should also satisfy this constraint. The representation equivalence in this case is just "equality on pairs of lists" because every tree has a unique representation as a pair of lists.

> $inv\ 1([\ ],\ [\ ],\ true\ )$.
> $inv\ 1([X\ 1\ |\ L\ 1],\ [X\ 2\ |\ L\ 2],\ true\ ) :- inv\ 1(L\ 1, L\ 2, true\ )$.
> $inv\ 1([\ ],[X\ 2\ |\ L\ 2],\ false)$.
> $inv\ 1([X\ 1\ |\ L\ 1],\ [\ ],\ false)$.
>
> $inv\ 2([\ ],\ true\ )$.
> $inv\ 2([X\ |\ L],\ true\ ) :- length([X\ |\ L],\ N),\ ge(X,\ 1),\ ge(N,\ X),$
> $\qquad\qquad prefix(L,\ X,\ L\ 1),\ postfix(L,\ X,\ L\ 2),$
> $\qquad\qquad inv\ 2(L\ 1,\ true\ ),\ inv\ 2(L\ 2,\ true\ )$.
>
> $repequiv([A\ 1,\ A\ 2],\ [B\ 1,\ B\ 2],\ true\ ) :- A\ 1 = A\ 2,\ B\ 1 = B\ 2$.

repequiv ([A 1, A 2], [B 1, B 2], *false*) :- *diff*(A 1, A 2), B 1 ≠ B 2.
repequiv ([A 1, A 2], [B 1, B 2], *false*) :- A 1 = A 2, B 1 ≠ B 2.
repequiv ([A 1, A 2], [B 1, B 2], *false*) :- *diff*(A 1, A 2), B 1 = B 2.

Given the specification of a data type, an implementation of it, and a definition of the representation invariant and representation equivalence, *Ver_Cond_Gen* generates the verification conditions as described below.

Verification Conditions for the Constructors

These conditions ensure that the values constructed using the predicates implementing the constructors satisfy the invariant. Thus, there is a verification condition for every predicate implementing a constructor that says "if the arguments to the predicate satisfy the invariant, then so does the value constructed by the predicate". For example, the verification conditions which ensure that the implementation satisfies the constraint expressed by *inv* 1 is given below.

invprop 1(L 1, L 2) :- *EMPTYTREE* ([L 1, L 2]), *inv* 1(L 1, L 2, B), B =*true* .
invprop 2(L 1, L 2, R 1, R 2) :-
        inv 1(L 1, L 2, *true*), *inv* 1(R 1, R 2, *true*),
        MKTREE ([L 1, L 2], N , [R 1, R 2], [T 1, T 2]), *inv* 1(T 1, T 2, B), B =*true* .

Just as a reminder, *invprop* 1 and *invprop* 2 are two clauses representing properties to be proved by the theorem prover. The logical meaning corresponding to *invprop* 1 is:

$$EMPTYTREE ([L\ 1,\ L\ 2]) \wedge inv\ 1(L\ 1,\ L\ 2,\ B) \supset B = true ,$$

where all the variables are universally quantified.

Verification Conditions for the Defined Operations

These conditions ensure that the implementation satisfies the homomorphism property. There is a verification condition corresponding to every clause in the specification of a defined operation. The verification condition for each clause is derived from the clause as follows:

(1) Subject every constructor term in the clause to the following steps:
   (a) Flatten the constructor term, and attach the resulting conjunction of predicates to the body of the clause. (Same as Step 1.a in Section 3.2.1.)
   (b) Replace every occurrence of the term by a new variable Z . (Same as Step 1.b in Section 3.2.1.)

(2) Replace every defined operation in the clause by its corresponding implementing predicate. (Same as Step 2 in Section 3.2.1.)

(3) Replace every equality on the representation values by the representation equivalence.

(4) Express the logical implication characterized by the PROLOG clause as a conjunction of goals according to the form required by *Ind_Prove* .

The verification conditions generated by *Ver_Cond_Gen* for the operations *isin* of *Tree* are given below, recall that *isin* is defined as:

isin (*emptytree* , *E* , *false*).
isin (*mktree* (*L* , *N* , *R*) , *N* , *true*).
isin (*mktree* (*L* , *N* , *R*) , *E* , *B*) :- *diff*(*N* , *E*), *isin* (*L* , *E* , *B* 1)
$\qquad$ *isin* (*R* , *E* , *B* 2), *or* (*B* 1, *B* 2, *B*).

Verification Conditions for ISIN

prop 1(*L* 1, *R* 1, *E*) :-
$\qquad$ *EMPTYTREE* ([*L* 1, *R* 1]), *ISIN* ([*L* 1, *R* 1], *E* , *B*), *B* = *false*.
prop 2(*L* 1, *R* 1, *N* , *L* 2, *R* 2, *N*) :-
$\qquad$ *MKTREE* ([*L* 1, *R* 1], *N* , [*L* 2, *R* 2], *T*), *ISIN* (*T* , *N* , *B*), *B* = *true*
prop 3(*L* 1, *R* 1, *N* , *R* 2, *L* 2, *E*) :-
$\qquad$ *MKTREE* ([*L* 1, *R* 1], *N* , [*L* 2, *R* 2], *T*), *ISIN* (*T* , *N* Result 1),
$\qquad$ *diff*(*N* , *E*), *ISIN* ([*L* 1, *R* 1], *E* , *B* 1), *ISIN* ([*L* 2, *R* 2], *E* , *B* 2),
$\qquad$ *or* (*B* 1, *B* 2, Result 2), Result 1 = Result 2.

5. The Theorem Prover Ind_Prove

In this section we present a brief and informal description of the theorem proving method used in the verification phase of the environment. A more detailed description can be found in [HsS84a].

The main task that our theorem prover needs to perform is to prove properties with universally quantified variables. PROLOG, which can be regarded as a prover for proving *existentially* quantified properties, is unable to fulfill this task. The conventional way of dealing with universally quantified variables in a refutational-type theorem prover (such as PROLOG) is to treat them as skolem constants (after negating the target sentence, of course) (e.g. [Sti84]). Such a method does not work satisfactorily if the domain of variables are defined inductively (such as *List*) since skolem constants cannot be unified with any of the constructors.

We solve this problem by introducing a deductive theorem proving method for first order inductive theory representable in Horn clauses. The basic inference mechanism in the theorem prover is backward deduction, the same as in PROLOG. The first major notion we introduce is a way of handling unsatisfiable goals whose unsatisfiability is due to the appearance of skolem constants. For example, given a goal is *append* (*sk* ,[ ], *X*), where *sk* is a skolem constant, *append* (*sk* ,[ ], *X*) is not satisfiable since *sk* unifies with neither [ ] nor [*A* | *L*]. However, we know that this goal *should* be satisfiable since *sk* , being a list, has to be either [ ] or [*A* | *L*] for some *A* and *L* . We handle this problem by delaying the evaluation of this goal until later by temporarily unifying *X* with a list *l* which satisfies *append* (*sk* ,[ ], *l*), without worrying about what *l* really is. In our notation, *X* is unified with Ω(*l* : *append* (*sk* ,[ ], *l*)). This method of delaying the evaluation of goals and binding variables is called Ω-*binding* , and *append* (*sk* ,[ ], *l*) is called the Ω-*constraint* of *X* . A goal which can be satisfied in such a way is called Ω-*satisfiable* . A similar notion has also been used by Kornfeld ([Kor83]) for enriching the unification to include equational axioms.

At the end of processing all the goals in the theorem to be proved (expressed as a Horn clause), the Ω-constraints will be put together in a certain way to produce a *Lemma* . The need of Ω-binding arises because the universally quantified variables have to be skolemized.

However, Ω-binding does not *solve* the problem created by skolemization but merely postpones the time of decision making to when the lemma is generated. Therefore it is important to have some mechanism for ensuring that the Ω-constraints thus generated are indeed "simpler" than the original problem. One way to achieve that is to delay the time of skolemization. For this purpose, we introduce a technique called *skolemize by need*. Under this method, we treat universally quantified variables as free variables, and skolemize them only when necessary (that is, when a value for that variable has to be determined). This technique produces three effects: (1) It prevents the variables from being instantiated indefinitely. (2) The variables are skolemized, automatically, according to the inductive structures of the constructing terms. (3) The Ω-bindings produced by such process usually contain unsatisfiable goals which are simpler than the original goals, and these unsatisfiable goals will sometimes lead to appropriate induction hypothesis. Because of the delaying of skolemization, the skolem constants so produced no longer cover the whole domain over which the universally quantified variables are defined. Therefore we also provide, in the prover, a mechanism of generating a complete set of skolemizations (not just one) to ensure the completeness. The method is very similar to the PROLOG backtracking mechanism, only we are more selective of the choice points for backtracking. We also use a *limited forward chaining* mechanism for producing potential induction hypothesis from the Ω-constraints.

The prover can be (and has been) built without too much difficulty in PROLOG since PROLOG already provides the basic mechanisms such as unification and backward deduction. However, we do need to add an additional *occur check* mechanism in PROLOG ([Pla84]) to avoid overlapping of variables which may lead to inconsistency.

Due to the lack of space, we refer the interested readers to [HsS84a] for a detailed description of the theorem proving method. Some examples of the proofs are given in Appendix II.

6. Conclusions

We have investigated the use of PROLOG as a uniform environment to carry out all three phases - specification, implementation, and verification - of systematic program development. For the specification part, we have proposed a methodology of designing data types in PROLOG that represents the constructors as functors and the defined operations as predicates. This approach to data types not only provides executable specifications, but also eliminates the need for an elaborate unification algorithm encountered in the other approaches. We have given several transformation techniques for transforming specifications into implementations. In particular, we have presented an automatic transformation method in which "cut" is produced mechanically without changing the semantics of the program. In order to verify PROLOG programs within PROLOG's own mechanism, we developed a deductive theorem proving method for the first order inductive theory representable in Horn clauses. This theorem prover, which can be easily incorporated into PROLOG, enables us to prove universally quantified inductive properties of PROLOG programs. It also does not employ, explicitly, any inductive inference rule. Methods for generating verification conditions are also given.

There is plenty of scope for further work in the area. In the data type development area we need to study more about the tradeoffs involved in representing the operations in functional style as opposed to in a predicate style. It would be interesting to extend our transformation method to data types (such as *Set*) where the constructors exhibit standard properties such as associativity and commutativity. It appears that when the equivalence class of constructor terms defined by the properties is finite, the transformation method can be extended by generating one clause for every term in the equivalence class. It would also be interesting to see if more sophisticated transformation techniques ([Sri83]) can be used to obtain better forms of direct implementation. In the theorem proving area we need to extend the form of the properties that can be proved beyond the Horn clause form that can currently be handled, such as incorporating Stickel's complete inference rule for PROLOG ([Sti84]) into our system. It is also necessary to study if the method can be used to disprove properties.

Acknowledgements

We are thankful to Eric Johnson, C. Mohan, Jean-Luc Remy, and David S. Warren for their helpful comments on earlier drafts of the paper.

1. References

[Dav82]   R. E. Davis, "Runnable Specification as a Design Tool", in *Logic Programming*, K. L. Clark and S. Tarnlund, (eds.), Academic Press, January 1982, 141-152.

[Ehr81]   H. Ehrig, "Algebraic Theory of Parameterized Specifications with Requirements", *6th CAAP*, 1981.

[Fag84]   F. Fages, "Associative-Commutative Unification", *7th Conf. on Automated Deduction*, Nappa Valley, CA, May, 1984, 194-208.

[GTW78]   J. A. Goguen, J. W. Thatcher and E. G. Wagner, "Initial Algebra Approach to the Specification, Correctness, and Implementation of Abstract Data Types", in *Current Trends in Programming Methodology*, vol. IV Data Structuring, R. T. Yeh, (ed.), Prentice Hall (Automatic Computation Series), Englewood Cliffs, NJ, 1978.

[GoT79]   J. A. Goguen and J. J. Tardo, "An Introduction to OBJ: A Language for Writing and Testing Formal Algebraic Program Specifications", *Proceedings of the Conference on Specification of Reliable Software*, Cambridge, MA 02139, 1979.

[Gog82]   J. A. Goguen, "Parameterized Programming", *Proceedings of the Workshop on Reusability in Programming*, 1982.

[GuH78]   J. V. Guttag and J. J. Horning, "The Algebraic Specification of Abstract Data Types", *Acta Informatica*, **10**, 1 (1978), 27-52.

[HaT82]   A. Hansson and S. Tarnlund, "Program Transformation by Data Structure", in *Logic Programming*, K. L. Clark and S. Tarnlund, (eds.), Academic Press, January 1982, 141-152.

[HsS84a] J. Hsiang and M. K. Srivas, "On Proving First Order Inductive Properties in Horn Clauses", Technical Report 84/75, SUNY at Stony Brook, Stony Brook, NY 11794, 1984.

[HsS84b] J. Hsiang and M. K. Srivas, "A PROLOG Environment for Developing and Reasoning about Data Types", Technical Report 84/074, SUNY at Stony Brook, Stony Brook, NY 11794, 1984.

[HuH80] G. Huet and J. M. Hullot, "Proofs by Induction in Equational Theories with Constructors", *21st IEEE Symposium on Foundations of Computer Science*, 1980, 797-821.

[HuO80] G. Huet and D. C. Oppen, "Equations and Rewrite Rules: A Survey", in *Formal Languages: Perspectives and Open Problems*, R. Book, (ed.), Academic Press, 1980.

[Hul80] J. M. Hullot, "Canonical Forms and Unification", *5th Conference on Automated Deduction*, Les Arcs, France, 1980, 318-334.

[KaS80] D. Kapur and M. K. Srivas, "Expressiveness of the Operation Set of a Data Abstraction", *Seventh Annual ACM Symposium on Principles of Programming Languages*, Las Vegas, Nevada, January 28-30, 1980, 139-153.

[Kor83] W. A. Kornfeld, "Equality in Prolog", *Proc. 8th IJCAI*, Karlsruhe, Germany, August 1983, 514-519.

[Mis84] P. Mishra, "Towards a Theory of Types in Prolog", *1984 International Symposium on Logic Programming*, Atlantic City, New Jersey, Feb. 6-9, 1984, 289-298.

[Mus80] D. R. Musser, "Abstract Data Types in the AFFIRM System", *IEEE*, **1**, 6 (Jan. 1980), .

[Pad82] P. Padawitz, "Correctness, Completeness and Consistency of Equational Data Type Specifications", in *Ph.D. Thesis,*, Technische Universitat, Berlin, 1982.

[Pla84] D. A. Plaisted, "The Occur-Check Problem in Prolog", *1984 International Symposium on Logic Programming*, Atlantic City, New Jersey, Feb. 6-9, 1984, 272-280.

[Sri83] M. K. Srivas, "A Rewrite Rule Based Approach to Program Transformation", *The Rewrite Rule Laboratory Workshop*, Schenectady, NY 12345, September 1983.

[Sti81] M. E. Stickel, "A Unification Algorithm for Associative-Commutative Functions", *J. ACM*, **28**, (1981), 233-264.

[Sti84] M. E. Stickel, "A Prolog Technology Theorem Prover", *1984 International Symposium on Logic Programming*, Atlantic City, New Jersey, Feb. 6-9, 1984, 212-219.

[SuY84] P. A. Subrahmanyam and J. You, "Conceptual Basis and Evaluation Strategies for Integrating Functional and Logic Programming", *1984 International Symposium on Logic Programming*, Atlantic City, New Jersey, February 6-9, 1984, 144-153.

Appendix I

Specification of Tree

Constructors

> $emptytree: \rightarrow Tree$
>
> $mktree: Tree \times Node \times Tree \rightarrow Tree$

Defined Operations

> $components: Tree \times Tree \times Node \times Tree$
>
> $isempty \qquad : Tree \times Boolean$
>
> $isnonempty: Tree \times Boolean$
>
> $isin \qquad : Tree \times Node \times Boolean$
>
> $components\,(emptytree\,,\ error\,,\ error\,,\ error\,)$.
>
> $components\,(mktree\,(L\,,\ N\,,\ R\,),\ L\,,\ N\,,\ R\,)$.
>
> $isempty\,(emptytree\,,\ true\,)$.
>
> $isempty\,(mktree\,(L\,,\ N\,,\ R\,),\ false\,)$.
>
> $isnonempty\,(emptytree\,,\ false)$.
>
> $isnonempty\,(mktree\,(L\,,\ N\,,\ R\,),\ true\,)$.
>
> $isin\,(emptytree\,,\ E\,,\ false)$.
>
> $isin\,(mktree\,(L\,,\ N\,,\ R\,),\ N\,,\ true\,)$.
>
> $isin\,(mktree\,(L\,,\ N\,,\ R\,),\ E\,,\ B\,) :- diff(N,\ E),\ isin\,(L\,,\ E\,,\ B_1)$
>
> $\qquad\qquad\qquad\qquad\qquad\quad isin\,(R\,,\ E\,,\ B_2),\ or\,(B_1,\ B_2,\ B\,)$.

Implementation of Tree

> $EMPTYTREE\,([[\ ],\ [\ ]])$.
>
> $MKTREE$ and $ISIN$ are given in Section 3.1.
>
> $ISEMPTY\,([[\ ],\ [\ ]],\ true\,)$.
>
> $ISEMPTY\,([X\ |\ L],\ [I\ |\ R\,]],\ false)$.
>
> $ISNONEMPTY\,([[\ ],\ [\ ]],\ false)$.
>
> $ISNONEMPTY\,([X\ |\ L],\ [I\ |\ R\,]],\ true\,)$.
>
> $COMPONENTS\,(T\,,\ Left\,,\ N\,,\ Right\,) :-$
>
> $\qquad LTREE\,(T\,,\ Left\,),\ NODEOF\,(T\,,\ N\,),\ RTREE\,(T\,,\ Right\,)$.
>
> $LTREE\,([[\ ],\ [\ ]],\ error\,)$.
>
> $LTREE\,([L_1,\ [I\ |\ L_2]],\ [T_1,\ T_2]) :-$
>
> $\qquad prefixof(L_1,I,\ T_1),\ prefixof(L_2,I,\ T_2)$.
>
> {$prefixof(L,I,\ T)$ *extracts a list of length I-1 at the head of L*}
>
> $RTREE\,([[\ ],\ [\ ]],\ error\,)$.
>
> $RTREE\,([L_1,\ [I\ |\ L_2]],\ [T_1,\ T_2]) :-$
>
> $\qquad postfixof(L_1,I,\ T_1),\ postfixof(L_2,I,\ T_2)$.
>
> {$postfixof(L,I,\ T)$ *extracts the tail of L starting from (I+1)th element*}

$NODEOF([[\ ],[\ ]],\ error)$.
$NODEOF([L,[I\mid R]],N):-$ $ithelementof(L,I,N)$.
$\{ithelementof(L,I,N)$ $checks$ if the ith $element$ of L is $N.\}$

Appendix II

In the following we show the proof of some of the verification conditions (derived in section 4) for the implementation of *Tree*. We present the proof of *invprop* 2 and *prop* 3 for the implementation of *isin*. The prover generates a set of instantiations, each with a *premise* (further constraint on the instantiations), and a *lemma*. Assuming that the instantiation is $\overline{X}_0$, the logical interpretation of the triplet is:

For every $\overline{X}_0$ which also satisfies *Premise*, if *Lemma* is true, then *prop* $(\overline{X}_0)$ is true.

1. Proof of Invprop2

In this case the proof generates a well-spanned set of four instantiations for the input variables. For the first and second instantiation the lemma generated is *true*. For the third and the fourth case, the lemma generated is an instance (for smaller argument values) of the property being proved, and hence forms the induction hypothesis.

$Invprop$ $2(L_1,L_2,R_1,R_2):-$
  inv $1(L_1,L_2,true)$, inv $1(R_1,R_2,true)$,
  $MKTREE([L_1,L_2],N,[R_1,R_2],[T_1,T_2])$, inv $1(T_1,T_2,B)$, $B=true$.

Instantiations	Premise	Lemma
$([\ ],[\ ],[\ ],[\ ])$	true	true
$([\ ],[\ ],[Y_1\mid R_1],[Y_2\mid R_2])$	true	true
$([X_1\mid L_1],[X_2\mid L_2],[\ ],[\ ])$	true	$invprop$ $2(L_1,L_2,[\ ],[\ ])$
$([X_1\mid L_1],[X_2\mid L_2],[Y_1\mid R_1],[Y_2\mid R_2])$	true	$invprop$ $2(L_1,L_2,R_1,R_2)$

2. Proof of Prop3

For *prop* 3, *Ind_Prove* generates nine sets of instantiations for the variables L and R which span the domain *List* $\times$ *List*. Every Lemma generated is either trivially true, or is implied by the induction hypothesis (derived from forward chaining), or can be proved to be true by applying *Ind_Prove* on it again. In the following the symbol $\neq$ is used as a synonym for the operation *diff* on nodes.

$prop$ $3(L_1,R_1,N,L_2,E):-$ $TREE([L_1,R_1],N,[L_2,R_2],T)$, $ISIN(T,N,Result\ 1)$,
    $N\neq E$, $ISIN([L_1,R_1],E,B_1)$, $ISIN([L_2,R_2],E,B_2)$,
    $or(B_1,B_2,Result\ 2)$, $Result\ 1=Result\ 2$.

Instantiations	Premise	Lemma
$L_1\leftarrow[\ ],N\leftarrow\hat{N},E\leftarrow\hat{E}$		
$R_1\leftarrow\hat{R}_1,R_2\leftarrow\hat{R}_2$		
(a) $L_2\leftarrow[\ ]$	$\hat{N}\neq\hat{E}$	true

(b) $L_2 \leftarrow [\hat{E} \mid \hat{L}_2]$ $\hat{N} \neq \hat{E}$ *true*

(c) $L_2 \leftarrow [\hat{Y} \mid \hat{L}_2]$ $\hat{N} \neq \hat{E}, \ \hat{Y} \neq \hat{E}$ *true*

$L_1 \leftarrow [\hat{E} \mid \hat{L}_1], N \leftarrow \hat{N}, E \leftarrow \hat{E}$
$R_1 \leftarrow \hat{R}_1, R_2 \leftarrow \hat{R}_2$

(a) $L_2 \leftarrow [\ ]$ $\hat{N} \neq \hat{E}$ *true*

(b) $L_2 \leftarrow [\hat{E} \mid \hat{L}_2]$ $\hat{N} \neq \hat{E}$ *true*

(c) $L_2 \leftarrow [\hat{Y} \mid \hat{L}_2]$ $\hat{N} \neq \hat{E}$ *true*

$L_1 \leftarrow [\hat{X} \mid \hat{L}_1], N \leftarrow \hat{N}, E \leftarrow \hat{E}$
$R_1 \leftarrow \hat{R}_1, R_2 \leftarrow \hat{R}_2$

(a) $L_2 \leftarrow [\ ]$ *true* $prop\,3(\hat{L}_1, \ \hat{N}, \ [\ ], \ \hat{E})$

(b) $L_2 \leftarrow [\hat{Y} \mid \hat{L}_2]$ $\hat{X} \neq \hat{E}$ $prop\,3(\hat{L}_1, \ \hat{N}, \ [\hat{Y} \mid \hat{L}_2], \hat{E})$

(c) $L_2 \leftarrow [\hat{E} \mid \hat{L}_2]$ $\hat{X} \neq \hat{E}, \ \hat{N} \neq \hat{E}$ $TREE([\hat{L}_1, \ \hat{R}_1], \ \hat{N}, \ [[\hat{E} \mid \hat{L}_2], \hat{R}_2], T),$
                                              $ISIN(T, \hat{E}, B), \ B = true.$

Proof of the Last Lemma

To complete the proof of *prop* 3 we have to prove the last lemma generated above. We use *Ind_Prove* once more to do this. The lemma is expressed as a new property to be proved as follows. Note that the relevant constraints in the *Premise* should be made as a part of the new property to be proved.

$newprop(L_1, R_1, N, L_2, R_2, E) :\text{-} \ N \neq E, TREE([L_1, R_1], N, [[E \mid L_2], R_2], T),$
                                $ISIN(T, E, B), \ B = true.$

Instantiations	Premise	Lemma
$([\ ], \ \hat{R}_1, \ \hat{N}, \ \hat{L}_2, \ \hat{R}_2, \ \hat{E})$	*true*	*true*
$([\hat{X}_1 \mid \hat{L}_1], \hat{N}, \ \hat{L}_2, \ \hat{R}_2, \ \hat{E})$	*true*	$newprop(\hat{L}_1, \ \hat{R}_1, \ \hat{N}, \ \hat{L}_2, \ \hat{R}_2, \ \hat{E})$

ALGEBRAIC SPECIFICATION OF SYNCHRONISATION AND ERRORS: A TELEPHONIC EXAMPLE

Brigitte Biebow (*) and Jacques Hagelstein (**)

(*) Laboratoires de Marcoussis
C.R.C.G.E.
Route de Nozay
F-91460 Marcoussis
France

(**) Philips Research Laboratory
Avenue van Becelaere, 2
B-1170 Brussels
Belgium

ABSTRACT

This paper presents an algebraic specification of the switching module, a component of a telephone switching system. This module exhibits interesting synchronisation properties which lead to consider it as a process. The specification is first presented without error handling, and then refined to include a non trivial error recovery strategy. Thus, we additionally show how error handling, which often obscures specifications, may be postponed and become a systematic refinement of a simpler specification.

1. Introduction

This paper aims at presenting an algebraic specification for a component of a telephonic exchange called a 'switching module', exhibiting synchronisation properties and possible erroneous behaviours. These two aspects admittedly raise problems in the abstract data type framework. We show, on this example, how these problems may be overcome. Incidentally, the switching module is usually implemented in hardware. This paper shows that a common specification language between hardware and software is by no means impossible.

Specification methods able to describe the behaviour of processes cover various levels of abstraction, from operational (e.g. Petri nets) to axiomatic ones (e.g. ACP). In this paper, we are specifically interested in specifying processes by using the classical algebraic approach to data type specification.

An algebra is formed by a collection of 'sorts' -- sets of objects -- and a collection of functions over the sorts. It may be defined by providing the signature of the functions and a set of axioms, thus enabling an axiomatic style of specification. Classically [GM 84], the sorts are used to model data types in programming languages, whereas the functions over the sorts model the functions defined in the programming language. Several approaches have been proposed to use the algebraic framework for the specification of processes.

ACP([BK 83]) provides operators to combine atomic actions into individual processes and sets of cooperating ones. These operators are defined axiomatically and form an 'algebra of communicating processes' in which specifications can be written. Currently, ACP suffers from a lack of integration with classical algebraic specifications of data types.

Another approach describes processes by means of auxiliary data types, specified in the algebraic style. In [Jul 83], processes communicate by applying the functions 'produce' (for the sender) and 'consume' (for the receiver) to a shared object belonging to a 'communication type'. This object is described axiomatically, but the specification has to include an operational part, described by means of a variant of weakest preconditions.

In this article, we propose an algebraic specification technique for processes which is more similar to the one used for abstract data types: in the same way as stacks belong to some sort in the algebra of stacks, processes will belong to some sort in some algebra. The elements of the sort will be the various possible states in which the process may be, all along its life. The functions applicable to these objects will correspond to the various events in which the process may be involved. These ideas will be developed in Section 3.

As proned in [Gog 77], the specification of a program should include all exceptional behaviours. All information necessary to the handling of the exceptional state, and only that information, should be kept in case of error. To follow these principles without obscuring the specification with too many details, we propose to provide the specification in three steps: first, just describing the circumstances of errors, secondly, providing error diagnostics, and thirdly, specifying the chosen error handling. These ideas will be developed in Section 4.

In the next section, we present an informal description of the switching module.

2. The switching module

The switching module is a component of a 'time multiplexed digital telephonic system'. A telephonic system is digital when the conversations are transmitted in digital form. To achieve this, the analogic signal delivered by the microphone is sampled 8000 times per second, i.e. every 125 microseconds. A sample takes slightly less than 4 microseconds to be transmitted. It is therefore possible for a line to transmit repeatedly the samples of 32 different conversations (figure 1). This technique is called "time multiplexing". The periodical interval of time allocated to a conversation is called a "channel", and there are thus 32 channels on a line. A channel is allocated to a user for the duration of his talk.

Still, a conversation is not transmitted on one single channel: it follows a path formed by several physical lines connected through nodes. It may be the case that it uses the channel 7 before a node and the channel 30 after it. Therefore, the nodes consist of

```
w1    w2                        w33    w34
0------4------8------------------125------129--------> time (μs)
```

w1 = 1st sample of conversation 1

w2 = 1st sample of conversation 2

...

w33 = 2nd sample of conversation 1

w34 = 2nd sample of conversation 2

figure 1

'switching modules' performing the switching of the channels. We assume that the network is synchronous (at least around a switching module), i.e. when it is channel 7's time before a node, it is channel 7's time after it too. Therefore, the switching module can only move the samples from one channel to another by delaying them. Of course, the amount of delay depends on the two channels which must be connected: if incoming channel 7 should be switched to 30, all samples reaching the switching module on channel 7 should be delayed by 23 channels, i.e around 90 μs.

Suppose the unit of time is 125/32 μs. Channel 1 is then handled at time 1, 33, 65, etc; channel 7 is handled at time 7, 39, 71, etc. Consider the voice sample or 'word' w received in the switching module at time 7, when channel 7 is handled. At the same time, an irrelevant word (for the considered conversation) goes out, sent on the outgoing channel 7. At time 30, an irrelevant word is received on the incoming channel 30, and the word w is sent on the outgoing channel 30.

Apart from the regularly incoming samples, there are two kinds of commands addressed to the switching module: 'connect' and 'disconnect' specifying two channels to connect or disconnect. Indeed, the channel connections are established and broken dynamically. An input channel may be connected to several output channels, but the reverse is not allowed. An output channel connected to no input channel will contain garbage.

The delicate points in the specification below come from synchronisation and error handling aspects:

* At the same time a word is received and a word is sent: input and output are synchronous.

* Errors happen when trying to disconnect two channels not connected together, or to connect an output channel which is already connected. This should not prevent the module to continue the transmission of words.

In the sequel, we make some simplifying assumptions, to avoid obscuring the specification with useless details. For instance, we assume that the connect and disconnect commands are immediately effective, whereas this could require some time. These simplifications can be removed without any problem, except the increasing size of the specification.

3. Specification of synchronisation in the switching module

3.1. Algebraic specification of processes

Algebraic techniques apply nicely to the specification of objects entirely characterised by the functions that one may invoke to create or modify them. Similarly, the state of a process is entirely characterised by the events that affected the process in the past, i.e. the information that was input and output, and, if relevant, the identification of the originators and destinators. In the spirit of the algebraic approach, we will thus consider process states as objects modified by the application of functions modeling the various events.

Example:
Consider a process which may receive from the outside the messages 'start', 'stop' and 'busy?'. It may issue the messages 'busy!' and 'notbusy!'. The signature of the algebra modeling the process's behaviour will thus include the following functions:

          start: Proc   -->   Proc
          stop: Proc   -->   Proc
          busy?:   Proc   -->   Proc
          busy!:   Proc   -->   Proc
          notbusy!:   Proc   -->   Proc

In addition, the function 'new' produces a process that no event has affected yet.

          new: -->   Proc

An expression such as 'stop(start(new))' describes the state of a process which was created, received the message 'start', and then received the message 'stop'.

The behaviour of the process will be described by stating which sequences of events lead to identical states. As usually, this is achieved by equating expressions formed with the available functions.

In the example above, the equation

          stop(new) = new

expresses that a message 'stop' has no effect on a newly created process.

The behaviour of the process is also described by stating which sequences of events are not allowed. For the process above, one may want to state that a stopped process may not issue 'busy!'. A discussion about how to state such facts is given in Section 4.

In the simple example above, the functions take no arguments in addition to the process itself. There is thus a function for each possible event. In general, a function will model a whole family of events, distinguished by the value of possible arguments of the function. It is up to the specifier to cluster the events in an appropriate way, but the problem is generally quite clear. For example, to specify a process able to receive a certain request accompanied by varying data, there would be a function identifying this kind of event and taking the data as argument.

Although it is not mandatory, we found it natural to let incoming messages appear as arguments of the function modeling the reception, and outgoing messages appear as additional values produced by the function modeling the emission. Consider for instance, a process of type 'Connector' which may receive the message 'connect' asking for the connection of two channels, and will, when the connection is completed, issue the message 'connected' specifying again the two channels. Its signature will include the functions

connect: Connector * Channel * Channel --> Connector
connected: Connector --> Connector * Channel * Channel

When several receptions or emissions are guaranteed to be synchronous, they form one single event and are thus modeled by one single function. This will be illustrated in the specification of the switching module.

3.2. Formal specification of the switching module

In the sequel, we will use the algebraic specification language PLUSS ([BBGGG 84]). It is based upon a set of specification-building operators derived from those of ASL ([Wir 83]) which allow to describe structured abstract data types specifications of realistic size. It includes the notion of multi-target algebras ([BGP 83]) which we will use to specify exception handling in algebraic data types. Errors will however only be considered in Section 4.

The algebraic model of the switching module is an object that records the history of events that have affected it until a certain moment. Those events, modeled by functions, are of the following kinds:

* creation of a new switching module that no event has affected yet

* switching of a channel, at regular intervals of time; this consists in the reception of a word belonging to that channel upstream from the switching module and the simultaneous emission of a word on the same channel downstream

* reception of a command to connect two channels

* reception of a command to disconnect two channels

The channel that is switched by the event of the second kind needs not be specified because the channels are handled in sequence: the nth switching handles the channel number n modulo 32.

The constructors of the sort Sm (for 'switching module') correspond to the events above. Note that the switching operation will be modeled by one single constructor, as the reception of one word and the emission of another one are simultaneous. The data that is received appears as argument while the data being produced appears as result. The constructors are the following ones:

init produces an initial state,

inout(s,w) models the switching of a certain channel on which w is received; the channel depends on the number of times 'inout' has been applied to produce the Sm s; the operation produces two things: a new Sm s' and a word w'; s' is identical to s, except that one more switching event has taken place, during which the word w has been received and w' has been sent; we shall note *inout1(s,w)* and *inout2(s,w)*, the first and second value of *inout(s,w)*,

* *connect(s,i,j)* produces a Sm *s'*, identical to *s* except that the input channel *i* is now connected to the output channel *j*,

* *disconnect(s,i,j)* produces an Sm *s'*, identical to *s* except that the input channel *i* is now disconnected from the output channel *j*.

We provide also some observers :

* *channel(s)* is the channel to which the next switching of the Sm *s* will refer,

* *identin(s,c)* is the input channel connected to the output channel *c* in the Sm *s*,

* *lastin(s,c)* is the last word input on the channel connected to the output channel *c* in the Sm *s*.

The specification of Sm uses the predefined specifications CHAN (integers from 1 to 32, with addition modulo 32) and WORD. The functions *is* and *isnot* are defined in CHAN and denote the equality and non-equality among objects of the sort.

specif SM =
  enrich WORD, CHAN *by*
  sorts Sm;
  functions

init:		-->	Sm;
inout:	Sm * Word	-->	Sm * Word;
connect:	Sm * Chan * Chan	-->	Sm;
disconnect:	Sm * Chan * Chan	-->	Sm;
channel:	Sm	-->	Chan;
identin:	Sm * Chan	-->	Chan;
lastin:	Sm * Chan	-->	Word;

  variables
    s,s' : Sm;
    w : Word;
    i,j,k,l : Chan;
% *i* and *k* are used for input channels, *j* and *l* for output channels. %

  axioms
% The following axiom is the heart of the specification. It states which word is output each time a switching takes place (i.e. at regular intervals). This word, the second value of *inout*, is the last word that entered the input channel to which the current output channel is connected. %

{Word}   inout2(s,w) = lastin(s,channel(s));

% The following axioms describe *channel*. They express that a new channel is handled each time *inout* is invoked. Note that channel(s) denotes the channel that the next *inout* will handle. %

{Chan}   channel(init) = 1;

$$channel(inout1(s,w)) = channel(s)+1;$$
$$channel(connect(s,i,j)) = channel(s);$$
$$channel(disconnect(s,i,j)) = channel(s);$$

% The following axioms describe *lastin*. *lastin(s,j)* is the last word entered on the input channel connected to j, i.e. on *identin(s,j)*. %

{Word} $channel(s)$ is $identin(s,j)$ ==> $lastin(inout1(s,w),j) = w;$
$channel(s)$ isnot $identin(s,j)$ ==> $lastin(inout1(s,w),j) = lastin(s,j);$
$lastin(connect(s,k,l),j) = lastin(s,j);$
$lastin(disconnect(s,k,l),j) = lastin(s,j);$

% The following axioms describe *identin*. %

{Chan} j is l ==> $identin(connect(s,i,j),l) = i;$
j isnot l ==> $identin(connect(s,i,j),l) = identin(s,l);$
j isnot l ==> $identin(disconnect(s,i,j),l) = identin(s,l);$
$identin(inout1(s,w),j) = identin(s,j);$

end SM;

Note that the words arriving on a channel connected to itself are not transmitted instantaneously, but delayed by 32 channels. Instantaneous transmission would have been allowed by replacing the first axiom by:

{Word} $inout2(s,w) = lastin(inout1(s,w),channel(s));$

4. Error handling

When defining an abstract data type, one has to consider so called error situations. These are produced by operations which are meaningless with the given arguments, for instance popping an empty stack.

Errors raise difficulties in the algebraic framework ([BG 83] for a survey, [Bid 84]), and it is tempting to just exclude them. This can be done by providing a conventional valid object as result of a meaningless operation. For instance, the following equation specifies that popping the empty stack has no effect:

$$pop(empty\text{-}stack) = empty\text{-}stack$$

This strategy has two drawbacks. First, it violates the principle of separation of concerns: both the reader and the writer of a specification will gain in considering first the normal cases, leaving the error handling for later. Second, it provides only a very specific way to handle errors, i.e. invisible recovery.

Other error handlings may be desirable: it may be needed to recognise in the value produced by a function, that an error just happened; this is not the case if the error produces a valid object. While doing so, it may also be needed to distinguish various errors one from the other. A classical example requiring a more flexible error handling than invisible recovery is a tolerant stack ([BBGGG 84]). It may be popped when empty, but only once before being pushed again. Popping the empty stack twice should lead to an unrecoverable error. This behaviour is described very easily if 'pop(empty-stack)' is an error object which behaves like 'empty-stack' when passed as argument to 'push' (error recovery), but produces a new error when passed to 'pop' (error propagation).

The second goal of this paper is to propose a method for the description of general error handlings. This strategy proceeds in three steps and is based on the definition of disjoints sorts, separating the valid objects from the erroneous ones.

4.1. Multi-target algebras

The simultaneous definition of several sorts is based on multi-target algebras ([BGP 83]), in which functions may produce values in several sorts:

pop: Stack   -->   Stack ∪ Stack-err;

When multi-target operators occur in a term, it is necessary to state the sort of the term, in a unique way. This is expressed by declarations, such as

{Stack-err} pop(empty-stack);

stating that 'pop(empty-stack)' belongs to the sort 'Stack-err'. The axioms and declarations are extended to positive conditional ones ([Bie 84]). Their general form is:

[{<sort>}]   [<condition> ==>] <term> [= <term>];

with the optional parts between brackets. Such an expression states that, [when the condition is verified], the left term belongs to the specified sort [and is equal to the right term]. The sort associated with an axiom indicates the sort on which the property expressed by the axiom is valid. This sort may be omitted if it is the same as the one of the previous axiom.

4.2. The method

This idea of multi-target algebras is used as follows to specify exceptions :

* In a first step, the domains of the functions include only valid objects, while the ranges may contain error objects. Declarations specify when errors take place, and when valid terms are produced. The handling of errors is thus not considered; only their production is specified.

* The second step still does not consider error handling: it provides error diagnostic, i.e. it specifies the constructors of the error sorts. Appropriate arguments are given to these functions and new axioms associate them with the error cases previously defined. These axioms replace the declarations introduced during step 1.

* In a last step, the desired error handling is described. The signature is modified to extend the domains of functions which can now accept erroneous arguments. The ranges of these functions may have to be extended too, depending on the chosen error handling. The axiom set has to be altered for two reasons: (1) to specify the behaviour of functions with arguments in the extension of the domain (specifying at the same

time the type of the result, in case of extended range), and (2) to adapt previous axioms relying on smaller domains or ranges. This will be illustrated in the sequel. New error objects and sorts may need to be defined, as a result of error propagation.

Note that the specification produced in the second step does not preclude any error handling if the term describing an error records any information that could be used for the error handling. This can be done by choosing appropriate arguments for the constructor of the error object.

Consider, for instance, the function 'def-array' which creates an array with given upper and lower bounds. It is an error to define an array with its upper bound inferior to its lower bound. Therefore, the first step of the error specification would include the signature:

| def-array: | Nat ' * Nat | --> | Array ∪ Array-err; |

and the declarations:

| {Array} | y >= x ==> def-array(x,y); |
| {Array-err} | y < x ==> def-array(x,y); |

In the second step, we would add the function:

| error-def-array: | Nat * Nat | --> | Array-err; |

intended to describe the error raised when 'def-array' is invoked with inappropriate arguments. The following axiom would replace the second one above:

| {Array-err} | y < x ==> def-array(x,y) = error-def-array(x,y); |

The term 'error-def-array(x,y)' records all information available about the error: the axiom associates the name 'error-def-array' with an improper use of 'def-array', while the arguments tells what indices produced the error. Certain error handlings may indeed require to know the value of x and y. For instance 'error-def-array(x,y)' could be handled as 'def-array(x,x)', i.e. the operation would define an array of one element, with x as index.

4.3. The tolerant stack

As a larger example, let us consider the stack that may be popped once when empty. We will define the sorts 'Stack' and 'Stack-err' for erroneous stacks. The first specification describes the valid behaviour and specifies when valid arguments lead to erroneous values. It includes the following functions (we omitted 'top'):

empty-stack:		-->	Stack;
push:	Stack * Elem	-->	Stack;
pop:	Stack	-->	Stack ∪ Stack-err;

No function may be applied to erroneous stacks, and only 'pop' may produce such stacks. The first set of axioms gives the usual property of stacks and tells when the value of 'pop' belongs to Stack or Stack-err (s ∈ Stack; x ∈ Elem) :

| {Stack} | pop(push(s,x)) = s; |
| {Stack-err} | pop(empty-stack); |

In a second step, we introduce constructors for the error sorts. There is only one declaration for erroneous objects. Thus, we need only introduce one function:

| bad-pop: | --> | Stack-err; |

Bad-pop does not take any argument, because there is no need to distinguish the various circumstances in which the error may take place (there is only one: popping the empty stack). The second declaration is replaced by the following axiom:

| {Stack-err} | pop(empty-stack) = bad-pop; |

In a third step, we want to specify how 'push' and 'pop' handle the error object 'bad-pop'. The two domains are extended to include 'Stack-err'. As 'push' will recover the error, its range is still limited to 'Stack'. However, 'pop' will produce an unrecoverable error, of the new sort 'Stack-err1', when given 'bad-pop' as argument. The arity of the functions thus becomes:

| push: | (Stack $\cup$ Stack-err) $*$ Elem | --> | Stack; |
| pop: | Stack $\cup$ Stack-err --> | | Stack $\cup$ Stack-err $\cup$ Stack-err1; |

New axioms are added to specify the behaviour of the functions on error arguments:

| {Stack} | push(bad-pop,x) = push(empty-stack,x); |
| {Stack-err1} | pop(bad-pop); |

Note that the second axiom completes the specification of the type of 'pop' for all kinds of arguments.

As Stack-err1 does not belong to the domain of 'pop' and 'push', terms such as 'pop(pop(bad-pop))' or 'push(pop(bad-pop),x)' simply do no exist in the described model. This is part of the error handling we chose to specify: no further computation is allowed after popping the empty stack twice. Another possibility would have been to allow such computations, and to continuously obtain the same object in 'Stack-err1'.

4.4. Error handling in the switching module

Let us now apply the previous strategy to the 'switching module' example. Errors may happen in the following cases:

* when disconnecting two channels which are not connected together,
* when connecting an output channel which is already connected (an output channel may only be connected to one input, although an input may be connected to several outputs).
* when determining the input channel connected to a non connected output channel,
* when determining the word coming out of channel j when there is no input channel connected to it.

For each sort in the range of 'connect', 'disconnect', 'identin' and 'lastin', we have to define a corresponding error sort. Let *Sm-err*, *Chan-err* and *Word-err* denote the error sorts corresponding respectively to *Sm*, *Chan* and *Word*. The functions 'is' and 'isnot' are defined in *Chan* ∪ *Chan-err* and denote the equality and non-equality among objects of the sorts.

We introduce a new observer, *free*, to ease the expression of error cases: *free(s,c)* is true if and only if the output channel *c* is not connected to any input channel in the Sm *s*. We thus use the predefined specification BOOL in addition to WORD and CHAN.

In the first step, we just define when errors take place (for brevity, we will denote *X* ∪ *X-err* by means of *Xer*):

functions

init:		-->	Sm;
inout:	Sm * Word	-->	Sm * Worder;
connect:	Sm * Chan * Chan	-->	Smer;
disconnect:	Sm * Chan * Chan	-->	Smer;
channel:	Sm	-->	Chan;
free:	Sm * Chan	-->	Bool;
identin:	Sm * Chan	-->	Chaner;
lastin:	Sm * Chan	-->	Worder;

variables

  s,s' : Sm;
  w : Word;
  i,j,k,l : Chan;

axioms

% The word output at each switching may be an erroneous one. %

{Worder} inout2(s,w) = lastin(s,channel(s));

% *channel* is never applied to an erroneous *Sm*. Its axioms are left unchanged %

{Chan}   channel(init) = 1;
       channel(inout1(s,w)) = channel(s)+1;
       channel(connect(s,i,j)) = channel(s);
       channel(disconnect(s,i,j)) = channel(s);

% The following axioms define *free*. %

{Bool}   free(init,j) = true;
       free(inout1(s,w),j) = free(s,j);
       j is l ==> free(connect(s,i,j),l) = false;
       j isnot l ==> free(connect(s,i,j),l) = free(s,l);
       j is l ==> free(disconnect(s,i,j),l) = true;
       j isnot l ==> free(disconnect(s,i,j),l) = free(s,l);

% *lastin(s,j)*, the last word entered on the input channel connected to *j*, is erroneous if *j* is free or if its connection to an input channel is too recent and no word arrived yet on this channel. %

{Word}	channel(s) is identin(s,j) ==> lastin(inout1(s,w),j) = w;
{Word-err}	l is j ==> lastin(connect(s,k,l),j);
	free(s,j) ==> lastin(s,j);
{Worder}	channel(s) isnot identin(s,j) ==> lastin(inout1(s,w),j) = lastin(s,j);
	l isnot j ==> lastin(connect(s,k,l),j) = lastin(s,j);
	l isnot j ==> lastin(disconnect(s,k,l),j) = lastin(s,j);

% *identin(s,c)* is erroneous if no input channel is connected to *c* in *s*. %

{Chan}	j is l ==> identin(connect(s,i,j),l) = i;
{Chan-err}	free(s,j) ==> identin(s,j);
{Chaner}	j isnot l ==> identin(connect(s,i,j),l) = identin(s,l);
	j isnot l ==> identin(disconnect(s,i,j),l) = identin(s,l);
	identin(inout1(s,w),j) = identin(s,j);

% The following declarations specify the type of *connect* and *disconnect*. %

{Sm}	free(s,j)) ==> connect(s,i,j);
	identin(s,j) is i ==> disconnect(s,i,j);
{Sm-err}	not(free(s,j)) ==> connect(s,i,j);
	identin(s,j) isnot i ==> disconnect(s,i,j);

In a second step, we define, for each declaration of an error sort, a constructor associated with the corresponding error. For brevity, we will limit ourselves to the constructors of Sm-err:

bad-connect:	Sm * Chan * Chan	-->	Sm-err;
bad-disconnect:	Sm * Chan * Chan	-->	Sm-err;

The following axioms replace the two last declarations above:

{Sm-err}	not(free(s,j)) ==> connect(s,i,j) = bad-connect(s,i,j);
	identin(s,j) isnot i ==> disconnect(s,i,j) = bad-disconnect(s,i,j);

In the third step, we will specify a non trivial error handling. As suggested in Section 2, bad connections or disconnections are without effect on the transmission of words but will prevent the effect of any other operation (i.e. further connect or disconnect). It is up to the controller of the switching module to reinitialise it in such cases. This is an example of partial recovery of errors.

To describe this behaviour, the second value of 'inout' will not be affected by the error, but its first value will belong to *Sm-err* if an error object is given as argument. Both 'connect' and 'disconnect' also produce an element of *Sm-err* when taking one as argument. The new arity of the functions is as follows (the domain of *channel* has not been extended to *Sm-err* as it is never applied to error objects):

init:		-->	Sm;
inout:	Smer * Word	-->	Smer * Worder;
connect:	Smer * Chan * Chan	-->	Smer;
disconnect:	Smer * Chan * Chan	-->	Smer;
channel:	Sm	-->	Chan;
free:	Smer * Chan	-->	Bool;
identin:	Smer * Chan	-->	Chaner;
lastin:	Smer * Chan	-->	Worder;
bad-connect:	Sm * Chan * Chan	-->	Sm-err;
bad-disconnect:	Sm * Chan * Chan	-->	Sm-err;

The axiom given for *inout* in the first step specifies its behaviour when its first argument belongs to *Sm* (the variable s is typed). The following ones are concerned with arguments in *Sm-err*. They specify a partial error recovery: words continue to be output as if no error had arisen. %

{Worder}   inout2(bad-disconnect(s,i,j),w) = inout2(s,w);
             inout2(bad-connect(s,i,j),w) = inout2(s,w);

On the other hand, the errors are propagated by *connect*, *disconnect* and the first value of *inout*:

{Sm-err}   inout1(bad-disconnect(s,i,j),w) = bad-disconnect(inout1(s,w),i,j);
             connect(bad-disconnect(s,i,j),k,l) = bad-disconnect(s,i,j);
             disconnect(bad-disconnect(s,i,j),k,l) = bad-disconnect(s,i,j);

The auxiliary functions *channel*, *free*, *lastin*, and *identin* are only used to define the word output by inout. As this word is not affected by connection errors, the functions will recover the error. We add the following axioms:

{Bool}   free(bad-disconnect(s,i,j),l) = free(s,l);
{Worder}   lastin(bad-disconnect(s,i,j),l) = lastin(s,l);
{Chaner}   identin(bad-disconnect(s,i,j),l) = identin(s,l);

Note that most axioms given for *free*, *lastin*, and *identin* in the first step rely on the assumption of a smaller domain. For instance,

{Bool}   j is l ==> free(disconnect(s,i,j),l) = true;

was only valid because *free* did only take elements of *Sm* as argument, and thus *disconnect(s,i,j)* was assumed not to be an error object. This is not the case any more. The condition of this axiom has to be strengthened to guarantee that 'disconnect(s,i,j)' is a valid object. We replace it by:

{Bool}   (identin(s,j) is i) and (j is 1) ==> free(disconnect(s,i,j),l) = true;

A similar transformation is applied to the other axioms, when needed. This completes the specification of the switching module, with error handling.

5. Conclusions

The first goal of the paper was to show that processes may, to a certain extend, be specified in the algebraic style, in the same way as passive objects. The key idea is in the appropriate interpretation of the meaning of a function. The advantage of this approach is to provide a uniform framework for the description of parallel and sequential parts of system. However, this goal is not yet reached. What we have illustrated is the local specification of the behaviour of a process, and not yet the specification of the interaction of several ones. This work is currently going on.

Another limitation of this formalism is that it does not, in its current form, allow for real-time specifications, i.e. specifications involving absolute values of time. For instance, we cannot say that 'inout' takes place every 125 μs. This limitation is common to most other specification techniques.

The second goal of the paper was to propose a systematic approach to the specification of error handling. This contribution is more of a methodological nature. The idea to distinguish the specification of normal cases and error situations is an illustration of the principle of separation of concern. Considering the size of an actual specification, its writing, reading or modification would nearly be possible without a clever application of this principle. But it is also important to introduce early the error cases. What we propose is to distinguish at the very beginning error cases from normal ones in an economic way, and to postpone the real choices of error handling.

6. Acknowledgements

We thank Professor Marie-Claude Gaudel for her helpful suggestions.

7. Bibliography

[BBGGG 84] M. Bidoit, B. Biebow, M-C. Gaudel, G. Guiho, C. Gresse, "Exception Handling: Formal Specification and Systematic Program Construction", International Conference on Software Engineering, Orlando, Florida, March 1984.

[Bid 84]   M. Bidoit, "Algebraic specification of exception handling and error recovery by means of declarations and equations", Proceedings ICALP 84, LNCS 172.

[Bie 84]   B. Biebow, "Application d'un langage de spécification algébrique à des exemples téléphoniques", 3rd cycle thesis of the University of Paris 6, Paris, France, February 1984.

[BG 83]   M. Bidoit, M-C. Gaudel, "Etude des méthodes de spécification des cas d'exceptions dans les types abstraits algébriques", Actes du Séminaire d'Informatique Théorique du LITP 1982-1983, Paris 6, Paris, France.

[BGP 83]   F. Boisson, G. Guiho, D. Pavot, "Algèbres à Opérateurs Multicibles", LRI report, Orsay, France, June 1983.

[BK 83]   J.A. Bergstra, J.W. Klop, "Process Algebra for Communication and Mutual Exclusion", Report IW 218/83, Mathematisch Centrum, Amsterdam.

[GM 84]   J.A. Goguen, J. Meseguer, "An initiality primer", SRI International, Computer Science Laboratory, Menlo Park CA 94025, USA.

[Gog 77]   J.A. Goguen, "Abstract errors for abstract data types", Description of Programming Concepts, E.J.Neuhol Ed., North Holland, New York, 1977.

[Jul 83]   J. Julliand, "Spécification algébrique de la communication entre processus parallèles", Technique et Science Informatiques, Vol. 2 Nr 4, 1983.

[Wir 83]   M. Wirsing, "Structured Algebraic Specifications: A Kernel Language", Technische Universität München, 1983.

MODELLING CONCURRENT MODULES

Rainer Isle
Klaus-Peter Löhr

Fachbereich Mathematik/Informatik
Universität Bremen
Postfach 330440, D-2800 Bremen 33

Abstract

The variety of module concepts for concurrent systems suggests looking for a
unified model that would serve as a basis for specification techniques and
languages. Starting from the client/server paradigm, a model for concurrent
modules is developed that is able to cope with incomplete service execution due to
blocking conditions. The model is shown to be applicable to different kinds of
modules known from programming languages. It is generalized to support so-called
implementation specification and interconnection of modules using different communication rules.

1. Introduction

If the maturity of a discipline is to be judged by the amount of agreement on its
basic issues and notions, then specification of concurrent program modules is still
in its infancy. This is in contrast to sequential programming. Although different
specification methods and languages exist for the design specification of sequential
systems, the basic notion of data abstraction is widely accepted. There are
different opinions on how to describe the behaviour of an abstract module (or
object), and on the composition of modules. But there is agreement that an
abstract data type has to be specified without resort to its possible implementation, in a way that allows both users and implementors to rely on the specification
only.

In the sequential case, a module is indeed a "passive object". Thus, a module can be
specified by associating certain mappings between abstract values of the module
with its operations (state machine approach), or by describing a set of possible
execution sequences (history approach), or by interrelating the visible effects of
the operations (algebraic approach). In any case, operation execution is considered indivisible or "timeless".

The situation is fundamentally different with concurrent systems where operations
may be executed concurrently and a process may block amidst an operation. Moreover, a module may not even be "passive", but may contain an active process.
Modules in concurrent systems will be collectively referred to as concurrent
modules throughout this paper, independent of their inner functioning.

Many programming language constructs have been proposed for the implementation of concurrent modules. Among the best known are the process (in different flavours), the monitor [Hoare 74] and the Ada task [Ada 82]. Note that each module concept has its specific paradigm of module interaction; see, e.g., [Wegner/Smolka 83] [Andrews/Schneider 83].

The fundamental difference between a sequential module and a concurrent module has given rise to completely different approaches to concurrent module specification. On the one hand, we have the extension of classical sequential techniques to support the specification of "guarded monitors": a passive module is used concurrently (but without overlapping), and blocking can occur at module entry only [Laventhal 79] [Keramidis/Mackert 79]. This works fine in simple cases, as long as no scheduling properties have to be specified and module composition and liveness properties are of no concern.

On the other hand, methods originally developed for fine-grain concurrency analysis have been extended for use in module specification. Temporal logic plays a prominent role here, and there is a multitude of sophisticated temporal logic approaches, differing both in style and the degree of "state machine orientation" (see, e.g., [Schwartz/Melliar-Smith 82] [Hailpern/Owicki 82] [Lamport 83]).

Much of the complexity of these approaches can be avoided if there is no need for complete liveness analysis. We propose a specification method based on state machines which produces specifications both compact and readable. The method

-   is general in that it allows any conceivable concurrent module to be modelled as a state machine;

-   it is flexible in that it supports module parametrization and composition, and allows to write partial specifications (sometimes called implementation specifications);

-   it is adaptable to existing sequential specification methods and languages, its essence being independent of the state machine view.

In section 2 of this paper, the basic ideas will be outlined. Section 3 deals with different possibilities to implement an abstract concurrent module. The notion of implementation specification (as opposed to service specification) is introduced in section 4; different paradigms of module interconnection are also discussed in this section. We conclude with section 5, commenting on context and perspective of our work.

2. Service Specification of a Module

2.1. The basic model

Let us think of a module as an independent agent that offers certain services. The agent will obey orders to execute these services: it acts as a server to certain clients producing the orders. At the moment, we do not care about the nature of clients or things such as "order transmission".

When a module accepts an order, the requested service is executed either instantaneously or with a certain delay. In the latter case, the completion of the service will be the byproduct of the acceptance of another order. In general, acceptance of an order implies the completion of 0, 1, or more orders, possibly including the order just accepted. Acceptance of an order, together with the resulting completion of previously accepted orders, is considered an indivisible, "timeless" action of the module.

A module M can be modelled as a special purpose state machine $M = (S,A,B,\tau,\rho,s_0)$, where S denotes the states, A the inputs, and B the outputs. τ and ρ are the state transition and output functions, respectively. $s_0 \in S$ is referred to as the initial state. S has a special structure, and so has B:

$$S = V \times N \times P(N \times A),$$
$$B = P(N \times R).$$

V stands for "value", N for natural numbers, P for powerset, A for "argument", and R for "result". The following must hold for τ, ρ, s_0:

$$\tau((v,n,P), a) = (v',n+1,P'), \qquad P' \subset P \cup \{(n+1, a)\}$$
$$\rho((v,n,P), a) = Q, \qquad Q_1 = (P_1 \cup \{n+1\}) - P'_1 \quad (*)$$
$$s_0 = (v_0,0,\phi)$$

Q_1 denotes the 1-projection of Q, i.e., if $Q = \{(n_1,r_1),...,(n_k,r_k)\}$ then $Q_1 = \{n_1,...,n_k\}$. ϕ denotes the empty set.

Given a certain state $s = (v,n,P)$, v is the abstract value of M, n identifies the last order accepted, and P is the set of orders accepted but not yet completed; it will be referred to as the "order list". An output Q can be seen as a set of completion notifications for previously accepted orders. Equation (*) specifies that, upon acceptance of an order, exactly those orders which are completed are removed from P.

The mappings τ and ρ need not be completely defined - but their domains are identical. We say that if $\tau(s,a)$ (or, equivalently, $\rho(s,a)$) is undefined, "M does not accept a in state s".

Given a module M as above, a sequence of arguments $a_1 a_2...a_i$ models a sequence of orders and determines a sequence of state transitions $s_0 \to s_1, s_1 \to s_2, ... , s_{i-1} \to s_i$ (if all are defined) and a corresponding sequence of sets of completion notifications $b_1 b_2...b_i$ for the orders given. Due to (*), there will be at most one notification for each order.

2.2. Describing a model

The behaviour of a module as modelled above can be described using any specification method/language that seems convenient. Throughout this paper, we will use a method in the tradition of the state machine view.

It must be emphasized, however, that the model is not tied to any specific language. As we do not want to elaborate on specification languages, we will use an ad-hoc language without giving precise syntax and semantics.

Let us first "structure" both the module state and the argument/result by allowing these to be tuples and their components to be typed. In addition, we use the notion of service with the meaning of "operation", "entry", or "port". Consequently, the flavour of "argument/result" changes a little: associated with each service are a certain number of arguments and a certain number of results, all of certain fixed types. An order is the request to execute a certain service with given arguments, and to deliver the results.

Accepting an order changes the state and may produce completion notifications. These effects are specified using an ad-hoc language reminiscent of sequential specification languages like Special [Robinson et al. 79] or Ina Jo [Eggert 80] [Cheheyl et. al. 81]. To give a flavour of both the method and the language, let us consider a simple example:

> We wish to specify a module that is capable of storing one value of a certain type, say *text*. There are two operations, *put* and *get*, for storing and removing, resp., such a value. *put*ting a value into the module can succeed only when no value is present. *get*ting a value from the module can succeed only if a value is present. There is one special requirement, though: *get* has a *boolean* argument *priority*; we want to specify a program module that, in the case of two "pending orders" with *priority* and **not** *priority*, resp., will complete the *priority* order upon arrival of a value.

Now turn to the following specification text:

```
module mailbox is
        put (message: in text),
        get (priority: in boolean; message: out text);
components box: text;
initially box = ?;
service put when box = ? is
        if orders = φ then
                box' = message
        else box' = ? and
                for that x in orders sat x.priority or that x in orders sat true
                return message' = this.message fi and
        return;
service get is
        box' = ? and
        if box ≠ ? then
                return message' = box fi;
end mailbox.
```

Although the reader may guess the meaning of many phrases in this example, several comments on the ad-hoc language used here are necessary.

(1) The module head contains the syntactical part of the specification (this corresponds to the "signature" in an algebraic specification and to the "definition module" of Modula-2 [Wirth 82]).

(2) The initial state is characterized by an assertion (it need not be unique).

(3) ? is a special value available for all types; it cannot be **returned**, though.

(4) Each service is specified by an assertion that relates old values of state components to new ones (the latter are denoted by primed component names). A component with no primed occurrence remains unaffected. Note that the description of the state transition may be highly non-determinate.

(5) The specification of a service may contain expressions of the form '**return** assertion' or '**for** order expression **return** assertion'. Such a return expression specifies the completion of the current order or the order indicated, resp. The assertion serves to characterize the return values.

(6) The expression '**that** x **in** set **sat** P(x)' denotes an arbitrary element in a given set satisfying P, or ? if no such element' is present. **or** means determinate choice if the operands are non-boolean: the first operand is selected if it is not ?; otherwise, the second operand is selected.

(7) The predefined identifier *orders* denotes the order list. Its elements are variant records, according to the information given in the module head.

A salient feature of the above specification is that overflow and underflow of the mailbox are prevented by different techniques. Overflow is prevented by simply not accepting a *put* order if the message cannot be deposited. A *get* order is always accepted; its completion, however, may be delayed until a message is available and can be granted - according to the priority discipline. Note that without accepting the *get* orders it would be impossible to express the priority scheduling.

2.3. Non-determinacy restricted by temporal logic assertions

Non-determinate service description as possible with an assertion-oriented specification language is a powerful tool. It allows for incomplete specification of modules in cases where abstraction from behavioral details is desired. It also allows to specify modules that are intentionally or de facto non-determinate.

In the latter case, it is often necessary to restrict the set of possible state sequences to a subset with certain properties. Such restrictions cannot be expressed by relating a state to its successor state. In this situation, temporal logic can be used to specify the desired properties of state sequences (see, e.g., [Manna/Pnueli 81]). The specification may contain a phrase like

assertion temporal assertion;

Note that an assertion of the form [] P, where P is a state predicate, introduces P as a module invariant. Unlike invariants known from other specification languages, P is not meant to be provable from the rest of the specification; its purpose is to restrict the module behaviour. - The introduction of the **assertion** clause makes the **initially** clause obsolete (as can be seen in the next example).

Consider the following example which specifies an unreliable transmission mediium. This might be, e.g., a communication line between two computers, one acting as a transmitter of certain "packets", the other acting as a receiver. There is a packet buffer at the receiver site, but no flow control to prevent overwriting of this buffer. Each packet sent will be received, although possibly damaged.

```
module line is
        xmit (data: in packet),
        recv (data: out packet);
components buffer: packet;
assertion buffer = ? and [] <> buffer ≠ ?;
service xmit is
        (buffer' = data or buffer' = ?) and
        return;
service recv when buffer ≠ ? is
        buffer' = ? and
        return data' = buffer;
end line.
```

The specification of *xmit* shows that transmission is unreliable. The temporal assertion, however, precludes permanent corruption of all packets.

2.4. Autonomous state transitions

It is easy to extend the basic model of 2.1. with autonomous state transitions. There are many practical cases where autonomous state transitions are useful. Typically, a process performing a certain background task over and over again will be modelled conveniently by using an autonomous state transition. As a simple example, consider the following *clock* module:

```
module clock is
        get time (t: out natural);
components time: natural;
assertion time = 0;
service get time is
        return t' = time;
auto tick is
        time' = time + 1;
end clock.
```

Note that the identifier *tick* serves documentation purposes only.

Autonomous transitions add to the degree of non-determinacy of a module. So it is not surprising that autonomous transitions will often be used in conjunction with a temporal assertion. The following example specifies a "bad memory" which is neither completely reliable nor completely broken:

```
module memory is
        read (v: out value),
        write (v: in value);
components cell: value;
assertion cell = ? and []<> (cell ≠ ? → ○ cell ≠ ?)
service read when cell ≠ ? is
        return v' = cell;
service write is
        cell' = v and return;
auto forget is
        cell' = ?;
end memory.
```

The temporal assertion contains the "next state" operator ○ . The assertion states that (1) the memory is an undefined state initially and (2) it will happen infinitely often that when a state is defined its successor state will also be defined. The latter requirement guarantees that a value written into the memory can be read again - at least from time to time.

Note that the **when** clause does not necessarily imply a "delay" of the *read* operation; whether *cell* = ? causes a "delay" or "exception" is beyond the expressiveness of the basic model (see, however, section 4.).

3. Correspondence between Modules and Programming Language Constructs

3.1. Processes with message passing

In a straightforward implementation, a module is realized as a sequential process interacting with its enviroment via message passing. There are different paradigms for inter-process communication. We assume the following basic chracteristics:

(1) The code of a process contains certain points where the process is willing to accept a message. If none is available (see below), the process waits for the arrival of a message.

(2) A message received by the process represents an order: it describes a service to be executed by the process.

(3) At any point, a process may decide to accept certain kinds of orders; these may be described by service names and/or certain predicates involving parameters and the process state.

(4) The process is able to signal the completion of an order by "sending an answer". It is irrelevant here, whether and how this answer is bound to the order, to a client process, to a third process, or whatever. Sending an answer does never imply waiting.

As is evident from (1) and (4), we abstract from the details of message/answer buffering, in fact from the whole inter-process communication scheme. E.g., we ignore issues like sending a message or receiving an answer. We just have an "environment" producing messages and swallowing answers. Issues of module interconnection are deferred to section 4.

Any process with the properties mentioned above can be modelled as a concurrent module. The activity between acceptance of a message and the next acceptance of a message is modelled as a state transition. If the locus of control is encoded in the module state, the **when** clause can be used to express that a process is choosy about when to accept which kind of order. The **when** clause also serves to reflect the predicates mentioned in (3). Note that the process has to take explicit measures for the bookkeeping on orders!

3.2. Processes with remote invocation

The Ada task [Ada 82] is an example for a process using the remote invocation paradigm. The task is an autonomous process with the following characteristics (cf. 3.1.):

(1) The code of a task contains accept statements carrying the names of task entries. Accept statements may be nested. At the beginning of an accept statement, the task waits for a corresponding entry call issued by a client task, then accepts the input parameters, executes the body of the accept statement, and delivers the output parameters to the client.

(2) An entry call accepted by a task represents an order: it describes a service to be executed by the task; executing the body of the accept statement is part(!) of the execution of the service (see below).

(3) Using the selective wait statement, a task can accept different service requests, whichever happens to arrive: a group of accept statements mentions the acceptable entry calls; moreover, each accept statement may be guarded by a **when** clause.

(4) The completion of an order accepted by a certain accept statement is signalled through termination of that statement. This comprises return of output parameters. Note that the client is waiting for the termination.

As with message passing, we presuppose that a task to be modelled as a concurrent module does not use another task (this restriction will be removed in section 4). The activity between acceptance of an entry call and the next acceptance of an entry call (possibly nested) is modelled as a state transition. If the task body consists of a loop containing a selective wait, but no other accept statements, this structure will be directly mirrored in the model specification. If the structure is different, the locus of control has to be encoded in the module state (as mentioned in 3.1.). Note that there is no explicit bookkeeping for orders! An order is represented by the activation of an accept body.

If a task uses the entry attribute e'count (denoting the number of pending calls for e), the model has to accept any call for e unconditionally. The service request will be registered in the order list so that the module behaviour can be made dependent on e'count. Clearly, the effect of service e will now be specified as the effect of a guarded autonomous transition.

Note that a selective wait can have an **else** part which will be executed if no other alternative can be selected. This can also be modelled using an autonomous transition.

3.3. Monitors

The monitor is the most natural generalization of the "module" as known from sequential programs. Different versions of synchronization within monitors have been proposed. We refer to the Hoare version [Hoare 74], but other versions could be taken as well.

Monitor activities are executed on behalf of a process calling one of the procedures exported by the monitor. The following characteristics of a monitor are pertinent to our modeling:

(1) A monitor is "active" when a process is within a monitor procedure and is not blocked. A monitor is activated when a process is entering it.

(2) A process entering a monitor is tantamount to the monitor accepting an order. The procedure called represents the service requested.

(3) If a monitor is ready to accept an order, it will accept any order. (This is different with "guarded monitors"!)

(4) An order is completed when a process leaves a monitor: termination of a procedure exported by the monitor means completion of the corresponding order.

If a monitor is modelled as a concurrent module, the exported procedures are modelled as the services. The activity within a monitor, lasting from an entry to the next entry, is described as the service effect. Different processes may take part in this activity, e.g., if a process wakes a blocked process using a signal operation. Furthermore, an activity period is not necessarily ended when a process leaves the monitor; monitor exit just means order completion. - No explicit bookkeeping on orders is necessary, since an order is represented by a procedure activation.

3.4. Synchronized sequential modules

A state transition in a concurrent module is an indivisible action. There is no concept of "overlapping transitions". Processes, tasks, and monitors correctly implement indivisible state transitions, due to their seriality and exclusion properties, respectively. It is nevertheless possible to weaken the restriction that two or more processes must not be proceeding simultaneously within an implementation of a module.

The important observation is that clients of a module, not aware of the module's implementation, are not even aware of exclusion or serialization measures within the module. These are exclusively in the module's responsibility. E.g., if a concurrent module is implemented as a single sequential program module containing some locking operations, this is perfectly alright as long as the clients receive the same services as they would receive from a monitor implementation. Service is a matter of specification, exclusion/locking is a matter of implementation.

Verifying such a module implementation is of course more difficult than verifying a monitor or process. In addition to proving the correctness of each individual operation, we have to prove the following:

Consider an arbitrary, overlapping execution E of orders $o_1,...,o_n$. Then there is a permutation $i_1,...,i_n$ of $1,...,n$ such that the net effect of the acceptances of $o_{i_1},...,o_{i_n}$ as specified for the abstract module is satisfied by the net effect of E.

Note that this notion of correctness does not guarantee determinacy, not even if the specification is determinate. This is not a weakness, though, it is the natural consequence of concurrent order arrival. Using data base terminology (see, e.g.,

[Ullman 80]), E involves a certain schedule for the transactions $o_1,...,o_n$; if the specification is determinate, we have to prove that all schedules are serializable.

If the specification is non-determinate, an overlapping execution may be allowed to produce a net effect that cannot be achieved by any serialization. This is because a determinate implementation will not usually exhaust all the possibilities allowed by a non-determinate specification. Thus, a correct implementation of a non-determinate module may well allow non-serializable schedules. A simple example will suffice to demonstrate this:

> module *growing* is
> > *increase*;
> components *counter: natural;*
> assertion *counter = 0;*
> service *increase* is
> > *counter' > counter* and return;
> end *growing.*

Implementing *increase* by the non-atomic assignment *counter := counter+1* on an integer variable *counter* with no locking is correct

- because any overlapping executions of the assignment will have a net effect that satisfies the net effect of a corresponding sequence of orders;

- despite the fact that, e.g., two overlapping executions may produce an effect different from that of two serial executions.

3.5. Multiple processes

We have seen that a module implementation may contain more than one locus of control at a given time. Similarly, it is possible that a module implementation is an arbitrary "non-sequential process", i.e., contains several permanent processes interacting in arbitrary ways. And vice versa, any concurrent system of arbitrary complexity can be modelled as a concurrent module - if its visible behaviour is that of a server. A simple example is the "resource" module of the language SR [Andrews 81] which may comprise multiple processes. The most general way to obtain a concurrent system is of course composing arbitrary abstract modules. This is the subject of the next section.

4. Building Modules from Modules

4.1. Implementation Specification

If an implementation of a module A makes use of another module B (or of several other modules), it is possible to "specify the implementation". With respect to the server B, A acts as a client. From this point of view, a state transition of A is caused not only by accepting an order, but also by taking notice of a completion notification from B which signals the completion of an order previously issued by A. Of course, the effect that A issues an order must be specifiable as well.

Let us assume that B is a private server of A, i.e., B has no other clients. Then we can picture the situation as follows:

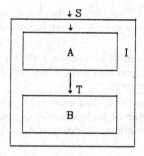

The clients of A rely on a certain service specification S. They don't know anything about B. The implementation of A relies on B's service specification T. The nature of this reliance is described by an implementation specification I for A.

As an example, let us consider the implementation specification for a scheduler A that controls access to a resource B; e.g., let A be a disk driver and B the corresponding disk drive (including the controller). A client of A sees an abstract disk which is described by the following service specification:

```
module disk is
        transfer (bn: in blockno; bl: in out block; dir: in (in,out));
components sector (1..last): block;
assertion true;
service transfer when 1 ≤ bn and bn ≤ last is
        if dir = in then return bl' = sector(bn)
        else sector'(bn) = bl and
            all i in 1..last sat (i ≠ bn → sector'(i)=sector(i)) and
            return fi;
end disk.
```

Of course, the specification doesn't say anything about scheduling, because scheduling does not affect the module's functional behaviour. For this reason, however, the specification can also be used for the disk drive! An implementation specification for the disk driver may look like this:

```
module disk driver
        using disk <transfer (bn: in blockno; bl: in out block; dir: in (in, out))>
        is transfer (bn: in blockno; bl: in out block; dir: in (in, out));
components devq: device queue; (* technical details are omitted *)
assertion length(devq) = 0;
accept transfer is
        devq' = enter(devq, this) (* realizes the scheduling discipline *)
        and
        if length (devq) = 1 then
            start disk.transfer(head (devq').bn) fi;
notice disk.transfer is
        devq' = body(devq) and
        if length(devq') > 0 then
            start disk.transfer(head (devq').bn, head (devq').bl,head (devq').dir)
        fi and
        for head(devq) return
            if dir = in then bl' = this.bl fi;
end disk driver.
```

We use the keyword **accept** instead of **service** in order to enhance the "implementation flavour".

A **start** expression specifies that a certain order is produced (like **return** produces a completion notification). At the moment, we don't care whether or not the server is ready to accept the order. A **notice** specification describes the effect of accepting a completion notification. Noticing will be selective in the general case: there will be different notice specifications for different services, and they may be guarded by **when** clauses.

The order list is not visible in this example. References to pending orders, however, are kept in *devq*, and the expression **for** *head(devq)* **return** ... specifies an order to be removed from the order list.

As indicated in the module head, *disk driver* refers to the *disk* module. *disk* can be seen as a formal parameter of *disk driver*. The semantics of *disk driver.transfer* depends on the specification given for *disk* and on the details of inter-module communication.

It should be noted that the **notice** concept is peculiar to concurrent systems. There is no need for it in sequential systems where an order will always be executed to completion prior to acceptance of the next order. (Cf. the **effect of** clause used in Special [Robinson, et al. 79].)

4.2. Module composition

The easiest way to model communication between modules is to assume the existence of a message pool which is capable of buffering an unlimited amount of orders and completion notifications. A state transition of a module (if not autonomous) removes a message from the pool and may enter new messages into the pool. If the state of a module allows consuming an order or completion notification present in the pool, that module is said to be "enabled". In a set of communicating modules, any enabled module may "switch" at any time. Each **service/accept/notice** will consume its messages in arrival time order.

It is readily clear that this modelling is appropriate for classical inter-process communication via mailboxes and ports. Interestingly, it is applicable to monitors as well. Consider the "weak monitor" first; it will release exclusion when calling another monitor [Haddon 77], which means that it will always be ready to consume any message sent to it. Thus, the infinite message pool is an adequate model although we don't see a message pool in the realization. (Note that queues of processes waiting to enter a monitor have nothing to do with the abstract message pool; they are a transient phenomenon of the implementation only, serving to achieve atomicity of state transitions.)

A problem arises with the regular, "strong" monitor and with the Ada task. Nested invocations may cause a module to get stuck with an invocation statement. However, since an invocation statement requests synchronous service we are in good shape: the implementation specification of the module has to specify that a transition producing an order will result in a state that refuses to consume any message different from the corresponding completion notification. So a simple implementation specification for a client module might look like this:

```
module client using server <s> is
        service 1, .... ; (* services offered by client! *)
components .... ,
            ready: boolean;
assertion ... ;
accept service 1 when ready is
        ... and start server.s
            and not ready ';
notice server.s is
        ... and ready ';
end client.
```

We can conclude that it is not necessary to have different models for module inter-connection; the "unlimited message pool" model will do. Communication peculiari-ties with different realizations of modules will be (and have to be) reflected in the implementation specifications.

4.3. A non-trivial example of module interconnection

Several authors have used the alternating bit protocol as a vehicle for demonstrat-ing specification techniques; see, e.g., [Schwartz/Melliar-Smith 82] [Lamport 83]. These papers also discuss the pros and cons of state machine orientation. Protocol specification using state machines is just a special case of our module specification. In considering the alternating bit protocol we will not encounter complex modules featuring order lists and delayed order completion; the example serves the mere purpose of demonstrating a non-trivial module interaction.

We assume to have two instances of an unreliable, unidirectional transmission line, similar to the *line* specified in 2.3. We would like to construct a reliable mailbox of finite capacity on top of the two lines. The mailbox should be similar to the mailbox specified in 2.2. The idea is to use one line for the transmission of messages, the other one for the transmission of acknowledgements. According to the alternating bit protocol, a message is tagged with a bit and transmitted repeatedly, until an acknowledgement carrying that tag is received; after this, repeated transmission of the next message is started, the tag being the complement of the last tag. The reli-able mailbox is to behave as follows:

```
module mailbox is
        send (message: in packet)
        receive (message: out packet);
components queue: infinite queue (* of messages *);
          capacity: natural (* limits number of queue elements *);
assertion length(queue) = 0 and [] capacity ≥ 1;
service send when length(queue) < capacity is
        queue' = enter(queue, message) and
        return;
service receive when length(queue) > 0 is
        queue' = body(queue) and
        return message' = head(queue);
end mailbox.
```

The mailbox is to be constructed from four components: a message line, an ack-nowledgement line, a sender module and a receiver module. The functional hierar-chy will look like this (cf. the picture in 4.1):

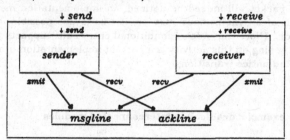

The details of the *sender/receiver* modules are decribed by the following implemen-tation specifications:

```
module sender
        using msgline, ackline <xmit(data: in message; tag: in boolean);
                                    recv(data: out message; tag: out boolean)>
        is send (msg: in message);
components buffer: message; bit: boolean;
assertion buffer = ? and not bit;
accept send when buffer = ? is
        buffer' = msg and return;
auto retransmission when buffer ≠ ? is
        start msgline.xmit(buffer, bit) and
        start ackline.recv;
notice ackline.recv is
        if tag = bit then
            bit' ≠ bit and buffer' = ? fi;
end sender.


module receiver
        using msgline, ackline <xmit(data: in message; tag: in boolean);
                                    recv(data: out message; tag: out boolean)>
        is receive(msg: out message);
components buffer: message; bit: boolean;
assertion buffer = ? and bit;
accept receive when buffer ≠ ? is
        buffer' = ? and return msg' = buffer;
auto retransmission is
        start ackline.xmit(nil, bit) and
        start msgline.recv;
notice msgline.recv is
        if tag ≠ bit and buffer = ? then
            buffer' = data and bit' = tag fi;
end receiver.
```

Let us investigate the interaction between these modules and the *line* modules. An *xmit* order is readily accepted by a *line* module, so an implementation of **start**...*xmit*.. will not require order queueing. The absence of state transitions **notice**...*xmit* specifies that the module is not interested in completion notifications; an implementation may either discard these - or they may be implicit in a synchronous interface to the line.

Treatment of *recv* orders is more subtle. Remember that such an order is not accepted until an uncorrupted packet is available. According to the above specifications, the lines are repeatedly "triggered", by means of **start** ... *recv*, to deliver a packet. When an uncorrupted packet is available, the state transition **notice**...*recv* may occur. Note that an implementation need not "buffer the trigger signals". On the other hand, it is by means of the triggering that arrival of an uncorrupted packet will indeed be noticed. An implementation may well decide to try execution of a synchronous *recv* or, if this is not possible, to proceed with retransmission. (Note that Ada's "conditional entry call" supports this kind of programming.) Looping on this activity is a correct implementation of what is specified by the **auto** and **notice** transitions.

4.4. Another example: deadlock in interconnected modules

We were able to specify the alternating bit protocol without recurrence to the notion of an order list. More general cases may require the usage of order lists for explicit specification of blocking. The added complexity introduces the danger of deadlock, as shown in the following example.

Our goal is to construct a module that represents two mailboxes which are functionally independent but share a common pool of message frames. Each mailbox is to be represented by a queue of numbers that serve to identify message frames in the pool. The head of the pool specification may read like this:

> module *text pool* is
>> enter *(message:* in *text; id:* out *natural),*
>> remove *(id:* in *natural; message:* out *text);*

As the pool has a finite capacity, say *cap,* an *enter* order will not be accepted when no empty frames are available. Completing the specification of the pool is left to the reader.

The desired module is constructed as indicated in this picture:

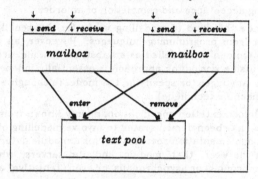

We omit the service specification of this module and turn our attention to the implementation specification of *mailbox.* If we have a monitor implementation in mind, we have to take into account the respective remarks in 4.2. This leads to the following specification:

> module *mailbox*
>> using *text pool* <enter*(message:* in *text; id:* out *natural),*
>>> remove*(id:* in *natural; message:* out *text)>*
>> is send *(message:* in *text),*
>>> receive *(message:* out *text);*
> components *queue: infinite queue (* of ids *),*
>> *locked: boolean;*
> assertion *length(queue) = 0* and not *locked;*
> accept send when *length(queue) < cap* and not *locked* is
>> start *text pool.enter(message)* and *locked';*
> notice *text pool.enter* is
>> *queue' = append(queue,id)* and not *locked'* and
>> for that *x* in *orders* sat *true* return;
> accept *receive* when *length(queue) > 0* and not *locked* is
>> *queue' = body(queue)* and *locked'* and
>> start *text pool.remove(head(queue));*
> notice *text pool.remove* is
>> not *locked'* and
>> for that *x* in *orders* sat *true* return *message' = this.message;*
> end *mailbox.*

Analysis of the module triple constructed from *text pool* and two instances of *mailbox* reveals that deadlock may occur. If the pool is exhausted it will not accept an *enter* order given by a mailbox, which means that the transition **notice text pool.enter** will not take place. If both the mailboxes experience this situation after a transition **accept send**, both will be in the *locked* state. As a consequence, they are disabled forever.

Of course, this effect is not too surprising to those who know of the problems with nesting strong monitors. Deadlock does not occur if the *locked* component is removed from the above example. The resulting specification describes the behaviour of a weak monitor.

5. Conclusion

It has been demonstrated that a simple state machine augmented with an order list is capable of modelling complex modules in a concurrent environment. The approach taken is applicable to modules obeying the client/server paradigm and rests on splitting acceptance and completion of an order.

We have seen how this kind of modelling works for different kinds of concurrent modules known from programming languages. Moreover, an arbitrarily complex concurrent system can be modelled as an abstract module, provided it acts like a server to the outside world. The approach is essentially independent of particular techniques and languages for specifying the model (although we found it practical to use a state machine technique).

The notion of implementation specification, mainly known from the area of protocol specification, has been demonstrated to involve modelling of inter-module communication. An implementation specification for a module determines the nature of communication between that module and its servers, whether buffered or unbuffered, synchronous or asynchronous, or even "tentative" as in the conditional entry call of Ada.

Work remains to be done in the area of verification. This includes both implementation verification and composition verification. While the former can be attacked along well-established lines of program verification, the ground is not well prepared for the latter (cf. [Lamport 83], footnote 2!). We are working on a formal framework that allows to prove that the behaviour of a system of interconnected modules with given specifications meets a specification given for that system.

It remains to be mentioned that the perspectives for prototyping concurrent systems seem promising. Executable service specifications will allow to exercise models. If implementation specifications are made executable as well, it will be possible to test concurrent systems built from concurrent module prototypes.

Acknowledgement

We would like to thank the referees for their comments which helped to improve the presentation.

References

[Ada 82] Reference Manual for the Ada Programming Language. ANSI/MIL-STD 1815A, Ada Joint Program Office, 1982

[Andrews 81] G.R. Andrews: Synchronizing Recources. ACM TOPLAS 3.4, October 1981

[Andrews/Schneider 83] G.R. Andrews/F.B. Schneider: Concepts and Notions for Concurrent Programming. ACM CS 15.1, March 1983

[Cheheyl et al. 81] M.H. Cheheyl/M. Glasser/G.A. Huff/J.K. Millen: Verifying Security. ACM CS 13.3, September 1981.

[Eggert 80] P.R. Eggert: Overview of the Ina Jo Specification Language. TR SP-4082, SDC Santa Monica, October 1980

[Haddon 77] B.K. Haddon: Nested Monitor Calls. ACM Operating Systems Review 11.4, October 1977

[Hailpern/Owicki 82] B. Hailpern/S. Owicki: Modular Verification of Concurrent Programs. Proc. 9. Ann. ACM Symp. on Principles of Programming Languages, Albuquerque 1982

[Hoare 74] C.A.R. Hoare: Monitors: An Operating System Structuring Concept. CACM 17.10, October 1974

[Keramidis/Mackert 79] S. Keramidis/L. Mackert: Specification and Implementation of Parallel Activities on Abstract Objects. Proc. 4. Int. Conf. on Software Engineering, München 1979

[Lamport 83] L. Lamport: Specifying Concurrent Program Modules. ACM TOPLAS 5.2, April 1983

[Laventhal 79] M.S. Laventhal: A Constructive Approach to Reliable Synchronization Code. Proc. 4. Int. Conf. on Software Engineering, München 1979

[Manna/Pnueli 81] Z. Manna, A. Pnueli: Temporal Verification of Concurrent Programs. In: The Correctness Problem in Computer Science (R.S. Boyer, J.S. Moore, Eds.). Academic Press, London 1981.

[Robinson et al. 79] L. Robinson/B.A. Silverberg/K.N. Levitt: The HDM Handbook. SRI International, Menlo Park 1979

[Schwartz/Melliar-Smith 82] R.L. Schwartz/P.M. Melliar-Smith: From State Machines to Temporal Logic: Specification Methods for Protocol Standards. IEEE Trans. Comm. 30.12, December 1982

[Ullman 80] J.D. Ullman: Principles of Data Base Systems. Computer Science Press 1980

[Wegner/Smolka 83] P. Wegner/S.A. Smolka: Processes, Tasks, and Monitors: A Comparative Study of Concurrent Programming Primitives. IEEE-SE 9.4, July 1983

[Wirth 82] N. Wirth: Programming in Modula-2. Springer-Verlag, Berlin 1982.

SYNTHESIS OF PARALLEL PROGRAMS INVARIANTS

E. Pascal Gribomont
Institut Montefiore
Université de Liège
4000 Liège, Belgium

ABSTRACT.

Most current methods for parallel programs design and verification are based on the concept of invariant. However, invariant synthesis is the most difficult part of those methods. This work presents a technique for invariant design usable for both parallel program synthesis and verification. This technique drastically reduces the risks of errors due to a bad statement serialization or to inadequate interprocess synchronization.

1. INTRODUCTION.

The verification and implementation of parallel programs meeting given requirements is difficult. Several methods have been proposed to specify and verify concurrent processes (see e.g. [1] and [11]). In most of these methods, the interesting properties of programs are often expressed as a relation between program variables and control points. Such a relation, named "safety property" or "invariance property", must remain true throughout the execution. To prove these properties, the invariant principle is generally used. Here we name "invariant" a safety property which is inductive, i.e. preserved by each statement of the program. Checking an invariant is straightforward and thus a simple way to prove some safety property is to find an invariant which implies this property. This approach was introduced by Floyd, Hoare and Dijkstra for sequential programming (see [3] for instance) and adapted to parallel programming by many authors e.g. Ashcroft, Owicki, Gries and Levin (see [1], [11] and [9]). Unfortunately, such methods have a major drawback : the design of parallel program invariants is not easy.

The technique we present in this paper is based on a very simple observation : simple programs generally admit simple invariants. Our design method consists in applying successive refinements to both the program and its invariant. The starting point is an abstract and simplified version of the program which usually admits a fairly simple invariant. The goal is of course the real program but also its complete invariant. Our method can also be used for program verification.

This research has been supported in part by IRSIA under grant number 80018.

The expression "refinement" has received many meanings, in the field of computer science (for instance, in the top-down sequential programming methodology). In this work, the two fundamental and opposite operations on a pair (program, invariant), called refinement and abstraction, have a precise meaning.

The main kind of refinement consists in transforming a non-elementary statement (like multiple assignment) into a sequence of simpler ones producing the same global effect. This transformation, called "splitting", does not change anything from a strict sequential point of view but introduces more interleaving between the processes, from the parallel point of view. The invariant must be adapted to take the new control points into account. More precisely, if I is the invariant of the program before splitting and J is the invariant after, we can write $J = I \land A$, where A is an unknown formula. This formula is a solution of a set of boolean inequations obtained from the text of the program before and after the transformation. These inequations are of two kinds : sequential constraints are related to the process containing the transformed statement and interaction constraints correspond to the other processes.

Another kind of refinement is the replacement of a high level communication statement by a lower level statement or set of statements. For instance, CSP-like communication statements, which allow only synchronous communication, can be replaced by classical send-receive statements, which allow asynchronous communication. Such transformations give rise to new control points, corresponding to states in which some messages have been sent but not yet received.

This incremental synthesis technique simplifies invariant design. At each step, the user has to perform a simple task : to state a system of boolean inequations and to find a solution of it (if possible). This method has been successfully applied to synthesize an invariant for the "On-the-fly garbage collector" due to Dijkstra (see [8] and [5]). Communicating processes have also been investigated by this technique. The algorithm of Ricart and Agrawala, which provides mutual exclusion in a computer network and was not formally verified (in fact, it contained a bug), has been studied by this method (see [7], [13] and [14]).

In the rest of this paper, the method is developed and applied to an example (a more detailed presentation of the method appears in [6]). While the example is rather short, the corresponding invariant is not trivial (see [4]). It emphasizes the difficulty of avoiding sequencing or synchronization errors in parallel programming.

2. EXAMPLE.

We wish to implement the mutual exclusion between the critical sections of two concurrent processes. More precisely, there are two cyclic processes attempting from time to time to execute a critical section. The implementation must be such that they will

never be both in their critical section. The solution presented here has been published with an informal proof by Peterson (see [12]).

2.1. Synthesis of a condensed version.

A starting point can be obtained from two simple classical algorithms, although they
both suffer from a critical drawback.

Algorithm 1.   (Initial conditions are immaterial).

	process P1		process P2
	Repeat forever		Repeat forever
	Non-critical section		Non-critical section
	T := 2		T := 1
	T = 1 ?		T = 2 ?
	Critical section		Critical section

If B is a condition, "B ?" means "wait until B". Variable T may be seen as the
"turn". Each process wishing to access its critical section first gives priority to
the other process; when it is given priority back, it enters its critical section.
This policy involves a difficulty : if one process never wishes to access its critical
section, the other will never get the opportunity to enter its own.

Algorithm 2.   (Initial conditions : $\sim Q1$ and $\sim Q2$).

	process 1		process 2
	Repeat forever		Repeat forever
	Non-critical section		Non-critical section
	Q1 := true		Q2 := true
	$\sim Q2$?		$\sim Q1$?
	Critical section		Critical section
	Q1 := false		Q2 := false

Variable Q_i (i = 1,2) means "process i requires access to its critical section".
There is a problem when both processes simultaneously require access : they will be
both deadlocked. Peterson has pointed out that his algorithm can be drawn from these
two primitive versions. We will in fact deduce Peterson's algorithm from them.

The two primitive algorithms can be merged. The access scenario to enter the critical
section will be :

- The process gives way to the other process and signals its request.
- The access will be granted if the process has the turn or if the other process
  does not require access.

When the critical section is completed,

  The process releases the request.

Two difficulties occur :

- Each process cyclically executes four actions about shared variables Q1, Q2 and T. These actions correspond to four different control points. An invariant taking the sixteen possible pairs into account is needed.
- We do not know if a process requesting access must first give priority and then signal its request or inversely. It is possible that only one of the two serialization proves acceptable.

Without knowing the answer to the last question, we can start with the following program :

        (Initial conditions : ~Q1 and ~Q2) :

process 1	process 2
Repeat forever	Repeat forever
Non-critical section	Non-critical section
T,Q1 := 2,true	T,Q2 := 1, true
(~Q2 ∨ T=1)?	(~Q1 ∨ T=2)?
Critical section	Critical section
Q1 := false	Q2 := false

This version is not fine-grained enough for an implementation : there is a multiple assignment. Also each process comprises three control points (see fig. 1); this makes it difficult to find an adequate invariant (if it exists). To find the invariant, we will first consider a condensed version of this algorithm. Afterwards, this version and its invariant will be refined by splitting.

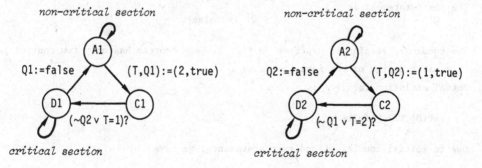

Figure 1.
A first version of the algorithm.

In the condensed version, the double assignment and the test will be abstracted into a single statement.

Let us first introduce some notation. If S is a (sequential) program and P,Q are two predicates, the formula

$$\{P\} \ S \ \{Q\}$$

means that if the execution of S is started in a state satisfying P and if this execution terminates, the final state satisfies Q. Two statements S1 and S2 are equivalent if for all predicates P and Q, we have

$$\{P\} \ S1 \ \{Q\} \ \equiv \ \{P\} \ S2 \ \{Q\}$$

If B is a predicate and S a statement, $(B \rightarrow S)$ is a statement; it means : "wait until B becomes true and then execute S". If B remains false forever, the execution of $(B \rightarrow S)$ will never terminate. Formally we can write

$$[\{P \wedge B\} \ (B \rightarrow S) \ \{Q\}] \ \equiv \ [\{P \wedge B\} \ S \ \{Q\}]$$

$$[\{P \wedge \sim B\} \ (B \rightarrow S) \ \{Q\}] \ \equiv \ true$$

Such statements are written "Await B then do S" in [11]. Another useful notation is the following. If S is a program, $<S>$ is an atomic statement producing the same net-effect as S. From the sequential point of view, there is no distinction between S and $<S>$.

For process 1, the abstracted statement

$$<(T,Q1 := 2,true) \ ; \ (\sim Q2 \vee T=1)? >$$

is equivalent to

$$< \sim Q2 \rightarrow (T,Q1 := 2,true)>$$

The last statement is

$$< Q1 := false>$$

The condensed version is depicted on fig. 2. Each process has only two control points. This makes design of the invariant easy :
Mutual exclusion requires :

    $at(D1,D2) \supset false$

Due to initial conditions and exit statements, we have :

    $at(A1,A2) \supset (\sim Q1 \wedge \sim Q2)$

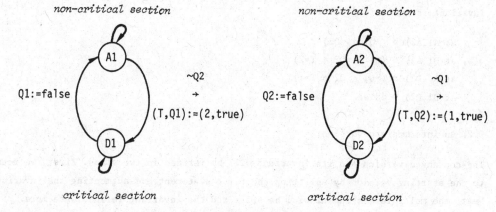

Figure 2.
The condensed version of the algorithm.

The invariant will be completed by two assertions :

at(A1,D2) $\Rightarrow$ I(A1,D2)
at(D1,A2) $\Rightarrow$ I(D1,A2)

where the formulas I(A1,D2) and I(D1,A2) satisfy the following conditions (we give only those related to I(D1,A2)).

$\{I(A1,A2)\} < \sim Q2 \rightarrow (T,Q1 := 2, true) > \{I(D1,A2)\}$
$\{I(D1,A2)\} < \sim Q1 \rightarrow (T,Q2 := 1, true) > \{I(D1,D2)\}$
$\{I(D1,A2)\}$ Q1 := false $\{I(A1,A2)\}$
$\{I(D1,D2)\}$ Q2 := false $\{I(D1,A2)\}$

These four constraints correspond to the four transitions starting from or ending to D1 or A2. These conditions form a set of inequations in the boolean lattice (B, $\supset$) where B is the set of predicates which only admit as free variables the program variables. These conditions amount respectively to the following :

$(Q1 \wedge \sim Q2 \wedge T=2) \supset I(D1,A2)$
$I(D1,A2) \supset Q1$
$I(D1,A2) \supset \sim Q2$
true

I(D1,A2) belongs to the boolean interval defined by :

$$(Q1 \wedge \sim Q2 \wedge T=2) \supset I(D1,A2) \supset (Q1 \wedge \sim Q2)$$

where $p \supset q \supset r$ is an abbreviation for $[p \supset q] \wedge [q \supset r]$. We will adopt here the strongest limit to gain as much knowledge as possible about the program but this is not mandatory. The formula I(A1,D2) is obtained symmetrically; the completed invariant is summarized below.

at(A1,A2) ⊃ (~Q1 ∧ ~Q2)
at(D1,A2) ⊃ (Q1 ∧ ~Q2 ∧ T=2)
at(A1,D2) ⊃ (~Q1 ∧ Q2 ∧ T=1)
at(D1,D2) ⊃ false

2.2. An intermediate version.

The condensed version and its invariant will be refined in two steps. First, we return to the starting version by splitting the first statement and augmenting the invariant. Next, the multiple assignment will be split and the invariant refined once more.

The splitting of the first statement in process 1 consists in introducing the control point C1 (see fig. 1). Two formulas I(C1,A2) and I(C1,D2) will complete the invariant. We first express the sequential constraints, related to process 1.

- about I(C1,A2) :

{I(A1,A2)} T,Q1 := 2,true {I(C1,A2)}
{I(C1,A2)} (~Q2 ∨ T=1)? {I(D1,A2)}
which reduces to :
(Q1 ∧ ~Q2 ∧ T=2) ⊃ I(C1,A2) ⊃ (Q1 ∧ T=2)

- about I(C1,D2) :

{I(A1,D2)} T,Q1 := 2,true {I(C1,D2)}
{I(C1,D2)} (~Q2 ∨ T=1)? {I(D1,D2)}
which reduces to :
(Q1 ∧ Q2 ∧ T=2) ⊃ I(C1,D2) ⊃ (Q2 ∧ T=2)

As before, we prefer the strongest limits of the intervals, with the aim of obtaining as precise an invariant as possible. By the way, let us notice that the following invariance properties are obvious :

at A2 ⊃ ~Q2   at D2 ⊃ Q2

The interaction constraints, related to process 2, are listed below :

{I(C1,A2)} (~Q1 → T,Q2 := 1,true) {I(C1,D2)}
{I(C1,D2)} Q2 := false {I(C1,A2)}

They express the fact that the second process respects the new part of the invariant. Checking these constraints is trivial.

The same splitting applies to process 2. Instead of deducing in a similar way the invariant part related to control point C2, we take symmetry into account. This leads to the following formulas :

$$I(A1,C2) = (\sim Q1 \wedge Q2 \wedge T=1)$$
$$I(D1,C2) = (Q1 \wedge Q2 \wedge T=1)$$

The assertion corresponding to the state (C1,C2) is determined by four constraints listed below,

$$\{I(A1,C2)\} \quad T,Q1 := 2,true \quad \{I(C1,C2)\}$$
$$\{I(C1,C2)\} \quad (\sim Q2 \vee T=1)? \quad \{I(D1,C2)\}$$
$$\{I(C1,A2)\} \quad T,Q2 := 1,true \quad \{I(C1,C2)\}$$
$$\{I(C1,C2)\} \quad (\sim Q1 \vee T=2)? \quad \{I(C1,D2)\}$$

which enforce the choice :

$$I(C1,C2) = (Q1 \wedge Q2)$$

The introduction of control point C2 gives rise to the following interaction constraints :

$$\{I(D1,C2)\} \quad (D1 \rightarrow A1) \quad \{I(A1,C2)\}$$
$$\{I(A1,C2)\} \quad (A1 \rightarrow C1) \quad \{I(C1,C2)\}$$
$$\{I(C1,C2)\} \quad (C1 \rightarrow D1) \quad \{I(D1,C2)\}$$

For instance, we make the first one explicit :

$$\{Q1 \wedge Q2 \wedge T=1\} \quad Q1 := false \quad \{\sim Q1 \wedge Q2 \wedge T=1\}$$

It is trivially true.

COMMENTS : Sequential constraints involve only one unknown formula but interaction constraints involve two of them. That is the reason why the sequential constraints are examined first. They delimit a boolean interval within which the solution must be picked. The choice of a solution satisfying also interaction constraints very often reduces to selecting one of the interval limits (in this example, we always picked the strongest limit). This is also true for more complex programs (examples are presented in [5] and [6]). Nevertheless, this simple tactic sometimes fails : a solution could exist in the interval although the limits do not satisfy the interaction requirements. We met with this situation only once (see [5] for more details). In fact, the method presented here yields inequations which can sometimes admit a number of solutions; the contrary would have been wonderful for a method not restricted to finite state programs.

The complete invariant of the intermediate version is summarized below.

$$at(A1,A2) \supset (\sim Q1 \wedge \sim Q2)$$

$$at(A1,C2) \supset (\sim Q1 \wedge Q2 \wedge T=1) \qquad at(C1,A2) \supset (Q1 \wedge \sim Q2 \wedge T=2)$$

$$at(A1,D2) \supset (\sim Q1 \wedge Q2 \wedge T=1) \qquad at(D1,A2) \supset (Q1 \wedge \sim Q2 \wedge T=2)$$

$$at(C1,C2) \supset (Q1 \wedge Q2)$$

$$at(C1,D2) \supset (Q1 \wedge Q2 \wedge T=2) \qquad at(D1,C2) \supset (Q1 \wedge Q2 \wedge T=1)$$

$$at(D1,D2) \supset false$$

2.3. The final version.

By now, each process comprises three statements, the first of which being a multiple assignment. Our last step will be the splitting of these assignments. The intermediate version invariant will help us to find how these statements can be split.

Let us observe that four cases can occur (while maintaining the symmetry).

1) The intended splitting would endanger mutual exclusion.
2) The splitting is allowed but variable T is to be assigned first.
3) The splitting is allowed but variables Q1, Q2 are to be assigned first.
4) The splitting is allowed and the assignment order is immaterial.

It is well known that intuitive reasoning about parallelism and synchronization is dangerous. The best way is to examine both possible splitting. This is what we will do.

The statement $< T,Q1 := 2,true >$ is split into : $T := 2; \quad Q1 := true$. The new control point is named B1. This splitting is not depicted on the figures. The sequential constraints are :

- about $I(B1,A2)$:

$$\{I(A1,A2)\} \ T := 2 \ \{I(B1,A2)\}$$
$$\{I(B1,A2)\} \ Q1 := true \ \{I(C1,A2)\}$$
which reduces to :
$$(\sim Q1 \wedge \sim Q2 \wedge T=2) \supset I(B1,A2) \supset (\sim Q2 \wedge T=2)$$

- about $I(B1,C2)$:

$$\{I(A1,C2)\} \ T := 2 \ \{I(B1,C2)\}$$
$$\{I(B1,C2)\} \ Q1 := true \ \{I(C1,C2)\}$$
which reduces to :
$$(\sim Q1 \wedge Q2 \wedge T=2) \supset I(B1,C2) \supset Q2$$

- about $I(B1,D2)$:

$$\{I(A1,D2)\} \ T := 2 \ \{I(B1,D2)\}$$
$$\{I(B1,D2)\} \ Q1 := true \ \{I(C1,D2)\}$$

which reduces to :

$(\sim Q1 \land Q2 \land T=2) \supset I(B1,D2) \supset (Q2 \land T=2)$

The formula (at B1 $\supset \sim$Q1) trivially holds. This leads to the following results :

$at(B1,A2) \supset (\sim Q1 \land \sim Q2 \land T=2)$
$at(B1,D2) \supset (\sim Q1 \land Q2 \land T=2)$

About the state (B1,C2), we have two possible assertions :

$at(B1,C2) \supset (\sim Q1 \land Q2 \land T=2)$

or

$at(B1,C2) \supset (\sim Q1 \land Q2)$

The interaction constraint

$\{I(B1,A2)\}$ $(A2 \rightarrow C2)$ $\{I(B1,C2)\}$

reduces to

$\{\sim Q1 \land \sim Q2 \land T=2\}$ $T,Q2 := 1,true$ $\{\sim Q1 \land Q2 \land T=2\}$

This eliminates the first possibility. The second one must also be rejected, due to

$\{I(B1,C2)\}$ $(C2 \rightarrow D2)$ $\{I(B1,D2)\}$

The intended splitting is thus impossible. This failure immediately provides a counterexample of bad execution, which is listed below.

control	Q1	Q2	T
(A1,A2)	F	F	-
(B1,A2)	F	F	2
(B1,C2)	F	T	1
(B1,D2)	F	T	1
(C1,D2)	T	T	1
(D1,D2)	T	T	1

The reverse splitting gives rise to the following statements (see fig. 3) :
(A1, Q1 := true ,B1) and (B1, T := 2 ,C1).

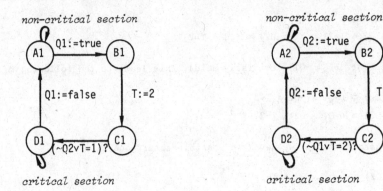

Figure 3.
The final version of the program.

We state now the sequential constraints related to node B1.

- about I(B1,A2) :

    {I(A1,A2)} Q1 := true {I(B1,A2)}
    {I(B1,A2)} T := 2 {I(C1,A2)}
    which reduces to :
    (Q1 ∧ ~Q2) ⊃ I(B1,A2) ⊃ (Q1 ∧ ~Q2)

- about I(B1,C2) :

    {I(A1,C2)} Q1 := true {I(B1,C2)}
    {I(B1,C2)} T := 2 {I(C1,C2)}
    which reduces to :
    (Q1 ∧ Q2 ∧ T=1) ⊃ I(B1,C2) ⊃ (Q1 ∧ Q2)

- about I(B1,D2) :

    {I(A1,D2)} Q1 := true {I(B1,D2)}
    {I(B1,D2)} T := 2 {I(C1,D2)}
    which reduces to :
    (Q1 ∧ Q2 ∧ T=1) ⊃ I(B1,D2) ⊃ (Q1 ∧ Q2)

Subject to verifying the interaction constraints, we choose the strongest limits of the three intervals. Here is the list of the interaction constraints, related to process 2.

    {I(B1,A2)} T,Q2 := 1,true {I(B1,C2)}
    {I(B1,C2)} (~Q1 ∨ T=2)? {I(B1,D2)}
    {I(B1,D2)} Q2 := false {I(B1,A2)}

It is easy to check that our choice is valid.

Control point B2 is introduced in the same way. The symmetry leads to the following choices :

$$I(A1,B2) = (\sim Q1 \wedge Q2)$$
$$I(C1,B2) = (Q1 \wedge Q2 \wedge T=2)$$
$$I(D1,B2) = (Q1 \wedge Q2 \wedge T=2)$$

We could compute $I(B1,B2)$ from the usual set of constraints but it is faster to observe that the formulas (at B1 $\supset$ Q1) and (at B2 $\supset$ Q2) obviously hold. The symmetry prevents us from fixing the value of T. This leads naturally to :

$$I(B1,B2) = (Q1 \wedge Q2)$$

Here is the complete invariant of the final version :

$$at(A1,A2) \supset (\sim Q1 \wedge \sim Q2)$$

$at(A1,B2) \supset (\sim Q1 \wedge Q2)$	$at(B1,A2) \supset (Q1 \wedge \sim Q2)$	
$at(A1,C2) \supset (\sim Q1 \wedge Q2 \wedge T=1)$	$at(C1,A2) \supset (Q1 \wedge \sim Q2 \wedge T=2)$	
$at(A1,D2) \supset (\sim Q1 \wedge Q2 \wedge T=1)$	$at(D1,A2) \supset (Q1 \wedge \sim Q2 \wedge T=2)$	

$$at(B1,B2) \supset (Q1 \wedge Q2)$$

$at(B1,C2) \supset (Q1 \wedge Q2 \wedge T=1)$	$at(C1,B2) \supset (Q1 \wedge Q2 \wedge T=2)$
$at(B1,D2) \supset (Q1 \wedge Q2 \wedge T=1)$	$at(D1,B2) \supset (Q1 \wedge Q2 \wedge T=2)$

$$at(C1,C2) \supset (Q1 \wedge Q2)$$

$at(C1,D2) \supset (Q1 \wedge Q2 \wedge T=2)$	$at(D1,C2) \supset (Q1 \wedge Q2 \wedge T=1)$

$$at(D1,D2) \supset false$$

3. SOME PROGRAM PROPERTIES.

The mutual exclusion is an immediate consequence of :

$$at(D1,D2) \supset false$$

This safety property is implied by the invariant. The primitive algorithms both suffer from deadlock; this is not the case for the final version. A deadlock could occur only if both processes were locked, necessarily at C1 and C2 respectively. The invariant implies :

$$at(C1,C2) \supset (Q1 \wedge Q2)$$

If $T = 1$, process 1 will go on, else process 2 will go on; deadlock is therefore impossible.

Individual starvation is also impossible. Although this fact is not a safety property, it can be deduced from the invariant. Let us suppose, for instance, that process 1 is locked, necessarily at C1. This implies $(Q2 \wedge T = 2)$. On an other hand, the invariant implies (at C1 ⊃ Q1). This leads to the "lock formula" of process 1 :

$$(Q1 \land Q2 \land T = 2)$$

Process 2 is not locked and will eventually set T to 1 or Q2 to false; afterwards, process 2 will never gain access until process 1 has executed its critical section.

COMMENTS : The invariant size seems to grow as the product of the processes sizes, which could be unacceptable for large programs. In fact, if suitable notations are used, the invariant size is a good measure of the program complexity : whenever a program can be written, its invariant can also be stated. For medium or large programs, abbreviation techniques are needed. These techniques do not solve by themselves the problem of "combinatorial explosion" but render it less critical. See [6] and [7] for some examples. In our case, the invariant can be shortened as follows :

$$(at\ A1 \equiv \sim Q1) \land (at\ A2 \equiv \sim Q2)$$
$$(at\ C1 \lor at\ D1) \supset (T=2 \lor at\ C2)$$
$$(at\ C2 \lor at\ D2) \supset (T=1 \lor at\ C1)$$

COMMENT : Our method, like other invariance methods, is especially devoted to invariance properties. Such properties assert that something bad never occurs (falsification of an invariant, deadlock, termination with incorrect results,...). Nevertheless, liveness properties, which assert that something good will eventually happen, can be established easier if adequate safety properties have been proved before. Notice that the invariant was needed to establish freeness of starvation. The same is also true in sequential programming : for instance, a proof of total correctness (liveness property) often begins with a proof of partial correctness (safety property). Without knowing safety properties, the proofs of liveness properties usually require more operational reasoning, which frequently leads to errors.

4. CONCLUSION.

The example shows that our method is useful even for small algorithms : it is sometimes difficult to find their invariants (see [4]). The need of an incremental methodology is still more pronounced for medium size or large programs. A problem which occurs frequently during the design of parallel processes is to know if some statement may be split or not. The methodology presented here provides reliable answer to such questions. If, in some case, a non-elementary statement may be split into several statements, these must be serialized in the right order. Our methodology helps to determine which order is acceptable. Mistakes of this kind occur frequently in parallel algorithms. It was the case for first versions of the "On-the-fly garbage collector" and the algorithm of Ricart and Agrawala previously mentioned (see

[8], [13] and [14]). Moreover, the study of these algorithms and others has made us believe that, contrary to a common view, the invariant method can be well adapted to parallel programming. Specifically, the size of the invariants remains acceptable.

The synthesis of invariants for concurrent programs has already been investigated. Clarke obtains the best invariant of a program as the least fixpoint of an equation written from the text of this program (see [2]). Another method has been developed by Manna and Pnueli (see [10]). Both methods apply only to a restricted class of parallel programs, which is not the case of ours.

REFERENCES.

[1] ASHCROFT, E.A., MANNA, Z., "Formalization of Properties of Parallel Programs", Machine Intelligence, vol. 6, pp. 17-41, 1970.

[2] CLARKE, E.M., "Synthesis of resource invariants for concurrent programs", ACM Toplas, Vol. 2, pp. 338-358, 1980.

[3] DIJKSTRA, E.W., "A discipline of programming", Prentice Hall, New Jersey, 1976.

[4] DIJKSTRA, E.W., "An assertional proof of a program by G. L. Peterson", EWD 779, 1981.

[5] GRIBOMONT, E.P., "Programmation parallèle", Internal Report, University of Liège, 1982.

[6] GRIBOMONT, E.P., "Proving parallel programs in an incremental way", submitted to Science of Computer Programming, 1983.

[7] GRIBOMONT, E.P., "Mutual exclusion in a computer network", submitted to Computer Networks, 1983.

[8] GRIES, D., "An Exercise in Proving Parallel Programs Correct", CACM, vol. 20, pp. 921-930, 1977.

[9] LEVIN, G.M., GRIES, D., "A Proof Technique for Communicating Sequential Processes", Acta Informatica, vol. 15, pp. 281-302, 1981.

[10] MANNA, Z., PNUELI, A., "Verification of concurrent programs : temporal proofs principles", Lecture Notes in Comp. Sc., vol. 131, pp. 200-252, Springer, 1981.

[11] OWICKI, S., GRIES, D., "An Axiomatic Proof Technique for Parallel Programs", Acta Informatica, vol. 6, pp. 319-340, 1976.

[12] PETERSON, G.L., "Myths about the mutual exclusion problem", Information Processing Letters, vol. 12, pp. 115-116, 1981.

[13] RICART, G., AGRAWALA, A.K., "An optimal algorithm for mutual exclusion", CACM, vol. 24, pp. 9-17, 1981.

[14] Corrigendum, CACM, vol. 24, p. 578, 1981.

ANALYZING SAFETY AND FAULT TOLERANCE USING TIME PETRI NETS[†]

N. G. Leveson and J. L. Stolzy
Information and Computer Science
University of California, Irvine
Irvine, California 92717

Abstract: The application of Time Petri net modelling and analysis techniques to safety-critical real-time systems is explored and procedures described which allow analysis of safety, recoverability, and fault-tolerance. These procedures can be used to help determine software requirements, to guide the use of fault detection and recovery procedures, to determine conditions which require immediate mitigating action to prevent accidents, etc. Thus it is possible to establish important properties during the synthesis of the system and software design instead of using guesswork and costly *a posteriori* analysis.

Introduction

Computers are increasingly being used as passive (monitoring) and active (controlling) components of real-time systems, e.g. air traffic control, aerospace, aircraft, industrial plants, and hospital patient monitoring systems. The problems of safety become important when these applications include systems where the consequences of failure are serious and may involve grave danger to human life and property.

Although in a batch system it is reasonable to abort execution and attempt to fix the problem when a failure occurs, control usually cannot be abandoned abruptly in an embedded system. Therefore, responses to hardware failures, software faults, human error, and undesired and perhaps unexpected environmental conditions must be built into the system. These responses can take three basic forms:

1) a *fault-tolerant* system continues to provide full performance and functional capabilities in the presence of operational faults.

2) a *fail-soft* system continues operation but provides only degraded performance or reduced functional capabilities until the fault is removed.

3) a *fail-safe* system attempts to limit the amount of damage caused by a failure. No attempt is made to satisfy the functional specifications except where necessary to ensure safety.

These responses are, for most situations, in the order of decreasing desirability although when the functional and safety requirements of the system are not identical (and especially when they are conflicting), they are not necessarily of decreasing importance.

The area of system safety is well-established, and procedures exist to identify and analyze electromechanical hazards along with techniques to eliminate or limit hazards in the final product (for a summary, see Malasky (1982)). Unfortunately, much more is known about how to engineer safe mechanical systems than safe software systems. With the increased use of software in safety-critical components of complex systems, government certification agencies and contractors are increasingly including requirements for software hazard analysis and verification of software safety (e.g. see MIL-STD-882b: System

[†]This work was partially supported by a MICRO grant co-funded by the State of California and Hughes Aircraft Co.

Safety Program Requirements). Modelling and analysis tools are desperately needed to aid in these tasks. This paper explores the application of Petri net modelling and analysis techniques to the design of safety-critical real-time systems. Because timing is crucial with respect to the control of real-time systems, Time Petri nets are used.

The next section describes the general approach to be taken. Following that, procedures are outlined for eliminating hazards from the system design. Then potential failures are added to the analysis procedures.

Safety Analysis

Whereas *system reliability* deals with the problems of ensuring that a system, including all hardware and software subsystems, performs a required task or mission for a specified time in a specified environment, *system safety* is concerned only with ensuring that a mishap does not occur in the process. Usually there are many possible system failures which have relatively little "cost" associated with them. Others have such drastic consequences that an attempt must be made to avoid them at all costs, perhaps even at the cost of attaining some or all of the goals of the system.[†] For example, an amusement park ride may have to be temporarily stopped because conditions are such (e.g. a foreign object is on the tracks) that a derailment is possible. Thus the response to a safety critical failure may focus on reduction of risk rather than attainment of mission [Leveson (1984)].

While software itself cannot be unsafe, it can issue commands to a system it controls which place the system in an unsafe state. Furthermore, the controlling software should be able to detect when factors beyond the control of the computer (e.g. environmental conditions) place the system in a hazardous state and to take steps to eliminate the hazard or, if that is not possible, initiate procedures to minimize the hazard. This then is the problem of *software safety*.

If software safety is to be studied and used as a measure of software quality, then some definitions are necessary. A *mishap* is an event or series of events which results in death, injury, illness, or damage to or loss of property or equipment. A *hazard* or *unsafe state* is a condition or state of the system with the potential for (i.e. some non-zero probability of) leading to a mishap. Hazards can be categorized by the aggregate probability of the occurrence of the individual conditions which make up the hazard and by the seriousness of the resulting mishap. Together these constitute *risk*.

The first step in a safety analysis is to identify the system hazards and assess their severity and probability (i.e. risk). The next step is to design the system so as to eliminate hazards or (if that is not possible) to minimize the risk by altering the design so that there is very little probability of the hazard occurring. This can be accomplished by first ensuring that the system as specified is safe, i.e. given that the specifications are correctly implemented and no failures occur, operation of the system will not result in a mishap. The next step in the design process is to identify and eliminate (by using fault tolerance techniques) single point failure modes which can lead to a hazard. Finally, techniques are used to ensure that the probability of multiple sequences of failures leading to a hazard is sufficiently low. If it is impossible to completely eliminate the possibility of a hazard, a design goal may be to minimize the effects of the hazard should it occur. In this case the system should detect the hazard and attempt to eliminate it, if possible; otherwise an attempt should be made to minimize any possible effects. In either case, in order to reduce risk, the *exposure time* (length of time of occurrence) of the hazardous conditions must be minimized. The goal of the techniques presented in this paper is to develop formal procedures to aid in this safety analysis process.

[†] In a system whose sole purpose is the sustaining of life, e.g. a pacemaker, these conflicts between safety and other system requirements do not occur.

It is important to stress the "system" nature of the problem. Software does not harm anyone -- only the instruments which it controls can do damage. Therefore, software safety procedures cannot be developed in a vacuum, but must be considered as part of the overall system safety. For example, a particular software error may cause a mishap only if there is a simultaneous human and/or hardware failure. Alternatively, an environmental event or failure may be involved in the software error. Mishaps are often the result of multiple failure sequences which involve hardware, software, and human failures. One modelling technique which has the potential for analyzing software for real-time systems within a system viewpoint is Time Petri nets. By combining hardware, software, and human components within one model, it is possible to determine, for example, the effects of a failure or fault in one component on another component. It is also possible to use the model to determine software safety and fault tolerance requirements. Writing correct software requirements is a difficult problem for which there are few analytical tools available. Techniques such as Failure Modes and Effects Analysis (FMEA) and Preliminary Hazard Analysis (PHA) [Malasky (1982)] have been developed to determine the system safety requirements. However, there is a need to be able to go from the system safety requirements to the software safety requirements. Using the hazardous states which have been identified in the PHA, it may be possible to work backward to the software interface using Petri net analysis techniques and thus to derive the software safety requirements.

Formal Definitions

A Petri net is composed of a set of *places* P, a set of *transitions* T, an *input* function I, an *output* function O, and an *initial marking* μ_0. The input function I is a mapping from the transition t_i to a bag of places $I(t_j)$ where a bag is a generalization of a set which allows multiple occurrences of an element. Similarly, the output function O maps a transition t_j to a bag of places $O(t_j)$. The initial placement of tokens on the places of the net is specified by μ_0 [Peterson (1981)]. Formally, this is written:

Definition: A *Petri net structure*, Φ, is a five-tuple, $\Phi = (P,T,I,O,\mu_0)$.

$P = \{p_1, p_2, ..., p_n\}$ is a finite set of *places*, $n \geq 0$.

$T = \{t_1, t_2, ..., t_m\}$ is a finite set of *transitions*, $m \geq 0$. The set of places and the set of transitions are disjoint, $P \cap T = \emptyset$.

$I: T \to P^\infty$ is the *input* function, a mapping from transitions to bags of places.

$O: T \to P^\infty$ is the *output* function, a mapping from transitions to bags of places.

Finally, $\mu_0: P \to N$ is the *initial marking* for the net where N is the set of non-negative integers.

Definition: The *multiplicity* of an input place p_i for a transition t_j is the number of occurrences of the place in the input bag of the transition, denoted $\#(p_i, I(t_j))$. The multiplicity of an output place is defined similarly and denoted $\#(p_i, O(t_j))$.

A graph structure is often used for illustration of Petri nets where a *circle* " $\bigcirc$ " represents a place and a *bar* " $|$ " represents a transition. Figure 1 shows a petri net. An arrow from a place to a transition defines the place to be an input to the transition. Similarly, an output place is indicated by an arrow from the transition to the place.

The dynamic aspects of Petri net models are denoted by markings which are assignments of *tokens* to the places of a Petri net. Markings may change during *execution* of a Petri net.

Definition: A *marking* μ of a Petri net Φ is a function from the set of places P to the nonnegative integers N, $\mu: P \to N$.

The execution of a Petri net is controlled by the number and distribution of tokens in the Petri net.

Definition: A transition t_j is *enabled* if and only if each of its input places contains at least as many tokens as there exists arcs from that place to the transition, i.e. $\mu(p_i) \geq \#(p_i, I(t_j))$ for all $p_i \in P$.

When a transition fires, all enabling tokens are removed from its input places, and a token is deposited in each of its output places. Transition firings continue as long as there exists at least one enabled transition.

When using Petri nets to model systems, places represent conditions and transitions are used to represent events. Figure 1 can be interpreted as a model of a simple railroad crossing. P_1, P_2, P_3, and P_4 represent the different conditions that can hold for the train (i.e. approaching, just before, within, and past the crossing, respectively). Similarly, transitions 1, 2, and 3 denote the events of signalling the train's approach, entering the crossing, and signalling the train's departure. The large box represents the controlling device or computer -- either hardware or software based. The states of the gate are represented by two places P_{11} (the gate is up) and P_{12} (the gate is down). Transitions 6 and 7 represent the events of raising and lowering the gate respectively.

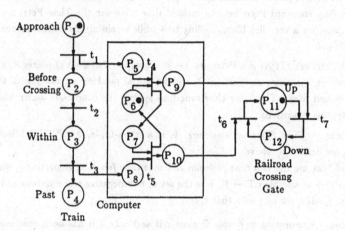

Figure 1. A Petri Net Graph

The state of the Petri net (and hence the state of the modelled system) is defined by the marking (the existing conditions). The change in state caused by firing a transition is defined by the *next-state function* δ.

Definition: The *next-state function* δ: $N^n \times T \to N^n$ for a Petri net $\Phi=(P,T,I,O,\mu_0)$ with marking μ and transition $t_j \in T$ is defined if and only if t_j is enabled. If $\delta(\mu,t_j)$ is defined, then $\delta(\mu,t_j) = \mu'$ where

$$\mu'(p_i) = \mu(p_i) - \#(p_i, I(t_j)) + \#(p_i, O(t_j)) \text{ for all } p_i \in P$$

Definition: For a Petri net $\Phi=(P,T,I,O,\mu_0)$ with marking μ, a marking μ' is *immediately reachable* from μ if there exists a transition $t_j \in T$ such that $\delta(\mu,t_j)=\mu'$.

The "reachability" relationship is the reflexive transitive closure of the "immediately reachable" relationship.

Definition: The *reachability set* $R(\Phi,\mu)$ for a Petri net $\Phi=(P,T,I,O,\mu_0)$ with marking μ is the smallest set of markings defined by:
1. $\mu \in R(\Phi,\mu)$
2. If $\mu' \in R(\Phi,\mu)$ and $\mu'' = \delta(\mu',t_j)$, for some $t_j \in T$, then $\mu'' \in R(\Phi,\mu)$.

Both trees and graphs have been used to represent the reachability state. In this paper, a reachability graph is used where the nodes of the graph are labeled with the present marking (i.e. the state) and the arcs represent transitions between states (see figure 2a).

Definition: A *path* in the reachability graph is a sequence of transitions $t_i,...,t_j$ starting at marking μ_{i-1} to μ_j such that $\delta(\mu_{n-1},t_n) = \mu_n$ for $n = i...j$

Definition: The *extended next-state function* δ^* is defined for a marking μ, and a sequence of transitions $s \in T^*$ by

$$\delta^*(\mu,t_j;s) = \delta^*(\delta(\mu,t_j),s)$$
$$\delta^*(\mu,\lambda) = \mu$$

To model time requires enhancements to the basic Petri net model. There have been several proposals for extending standard Petri nets to include time. We use the Time Petri net approach of Merlin (1974) as it provides a very flexible modelling tool while retaining the instantaneous firing feature of the untimed Petri net.

A Time Petri net (TPN) is a Petri net, i.e. it is composed of a set of places P, a set of transitions T, an input function I, an output function O, and an initial marking μ_0 along with the added *firing time functions* Min and Max. The firing time functions specify the conditions under which a transition may fire. Formally, this is written:

Definition: A *Time Petri net structure*, Φ, is a seven-tuple, $\Phi=(P,T,I,O,Min,Max,\mu_0)$. P, T, I, O, and μ_0 are defined as above.

Min and Max are the *min time function* and *max time function*, respectively, where

Min:$T \rightarrow R$ and Max:$T \rightarrow R$, R is the set of non-negative real numbers and

$Min_i \leq Max_i$ for all i such that $t_i \in T$.

Definition: A transition is *firable* at time τ if and only if it has been continuously enabled during the interval $\tau - Min(t_j)$ to τ. The firable transition may fire at any time τ for $Min(t_j) \leq \tau \leq Max(t_j)$. A transition must fire at time τ if it has been continuously enabled during the interval $\tau - Max(t_j)$ to τ.

Note that the Time Petri net is equivalent to a standard Petri net if all Min times are 0 and all Max times are set to ∞. Also note that the markings of the states of the Time Petri net reachability graph will be equal to or a subset of the markings of the equivalent untimed Petri net. This is true since the enabling rules for the time Petri net are the same as for a Petri net. The difference lies in the additional restrictions placed on the firing rules. Thus adding timing may restrict the set of possible markings, but will never increase it. Since we are basically interested in determining worst cases (including the potential effects of timing failures), much of our analysis will involve deriving the untimed reachability graph and then determining 1) the timing constraints of the final system necessary to avoid high-risk states, and 2) the run-time checks, e.g. watchdog timers, needed to detect critical timing failures.

Eliminating High-Risk States from the Design

A mishap is an unplanned event or series of events that results in death, injury, illness, or damage to or loss of property or equipment. Mishaps can be classified as to severity from catastrophic to negligible.

Definition: A *hazard* is a set of conditions within a state from which there is a path to a mishap. A state σ is hazardous if and only if there exists a mishap state σ_m and a sequence of transitions $s \in T^*$ such that $\delta^*(\sigma,s)=\sigma_m$.

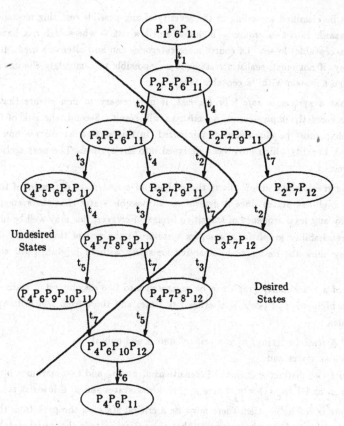

Figure 2a. Reachability Graph for Figure 1

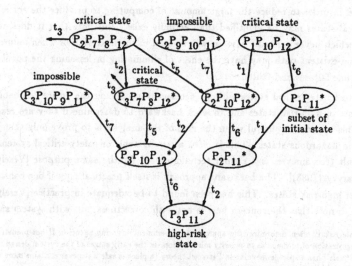

Figure 2b. Example of Critical State Algorithm

Hazards can be classified according to the severity of any possible resulting mishap. For simplicity we will divide hazards into two groups -- high-risk and low-risk -- where high-risk hazards can lead to catastrophic (unacceptable) losses. Of course more categories can and often are used. It is important to note that in many, if not most, realistic systems it is impossible to completely eliminate risk. The goal instead is to design a system with "acceptable risk." [†]

To show that a system is *safe* [‡] or *low-risk*, it is necessary to first ensure that given that the specifications are correctly implemented, no mishaps will result. Second, the risk of faults or failures leading to a mishap must be eliminated or minimized. In this section we discuss how to identify and eliminate high-risk hazards which have been designed into the system. The next section will treat the problem of failures.

Creating the reachability graph allows the designer of a system to determine if the system design can "reach" any high-risk states since it determines all possible states that the system can reach from the initial state by any legal sequence of transition firings. However, this may well be impractical due to the size of the reachability graph for a complex system. In the rest of this section, we describe techniques which may allow the design to be analyzed for safety without producing the entire reachability graph.

The states of a reachability graph can be separated into two disjoint sets: states from which it is possible to reach high-risk and possibly also low-risk states and those from which it is possible to reach only low-risk states.

Definition: A state (marking) μ_c is a *critical state* if and only if

a) $\mu_c \in$ low-risk states and

b) there exist two distinct sequences of transitions s_1 and s_2 and two markings μ_i and μ_j such that $\delta^*(\mu_c, s_1) = \mu_i$ and $\delta^*(\mu_c, s_2) = \mu_j$ where $\mu_i \in$ high-risk states and $\mu_j \in$ low-risk states.

If a high-risk state is reachable, then there must be a critical state on the path from the initial state to the high-risk state (this includes the possibility that the critical state is the initial state). Otherwise, the design needs to be completely redone since all executions result in high-risk states.

To eliminate hazards, it is not necessary to produce the entire reachability graph but only to determine the critical states and to disallow the unwanted transition in each case. Some of our techniques are conservative, i.e. in order to reduce the large amount of computing to produce the entire graph, a larger number of critical states may be identified than actually exist. But note that it does no harm to eliminate a hazard which never existed. Also, as will be seen in the next section when failures are discussed, eliminating a non-existent path may have the effect of eliminating or lessening the possibility of mishaps caused by run-time failures and faults.

One way to locate critical states without necessarily producing the entire reachability graph is to start with the set of high-risk states and to work backward to determine if they are reachable from the initial state. This approach is useful when the goal of the analysis is to prove only that the system cannot reach certain hazardous states. This is often a requirement for safety-critical systems, e.g. see MIL-STD-882b. Fault tree analysis is a similar technique used for the same purpose [Vesely *et. al.* (1981), Leveson and Harvey (1983)]. The backward approach is itself practical only if one considers a relatively small number of high-risk states. This has been found to be adequate in practice [Vesely *et. al.* (1981)]. It is important to note that the concern here is not with correctness, but with system safety. That is, a

---

[†] What is acceptable risk is often determined by appropriate government licensing agencies. If not predetermined by law, the definition and categorization of mishaps as to severity must be done in the early stages of the system design.

[‡] Because the term "safe" has a specific meaning in Petri net theory (a place is safe if it never contains more than one token), we will use the term "low-risk" where necessary to avoid confusion.

system is "safe" if it is free from mishaps even if it also does not accomplish its "mission" or functional objectives.

To determine if a state can be reached using backward reachability graphs, it is necessary to temporarily ignore timing constraints. The procedure is to first construct the *inverse* untimed Petri net.

Definition: The *inverse* Petri net, Φ^{-1} for a Petri net $\Phi=(P,T,I,O)$ is defined by interchanging the input and output functions, $\Phi^{-1} = (P,T,O,I)$.

A reachability graph is then constructed using the inverse Petri net and the high-risk state as the initial marking. If the original initial state is reachable, then the mishap may be possible.

Theorem: A high-risk state σ_m is in the reachability set $R(\Phi,\sigma_0)$ if and only if given an initial state σ_0, $\sigma_0 \in R(\Phi^{-1},\sigma_m)$.

The proof can be shown by induction on the sequence of transition firings. By definition if $\mu = \delta(\mu',t)$ then $\mu' = \delta^{-1}(\mu,t)$. This allows the sequence of transitions from σ_0 to σ_m to be traversed in reverse order.

Even though a high-risk state is reachable in the untimed Petri net, it may not be reachable when time constraints are considered. Two approaches are possible. The first is to use the time constraints and work forward from the initial state to determine if the timing constraints have eliminated this path from the timed reachability graph. The other is to assume the worst and just modify the design to ensure that the path is eliminated.

This backward approach is helpful only if the resulting reachability graph is smaller than the original. If the state is reachable, then the backward reachability graph can never be larger than the original reachability graph. Unfortunately, if the high-risk state is not reachable, it is possible for the backward reachability graph to be larger than the original graph and even to be infinite. Therefore, again it may be impractical to generate the entire backward reachability graph.

But if the goal is to ensure that high-risk states can never be reached, it is possible to simply work backward to the first "critical" state (in this case to a state in the reachability graph which has two successors) and to use design techniques such as those outlined below to ensure that the bad path is never taken. It is unimportant as to whether this path actually is reachable since eliminating the possibility of a mishap which would not have occurred does no harm. It is also unimportant if this is truly a critical state as defined above (one path leads to low-risk states) since if the uneliminated path also leads to a mishap, this will be determined in a later step, and this second path will also be eliminated.

The analysis procedure starts with the set of high-risk conditions. For each member of this set, the immediately prior state or states are generated. Each of these "one-step-backward" states is then examined to see if it is a potentially critical state and can be used to eliminate one path to the high-risk state. Note that we are not dealing with complete states but only with partial states. That is, some conditions in the state are unimportant as far as risk goes. Furthermore, we do not know what the complete final states are. Therefore there may be some "don't care" places in each state which are "filled in" in the process of executing the algorithm. Finally, we need only to look forward one step from each potentially critical state in order to label it as critical (i.e. there exists a next-state which is low-risk). This is because if this path also leads to a high-risk state, then it will be eliminated by the algorithm in a later step. The details of the algorithm follow:

```
Put initial set of high-risk conditions into S = states_to_process
while  S is not empty
  do
    let c be one of S;
    if c is a subset of the initial state then
        high-risk state reachable and need to redesign
    else
      do  {work backwards to critical states}
        next_back_states = ∅
        {determine which transitions are enabled}
        for each transition t ∈ T
          do
            let R = O(t) ∩ c;
            TE = O(t) − R;
            SE = c − R;
            if R ≠ ∅ then {t is enabled − generate the corresponding next backward states}
                Next_back_states = Next_back_states ∪ δ⁻¹(R ∪ TE ∪ SE,t);
          od
        for each next_back_state b
          do
            Forward_states = set of immediately reachable states δ(b,t)
            Other_states = Forward_states − [Forward_states ∩ {S ∪ Next_back_states}]
            case b
              b ∈ states_considered : exit;
              b is illegal according to system invariants : exit;
              b is high risk : add b to S;
              b is low-risk and there exists a f ∈ other_states such
                  that f is low-risk {therefore b is potentially critical}: add b to set of critical states;
              else {b is low-risk but not critical - necessary to go backwards again}
                      add b to S;
            esac
          od
        move c from S to states_considered;
        augment design by eliminating bad transitions from critical states;
      od
end while
```

Using the train example again, figure 2b shows the partial graph generated by the algorithm for the high risk state where the train is approaching (P_3), the gate is up (P_{11}), and any other "don't care conditions" (denoted by the "*") may also hold. Propagating this state backwards, we reach the initial state, impossible states, and critical states. From this we derive the information that in order to avoid the high-risk state, the design must be modified to ensure that transition t_3 has priority over transition t_5 and that transition t_6 has priority over transition t_1.

When a critical state is identified, it is necessary to modify the Petri net in some way to ensure that the good path is always taken, i.e. that another transition always is performed before or has priority over the critical transition.[†]

There are many possible ways to modify the system design in order to eliminate the high-risk states. One common approach is to use an interlock. Interlocks are used to ensure correct sequences of events. An example of a hardware interlock is an access panel or door to equipment where a high voltage exists. Software interlocks include monitors and batons. To model an interlock in a Petri net, assume that t_i is the desired transition, while t_j is the undesired transition. It is possible to force the system always to take the desired path (i.e. to eliminate the undesired path from the reachability graph) by making the following changes to the two transitions in the Petri net. Add a new place (the interlock I) to the output bag of t_i and to the input bag of t_j. This ensures that transition t_i always has priority over transition t_j. There may be multiple desired transitions and an interlock must be applied to each. See figure 3a for an example.

The above type of interlock is used to ensure that one event always precedes another event (e.g. a baton in software). Another type involves ensuring that an event does not occur while a condition is true. This is implemented in the Petri net by using a locking place (see figure 3b). This corresponds to a critical section in software.

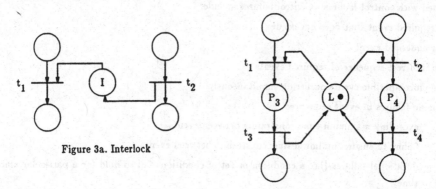

Figure 3a. Interlock

Figure 3b. Locking Place

In the train example, an interlock can be added between t_7 and t_2 (see figure 5a) in order to eliminate the high-risk states. The interlock is included within the computer-controller, but alternatively it might have been part of the hardware. One physical implementation of such an interlock might be a computer-controlled warning signal for the train.

Another way to ensure that one transition will always fire when both are enabled is to enforce timing constraints or timing conditions in the designed system. In order to ensure that a transition t_j (which leads to the high-risk state) does not fires whenever t_i and t_j are both enabled (i.e. the high-risk state is eliminated from the reachability graph), the following timing constraint must be enforced: the maximum time that it may take for the higher priority transition (t_i) to fire must be less than the minimum time for the lower priority transition (t_j) to become enabled and to fire. Each of these time quantities must be the total time that the enabling conditions have been met, not just the individual transition time limit.

One method of determining these quantities is to use the reachability graph to find the maximum (or minimum) valued path leading to the transition which has the required conditions continually enabled. In the system modelled in figure 1, the desired goal is to have condition P_{12} occur before

---

[†]To require that a transition t_i always have priority over a transition t_j in all situations may be more strict than absolutely necessary but this is true of most safety devices and is one reason why safety occasionally conflicts with other system qualities such as performance.

condition P_3. In terms of the reachability graph this means that when in state $P_2 P_5 P_6 P_{11}$ or $P_2 P_7 P_9 P_{11}$, transition t_2 must not be firable. In the first case, the constraint necessary for t_4 to fire before t_2 is simply that $Min(t_2) > Max(t_4)$. For the second case it is a bit more complicated since firing t_1 results in t_2 being enabled. The constraint in this case is $Min(t_2) > Max(t_7) + Max(t_4)$.

Timing constraints are enforced in systems by either verifying that the design makes it impossible for the constraint to be violated or by using watchdog timers and other devices to determine when the constraint is about to fail and to insert recovery techniques into the system design (either software or hardware). An example is shown in the next section.

Adding Failures to the Analysis

Once the design is determined to have an acceptable level of risk, run-time faults and failures must be considered. Designing for fault tolerance and safety requires being able to model failures and faults and to analyze the resulting model. Using definitions from Kopetz (1982), a failure is defined as an event while a fault is a state. A failure always results in a fault and is called a fault-starting event. The fault remains in the system until the occurrence of a terminating event for this fault. In this paper, we are concerned with control failures. Control failures include:

- a required event that does not occur
- an undesired event
- an incorrect sequence of required events
- two incompatible events occurring simultaneously
- timing failures in event sequences
  - exceeding maximum time constraints between events
  - failing to ensure minimum time constraints between events
  - durational failures (i.e. a condition or set of conditions fail to hold for a particular amount of time)

Each of these types of failures must be able to be modelled in the Petri net. Merlin and Farber (1976) modelled failures in Petri nets as a loss of token or generation of a spurious token. Azema and Diaz (1977) took a similar approach. This was appropriate since Merlin's goal was to analyze failures in communication systems where the primary type of fault is the loss of a message due to failure of the underlying communication medium. However, when dealing with analysis of failures in more general situations, it is often useful to be able to determine the state that a system is in after the failure has occurred (i.e. the fault). For example, if a token is lost when the system is in a state where a particular bit is one, it is important to know whether the failure results in a "stuck at one" state or a "zero" state for the bit. This is because a fault remains in the system until a terminating event for the fault (the faulty condition is no longer true or loses its token). Because of the faulty state or condition, it is possible for further failures to occur which cause further faults. Thus the type of fault which results from the failure must be included in the model in order to analyze the consequences of failures on the system (and thus to differentiate between high and low cost failures). For analysis and readability purposes, it is also useful to model failure events in a different way than normal, expected events.

For these reasons, we introduce a new type of transition, a *failure transition* which acts like other transitions but is denoted by a double bar and a *fault condition* which is denoted by a double circle.[†] For

---

[†] Merlin actually includes failure transitions in his reachability graph (which he calls the error token machine), but does not put them in the Petri net itself.

a Petri net, Φ, the set of transitions becomes $T = T_L \cup T_F$ where T_L are legal transitions and T_F are failure transitions and $T_L \cap T_F = \emptyset$. Similarly, the set of places is now $P = P_L \cup P_F$ where P_L are legal places and P_F are faults and $P_L \cap P_F = \emptyset$. Examples of modelling some of the above types of control failures can be found in figure 4. The failure transitions shown are infinitely fire-able. To make analysis practical, a place which acts as a counter can be added to the failure transition. The number of tokens initially contained in this place controls the maximum number of times the transition (failure) can fire. Realistically, most systems are designed to handle and recover from a maximum number of faults, and the tokens in the counter are the Petri net equivalent of this ceiling value.

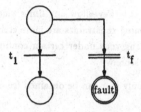

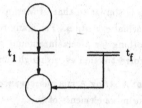

Figure 4a. Desired Event t_1 Does Not Occur   Figure 4b. Undesired Event t_1 Occurs

We now have two types of states: faulty states and legal states.

Definition: A state σ is a *legal state* if and only if there exists a path in the failure reachability graph from the initial state σ_0 to σ which contains only legal transitions, i.e. if σ_0 is the initial state, there exists a sequence of legal transitions $s \in T_L^*$ such that $\delta^*(\sigma_0, s) = \sigma$.

Definition: A state σ is a *faulty state* if and only if every path to σ from the initial state σ_0 contains a failure transition i.e. for every sequence $s \in T^*$ where $\delta^*(\sigma_0, s) = \sigma$ there exists a t_f such that $t_f \in T_F$ and $t_f \in s$

Once failures are included in the model, it is necessary to decide what qualities of the design are important to analyze with respect to control failures. Three such qualities are control fault tolerance, recoverability, and fail-safety. Control fault tolerance implies that a system continues to function correctly (i.e. to provide the service required by its specification) in the presence of component failure. Recoverability implies that a system continues to provide service although the service may be (temporarily) degraded (i.e. may not satisfy *all* the requirements of the specification). A system is fail-safe if component faults do not lead to a catastrophic system failure (mishap) although the system may not provide any service except that required to prevent the catastrophic failure. Each of these qualities can be defined in terms of Petri nets as follows:

Definition: A process is *recoverable* if after the occurrence of a failure, the control of the process is not lost, and in an acceptable amount of time, it will return to normal execution. Formally, a process is recoverable from a failure $t_f \in T_F$ if and only if in the failure reachability graph (FRG):

Let Σ_F be the set of faulty states and let Σ_L be the set of legal states

1) the number of faulty states is finite,

     $cardinality(\Sigma_F) < \infty$

2) there are no terminal faulty states,

     for all $\sigma \in \Sigma_F$, σ is firable

3) there are no directed loops including *only* faulty states,

there does not exist a sequence $t_1 \dots t_n$ in the FRG such that for $\sigma_i \in \Sigma_F$,
$\delta(\sigma_i, t_i) = \sigma_{i+1}$ for i=1...n-1 and $\sigma_1 = \sigma_{n+1}$

4) the sum of the maximum times on all paths from the failure transition to a correct state is less than a pre-defined acceptable amount of time.

For every path $(t_1, \dots, t_n)$ from $\sigma_1 \in \Sigma_F$ to $\sigma_2 \in \Sigma_L$,
$\Sigma \, Max(t_j) < T_{acceptable}$ for $j = 1 \dots n$

This definition is similar to that of Merlin and Farber (1976), but they allow any finite amount of time to return to normal execution. For many real-time systems, timing constraints are more strict than this. Thus doing nothing for a certain amount of time can be as dangerous under certain conditions as performing an incorrect action even though control is ultimately restored.

Definition: A string A is a *subsequence* of string B if and only if A can be obtained from B by deleting zero or more elements of B.

Definition: A process is *fault-tolerant* for a control failure $t_f \in T_F$ if and only if a) it is recoverable and b) a correct behavior path is a subsequence of every path from the initial state to any terminal state. A correct behavior path is a path in the FRG from the initial state to final state which contains no failure transitions, i.e. a sequence of transitions $t_1 \dots t_n \in T^*$ such that for all i, $t_i \in T_L$ and $\delta(\sigma_{i-1}, t_i) = \sigma_i$, for i=1...n, σ_n is not firable

Note that for nonterminating or cyclic processes, σ_n may not be a terminal state but may instead be the initial state.

Definition: A system is *fail-safe* if and only if all paths from a failure F in the FRG contain only low-risk states, i.e. for all states σ_f and sequences s_1 such that $\delta^*(\sigma_0, s_1 F) = \sigma_f$ there does not exist a sequence s_2 and state $\sigma_h \in$ high-risk states such that $\delta^*(\sigma_f, F s_2) = \sigma_h$. Note that the system may never get back to a legal state.

The above definitions can be extended to include the possibility of n failures, thus a system, for example, may be n-fault tolerant, n+1-recoverable, and n+2-fail-safe.

Two analysis approaches are possible. The first is to determine, perhaps through past experience, which failures are most likely, and then to create the resulting Failure Reachability Graph (FRG) and analyze it for the above properties. This may be very costly (and possibly impractical) for complex systems with many possible failure modes. Also, in software it is difficult to determine directly which failures are the most likely.

An alternative approach is to take the safety viewpoint and consider only those failures with the most serious consequences. Since this is the requirement of most safety certification programs, there is a practical application for this type of analysis. In this approach, single-point failures and failure sequences which can lead to high-risk states are determined through the analysis after which the design can be augmented with fault-detection and recovery devices to minimize the risk of a mishap. If risk cannot be lowered sufficiently through these devices (e.g. there is an unacceptable probability they will fail or there are uncontrollable variables such as human error involved), it is also possible to add additional safety devices to the design. For example, the designer may add hazard-detection and risk-minimization mechanisms which attempt to ensure that if a hazardous state is reached, the risk will be eliminated or minimized by fail-safe techniques which change the state to a no-risk or lesser-risk state

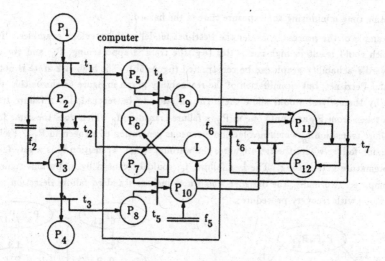

Figure 5a. A Petri Net Graph with Failures

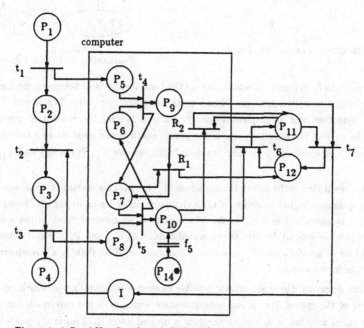

Figure 6. A Petri Net Graph with Failure Transition and Recovery

while at the same time minimizing the exposure time of the hazard.

As an example of the process, consider the Petri-net model in the previous examples. If interested in failures which could result in high-risk states (e.g. the train is approaching, P_3, and the gate is up, P_{11}), a backward reachability graph can be constructed (figure 5b). The high-risk state is not reachable from the regular Petri net, but examination of the reachability graph in figure 5c shows that three single failures (each by themselves) would allow the high-risk state to be reached, i.e. a failure transition f_2 which takes a token from P_2 and puts one in P_3, a failure transition f_6 which does the same for P_{12} and P_{11}, and a failure transition f_5 which involves an erroneous generation of a token in P_{10}. Failure transition f_2 is a human failure where the train ignores the warning signal. Transition f_6 is a gate failure which results in a premature gate raising. The last failure, f_5, could be caused by a spurious signal from the controlling computer. Normally, the designer would now include standard failure detection mechanisms in the design along with recovery procedures.

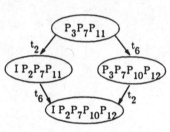

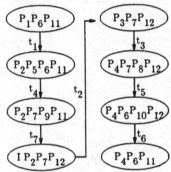

Figure 5b
Backwards Reachability Graph

Figure 5c
Reachability Graph for Figure 5a

Failure transition f_5 in figure 5a was chosen as the basis for the fault tolerance mechanism shown in figure 6. This failure models a spurious output signal from the computer. Transitions R_1 and R_2 are used for fault detection and subsequent recovery. After a failure, there are two possible situations depending on the current state of the gate. If the gate is up then one response to a spurious up signal is to ignore it (shown in transition R_2). The enabling conditions are P_{11} (gate up) and P_{10} (signal from the computer).

The second possibility is the safety critical situation. In this case a train in approaching, the gate is down, and the erroneous signal is given to raise the gate. In order to detect the problem, redundant information must be contained in the system. The model has an internal "view of the world" contained in P_6 and P_7 which correspond directly to the actual conditions P_{11} and P_{12}. Fault detection is accomplished by checking to see if P_7 and P_{11} occur at the same time. If so, there is a discrepancy between the real world and the internal state.

Upon failure detection, there are several possible recoveries -- depending on which model is accepted as the true state of the system (i.e. is the computer state wrong or is the gate really up when it should be down). The safest solution is to assume the gate is up and lower it. This is the purpose of transition R_1. Figure 7 shows the reachability graph for this net. The untimed reachability graph shows that for the state labelled 4 (conditions P_2, P_7, P_9, P_{11}, and P_{14}), recovery is initiated when a failure has not occurred. Further investigation reveals that there is a point in time when the computer state is legitimately inconsistent with the actual world (after t_4 has fired but before t_7 fires). One solution is to put a time constraint on R_1 such that the minimum time of R_1 is greater than the maximum time of t_7. This forces failure detection to wait until a consistent state has been permitted.

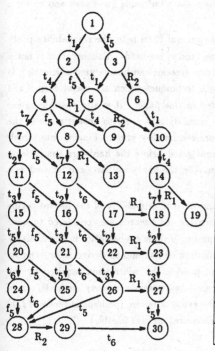

354

State #	Places	State #	Places
1	$P_1 P_6 P_{11} P_{14}$	16	$P_3 P_7 P_{10} P_{12}$
2	$P_2 P_5 P_6 P_{11} P_{14}$	17	$P_2 P_7 P_{11} I$
3	$P_1 P_6 P_{10} P_{11}$	18	$P_2 P_7 P_{12} I$
4	$P_2 P_7 P_9 P_{11} P_{14}$	19	$P_2 P_7 P_9 P_{12}$
5	$P_2 P_5 P_6 P_{10} P_{11}$	20	$P_4 P_6 P_{10} P_{12} P_{14}$
6	$P_1 P_6 P_{11}$	21	$P_4 P_7 P_8 P_{10} P_{12}$
7	$P_2 P_7 P_{12} P_{14} I$	22	$P_3 P_7 P_{11}$
8	$P_2 P_7 P_9 P_{10} P_{11}$	23	$P_3 P_7 P_{12}$
9	$P_2 P_7 P_9 P_{12} P_{14}$	24	$P_4 P_6 P_{11} P_{14}$
10	$P_2 P_5 P_6 P_{11}$	25	$P_4 P_6 P_{10} P_{10} P_{12}$
11	$P_3 P_7 P_{12} P_{14}$	26	$P_4 P_7 P_8 P_{11}$
12	$P_2 P_7 P_{10} P_{12} I$	27	$P_4 P_7 P_8 P_{12}$
13	$P_2 P_7 P_9 P_{10} P_{12}$	28	$P_4 P_6 P_{10} P_{11}$
14	$P_2 P_7 P_9 P_{11}$	29	$P_4 P_6 P_{11}$
15	$P_4 P_7 P_8 P_{12} P_{14}$	30	$P_4 P_6 P_{10} P_{12}$

Figure 7. Reachability Graph for Figure 6

In summary, analysis of the failure reachability graph with respect to the definitions of fault tolerant, recoverable, and fail-safe design will aid the designer in adding appropriate failure detection and recovery techniques to the system. When interested solely in a safety analysis, backward procedures can be used to determine which failures and faults are potentially the most costly and thus need to be augmented with fault tolerance mechanisms and also to determine where and how safety mechanisms should be used. This may be particularly useful for the software components of the system since it is difficult to determine which faults are most likely to occur and the potential number of failures to model may be very large. Furthermore, it is possible to treat the software at various levels of abstraction, e.g. only failures of the interfaces of the software and non-software components may be considered or more detailed failures of only those particular modules which are determined to be critical may be modelled.

Conclusions

The use of Time Petri nets in design and analysis of safety-critical, real-time systems has been described and the basic model extended to allow modelling failures and faults. This allows the system to be analyzed for properties such as fault-tolerance and safety, to determine which functions are most critical and thus may need to be made fault-tolerant (assuming that it may be too costly to ensure complete fault-tolerance), to determine conditions which require immediate mitigating action to prevent accidents, to determine possible sequences of failures which can lead to accidents, etc. Thus it is possible to establish important properties during the synthesis of the design instead of using guesswork and costly *a posteriori* analysis (including formal analysis and testing).

Unfortunately, Petri nets can be difficult to analyze. For general Petri nets, the reachability problem, though decidable, has been shown to be exponential time- and space-hard. Although this is not a necessary property of Petri net models (many important and real systems can be analyzed efficiently), it is a possible result when complex systems are modelled. Some techniques which are useful even if the entire reachability graph is not completed have been presented in this paper. It is also possible to use the failure-enhanced Time Petri net model as the basis for a simulation in order to answer some of the same questions which could have been answered by the failure reachability graph. Finally, many real-time systems require the computer software to be written and tested before the hardware components have been completed. Since the Time Petri net model is executable, the hardware parts can be used as a test bed for the software development process.

In this paper, only severity of hazards was considered and not the probability of the hazard occurring or of leading to a mishap. This is a pessimistic approach (i.e. all hazards are considered to have equally high probabilities). We are currently devising techniques to include probabilities in the analysis. This will enable the designer to use a more sophisticated definition of risk and to derive measurements for risk (and thus safety) from the model. This in turn can provide the information required by the designer to make difficult tradeoff decisions, e.g. what if there are two possible recovery methods, one of which is more likely to work but also has worse penalties in the event of failure (perhaps in terms of taking so long to execute that no other alternatives or fail-safe procedures are still feasible).

References

[1]   Azema, P., and Diaz, M. "Checking Experiments for Concurrent Systems," *FTCS-7*, June 1977, p. 206.

[2]   Malasky, S.W. *System Safety: Technology and Application*, Garland STPM Press, New York, 1982.

[3]   Kopetz, H. "The Failure Fault (FF) Model," *FTCS-12*, Santa Monica, Calif., June 1982, pp. 14-17.

[4]   Leveson, N.G. and Harvey, P.R. "Analyzing Software Safety," *IEEE Transactions on Software Engineering*, vol. SE-9, no. 5, Sept. 1983.

[5]   Leveson, N.G. "Software Safety in Process-Control Systems," *IEEE Computer*, February 1984.

[6]   Merlin, P.M. "A Study of the Recoverability of Computing Systems," Ph.D. Thesis, Information and Computer Science Department, University of California, Irvine, 1974.

[7]   Merlin, P.M. and Farber, D.J. "Recoverability of Communication Protocols -- Implications of a Theoretical Study," *IEEE Transactions on Communications*, vol. COM-24, no. 9, September 1976, pp. 1036-1043.

[8]   MIL-STD-882b, System Safety Program Requirements, U.S. Department of Defense, April 1984.

[9]   Peterson, J.L. *Petri Net Theory and the Modeling of Systems*, Prentice Hall, 1981.

[10] Vesely, W.E., Goldberg, F.F., Roberts, N.H., and Haasl, D.F. *Fault Tree Handbook*, NUREG-0492, U.S. Nuclear Regulatory Commission, January 1981.

Algebraic Specification
Of A Communication Scheduler

Mathai Joseph

Computer Science Group
Tata Institute of Fundamental Research
Colaba, Bombay 400 005 INDIA

Abha Moitra

Department of Computer Science
Cornell University
Ithaca NY 14853

ABSTRACT

A distributed programming language normally incorporates one mechanism by which processes communicate with each other. This mechanism can be used to transfer information or to synchronize the flow of control in the program. Different communication mechanisms have been proposed for different languages. In this paper, we provide a common framework in which these mechanisms can be examined independently of the languages in which they may be embedded. Operationally, this framework is a communication scheduler : formally, it is specified algebraically as a data type. A number of different communication mechanisms, such as synchronous and asynchronous message passing, broadcasts and remote procedure calls, are modelled and, as an illustration of how global properties can be analysed, we consider the problem of deadlock detection.

1. INTRODUCTION

Modularity and abstraction are used in program construction so that a complex problem can be solved using a program with a number of small and relatively simple components. In sequential programs, these components are usually procedures, functions, or class-like encapsulations, while concurrent and distributed programs may also contain independently executing processes or tasks. Different kinds of components are distinguished by the form of control used to invoke their actions and by the means used to propagate information from one component to another. Thus, between the components of a sequential program, procedure (or function) calls and returns are normally used to transfer information and control, and block structure has been used to statically control access to data. Many schemes have been proposed for inter-process communication in concurrent and distributed programs and different languages have used, for example, synchronous message transfer [10], asynchronous message transfer [5], coroutine calls [15] and remote procedure calls [13]. In several of these schemes, sending data in a message is the common means of transferring information from one process to another, but the synchronization disciplines used for message transfer differ considerably and have important effects on global properties of the program, such as termination and deadlock. For example, the minor variation over standard CSP [10] needed to introduce output commands in guards adds to the symmetry and elegance of the language, makes it easier to avoid deadlock in certain cases, but certainly leads also to some implementational complexity [1].

Proof of the properties of a program written in a distributed programming language usually requires global reasoning about the whole program to be combined with local reasoning for each process. Such a proof can be established using a proof system which provides rules for each statement and for the particular communication mechanisms used in that language. Proof of a distributed program is usually more complex than that of a similar sequential program and the additional complexity is almost solely an outcome of the process interactions that take place through interprocess communication. Each proof system is specific to one programming language, and therefore to one set of communication mechanisms.

It is therefore of interest to model a multiplicity of communication mechanisms in a common framework so that their intrinsic properties can be examined independently of the operational details of the languages in which they may be embedded. We shall attempt to do so in this paper, using an algebraically specified communication environment in which the components of the distributed or concurrent program are defined as modules. The environment will be defined by a set of operations whose semantics are described by axioms; algebraic specification of this form has been used for defining abstract data types (e.g., Goguen, Thatcher and Wagner [8], and Guttag and Horning [9]), so we could consider this environment to be a 'communication data type' [3].

2. ALGEBRAIC SPECIFICATION

The algebraic specification of a data type consists of the definition of the set of operations, or functions, of the data type together with axioms which provide the semantics of the operations. We shall not describe the method of algebraic specification in detail (the interested reader is referred to [8], [9]) but we can illustrate it, and the syntax we shall be using, by defining a simple data type.

The operations of a data type will be defined using the following syntax :

$$[<\text{mnemonic}> =] <\text{operation name}> : <\text{domain}> \rightarrow <\text{range}>$$

Axioms will be numbered in sequence (for easy reference), sometimes given a mnemonic name, and written as algebraic equations with expressions on the left and right hand sides, the latter containing values of type range and logical expressions of the form *if..then..else.. .*

2.1. A Simple Data Type

Let us define *MNSEQ* a data type which models an abstract sequence of items of type *mod-name*. *MNSEQ* is defined using seven operations and eleven axioms, and *mod-name* is just a sequence of characters. We shall assume that the data type *BOOLEAN* is predefined.

MNSEQ

```
NS = NewSeq :                        → mnseq
     Insert   : mnseq X mod-name → mnseq
     In       : mnseq X mod-name → boolean
     Empty    : mnseq                 → boolean
     Del1     : mnseq X mod-name → mnseq
     DelAll   : mnseq X mod-name → mnseq
     Concat   : mnseq X mnseq     → mnseq
```

for all s,s1 in mnseq and m,m1 in mod-name

1 In(NS,m) = false
2 In(Insert(s,m),m1) = if Eq(m,m1) then true else In(s,m1)

3 Empty(NS) = true
4 Empty(Insert(s,m)) = false

5 Del1(NS,m) = NS
6 Del1(Insert(s,m),m1) = if Eq(m,m1) then s else Insert(Del1(s,m1),m)

7 DelAll(NS,m) = NS
8 DelAll(Insert(s,m),m1) = if Eq(m,m1) then DelAll(s,m1) else Insert(DelAll(s,m1),m)

9   Concat(NS,s) = s
10 Concat(s,NS) = s
11 Concat(s,Insert(s1,m)) = Insert(Concat(s,s1),m)

where we assume the existence of a operation *Eq* to determine equality between two objects of type *mod-name*.

The operation *Del1* deletes the first occurrence and the operation *DelAll* deletes each occurrence of an element from the sequence : thus use of *DelAll* results in the sequence being treated more as a set than a sequence. The data type *MNSEQ* will be used later in the definition of other data types.

2.2. Design of Algebraic Specification

It is well known ([11], [14]) that it is not possible to specify every computable operation with a finite number of axioms. Majster [11] therefore proposed the use of hidden operations, where a hidden operation is one that may only be invoked from some operation of the data type, and which is not accessible from outside the data type; using hidden operations it is always possible to give a finite specification for any computable operation [14]. We make extensive use of hidden operations in this paper; a '#' symbol preceding a operation identifies it as being a hidden operation.

Though algebraic specifications have been formalized and used for a number of years, very few data types have actually been defined in this methodology. We believe this is probably due to the fact that writing algebraic specifications is still an art. In this paper we shall also try to motivate the development of the various data types introduced in this paper.

A particular data type can be algebraically described in a number of different ways. It is therefore important to know why a particular algebraic specification is chosen. So, we shall often indicate the choices possible as well as the consequences of each decision. Further, the requirements placed on a data type are typically in terms of the semantics that should be provided for the operations. But since hidden operations are not available to a user of the data type, there is no obvious guideline for deciding what hidden operations should be introduced but we shall attempt to explain the basis for our choices.

3. MODELLING COMMUNICATION

Communication between concurrent or distributed processes requires action through some mediating agency such as shared memory, a communication medium, a 'transport layer', or an operating system. This agency provides a name space in which processes are assigned unique identification, and a means of conveying messages from one named process to another : in other words, the agency is the environment in which interprocess communication takes place and we shall refer to it subsequently as the 'communication environment', or just as the 'environment'. To relate the syntax and semantics of the algebraic specification with the more familiar operational view, we shall 'annotate' the axioms with operational descriptions of their semantics.

Initially the environment is empty and each module that is to participate in communication must be defined in the environment using the operation *EnterModName*. A module then indicates its willingness to communicate using the operation *Request*, which requires as arguments the name of the module and two objects of type *mnseq* which contain the names of the modules to which it is ready to send messages and from which it will accept messages respectively. This corresponds to a non-deterministic construct in a programming language, where one of a set of input or output commands may be selected for execution (as is the case in extended CSP [1]). An additional constraint in a programming language would be that for communication to take place, the type of the message to be input in one process must be identical to that to be output by another process. For simplicity, we shall assume that separate syntactic checks ensure this and ignore message types in this analysis. In synchronous communications, which we shall be modelling initially, the first process to attempt a communication must wait until a matching request comes from some other process. Another operation that must be provided is to allow a module to be removed from the environment, *RemoveMod-Name*.

The semantics of the operation *Request* can be informally described as follows.

Request(e,m,s1,s2)

= if mod-name m is not defined in the environment e then drop this request   (1)

    else if m is attempting to wait for itself then drop this request   (2)

    else if none of the mod-names in s1 and s2 is present in the environment e   (3)
      then error

    else if m already has a request pending in the environment e   (4)
      then drop this request

    else if possible match this request with a pending request   (5)

    else if by adding this request all modules will have a request pending   (6)
      then deadlock-error

    else keep this request pending (to be satisfied later)   (7)

The test in (1) can be accomplished by introducing a new boolean operation *IsModNameInEnv*. This operation could be kept as a hidden operation but since there might be other uses for it we can allow it to be invoked by a user. The test in (2) can be handled by making use of the operation *In* defined in *MNSEQ*. The test in (3) can be done by introducing a new operation *Strip* which takes as arguments an environment and a *mnseq* and returns a *mnseq* which is the sequence of all *mod-name* in the input *mnseq* that are also present in the environment.

Before we consider the other tests that have to be performed, we must first decide on how a pending request will be kept (7). The simplest solution would be to rewrite (7) as

    else Request(e,m,s1,s2)   (7′)

but then if *Request(e,m,s1,s2)* is encountered there is no way of knowing whether this is a new request for which tests have not been performed or whether it is a pending request for which the tests have been done but for which there was no matching communication. Such a distinction has to be made to specify, among other things, the test in (4). So, we should introduce a new operation, say *NewFn1*, and rewrite (7) as

    else NewFn1(e,m,s1,s2)   (7′′)

Algebraic specifications are defined in a hierarchical fashion : a new type is defined using some predefined types. For example, here we are trying to define a new type *env* using the predefined types *mnseq*, *boolean*. For any data type, we can define a minimal set of operations that are sufficient to describe every possible element of the new type [9]. In the present case, the operations *EnterModName*, *NewFn1* and *CreateEnv* are the minimal operations that are sufficient to describe every element in the type *env*. So, any environment will be of the form

    {EnterModName, NewFn1}* CreateEnv

This means that the various operations that test whether or not an environment satisfies a particular property must typically be defined using three axioms. (Of course, if enough additional operations are introduced, each original operation can be defined using one axiom only but then this axiom can get quite complicated [12].) However the specification can be simplified if we could get an arbitrary environment to be of the form

    {NewFn2}* CreateEnv

where *NewFn2* is some new operation.

This can be accomplished in the following way :

EnterModName(e,m) = if the mod-name m is in the environment e then e
else AddModName(e,m,NS,NS)

and (7) is written as

else change AddModName(e′,m,NS,NS) in e to AddModName(e′,m,s1,s2)

In *AddModName(e,m,s1,s2)*, module *m* is not waiting for any communication if and only if both *s1* and *s2* are empty; otherwise it is waiting for a communication.

The operations and axioms of the communication data type *SYNCH-COMM* are given below. In this data type, communication between modules is synchronous, i.e. a module making a communication request is blocked until its message is transmitted and this takes place when the sender and the receiver are both ready. We assume that each domain is extended to include appropriate error elements [7].

SYNCH-COMM

CE	= CreateEnv	:	$\rightarrow$ env
EMN	= EnterModName	: env X mod-name	$\rightarrow$ env
#AMN	= AddModName	: env X mod-name X mnseq X mnseq	$\rightarrow$ env
Req	= Request	: env X mod-name X mnseq X mnseq	$\rightarrow$ env
#Add		: env X mod-name X mnseq X mnseq	$\rightarrow$ env
CMatch	= CanBeMatched	: env X mod-name X mnseq X mnseq	$\rightarrow$ boolean
#Match		: env X mod-name X mnseq X mnseq	$\rightarrow$ env
RMN	= RemoveModName	: env X mod-name	$\rightarrow$ env
#DMN	= DeleteModName	: env X mod-name	$\rightarrow$ env
ISMNE	= IsModNameInEnv	: env X mod-name	$\rightarrow$ boolean
Wait	= Waiting	: env X mod-name	$\rightarrow$ boolean
AllWait	= AllWaiting	: env	$\rightarrow$ boolean
Strip		: env X mnseq	$\rightarrow$ mnseq

for all e in env, m,m1 in mod-name, s1,s2,s3,s4 in mnseq

1 EMN(e,m) = if ISMNE(e,m) then e else AMN(e,m,NS,NS)

Each module in the environment is unique; a new *mod-name* is added to the environment along with two *mnseq* objects (initially empty) that will be used to contain the names of the modules to which communications may be sent and from which communications may be received.

2 Req(e,m,s1,s2) = if ¬ISMNE(e,m) then e
else if In(s1,m) ∨ In(s2,m) then e
else if Empty(Strip(e,s1)) ∧ Empty(Strip(e,s2)) then error
else if Wait(e,m) then e
else if CMatch(e,m,s1,s2) then Match(e,m,s1,s2)
else if AllWait(Add(e,m,s1,s2)) then deadlock-error
else Add(e,m,s1,s2)

Requests for communication may only be received from modules defined in the environment. The object *s1* contains the names of modules to any of which module *m* is prepared to send messages, and *s2* the names of modules from any of which *m* is ready to accept messages. *s1* and *s2* should not contain *m*, nor should they both be empty. To simulate synchronous communication, a request from a module that is already waiting for a previous communication is ignored. Each request is tested for a match with other pending requests; a request that can be matched is satisfied immediately. If a request from a module cannot be matched immediately, and all the other modules have either terminated or are also waiting for communication, then no progress by any module is possible and the system is deadlocked. (If only part of the system is deadlocked but progress can be made by some modules, the processing of further communication requests is carried on.) If a request cannot be matched, and the entire system is not deadlocked, then that request is added to the list of pending requests.

For the present, we take the simple and straightforward view that deadlock occurs only if no module can make any further progress. Later, we will also show how it is possible to detect a partial deadlock.

3 CMatch(CE,m1,s1,s2) = false
4 CMatch(AMN(e,m1,s3,s4),m,s1,s2) = if Eq(m,m1) then CMatch(e,m,s1,s2)
    else if In(s2,m1) ∧ In(s3,m) then true
    else if In(s1,m1) ∧ In(s4,m) then true
    else CMatch(e,m,s1,s2)

A request can be matched with a pending request if the names of the modules *m* and *m1* appear in complementary send and receive requests (i.e. in the objects *s2* and *s3*, or in the objects *s1* and *s4*).

5 Match(CE,m,s1,s2) = error
6 Match(AMN(e,m1,s3,s4),m,s1,s2) = if Eq(m,m1) then AMN(Match(e,m,s1,s2),m1,s3,s4)
    else if In(s2,m1) ∧ In(s3,m) then AMN(e,m1,NS,NS)
    else if In(s1,m1) ∧ In(s4,m) then AMN(e,m1,NS,NS)
    else AMN(Match(e,m,s1,s2),m1,s3,s4)

In axiom 6, checks are made for inclusion of *m1* and *m* in *s2* and *s3*, respectively, and then in *s1* and *s4*. Note that this order can be reversed. When two requests match, they are cancelled (this is done by setting the associated *mnseq* objects to the value *NS*).

7 Add(CE,m,s1,s2) = error
8 Add(AMN(e,m1,s3,s4),m,s1,s2) = if Eq(m,m1) then AMN(e,m,s1,s2)
    else AMN(Add(e,m,s1,s2),m1,s3,s4)

For a request that cannot immediately be matched, *Add* associates the request with the appropriate *AMN* operation for that module. Thus the objects *s1* and *s2* associated with an unmatched request will replace the empty *mnseq* objects associated with that module.

9 RMN(e,m) = if Wait(e,m) then e else DMN(e,m)

10 DMN(CE,m) = CE

11 DMN(AMN(e,m1,s1,s2),m) = if Eq(m,m1) then DMN(e,m)
                         else if ¬(Empty(s1) ∧ Empty(s2)) ∧ Empty(DelAll(s1,m))
                                  ∧ Empty(DelAll(s2,m)) then error
                         else AMN(DMN(e,m),m1,DelAll(s1,m),DelAll(s2,m))

A module may be removed only if it is not awaiting any communication. If the removal of a module causes some other module to wait on empty objects *s1* and *s2* then an error is raised.

12 ISMNE(CE,m) = false
13 ISMNE(AMN(e,m,s1,s2),m1) = if Eq(m,m1) then true else ISMNE(e,m1)

14 Wait(CE,m) = false
15 Wait(AMN(e,m,s1,s2),m1) = if ¬Eq(m,m1) then Wait(e,m1)
                         else if Empty(s1) ∧ Empty(s2) then false
                         else true

A module which is not waiting for any communication will have empty objects *s1* and *s2*.

16 AllWait(CE) = true
17 AllWait(AMN(e,m,s1,s2)) = if Empty(s1) ∧ Empty(s2) then false else AllWait(e)

AllWait checks whether there are any modules in the environment that are not waiting for a communication : thus axiom 16 follows because in this case the environment is empty.

18 Strip(e,NS) = NS
19 Strip(e,Insert(s,m)) = if ISMNE(e,m) then Insert(Strip(e,s),m) else Strip(e,s)

Strip takes an *mnseq* object as an argument and deletes all *mod-name* in it that are not defined in the environment.

4. DEADLOCK

In the previous section we had assumed that it is necessary to detect a deadlock only if no module could make any further progress. While every deadlock situation will eventually lead to a situation in which no module can make any further progress, it would be preferable to detect even a partial deadlock as soon as it occurs. In this section we show that a deadlock of some processes can be detected even when there are other processes that can make further progress. The procedure for deadlock detection is formulated to minimize the amount of computation that is required when a new unmatched communication request is added to the environment. This procedure works as follows.

Let e be an environment with n modules m_1, m_2, .. m_n and let $Safe(e,m_i)$ be the set of modules that must be unblocked for execution of m_i to be possible. Initially, when there is no communication request pending in an environment e, $Safe(e,m_i) = \emptyset$ for all $1 \leq i \leq n$. When a new communication request of the form

m_j waiting on m_{j1}, m_{j2}, .., m_{jk}

that cannot be immediately satisfied is added to the environment e to give a new environment e', the operation $Safe$ is redefined as follows :

$$Safe(e', m_j) = Safe(e, m_{j1}) \cup Safe(e, m_{j2}) \cup .. \cup Safe(e, m_{jk}) \cup \{m_{j1}, .., m_{jk}\}$$

$$\text{for } 1 \leq i \leq n, i \neq j, \quad \text{if } m_j \in Safe(e, m_i) \text{ then } Safe(e', m_i) = Safe(e, m_i) \cup Safe(e', m_j)$$
$$\text{else } Safe(e', m_i) = Safe(e, m_i)$$

A deadlock occurs in an environment e if there is some $1 \leq i \leq n$ such that $m_i \in Safe(e, m_i)$. This formulation of deadlock detection can be easily incorporated into the data type $SYNCH\text{-}COMM$ by adding another $mnseq$ argument to the operation AMN to keep track of the 'safe' set for that module. We do not present the new data type here as it involves a straightforward change to the data type $SYNCH\text{-}COMM$.

There are several ways in which deadlock may be detected. We have distinguished between partial and complete deadlocks, referring by the later term to the case where all the modules left in the environment are blocked awaiting communication. But a partial deadlock will also eventually become a complete deadlock. On the other hand, there is a specific communication request that completes the condition for a partial deadlock and it is naturally desirable that this be detected as soon as it occurs. In terms of our model, this condition is represented by the truth of the relation $m_i \in Safe(e, m_i)$ for some i, $1 \leq i \leq n$.

Since this scheme detects partial deadlocks, it is closer in form to one described by Chandy, Misra and Haas [2] than, for example, the work on termination detection (e.g., [4], [6]) which tests for a global property. But it differs from all such work because, by its applicative nature, it does not rely on implementational details like the propagation of test messages such as probes [2] or signals [6] to detect deadlocks. This is a consequence of the fact that we are modelling the communication environment, rather than individual modules. For this reason also, it is not necessary to define a spanning tree or a ring along which to send deadlock detection signals.

As deadlock detection takes place before every unmatched communication request is added to e, the total associated cost is proportional to the number of such requests. Further, for each unmatched communication request, the cost of deadlock detection is proportional to the total number of modules in the environment e (one pass over the environment e is enough to update all 'safe' information).

5. MESSAGE QUEUES

Under the discipline of synchronous communication, there can be at most one request pending from a module so it follows that two successive messages sent from one module to another will reach in the order in which they were sent. Can it also be ensured that messages are accepted by modules according to the order in which they were received? This is easily done by replacing axioms 7 and 8 by the following axioms :

7a Add(CE,m,s1,s2) = AMN(CE,m,s1,s2)
8a Add(AMN(e,m1,s3,s4),m,s1,s2) = if Eq(m,m1) then Add(e,m,s1,s2)
  else AMN(Add(e,m,s1,s2),m1,s3,s4)

which will result in message propagation having a first-in-first-out order. By suitably extending the operations *AMN* and *Add*, it can also be arranged for modules to be assigned priorities so that message transmission follows the order imposed by these priorities.

Note that in the last line of axiom 2 in *SYNCH-COMM* we could have used

  else AMN(Del(e,m),m,s1,s2)

where *Del* would replace *AMN(e′,m,NS,NS)* in *e* by *e′*. But then such a choice would have made it more difficult to alter *SYNCH-COMM* to ensure that modules receive messages only in the order in which they were sent.

6. REMOTE PROCEDURE CALLS

An extended form of synchronous communication can be used to describe remote procedure calls from one module to another. Syntactically, a successful remote procedure call from module *m* to module *m1* can be simulated by four operations : a send request for the call from *m* to *m1*, acceptance of this request by *m1*, a send request for the reply from *m1* to *m*, and receipt of this by *m*. But defining this protocol literally in the axioms has several deficiencies : for example, the call by *m* and its acceptance by *m1* may be followed by other communication requests from *m* before waiting for a reply from *m1*, or the definition of the axioms may be such as to prevent nested remote procedure calls (i.e. calls from *m1* to other modules before a reply is sent to *m*).

It is necessary to introduce some new operations : let *RPC* be the remote procedure call and *Serve* the request to accept such a call :

  RPC   : env X mod-name X mod-name → env
  Serve : env X mod-name   → env

The corresponding axioms are :

20 Serve(e,m) = Req(e,m,NS,DelAll(NewFn3(e),m))

21 RPC(e,m,m1) = if ¬ISMNE(e,m) then e
    else if Eq(m,m1) then e
    else if Empty(Strip(e,{m1})) then error
    else if Wait(e,m) then e
    else if CMatch(e,m,{m1},NS)
      then Req(Match(e,m,{m1},NS),m,NS,{m1})
    else if AllWait(Add(e,m,{m1},NS)) then deadlock-error
    else RP(Add(e,m,{m1},NS),m,m1)

22 RP(e,m,m1) = if Wait(e,m) then RP(e,m,m1) else Req(e,m,NS,{m1})

where *NewFn3(e)* returns the set of all the modules in the environment *e* ; *RP* is a constructor type operation for which new axioms have to be defined and *{m1}* = *Insert(NS,m1)*.

This is a relatively simple solution, but it introduces an additional constructor type operation *RP*. Another solution would be to 'tag' the existing constructor type operations so as to distinguish between *RPC* and ordinary *Req* operations. This type of solution will be used later in this paper for broadcast communication.

7. ASYNCHRONOUS MESSAGE PASSING AND BROADCAST

The addition of fully general asynchronous communication between modules requires unbounded buffering, because a module may send an unlimited number of asynchronous messages to one or more other modules. In any specific case, the number of asynchronous messages sent by one module and still to be received by another module would be limited only by module termination, or by the sender attempting a synchronous communication or a remote procedure call, both of which block the module's execution until completed. There are two constraints on asynchronous communication : messages sent from one module to another must be received in the order in which they were sent, and no more messages may be received than are sent. Permitting a module to send a message to a number of other modules, in a single operation, is equivalent to a multicast or a broadcast operation. Conversely, there is no essential difference between a broadcast operation with just one destination module and simple asynchronous send. We shall therefore consider the problem of modelling broadcast communication.

The data type *SYNCH-COMM* has two constructor type operations [9], *CE* and *AMN*. One way of adding broadcasts to this data type would be to introduce another constructor type operation, e.g. *BroadCast(e,m,s1)*, which would allow more than one broadcast request to be pending for the same module. The addition of a new constructor type operation *BC* would require some of the existing axioms to be rewritten and the number of axioms required would also increase. (Typically, if an operation was originally defined for *CE* and *AMN*, it would then have to be defined for *CE*, *AMN* and *BC*.)

A simpler way of introducing the facility for broadcasts, and one we shall follow here, is to add an argument to the operation *AMN*.

```
BC = BroadCast    : env X mod-name X mnseq                    → env
AMN = AddModName : env X mod-name X mnseq X mnseq X mnseq → env
```

Both *Req* and *BC* will be handled by the operation *AMN* (and the number of constructor type operations will therefore not increase.) The third argument for *AMN* is the set containing the names of modules to which messages are to be broadcast. In this set, the oldest broadcast requests will be at the front, thus guaranteeing a first-come-first-served order for broadcasts to the same module. The new data type, *ASYNCH-COMM*, is defined below.

ASYNCH-COMM

CE	= CreateEnv	:	→ env
EMN	= EnterModName	: env X mod-name	→ env
#AMN	= AddModName	: env X mod-name X mnseq X mnseq X mnseq	→ env
#Add		: env X mod-name X mnseq X mnseq X mnseq	→ env
Req	= Request	: env X mod-name X mnseq X mnseq	→ env
BC	= BroadCast	: env X mod-name X mnseq	→ env
CMatch	= CanBeMatched	: env X mod-name X mnseq X mnseq	→ boolean
#Match		: env X mod-name X mnseq X mnseq	→ env
RMN	= RemoveModName	: env X mod-name	→ env
#DMN	= DeleteModName	: env X mod-name	→ env
ISMNE	= IsModNameInEnv	: env X mod-name	→ boolean
Wait	= Waiting	: env X mod-name	→ boolean
AllWait	= AllWaiting	: env	→ boolean
Strip		: env X mnseq	→ mnseq

for all e in env, m,m1 in mod-name, s1,s2,s3,s4,s5,s6 in mnseq

1 EMN(e,m) = if ISMNE(e,m) then e else AMN(e,m,NS,NS,NS)

2 Req(e,m,s1,s2) = if ¬ISMNE(e,m) then e
$\qquad$ else if In(s1,m) ∨ In(s2,m) then e
$\qquad$ else if Empty(Strip(e,s1)) ∧ Empty(Strip(e,s2)) then error
$\qquad$ else if Wait(e,m) then e
$\qquad$ else if CMatch(e,m,s1,s2) then Match(e,m,s1,s2)
$\qquad$ else if AllWait(Add(e,m,s1,s2,NS)) then deadlock-error
$\qquad$ else Add(e,m,s1,s2,NS)

3 BC(e,m,NS) = e
4 BC(e,m,Insert(s1,m1)) = if ¬ISMNE(e,m) then e
$\qquad$ else if In(s1,m1) ∨ Eq(m,m1) then BC(e,m,s1)
$\qquad$ else if ¬ISMNE(e,m1) then BC(e,m,s1)
$\qquad$ else if Wait(e,m) then e
$\qquad$ else if CMatch(e,m,Insert(NS,m1),NS)
$\qquad\qquad$ then BC(Match(e,m,Insert(NS,m1),NS),m,s1)
$\qquad$ else BC(Add(e,m,NS,NS,Insert(NS,m1)),m,s1)

5 CMatch(CE,m1,s1,s2) = false
6 CMatch(AMN(e,m1,s3,s4,s5),m,s1,s2) = if Eq(m,m1) then CMatch(e,m,s1,s2)
$\qquad\qquad\qquad\qquad$ else if In(s2,m1) ∧ In(s3,m) then true
$\qquad\qquad\qquad\qquad$ else if In(s1,m1) ∧ In(s4,m) then true
$\qquad\qquad\qquad\qquad$ else if In(s2,m1) ∧ In(s5,m) then true
$\qquad\qquad\qquad\qquad$ else CMatch(e,m,s1,s2)

7 Match(CE,m,s1,s2) = error
8 Match(AMN(e,m1,s3,s4,s5),m,s1,s2)
$\qquad$ = if Eq(m,m1) then AMN(Match(e,m,s1,s2),m1,s3,s4,s5)
$\qquad$ else if In(s2,m1) ∧ In(s3,m) then AMN(e,m1,NS,NS,s5)
$\qquad$ else if In(s1,m1) ∧ In(s4,m) then AMN(e,m1,NS,NS,s5)
$\qquad$ else if In(s2,m1) ∧ In(s5,m) then AMN(e,m1,s3,s4,Del1(s5,m))
$\qquad$ else AMN(Match(e,m,s1,s2),m1,s3,s4,s5)

9 Add(CE,m,s1,s2,s3) = error
10 Add(AMN(e,m1,s4,s5,s6),m,s1,s2,s3)
$\qquad$ = if ¬Eq(m,m1) then AMN(Add(e,m,s1,s2,s3),m1,s4,s5,s6)
$\qquad$ else if Empty(s3) then AMN(e,m,s1,s2,NS)
$\qquad$ else AMN(e,m,s4,s5,Concat(s3,s6))

11 RMN(e,m) = if Wait(e,m) then e else DMN(e,m)

12 DMN(CE,m) = CE
13 DMN(AMN(e,m1,s1,s2,s3),m)
       = if Eq(m1,m) then DMN(e,m)
         else if ¬(Empty(s1) ∧ Empty(s2)) ∧ Empty(DelAll(s1,m)) ∧ Empty(DelAll(s2,m))
            then error
         else AMN(DMN(e,m),m1,DelAll(s1,m),DelAll(s2,m),DelAll(s3,m))

14 ISMNE(CE,m) = false
15 ISMNE(AMN(e,m,s1,s2,s3),m1) = if Eq(m,m1) then true else ISMNE(e,m1)

16 Wait(CE,m) = false
17 Wait(AMN(e,m,s1,s2,s3),m1) = if ¬Eq(m,m1) then Wait(e,m1)
                                  else if Empty(s1) ∧ Empty(s2) then false
                                  else true

18 AllWait(CE) = true
19 AllWait(AMN(e,m,s1,s2,s3)) = if Empty(s1) ∧ Empty(s2) then false else AllWait(e)

20 Strip(e,NS) = NS
21 Strip(e,Insert(s,m)) = if ISMNE(e,m) then Insert(Strip(e,s),m) else Strip(e,s)

The data type *ASYNCH-COMM* can be augmented in a straightforward way to provide operations for deadlock detection. In the term *AMN(e,m,s1,s2,s3)*, *s3* is not involved in deadlock detection and hence the extension for *ASYNCH-COMM* would be very similar to that suggested for *SYNCH-COMM*.

Relatively few changes were needed to convert *SYNCH-COMM* to *ASYNCH-COMM*, and the operations and axioms of the new data type show a high degree of similarity with those defined earlier. This was accomplished partly by treating *mnseq* objects both as sequences (using the operation *Del1*) and as sets (using the operation *DelAll*). Another reason for achieving this high similarity was that the number of constructor type operations in both data types was the same. It is also interesting to note that the blocking effect of synchronous communication can be preserved, despite the introduction of asynchronous communication, merely by choosing an appropriate order of checking in the axioms. Thus, by axiom 4, no broadcast requests (*BC*) are accepted from a module waiting for a synchronous communication request (*Req*) : when a new request is added, synchronous communication requests are matched before broadcast requests (axiom 8).

CONCLUSIONS

In this paper we have modelled a number of different interprocess communication schemes used in concurrent and distributed programming by specifying them algebraically as abstract data types.

Two criteria can be used to judge the usefulness of such specifications. First, how faithfully do they represent the commonly understood semantics of the communication mechanisms? Secondly, how well do the specifications for different communication mechanisms illustrate any inherent similarities between them?

The importance of achieving the first criterion lies in the fact that, in practice, each communication mechanism is defined either informally, or operationally as part of a programming language. Once a formally defined and operationally acceptable specification has been produced, there appears to be many operational similarities between the mechanisms.

The design of the specifications described in this paper proceeded with these criteria acting as constraints. The specification of the data type *ASYNCH-COMM* shows that mechanism as different as broadcasts and synchronous communication can be modelled in a common framework. Simple extensions to this data type permit more complex operations, such as remote procedure calls, to be specified. Global properties, like the presence of deadlocks, can also be quite easily considered.

REFERENCES

1. A.J. Bernstein, Output guards and nondeterminism in "Communicating Sequential Processes", *ACM Trans. Prog. Lang. and Sys.*, *2*, 2, April 1980, pp. 234-238.

2. K.M. Chandy, J. Misra, L.M. Haas, Distributed deadlock detection, *ACM Trans. on Comp. Sys.*, *1*, 2, May 1983, pp. 144-156.

3. P.R.F. Cunha, T.S.E. Maibaum, A communication data type for message oriented programming, *Proc. IV Intl. Symp. on Prog.*, Springer-Verlag, Lecture Notes in Computer Science, Vol. 83, 1980, pp. 79-91.

4. E.W. Dijkstra, C.S. Scholten, Termination detection for diffusing computations, *Inf. Proc. Lett.*, *11*, 1, August 1980, pp. 1-4.

5. J.A. Feldman, High level programming for distributed computing, *Comm. ACM, 21*, 11, November 1978, pp. 934-941.

6. N. Francez, Distributed termination, *ACM Trans. on Prog. Lang. and Sys.*, *2*, 1, January 1980, pp. 42-55.

7. J.A. Goguen, Abstract errors for abstract data types, in *Formal Description of Programming Concepts*, E.J. Neuhold (Ed.), North Holland, 1978, pp. 491-525.

8. J.A. Goguen, J.W. Thatcher and E.G. Wagner, An initial algebra approach to the specification, correctness, and implementation of abstract data types, in *Current Trends in Programming Methodology Vol. IV : Data Structuring*, R.T. Yeh (Ed.), Prentice-Hall, Englewood Cliffs, 1978, pp. 80-149.

9. J.V. Guttag and J.J. Horning, The algebraic specification of abstract data types, *Acta Inform.*, *10*, 1, 1978, pp. 27-52.

10. C.A.R. Hoare, Communicating sequential processes, *Comm. ACM, 21*, 8, August 1978, pp. 666-677.

11. M.E. Majster, Limits of the 'algebraic' specification of abstract data types, *SIGPLAN Notices, 12*, 10, October 1977, pp. 37-42.

12. A. Moitra, Direct implementation of algebraic specification of abstract data types, *IEEE Trans. on Software Eng., SE-8*, 1, January 1982, pp. 12-20.

370

13. B.J. Nelson, Remote procedure call, Tech. Rep., Computer Science Department, Carnegie-Mellon University, May 1981.

14. J.W. Thatcher, E.G. Wagner and J.B. Wright, Data type specification : parameterization and the power of specification techniques, in *Proc. of the Tenth Annual ACM Symp. on Theory of Computing* (1978) 119-132.

15. N. Wirth, *Programming in Modula 2*, Springer-Verlag, 1982.

THE INTEGRATION AND DISTRIBUTION PHASE IN THE SOFTWARE LIFE CYCLE

G. CASAGLIA - F. PISANI

OLIVETTI - DIDAU/DSM

VIA JERVIS, 77 - 10015 IVREA - ITALY

ABSTRACT

The software production process may be seen as three main phases:
definition and design, implentation and distribution. It is obvious that in a
industrial environment the phases must have a comparable throughput.
In past years at Olivetti, design and implementation has been significantly
increased, introducing a new set of programming tools such as:
- UNIX os plus a number of related tools (make, berkleynet, mail,....)
- Pascal+: an enhanced version of Pascal including monitors, as system programming language.
Special care has also been given to the final part of production process where
all software components are integrated, finally tested and distributed to subsi-
diares and then to customers.
A number of management procedures and automated tools have been defined with the
purpose of enhancing such integration/distribution process; among these, worth of
note are the integration plan, describing the process managed by an integration
control board, and release committee.
Two level distribution data base, system test and amendment data base are some
tools supporting the process.
The presentation will sketch the whole software life cycle and then will
concentrate in the description of the integration-distribution process. According
to our experience this step may introduce a significant bottleneck. Removing such
bottleneck can significantly increase the performance (and quality) of the entire
process.
A detailed analysis of critical points and problems to be solved is derived,
following our experience in developing an entirely new operating system.

1. INTRODUCTION

In 1980, starting a completely new software project, it was decided to introduce
a new software life cicle and a completely new set of tools for software
production. At that time software implementation was based on a number of
different tools, depending on different projects, but a limited number of
scenarios can be described:

i) small projects using target machine as support, and assembly languages plus
   various types of debugging aids.

ii) medium size projects accessing IBM T.S. system, using cross-tools and
    various means for transferring object code from cross-system to target
    systems (i.e. down- line loading, transport via compatibile media and so
    on). Assembler and, in some cases high-level languages, were used in system
    software implementation.

iii) medium size projects using IBM RJE facilities, plus cross-tools and assembly

languages.
Each project adopted a specific-implicit-life cycle model.

Due to the characteristics of the new project, large system software for a new line of minicomputers with a significant number of successive releases to be produced, it was decided to define a uniform software production environment, suitable for all development groups. A plan to have all groups migrating from their "private" environment to the new "software factory" was also defined.

The key points on which the new "software factory" was based are the following:

.   use of minicomputers as development systems (PDP-11/70 and VAX), in order to be able to dedicate computing power to each project group and to be able to expand such capacity, according to the specific needs of such project groups.

.   use of UNIX as operating system and the related development tools, as the most advanced development environment.

.   distribution of a large number of terminals to the different project groups.

.   use of Pascal as high level development language.

.   network interconnection of all development systems in order to have the different groups exchange mail, documentation, source modules.

.   connection target systems to development systems for down-line loading of programs.

.   definition of a suitable global software life cicle.

2.   PRESENT SITUATION

Today the environment is completed and successfully operational.
Just to give some idea, the present situation is as follows:

-   About 30 development systems (PDP-11/70, VAX) are installed in seven different locations: four in Italy and three in the USA.

-   A network is connecting all of them using dedicated, switched lines and satellite links.

-   About 900 terminals are connected to the development systems serving about 1100 people involved in planning, implementation, QC, Sw distribution. This gives 1 terminal per 1.2 person.

-   90% of all the software produced is written in Pascal.

Fig. 2.1 is showing the general topolog of the network, being this the powerfull base supporting the development tools and metodology.

In the first two years of the project much care was dedicated to the environment and tools affecting productivity in the implementation phase (i.e. implementation language, debugging tools, computing equipments).
While more can be done in this area, that seems to be the area on which research efforts are concentrated, the two following years of our project have shown a large impact of the integration/distribution phase on global productivity.
The following sections are firstly dedicated to analize the global production process we have adopted and then to discuss some implications and then to consider possible evolutions or alternatives.

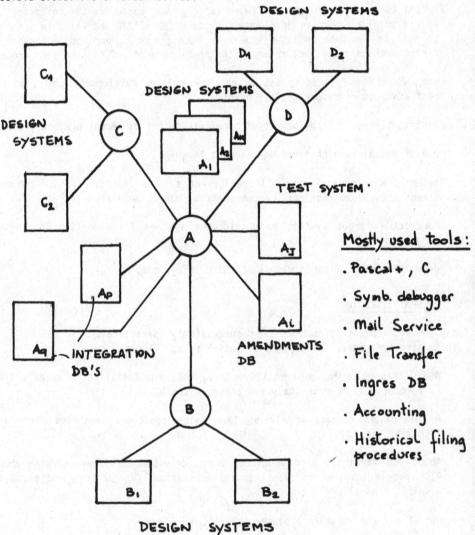

Fig. 2.1   Development Network Topology

3. ORGANISATIONAL ISSUES AND FLOW OF THE DEVELOPMENT PROCESS

Groups dedicated to the implementation of the software system, were organised according to a functional structure, like the one sketched in fig. 3.1

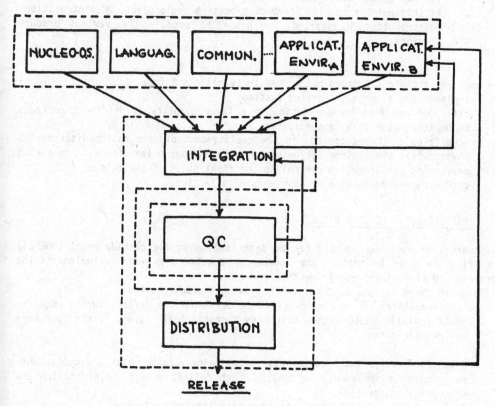

Fig. 3.1.   Functional structure organisation

The main characteristics of such structure are:

- Implementation of all software parts is done in parallel up to completion of all components according to the functional specs, practically without feedbacks from Integration and CQ phases before the end of implementation phase.

- Quality control is performed in a large single external organisation independent from the implementation groups.

- Integration control and distribution is performed by a third independent group.

- The production process is practically divided in two parts:
    - Implentation
    - CQ, Integration/Distribution

- The process can be described as follows:
  - implementation of different components is completed independently
  - components are then Quality Controlled
  - they are then funneled to the integration process, integrated to form the complete system and then quality controlled, according to the various system-configuration.
  - At this point a complex feedback process among project, QC, integration-/distribution is started, in order to produce the various product versions.

In past years these structure has proved to be efficient for:
- implementing a large integrated systems
- efficient and fast implementation of a large quantity of different packages to be integrated in a unique systems
- organizing a strong control in the quality-control integration/distribution phases while the implementation phase is technology driven for a large period
- performing configuration control in the final phase of the release
- producing and managing a release version at a time.

4. PRESENT SOFTWARE LIFE CYCLE.

Software life cycle we adopted can be described using the cascade model (BOE 81) modified in order to reflect the independence between sw modules implementation process and product release production process.
Life cycle shown in fig. 4.1, has the following characteristics:
- Functionalities of sw components to be developed are defined during require-ments analysis phase (REQA) driven by technological issues, rather than mar-ket requirements.

- Development of software components is following a rather standard cycle, whe-re components implementation and QC test definition and implementation are proceeding in parallel.
Implementation of all components is proceeding independently.

- Market requirement are introduced later in the development process, in order to define the set of components to be included in a product release.
Such definition, plus the components definition, allows the definition of the actual Product Release Contents (PREQA), and the definition of Integra-tion and Test Strategy (Integration Tree, Test Plan, ect.)
It is in this phase that additional developments are defined to complete Pro-duct Release Functionalities.

- Integration and test phase include high interaction among development gro-ups. Distribution kit is prepared and tested during this phase.

- Integration phase ends with the actual delivery of the release to a System Test phase, validating functional contents through home tests (application environment emulation) and through beta test (pilot user environment test).

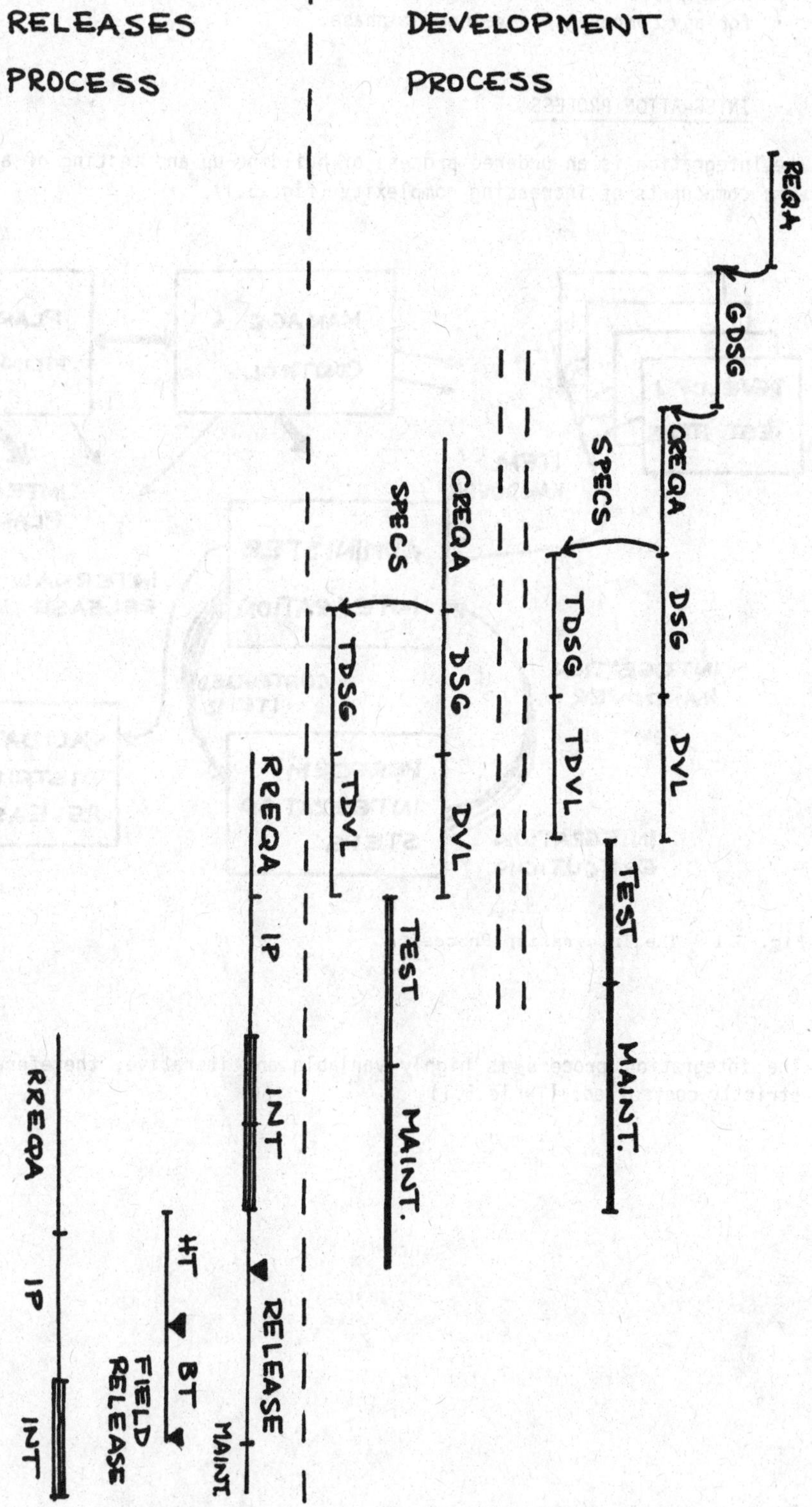

RELEASES PROCESS

DEVELOPMENT PROCESS

Fig. 4.1 Software Life Cycle

REQ+

GDSG

CREQA

SPECS

DSG

DVL

TEST

MAINT.

SPECS

CREQA

DSG

DVL

TDSG , TDVL

TEST

MAINT.

SPECS

TDSG , TDVL

RREQA

IP

INT

RELEASE

HT

BT

FIELD RELEASE

MAINT.

RREQA

IP

INT

A complete life cycle include three-four time integration phase iteration for any components development phase.

5. INTEGRATION PROCESS

The Integration is an ordered process of building-up and testing of a set of software components of increasing complexity (fig. 5.1).

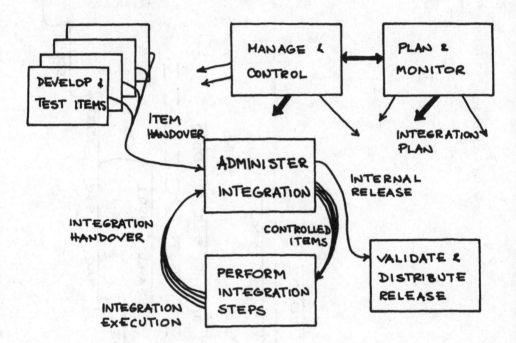

Fig. 5.1   The Integration Process

The integration process is highly variable and iterative, therefore it must be strictly controlled. (Table 5.1)

- Integration Programming

    • Includes technical planning, monitoring replanning

- Integration Execution

    • Construction and test

- Integration Administration

    • Includes Error handling

- Integration Control

    • Management & Change Change Control

Tab. 5.1 Integration Activities

Control of the process can be obtained having a high visibility of the process; such visibility is obtained having the software components flowing through three different and independent organisations:
- Development groups seen as producer of the components and the related documentation.

- Integration, in charge of receiving, managing and controlling the software library and organizing the documentation needed to build the product release.

- Quality Insurance, controlling the quality of the software received from Integration.

Fig. 5.2 shows the information flow among the different organisations.
An integration control board coordinate change control and conflict resolution activities, in order to have a smoothly converging process.

A typical Integration cycle is shown in fig 5.3, where critical mile stones are:
- delivery to integration of the last relevant software component;
- execution of a complete test phase, accepting software changes for errors during the test phase;
- non-regression test on final sw version, accepting controlled and authorized software changes;
- production of distribution kit.

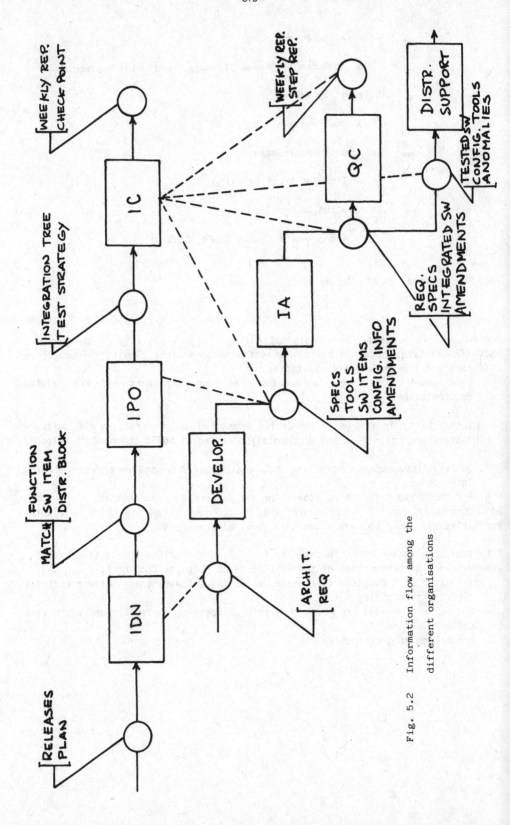

Fig. 5.2   Information flow among the different organisations

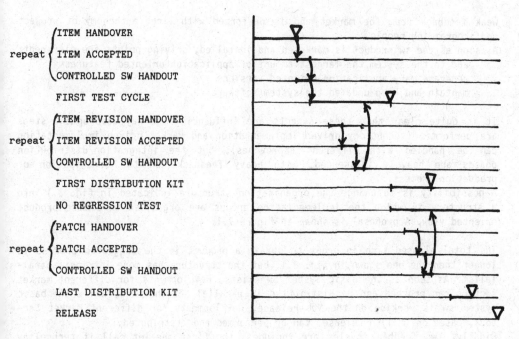

```
        ⎧ITEM HANDOVER
repeat ⎨ ITEM ACCEPTED
        ⎩CONTROLLED SW HANDOUT

         FIRST TEST CYCLE

        ⎧ITEM REVISION HANDOVER
repeat ⎨ ITEM REVISION ACCEPTED
        ⎩CONTROLLED SW HANDOUT

         FIRST DISTRIBUTION KIT

         NO REGRESSION TEST

        ⎧PATCH HANDOVER
repeat ⎨ PATCH ACCEPTED
        ⎩CONTROLLED SW HANDOUT

         LAST DISTRIBUTION KIT

         RELEASE
```

Fig. 5.3   Integration Life Cycle

6.   INTERMEDIATE STATUS.

The environment described has shown the following caracteristics:
.   Provides an efficient implementation process

.   Implementation process, not integrated with the functional specs definition and plan definition, gives too loose connection and feedbacks between this two phases which are proceeding practically in parallel, up to the integration phase.

.   Strong QC and Integration phases at the end of the process; this gives:
+   capacity of producing large complex configurations; but
+   long feedback-time among definition, implementation and integration
.   potential boottleneck in the final phase, as soon as the first versions are available and a significant number of different releases has to be managed.

7.   EVOLUTION OF PRODUCTION PROCESS AND SOFTWARE LIFE CYCLE.

As the first release of the new product was distributed it became apparent a new problem, we can try to summurize as follows:

Present structure is targeted to manage a very long implementation period of a sophisticated technology driven software system; i.e. implementation period has weak feedback from the market and is performed with large authonomy of project and programming people.

As soon as the sw product is marketed and installed, driving points are different:

. add to the system the largest amount of application oriented features

. generate many application oriented versions

. mantain and keep updated the system software.

It is quite clear that these aspects are influencing the way development steps are performed (technology driven implementation and market driven implementation can be handled with different approaches), but the integration/distribution phases are heavely influenced, with heavy feedbacks on the organisation of production process.

A possibility is to change the organisation structure indicated in fig. 3.1 into a structure in which the implementation groups are organised in a more product oriented view. A proposal is shown in figure 7.1.

The total elapsed time in order to obtain a product in the suggested process is longer then the one shown in fig. 3.1, but the structure has more intrinsic parallelism. As soon as the Basic System SW exists, developments for different market sectors can proceed and be distributed in parallel. Furthermore, while the basic system sw is working on the Nth release, developments for different Market Sectors, based on (N-1)th release, can be performed and distributed.

Finally, two feedback cycles are included; the first one-let call it technology driven - targeted to keep updated the basic System Software and the second one - let call it product driven - targeted to a fast reaction to market requirement. The second one can be significantly faster than the one in fig. 3.1, in which technology and product feedbacks are mixed and therefore the product feedbacks can be conditioned or even de-prioritized, in order to support apparently more urgent technological requirements.

In order to stress all the consequences from such production process organisation, it is interesting to structure a new software life cycle, that we can call the "Technology Market Compound Life Cicle" (See fig. 7.2).

Again, supported by the production process organisation shown in fig. 7.1, we have to pipelined phases with high degree of parallelism, which sharply separate the process of producing a new technologically advanced system and the process of releasing products driven by market requirement.

Important points to note on fig. 7.2 are:

. Architecture Definition is corresponding, at the technology level, to Product Definition at Market Level.

. The different steps of such life cycle may be described in greater details utilising one of the well known models (for example "Cascade" (BOE 81) or "Iterative"(BAL 84)), even if in this case we have sketched Baltzer's approach.

. Congifuration management is a very important phase also in technology driven development, where the fast prototiping technique is introducing a potentially unstructured development process.

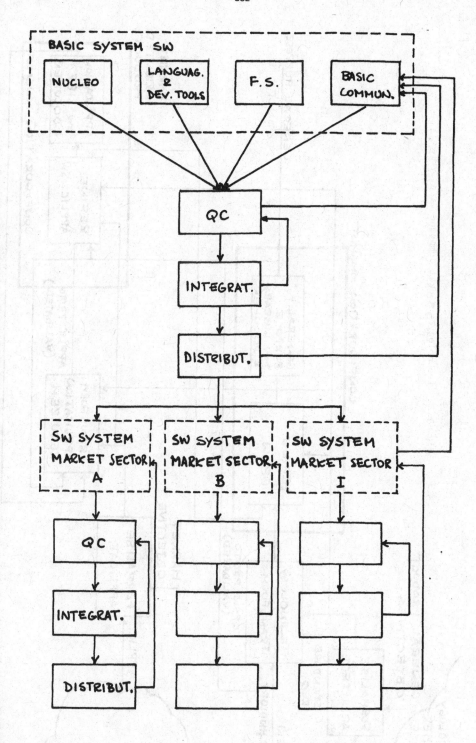

Fig. 7.1   Technology – Market Compound Production Process

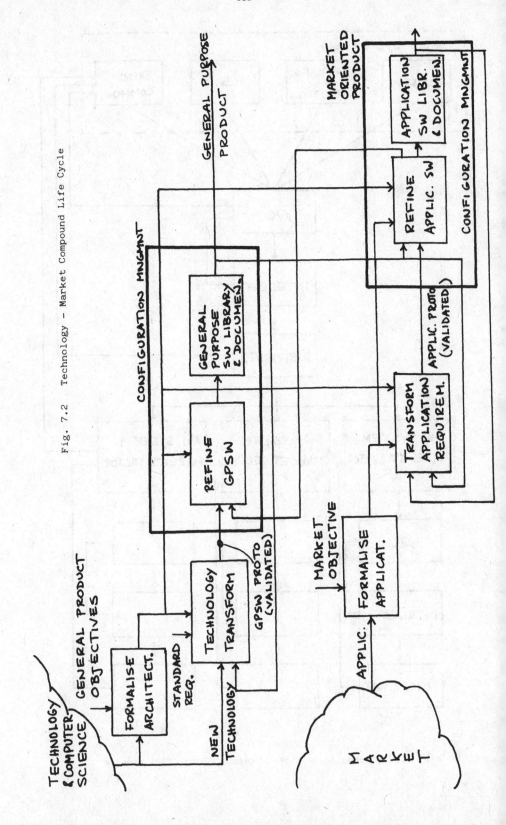

Fig. 7.2 Technology – Market Compound Life Cycle

Many parallel Market oriented cycles may be connected to one Technology cycles and therefore two different phases and distinct organisations are needed for Configuration Management.

8. <u>CONCLUSIONS</u>

Large enphasis is often given to programming tools, metodology and equipments, in order to increase software productivity. At Olivetti, starting a completely new project, a significant effort was dedecated to adopt modern and up-to-date tools and metodology. The project - "design and implementation of an entirely new general purpose multifunctional operant system and environment software for a minicomputer line" - found very beneficial the use of new tools up to the end of the first release.

A cascade software life cycle was adopted, with a large parallelism in the implementation fase and a single sequential integration, quality control and distribution phase.

When the software project is completely new and very complex, if the functional specs are well defined, this life cycle offers a strong control of the production process. It increases the probability of obtaing required functional characteristics while it offers lower control on delays and cost, because of lack of significant number of frequent feedbacks. Furthermore, the single integration quality control and distribution phase become to limiting, in order to exploit market potential of new system software while copying with it evolution.

A new process organisation, and software life cycle has been suggested in order to have a two phases process: one dealing with technologycal evolution and the other with market requirements. Each phase is supporting parallel development activities and offers many short feedback loops.

Because we are starting to experiment such approach, we are unable to report risults or criticisms.

BIBLIOGRAPHY

(BAL 84) R. Baltzer - Programming in the 1990's, Information Sciences Institute 1984.

(BOE 81) B.W. Boehm - Software Engineering Economics, Prentice Hall Inc, Englewood Cliffs.

FORMALIZED SOFTWARE DEVELOPMENT IN AN INDUSTRIAL ENVIRONMENT

Otthein Herzog

IBM Germany, Dept. 3100

P.O.Box 80 0880

D-7000 STUTTGART, F. R. G.

ABSTRACT

In the IBM Boeblingen Laboratory some software was experimentally developed in the framework of a "traditional" life-cycle model where precise semantics were introduced very early in the development process through the use of a formal specification method.

As a typical example for these ongoing efforts, the development of a medium-size software product is presented where a first informal global data flow specification was described using simple graphical conventions. The result of this development step was refined and formalized using the formal specification technique proposed in [JON80].The specification and design language SLAN-4 [BEI83] was used to document this specification. The experiences are outlined which were gained by this development approach.

1. The Software Life Cycle - a Specification in itself

There is a widely accepted software life-cycle the steps of which may be called differently but which usually are established in the following way:

1. Requirements collection: evolving a functional concept.

2. Specification: describing an appropriate global system architecture.

3. High Level Design: structure the system.

4. Low Level Design: getting the algorithms straight.

5. Implementation: coding.

6. Test: probing functions and quality.

7. Maintenance: maintaining proper functioning.

Obviously, this is a specification of a software development process which can be implemented in many different ways - and there are many methods and tools stating exactly this fact. However there does not seem to be a coherent method yet which has been widely accepted since different methods are normally used in the different development phases, and in addition, most of the methods appear to be aimed at specialized development areas such as certain types of applications or of system oriented software, e. g. teleprocessing protocols.

Before proceeding to the approach taken in the experiment some observations about implementations of this development process in general are worthwhile to be mentioned:

● Documents

The outcome of each development step should be a document or even a collection of documents which serves external or internal purposes, e. g.

- a functional description of a proposed software system to be used in negotiations with future users,
- a functional system decomposition to be used by the designers,
- a system specification to be used by designers as input to base the high level design on, by test designers to plan the test phases or by technical writers to develop the documentation,
- the programs themselves.

The collection of the documents written during development constitutes what is called software.

● Formalism

It is commonly accepted that the very first concept of a software system is conveniently described in an informal way. But in general the managers, designers, analysts and programmers got used to work with documents written in natural language, mostly English, which is in addition a foreign language for many people in the programming community.

As a common practice, these informal documents are augmented by flow charts, data flow diagrams, data definitions, and programming language control constructs (pseudocode) to describe additional details.

In this way there is an increasing formalism in the documents resulting from the development steps, but a complete formal description can be accomplished only at the coding level. There are some consequences of this approach: the documents

- tend to be very long,
- are ambiguous, inconsistent and incomplete,
- cannot be refined without implicit assumptions and interpretations.

● **Validation and Verification**

There is no question that each subsequent development step has to be an implementation of the preceding phase. But given the restriction that the early development steps are not documented in a formal way it is not possible to effectively use automated verification in these phases. Inspections and walkthrus are used instead facing all the limitations of the human mind confronted with large volumes of documentation.

This basically leads to the high specification and design error rate of up to 60% [MEN82] which is uncovered during the regular use of software. Although up to 50% of the development costs are usually spent in the test phase these specification and design errors are detected very late in the process and thus are very costly to correct since it might even be necessary to back up several development steps to effectively correct this type of errors.

Taking all these observations into consideration the formalization of the early development steps should be at least a partial solution to this problem. It should improve the early error detection and should help to avoid early errors. Which are the properties of methods to satisfy these strong requirements? They

- enforce a coherent, precise and minimal description of a system's behaviour which is complete in respect to its purpose,
- are interface oriented,
- describe the essentials of the problem solution, not implementation details,
- offer non-procedural description elements which usually lead to conciser system descriptions than algorithmic ones,
- stress the description of system interdependencies,
- build a bridge of understanding between the users, requirement planners, designers, and implementors.

The following objectives refine some of these properties: "Good" specification and design methods

- add discipline to the specification and design process,
- separate "WHAT" from "HOW",
- rigorize the system interface definitions,
- encourage levels of abstraction,
- promote hierarchical architectures,
- support maintainability of documents,
- are independent of hardware.

In addition it is necessary to support such a method by a language which can be implemented in an environment providing the necessary tool support. The items mentioned in [MAR83] give an impression of the important issues:

- The specification language must be rigorously defined.

- There has to be an interactive graphics facility.

- A mathematical basis allows for checking the logic structure.

- Rigorous refinement steps must be possible.

- Ultimately, code must be generated from the specification.

- The definition levels must be integrated: One language has to cover all development phases to ease the maintenance of front-end documents.

- Integrated top-down and bottom-up specification must be possible.

- An evolving library of reusable parts must be available.

- Integrated checking must guarantee interface consistency.

- Documents are easy to change, also by persons which did not create them.

- All elements of a system should be traceable.

2. An experiment to formalize early development phases

In the IBM Boeblingen laboratory the specification and design language SLAN-4 has been developed [BEI83] which satisfies almost all the requirements against such a language. It provides constructs for the algebraic specification and implements also essential parts of the Vienna Definition Method ("VDM")[BJO78]. Some experiments were conducted to use this method and this language to determine the effects of the formalization of early development phases.

A medium-size software product including an interactive user interface was specified using a combination of a simple graphical notation for the global data flow and SLAN-4 for the formal specification of the operations to be performed by the individual modules. This formal specification was expressed using SLAN-4 syntax with **pre-** and **post**-conditions for each of the operations.

The Software System

The system addresses a networking environment, resides on a host machine and allows a network administrator to

● maintain a data base on network resources (repository of the hardware and software configuration),

● report on the stored information,

● retrieve and send data from and to nodes,

● get status information from the nodes, and

● send messages to the nodes.

It offers the user an interactive front-end with guidance to the main system functions through a small number of selection menus.

The total size of the system is 17,300 lines of an IBM internal very high-level language code, not including 4,000 lines of HELP text, which is available on-line during a session.

Specification and Design

The development was done top-down with very few iterations and included a mixed design strategy:

1. The global flow was designed using an outside-in method starting from the functional description of the user interface.

2. The functional specification resulted in a hierarchical decomposition of the system including the panels required for the user interaction within the individual functions. Again, the user interface determined here essential parts of the specification.

   For the functional specification itself, the global data state and the data interfaces for each module were specified. Then the elaboration of the pre- and post-conditions allowed the developers to check the completeness and consistency of the interfaces.

The specification phase was completed after a thorough inspection of the specification document which was very effective because of the unambiguous description of the system.

3. For the low level design step, the data object declarations were carried over to the design/implementation language and the algorithms were developed using well-known sequencing control structures to implement the specified functions.

   The final layout of the selection menus and the data entry panels was defined in such a way that a prototype of the system was the outcome of the low level design. This step was also concluded by a design inspection.

Implementation and Test

1. A very high level implementation language was used to directly implement the design. This language offered very high level data types, such as sets, bags, lists and arrays.

   The development team was thus able to also use the data types selected during the specification phase in the low level design and also in the implementation phase.

2. After the code inspections the test of the system was carried out in different steps:

   a. Each developer performed a structural unit test taking the internal structure of the code into account.

   b. Then the code was transferred to a test team which subsequently did a function test against the specification. The next test phase was a component test against the user documentation to assure the proper cooperation among the different functional components. Finally a system test was performed varying hardware and software configurations.

   The test period lasted four months. The errors found were formally reported and the valid errors were corrected in all affected documents including the specification, since this document was supposed to be the description of the system for the maintenance team.

Evaluation of the experiment

The following points resulted from the methods and the languages used:

- The method was applicable to a software system without heavy external interfaces.
- Module interfaces could be explicitly documented.
- Abstract data types were successfully used.
- Each module could be described in a non-procedural way independently from the final implementation.
- The precise module semantics and the complete interface description led to very stable interfaces between the individual modules which were in most cases only changed by new requirements.
- During four months of function, component and system testing, 5.84 valid program errors were found per 1000 lines of code. This compares to 20 to 40 errors usually found during such a test cycle for software of comparable complexity. The main reasons for this result were the early formalization which helped to avoid errors and to reduce the error propagation through the subsequent development steps and the availabilty of the same high level data types in the specification, design and implementation languages. This avoided errors introduced by implementations of abstract data types.

  However, an analysis of the errors found showed the interesting result that an integrated formalized description of the global data flow would have avoided some errors which were found during the test cycle.
- There was also a considerable positive effect on productivity.
- Although the method and the language was new to the majority of the development team, the early development phases did not need more time than "conventional" specification and design methods.
- The specification was invariant against small requirement changes. During the development a considerable change in the requirements for the user interface could be easily incorporated in the existing specification document.

3. References

[BEI83]   F. Beichter at al.: SLAN-4: A Language for the Specification and the
           Design of Large Software Systems.-
           IBM Journal of Res. and Dev. Vol 27(6), Nov. 1983, p. 558 - 576

[BEI84]   F. Beichter at al.: SLAN-4: A Software Specification and Design
           Language.-
           IEEE Trans. Software Eng. Vol. SE-10(2), March 1984, p. 155 - 162

[BJO78]   D. Bjorner, C. B. Jones (Eds.): The Vienna Development
            Method: The Meta-Language.-
           Springer (1978)

[COT84]   I. D. Cottam: The Rigorous Development of a System Version Control
           Program.-
           IEEE Trans. Software Eng. Vol. SE-10(2), March 1984, p. 143 - 154

[JON80]   C. B. JONES: Software Development - A Rigorous Approach.-
           Prentice Hall (1980)

[MAR83]   J. Martin: Fourth Generation Languages, Vol. 1.-
           Savant Research Studies (1983)

[MEN82]   K. S. Mendis: Quantifying Software Quality.- Quality Progress, pp.
           18-22, May 1982.

[PEP84]   P. Pepper (Ed.): Program Transformation and Programming
           Environments.
           Report on a Workshop directed by F. L. Bauer und H. Remus.-
           Springer (1984)

OBJECT ORIENTED CONCURRENT PROGRAMMING AND INDUSTRIAL SOFTWARE PRODUCTION

Akinori Yonezawa* and Yoshihiro Matsumoto**

*) Department of Information Science
Tokyo Institute of Technology
Ookayama Meguro-ku, Tokyo 152

**) Toshiba Corporation
Heavy Apparatus Eng. Lab.
1, Toshiba-Cho, Fuchu, Tokyo 183

0. Abstract

A framework of object oriented parallel computations is presented and a programming language called ABCL whose semantics faithfully reflects this computation model is illustrated. A methodology for industrial software production based upon the computation model is discussed.

1. Introduction

Objects in the object oriented programming are conceptual entities which model the functions and knowledge of "things" that appear in problem domains. The fundamental aim in the object oriented programming is to make the structure of a solution as natural as possible by representing it as interactions of objects.

Currently proposed formalisms for object oriented programming (e.g., [GR83] [WM81]) confine themselves in the sequential world. This is too restrictive. Parallelism is ubiquitous in our problem domains. Behaviors of computer systems, human information processing systems, corporative organizations, scientific societies etc. are results of highly concurrent (independent, cooperative or contentious) activities of their components. To model and study such systems, or design various software systems and solve problems by the metaphor of such systems, it is necessary to develop an adequate formalism in which various concurrent activities and interactions of "objects" can be naturally expressed and which is also executable as computer programs.

We have already proposed such a formalism, namely a programming language called ABCL[YO84]. The problem domains to which we apply our formalism include distributed problem solving and planning in AI, modeling human cognitive processes, designing real-time systems and operating systems, and designing and constructing office information systems. Some of characteristic example programs in these domains are also given in [YO84].

2. A Model of Computation

Our computation model for object oriented concurrent programming is a direct descendant of the Actor computation model which was proposed and studied by C. Hewitt and his group at MIT[HE73][HB77][YO77][YO79]. This section gives an intuitive account of what we mean by "objects". The properties of objects explained in this section are those which are inherited from the notion of "actors".

In our computation model, computations are performed by concurrent message passing among procedural modules called objects. Objects model conceptual or physical entities which appear in problem domains. Messages correspond to requests, inquiries or replies.

Each object has its own processing power and it may have its local memory. An object is always in one of two modes, active or inactive and it becomes active when it receives a message. Each object has its own description which determines what messages it can accept and what computations it performs. Upon receiving a message, an object can make simple decisions, send messages to objects (including itself), create new objects and change its local memory according to its description. After performing the described computation, an object becomes inactive until it receives a new message.

Though message passings in a system of objects may take place concurrently, we assume message arrivals at an object be linearly ordered. No two messages cannot arrive at the same object simultaneously and a single message queue sorted in the arrival order is assumed for each object. When a message arrives at an object, if the object is not active and no messages are in the queue, then the message is received by the object. If the object is active or messages are already in the queue, the message is put at the end of the queue.

There are two classes of objects, "serialized" objects and "unserialized" objects. A serialized object is activated by one message at a time. While a serialized object is being activated by a message, it is locked and cannot receive a new message. We do not assume this property for unserialized objects. In the subsequent discussion we focus our attention on serialized objects.

3. Types of Message Passings and Continuations

To study the versatility of our model of computation, we modeled and described various parallel or real-time systems using a simple set of notations. In the course of this process, we made a simple assumption on the message arrival and also found it sometimes necessary to distinguish three types of message passings which are not included in the original Actor model of computation.

[Arrival Ordering Preservation Assumption]

When two messages are sent to an object T by the same object O, the time ordering of the two message transmissions (according to O's clock) must be preserved in the time ordering of the two message arrivals (according to T's clock).

This assumption was not included in the original Actor model of computation[HB77]. Without this, however, we cannot model, for example, a computer terminal or displaying device as an object. The terminal object must receive character messages in the same order as their transmissions from an object that models an output handling program in an operating system.

["Past" Type Message Passings]

    Suppose an object O is being activated and it sends a message M to an object T. Then O does not wait for M to be received by T. It just continues its computation after the transmission of M (provided that the transmission of M is not the last action during the current activation of O).

We call this type of message passings "past" type because sending a message finishes before it causes the intented effects to the message receiving object. Let us denote a past type message passing by the following notation.

$$[T <= M] \tag{1}$$

The past type corresponds to the situation where one requests or commands someone to do some task and simultaneously he proceeds his own task without waiting for the requested task to be completed. This type of message passings substantially increase concurrency of activities within a system. (Past type message passings can further be divided into two kinds which may reflect two different implementation strategies. In one kind, an object which transmits a message does not continue its computation until the arrival of the message is assured, while in the other kind, the object continues its computation as soon as the message leaves the object. Of course the latter kind allows higher concurrency than the former one, but may sacrifice the robustness against various unexpected errors in the system's components.)

["Now" Type Message Passings]

    When an object O sends a message M to an object T, O waits for not only M to be received by T, but also waits for T to return some information to O. If T does not return anything, O waits until T's current activation caused by M ends.

This is similar to ordinary function/procedure calls, but it differs in that T's activation does not have to end with sending some information back to O. T may continue its computation during the same activation caused by M. A now type message passing is denoted by

$$[T <== M] \tag{2}$$

Returning information from T to O may serve as an acknowledgement of receiving the message (or request) as well as reporting the result of a requested task. Thus the message sending object O is able to know that his message was surely received by the object though he may waste time in waiting. The returned information (certain values or signals) is denoted by the same notation as the message passing. Namely, (2) denotes not merely an action of sending M to T by a now type message passing, but also denotes the information returned by T. If the activation of T ends without returning any information, we assume, by convention, (2) denotes some special value (e.g. nil).

Now type message passings provide a quite convenient means to synchronize concurrent activities performed by independent objects when it is used together with the parallel construct that will be discussed in a later section. (It should be warned that recursive now type message passings cause local deadlock.)

["Future" Type Message Passings]

Suppose an object O sends a message M to an object T expecting a certain request-ed result to be returned from T. But O does not need the result immediately. In this situation, O does not have to wait for T to return the result after the transmission of M. It continues its computation immediately. Later on when O needs that result, it checks O's internal memory area that was specified at the time of the transmission of M. If the result is ready, it is used. Otherwise O waits there until the result is obtained.

A future type message passing is denoted by

$$[x := [T <= M]] \tag{3}$$

where x is the specified memory area (or a variable). A system's concurrency is increased by the use of future type message passings. If the now type were used instead of future type, O would have to waste time by waiting for the currently unnecessary result to be produced. The future type message passing feature has been incorporated in previous object oriented programming languages [LI81][FU84].

Since the now type and future type message passings are not allowed in the Actor computation model, an actor A which sends a message to a target actor T and expects a response from T must terminate its current activation and A must wait for the response to arrive as just one of incoming messages. To discriminate T's response from other incoming messages, A must make some provision before it sends the message to T. Also the necessity of the termination of A's current activation causes unna-tural breaking down of A's task into small pieces.

In the above discussion, the contents of a message was left vague. We should make it clear in order to make a more precise account of how various information flows among objects through message passings. A message consists of two parts, an RR-part and a C-part. An RR-part which stands for a request/reply part tells the message receiving object about the contents of a request or it is used to carry a reply or result of a requested task.

When a message is sent by a "past" type message passing to request an object to do some task, it is sometimes useful for the message sending object to have a means to specify a destination object where the result of the requested task should be sent. We call this destination object a "continuation". A C-part which stands for a continuation-part provides this means. (Without an explicit indication of the desti-nation, the only thing one can do is either to have the object which carries out the requested task keep the result within itself, or to have the result sent to some default object.) In our notational convention, a message is expressed by a pair whose first and second parts are separated by a period. The first part and second part correspond to its RR-part and C-part, respectively. Namely, it is of the form

[<RR-part> . <C-part>].

When the C-part of a message need not be specified, it is left blanked. In this case the message is a Lisp singleton list of the following form

```
[<RR-part>]
```

where the period after <RR-part> is omitted. In fact, the C-parts of messages sent by "now" or "future" types must be void, because the destination to which the result is supposed to be sent is predetermined. Namely, a "future" type message passing itself specifies a part of the internal memory (or a variable) of the message sending object. For the case of "now" type, we can view this type of message passings as a special case of "now" type message passings.

4. A Language ABCL

In order to describe behaviors of objects in more precise and concrete terms, we need to develop a language. We have tentatively designed and implemented a programming language called ABCL (An object-Based Core Language). The purpose of designing this language is manifold. It is intended to serve as an experimental programming language to construct software in the framework of object-based concurrent programming. The kind of the application domain we emphasize includes the AI fields and we plan to use this language as an executable thought-tool for developing the paradigm of distributed problems solving [YO84][SI81] and cognitive models. It is also intended to serve as an executable language for modeling and designing of various parallel or real time systems. Thus ABCL serves as a language for rapid prototyping[SI82].

The primary design principles of this language are:

[1] Clear semantics: the semantics of the language should be as close to the simple underlying computation model as possible.

[2] Practicality: various features of Lisp can be directly utilized to exploit efficiency and programming ease as long as the framework of the object oriented programming style is maintained.

The purpose of the present paper is not to introduce the details of the language, we keep its explanation minimum. For those who are interested in the language, see [YO84][MY84].

4.1. Defining Objects

Each object has a fixed set of message patterns it accepts. To define the behavior of an object, we must specify what computations or actions it will perform for each such message pattern. The description of computation for each message pattern is called a "script". If an object has its local memory, its computations may be affected by the current contents of such memory. Thus in order to define an object with local memory, we must also describe how the object's local memory is represented. Representations of local memory are variables or internal objects which have its own local memory.

To write a definition of an object in ABCL, we use a notation of the following form (4). (state: ...) declares the representation of local memory and initializes it. Scripts are basically expressed in terms of message passings, referencing to variables and calculating values or manipulating list structures using Lisp functions. These actions are performed sequentially unless special parallel execution constructs are used.

```
[object <object-name>
   (state: <representation of memory> )

   (=> [<pattern>]   <script>   )                                    (4)
    ...
    ...
   (=> [<pattern>]   <script>   )     ]
```

As an illustrative example, let us consider an object which models the behavior of a semaphore. A semaphore has a counter to store an integer with a certain initial value (say 1) and also it has a queue for waiting processes which is initially empty. We represent the counter as a variable and the queue as an (internal) object which behaves as a queue. A semaphore accepts two patterns of messages, [p-op: . C] and [v-op: . C] which correspond to the P-operation and V-operation. In ABCL, symbols ending with a colon in messages or message patterns are constants, whereas symbols starting with a capital letter or "_" are pattern variables which bind components of incoming messages. (p-op: and v-op: are constants. C is a pattern variable which binds the C-part (, namely the continuation) of an incoming matching message.)

Using the notation (4), a definition of the semaphore object is shown below.

```
[object aSemaphore
   (state: [counter := 1]                        ; := means assignment.
           [process_q = [CreateQ <== [new:]]])   ; = means binding.

   (=> [p-op: . C]  <script for P-operation>   )

   (=> [v-op: . C]  <script for V-operation>   ) ]
```

Note that a "now" type message passing is used to create a queue object and it is bound to a symbol process_q.

4.2. Creating Objects

CreateQ in the above example is an object which creates and returns a new object which behaves as a queue. We assume it is defined elsewhere. CreateQ can be viewed as a class of queues and the created queue object as an instance of the queue class (if we use the terminology of AI or SmallTalk[GB83]). In ABCL, rather complicated notions such as classes and meta-classes are unified as the notion of objects, which allows us to manipulate classes and meta-classes as objects.

Objects which create and return an object are often defined in the following fashion.

```
[object CreateSomething
  (=> [<initial-information> . <continuation>]

    [<continuation> <= [[object ...              ; a newly created object is
                         (=> [...] ...)          ; sent to <continuation>
                         ...
                         (=> [...] ...)]

                  nil]]
  )]
```

Namely, a message whose RR-part is a newly created object defined by [object ....]
and whose C-part is nil is sent to <continuation>. Creating a new object and sending
it back to the continuation is one of typical situations where a message with its
C-part being nil is sent to the original continuation. A simple abbreviated notation in ABCL expresses this scheme of message transmission.

```
        (=> [<request>]     ... !<expression> ...),
```

This is equivalent to

```
    (=> [<request> . <continuation>]
        ... [<continuation> <= [<expression> . nil]] ...).
```


5. Parallelism and Synchronization

5.1 Parallelism

Using the abbreviated notation explained in the previous section, the object which
creates and returns a semaphore object is defined in Figure 1. In the script for
p-op:, (subl counter) is an invocation of a lisp function subl and the result
updates the contents of counter. When process_q object is empty in executing the
script for v-op:, a [go:] message is sent to the continuation which is bound to C;
otherwise the first process that has been waiting is removed from the queue and
[go:] messages are sent to this process and the continuation simultaneously.

As noted earlier, a script is usually executed sequentially. But when a special
construct denoted by

```
        { El , ... , Ek }
```

is executed, the executions of El,...,Ek start simultaneously. The execution of
this construct, which we call a "parallel construct", does not end until the executions of all the components El,...,Ek end. When the components of a parallel construct are all past type message passings, the degree of parallelism caused among
the message receiving objects is not much greater than the degree of parallelism
caused by the sequential execution of the components because of very small time cost
of a message transmission. But if a parallel construct contains now type message
passings, the possibility of exploitation of parallelism among the message receiving
objects is very high.

```
[object CreateSemaphore
  (=> [init: N]                ;when [init: ...] is sent, the following object
                               ;is created and returned.
   ![object                    ; definition of a semaphore object begins.
      (state:
        [counter := N]
        [process_q = [CreateQ <== [new:]]])

      (=> [p_op: . C]
        [counter := (sub1 counter)]
        (case (> 0 counter)
          (is t                ; if counter is negative
           [process_q <= [enqueue: C]])
          (otherwise
           [C <= [go:]])))

      (=> [v_op: . C]
        [counter := (add1 counter)]
        (case [process_q <== [dequeue:]]
         (is nil                ; if process_q is empty
          [C <= [go:]])
         (is FrontProcess      ; the head of process_q is bound to FrontProcess
          { [FrontProcess <= [go:]],
            [C <= [go:]] }     )))
   ] )]
```

Figure 1. Defining a Semaphore Object

After having explained parallel constructs, it is an appropriate time to review the
basic types of parallelism provided in ABCL.

[1] concurrent activations of independent objects.

[2] parallelism caused by past type message passings.

[3] parallelism caused by parallel constructs.

5.2. Synchronization

Parallel constructs are also powerful in synchronizing the behaviors of objects
because the semantics of a parallel construct requires that its execution completes
only when the executions of all the components complete. When a parallel construct,
in a script, contains a now type message passing, all the intended actions of the
message receiving objects must be completed before going on to the execution of the
rest of the script. (Note that we need no synchronization if all the components of
a parallel construct are past type message passings.)

For example, suppose the movement of a robot arm is actuated by three step motors,
each being responsible for the movement along different coordinates[KS84] and for

each motor there is an object operating it. In order to pick up something by the fingers attached to the arm, the control program sends signals to the three objects in parallel, and it must wait until the rotations of all the three motors stop. See a fragment of the program below.

```
... { [motorX <== [step: 100]], [motorY <== [step: 150]], [motorZ <== [step: -30]] }
    <command to pick up>  ...
```

We conclude this section to remind one that ABCL provides the following four basic mechanisms for synchronization.

[1] serialized object: the activation of a serialized object takes place one at a time and a single first-come-first-served message queue is associated with each object.

[2] now type message passing: it does not end until a certain result is returned or the activation of the message receiving object comes to end.

[3] future type message passing: when the specified variable is referred to, the execution is suspended if the contents is not updated yet.

[4] parallel construct: as discussed above.

Although we have shown an implementation (or modeling) of semaphores in terms of the object paradigm, we think semaphores are too primitive and unstructured as a basic synchronization mechanism. Thus we have no intention of using semaphore objects to synchronize behaviors of objects. Our experience of writing programs which require various types of synchronization suggests that combinations of the four mechanisms listed above seem sufficiently powerful for dealing our current problems.

6. Use of ABCL for Industrial Software Production

Software design in the practical software manufacturing is a refinement process in which requirements specified in a problem domain are gradually transformed into programs. In the waterfall type lifecycle models, the refinement is done through multiple numbers of consecutive phases. In an earlier phase, a specification may be transformed into the second specification which has more concreteness, or less abstraction. In later phases, a program written in a higher language will be translated into the program written in a lower language. Dijkstra described the concept of abstract machine $M(i)$ and description $D(i)$ on abstract level i such that execution of $D(i)$ on $M(i)$ satisfies the purpose of code $D(0)$ which is to be executed on a real machine $M(0)$. At the next lower level, level$(i-1)$, $D(i-1)$ is executed on $M(i-1)$ [DI72].

The phases, descriptions and abstract levels in our practical software production are defined as follows [MA84]:

i=4; D(4): requirements specification,
i=3; D(3): functional design specification or external design specification,
i=2; D(2): program design specification or detail design specification,
i=1; D(1): program text,
i=0; D(0): binary code.

phase(4): requirements analysis and definition,
phase(3): functional design,
phase(2): program design,
phase(1): programming,
phase(0): translation or compilation.

It has been our consistent desire that the designer does not have to go down into too much low level description. In this sense, we owe compilers and assemblers for staying away from level 0, but the actual productivity value is still much to be improved. If we could have a language in which we could write a specification of a higher abstract level (i.e., the functional design or program design level) and translate it into binary code, it will bring us a great benefit' for increasing the productivity. The descriptions of higher abstract levels reflect the designer's internal models or concepts more directly than those of lower levels do. Therefore the languages which could meet our desire of describing specifications of higher levels should be those which could describe human (expert) knowledge in more direct forms. Our object oriented concurrent language ABCL seems to be one candidate of such desired languages.

We will give a simple example selected from our actual software and show how ABCL has been used for this example. This example is a part of software to print out the operational guidance messages for human operators in local dispatch control stations of an electric power system.

In response to requests from the central supervisory office, an operator disconnects facilities which are required to be checked, repaired or cleaned. The facilities may be transmission lines, electric bus lines in a substation, or transformers. When a facility is disconnected, it will become out of service. Therefore the operator must put alternative facilities into service so that they will substitute for the functions of the disconnected facility. By setting up an alternative circuit which rounds about the facility to be disconnected, the consumer of electric power will not be affected.

The programs written in ABCL in Figure 2 and Figure 3 show a part of the software which reasons the method to set up this round about operation. The programs describe a knowledge to disconnect a transmission line named "LINE-N". Figure 3 describes the knowledge before it is instantiated. The description in Figure 2 instantiates it so that the newly created object whose name is now Disconnect_operation_for_LINE_N contains the knowledge to disconnect the transmission line "LINE-N". This knowledge is modelled as the object described in line 4 to line 17 in Figure 3, where the value of the pattern variable "Line_name" is "LINE-N".

```
1  [Disconnect_operation_for_LINE_N =
2           [Create_line_disconnect_knowledge <== [for: LINE-N]]]

3  [Disconnect_operation_for_LINE_N <=
4     [disconnect_transmission_line_and_report_to: . Supervisor]]
```

Figure 2.

```
1   [object Create_line_disconnect_knowledge
2     (=> [for: Line_name]
3
4     ![object Me
5       (state:
6         [caller_name := nil]
7         [load_facility_list := (func$fetch_local_facility_for  Line_name)]
8         [substation_operation = [Create_substation_operation <= [new:]]])
9
10      (=> [disconnect_transmission_line_and_report_to: . Caller]
11        [caller_name := Caller]
12        [substation_operation <=
13          [handle_outservice_of: load_facility_list and_report_to: . Me]])
14
15      (=> [substation_operation_finished:]
16        (func$disconnect_transmission_line  Line_name)
17        [caller_name <= [transmission_line_disconnected:]])] )]
```

Figure 3.

The object "Disconnect_operation_for_LINE_N" is activated when it receives messages with the patterns shown in line 10 and 15. When it receives a message of the pattern in line 10, the name of the object which is bound to the pattern variable "Caller" is stored in the variable "caller_name", and it activates the object "substation_operation" by sending the message shown in line 13, and then it becomes inactive. When the substation object finishes its operation, it is supposed to send back to Disconnect_operation_for_LINE_N a message of the pattern shown in line 15. Thus Disconnect_operation_for_LINE_N becomes active again and does the disconnecting of transmission lines for LINE-N (line 16) and finally it sends to the original caller (here, Supervisor) a message indicating the end of the operation (line 17).

The programs shown reflect the knowledge of the operator more directly because it simulates the behavior of the operator who first becomes active by the instruction from the central office, analyzes it, transmits his instructions to his subsidiaries, disconnects his facility and then reports the completion to the central office.

A create-object such as the one shown in Figure 3 is defined for each type of facility. For example, we have Create_transformer_disconnect_knowledge for the transformer. The collection of such objects is called "knowledge base" in our system. This knowledge base is accessed and maintained through the knowledge base management system.

The object defined in Figure 3 illustrates just one type of objects which represent "knowledge chunk" in the form of state changes. We have other types of objects. For example, a type of object represents a block of production rules. Another type of object can represent a set of fuzzy logic. We are convinced that all these types of objects are required in order to implement our system which supports plant operators.

7. Concluding Remarks

7.1. Programming Environments

The first stage of (concurrent) programming in the object oriented style is to determine, at a certain level of abstraction, what kinds of objects are necessary and natural to have in solving the problem concerned. At this stage, message passing relations (namely what objects send messages to what objects) are also determined.

Since it is often useful or even necessary to effectively overview the structure of a solution or result of modeling, those identified objects and message passing relations should be recorded and be retrieved or even manipulated graphically. For this purpose, we are currently designing and implementing a programming aid system on a SUN-II Workstation with multi-window facilities and a standard pointing device. A typical action using this system might be to add a node to a graph which represents message passing relations among objects (where nodes correspond to objects), point the node by a mouse to get a pop-up menu and select/perform operations such as editing and compiling the program for the object.

7.2. Other Examples

A wide variety of example programs have been written in ABCL and we are fairly convinced that essential part of ABCL is robust enough to be used in the intended domains. Examples we have written include distributed problem solving by a project team[YO84], parallel discrete simulation[YO84a], deamons, production rules, robot arm control[KS84], bounded buffers, integer tables[HO78], simulation of data flow computations, process schedulers etc. Also a simplified example of a mill speed control program[MA84] written in ABCL is given in the Appendix below.

Acknowledgements

The first author expresses his deep appreciation to H. Matsuda and E. Shibayama who made various contributions to the present work including the design and implementation of ABCL.

References

[DI72] Dijkstra, E.W.: Notes on Structured Programming, Structured Programming, (Eds. O.J. Dahl, et al.), Academic Press, 1972.

[FU84] Fukui, S.: An Object Oriented Parallel Language, Proc. Hakone Programming Symposium, (1984), in Japanese.

[GR83] Goldberg, A. and Robson, D.: SmallTalk80 - The Language and its Implementation -, Addison Wesley, 1983.

[HB77] Hewitt, C. and Baker, H.: Laws for Parallel Communicating Processes, IFIP-77, Toronto, (1977).

[HE73] Hewitt, C. et al.: A Universal Modular Actor Formalism for Artificial Intelligence, Proc. Int. Jnt. Conf. on Art. Int., (1973).

[HO78] Hoare, C.A.R.: Communicating Sequential Processes, CACM, Vol. 21 No. 8, 1978.

[KS84] Kerridge, J. M. and Simpson, D.: Three Solutions for a Robot Arm Controller Using Pascal-Plus, Occam and Edison, Software - Practice and Experience - Vol. 14, (1984), pp.3-15.

[LI81] Lieberman, H.: A Preview of Act-1, AI-Memo 625, MIT AI Lab., (1981).

[MA84] Matsumoto, Y.: Management of Industrial Software Production, IEEE Computer Vol. 17, No. 2, (1984), pp.59-72.

[MY84] Matsuda, H. and Yonezawa, A.: ABCL User's Manual, Internal Memo, Dept. of Information Science, Tokyo Institute of Technology, November 1984.

[SI82] Special Issue on Rapid Prototyping, ACM SIG Software Engineering Notes Vol. 7, No. 5, December 1982.

[SP81] Special Issue For Distributed Problem Solving, IEEE Trans. on Systems, Man and Cybernetics, Vol. SMC-11, No.1, (1981).

[WM81] Weinreb, D. and Moon, D.: Flavors: Message Passing in the Lisp Machine, AI-Memo 602, MIT AI Lab., (1981).

[YO77] Yonezawa, A.: Specification and Verification Techniques for Parallel Programs Based on Message Passing Semantics, (Ph.D. Thesis), TR-191 Laboratory for Computer Science, MIT, 1977.

[YO79] Yonezawa, A. and Hewitt, C.: Modelling Distributed Systems, Machine Intelligence, Vol. 9 (1979).

[YO84] Yonezawa, A, Matsuda, H and Shibayama, E: An Object Oriented Approach for Concurrent Programming, Research Report C-63, Dept. of Information Science, Tokyo Institute of Technology, November 1984.

[YO84a] Yonezawa, A.: Discrete Event Simulation Based on An Object Oriented Parallel Computation Model, Research Report C-64, Dept. of Information Science, Tokyo Institute of Technology, November 1984.

Appendix   Mill Speed Control Program

A simple ABCL program for controlling mill roller speed is given below.
Input_Handler object receives sensor data which consist of 6 heat sensor values
(h1-h6), a load cell value (ls), and an emergency stop flag (stp). Speed_Selection
object determines the right speed of the mill roller by considering the current
position of the slab and the data sent from Input_Handler. Speed_Control object
sets the actual speed of the roller. Note the concurrency among the three object.

```
                                    *****************
            Sensor Value    ==>     * Input_Handler *
                                    *****************

                                         ||
                                         vv

     *****************                *******************
     * Speed_Control *     <==        * Speed_Selection *
     *****************                *******************
```

```
[object Input_Handler
  (=> [sensor_value: Frame]
   (case Frame
    (is [h1: 0 h2: 0 h3: 0 ls: 0 h4: 0 h5: 0 h6: 0 stp: 0]
      [Speed_Selection <= [input: 'i1]] )

    (is [h1: 1 h2: 0 h3: 0 ls: 0 h4: 0 h5: 0 h6: 0 stp: 0]
      [Speed_Selection <= [input: 'i2]] )

    (is [h1: 0 h2: 1 h3: 0 ls: 0 h4: 0 h5: 0 h6: 0 stp: 0]
      [Speed_Selection <= [input: 'i3]] )

     ... <cases for 'i4 to 'i8 are omitted> ...

    (is [h1: 0 h2: 0 h3: 0 ls: 0 h4: 0 h5: 1 h6: 0 stp: 0]
      [Speed_Selection M= [input: 'i9]])

    (is [h1: 1 h2: 0 h3: 0 ls: 0 h4: 0 h5: 0 h6: 1 stp: 0]
      [Speed_Selection <= [input: 'i10]] )

    (is [h1: _ h2: _ h3: _ ls: _ h4: _ h5: _ h6: _ stp: 1]
      [Speed_Selection <= [input: 'i11]])

    (otherwise
      [Speed_Selection <= [input: 'i12]]) ))]
```

```
[object Speed_Selection
  (state: [current_slab_loc := 'no_slab])

  (=> [input: Status]
    (case (list current_slab_loc Status)

      (is ['no_slab 'i1]
        [Speed_Control <= [speed: idle:]] )

      (is ['no_slab 'i2]
        [current_slab_loc := 'coming]
        [Speed_Control <= [speed: low:]] )

      (is ['coming _I]
        (case (member _I '(i3 i4 i5))
          (is t
            [Speed_Control <= [speed: low:]])))

      (is ['coming 'i6]
        [current_slab_loc := 'rolling]
        [Speed_Control <= [speed: high:]] )

      (is ['rolling 'i6]
        [Speed_Control <= [speed: high:]] )

      (is ['rolling 'i7]
        [current_slab_loc := 'leaving]
        [Speed_Control <= [speed: low:]] )

      (is ['leaving _I]
        (case (member _I '(i7 i8 i9 i10))
          (is t
            [Speed_Control <= [speed: low:]])))

      (is ['leaving 'i1]
        [current_slab_loc := 'no_slab]
        [Speed_Control <= [speed: idle:]] )

      (otherwise
        [Speed_Control <= [speed: stop:]]) )) ]


[object Speed_Control
  (=> [speed: SP]
    (case SP
      (is idle:     (set_roller_speed 'idle))

      (is low:      (set_roller_speed 'low))

      (is high:     (set_roller_speed 'high))

      (is stop:     (set_roller_speed 'stop)) ))]
```

EXPERIENCE OF INTRODUCING THE VIENNA DEVELOPMENT METHOD

INTO AN INDUSTRIAL ORGANISATION

M.I. Jackson, B.T. Denvir
STC Standard Telecommunication Laboratories Limited
London Road
Harlow, Essex,
CM17 9NA, England.

R.C. Shaw
STC IDEC
Six Hills Road,
Stevenage, Herts,
SG1 1YB, England.

1. INTRODUCTION

Formal specification techniques are frequently advocated as a basis
for improved software development methods leading to greater product
quality and reduced life cycle costs. Although a great deal of
research has been done into formal specification languages and
techniques, relatively little experience has been gained of the
impact of such approaches in industrial environments.

In order to introduce such approaches effectively, a number of
difficulties have to be overcome, such as the education and training
of industrial personnel, the development of appropriate standards,
the phased introduction of formal specification techniques alongside
established methods and practices etc.

The paper addresses some pragmatic approaches to problems such as
those described above. It is based on experience gained within STC
of the introduction of the Vienna Development Method (VDM) over the
last two years.

2. BACKGROUND TO VDM WITHIN STC

The Systems and Software Technology Division of STC Standard
Telecommunication Laboratories Ltd., has been conducting research
into formal (i.e. mathematically-based) approaches to system
development since 1979. Particular emphasis has been placed on
improved specification techniques, since weaknesses in this area are
known to cause serious design errors often discovered late in the
development process with commensurately increased costs of removal.

In 1982, a major new project established in the office systems area
requested advice on formal specification methods from STL. Of the
methods under consideration at that time, one in particular, the
Vienna Development Method (VDM), was recommended for consideration.

An attractive feature of VDM is that it provides a framework for
development; formal notations are used for defining system behaviour
at various levels of refinement during the development process and
the necessary obligations to be satisfied for verifying that a
refined description satisfies a more abstract description are clearly
defined. However, a spectrum of verification techniques may be
applied by the user to satisfy these obligations, ranging from
totally formal proof techniques (used where high reliability is
required) to informal justification of correctness (more practicable
on a day-to-day basis). This flexibility to apply the disciplines of
the method with varying degrees of formality within a formal
framework identifies VDM as a "rigorous" (as opposed to fully formal)
method and accounts to a great extent for its success in practical
situations.

VDM originated in the IBM Vienna Research Laboratories and is most
closely associated with the names of D. Bjorner and C.B. Jones. Our
reasons for recommending it were largely pragmatic, for example:

(i)   Considerable user experience of the method already existed
        within organisations such as IBM and the Danish Datamatik
        Centre. A number of case studies have been published, for
        example, in the recent book by Bjorner and Jones (BJO82).
        The strengths and weaknesses of the method are
        well-understood. (The reader is referred to the critical
        appraisal by Prehn et. al. [PRE83] for more information.)

(ii)   Training and consultancy in the method were available. Prof. C.B. Jones, now of Manchester University, was willing to present an established 2-week training course for the project team and to provide continual support to STC through consultancy.

(iii)   A well-written and accessible text book produced by Professor Jones, was available to support the course material [JON80].

VDM was thus seen to be among the most mature methods of system development and, therefore, suitable for industrial exploitation.

3. VDM EVALUATION

In the Summer of 1982 an evaluation exercise was conducted in order to assess the suitability of VDM as a specification vehicle for the proposed project. This exercise was organised as follows:

- A subsystem of the project was chosen by management as the case study to be used.

- A small group of analysts, having no previous familiarity with formal methods, were selected and introduced to VDM.

- Two STL staff members already familiar with VDM, were asked to support the analysts as consultants (alongside Professor Jones). Consultancy activity was intensive at the beginning of the exercise, but was conducted at a rate of a one-day review meeting every two weeks thereafter.

- An observer, independent of the analysts and consultants, was appointed to identify assessment criteria before commencement of the evaluation, to observe the conduct of the exercise and its outputs, to write the final evaluation report and to produce recommendations to management.

- The Chief System Designer was involved from time to time to answer questions regarding the requirements and to play the role of "customer".

The Evaluation exercise took as its input an English language
statement of requirements. Its outputs were the VDM specification
corresponding to the statement of requirements, the Evaluation Report
and future plans and recommendations for VDM. The conclusions drawn
can be summarised as follows:

(i)   Overall VDM was found to be very effective. The
           identification of abstract data structures in the VDM
           specification was found to be a powerful concept, amenable
           to "brain-storming" activity. The production of the formal
           specification helped in identifying the best choice of
           operations and functions available to users of the system.
           A number of versions of the specification were produced and
           each was validated by discussion with the "customer"; this
           systematic, iterative approach continued until a
           satisfactory version, acceptable to the "customer", was
           produced.

(ii)   VDM provided a number of useful thinking 'tools' the effects
           of which were evaluated as follows:

           -    The designer was forced and able to consider many more
                aspects of the requirements than with previous
                (non-formal) analysis techniques.

           -    VDM enhanced the analytical potential of the analysts
                by allowing them to reason about the abstract models
                developed in the specification process.

           -    VDM allowed the analysts to distinguish more easily
                between WHAT the system should do and HOW it should
                work.

(iii)   VDM is capable of producing a precise, consistent and
           unambiguous specification. In the evaluation exercise it
           revealed many (unrealised) anomalies and inadequacies in the
           informal statement of requirements. Although no formal
           validation of the specification was carried out, the
           analysts were able to reason informally about the
           specification and there was a higher degree of confidence in
           the specification than normal.

(iv)   The initial statement of requirements was found to be too
         brief, incomplete and ambiguous in places, to have an
         inadequate description of the data objects and the user
         operations of the system, and to include unnecessary
         implementation detail in places. (In spite of these faults
         it was considered, however, to be a fairly typical
         "marketing" style specification.) After producing the VDM
         specification, the analysts were able to derive
         systematically from it an English language version which was
         superior in all the above respects to the original and which
         could form a very suitable basis for marketing/customer
         documentation.

(v)   One of the benefits of using VDM was that essential
         decisions had to be made during the specification phase
         (where they could be discussed with the customer), whereas
         with traditional methods these were often not made until
         detailed design or even implementation.

(vi)   There were a number of shortcomings in the basic method
         which needed to be remedied before it could be used on the
         project. These included:

    -    A well-defined concrete syntax which could be input and
         output by the terminals and printers used on the
         project, so that specifications could be held within
         the project database and subject to normal disciplines
         of version control etc.

    -    Better structuring facilities which would allow the
         factoring of large specifications into modules with
         well-defined interfaces and tight control of the scope
         of names. This is necessary to support the development
         of large specifications by different analysts, possibly
         in different teams.

    -    More convenient facilities for defining and handling
         errors in a system specification, i.e. to factor the
         description of error behaviour from that of normal
         behaviour.

- The lack of an extended linguistic framework in which
the VDM abstract specifications could be represented
alongside more conventional pseudo-code designs
developed subsequently to match the specfication.

As a result of the evaluation exercise, project management recognised
the positive benefits of using VDM and decided to incorporate it as a
project method. Consequently a training programme, a language
development and support tools activity and a maintenance and
coordination activity were initiated.

4. TRAINING PROGRAMME

The first two week VDM course, presented by Professor Jones, was held
in the Autumn of 1982 and was attended by 10 students, seven of whom
were from the project and three of whom were prospective lecturers.
The seven project members were all senior staff, being project
managers (1), technical consultants (3) and team leaders (3).
Subsequently, further training courses were given for the benefit of
other project staff. These were given by the STC staff trained as
lecturers.

As a result of growing interest in VDM within the Company, a variety
of courses have been developed. These comprise:

(i)   A Perspective on VDM. This is a three day non-residential
course aimed at project managers, team leaders, technical
consultants and support staff involved in activities such as
quality assurance, technical documentation or marketing and
who require a sound understanding of VDM. Its objectives
are to provide a broad appreciation of formal methods, the
ability to read and review VDM specifications, and the
ability to control the introduction and use of VDM into a
project.

(ii)   VDM Foundation course. This is a 10-day residential course
for technical staff wishing to produce system specifications
written in VDM and for those who need design systems to
satisfy VDM specifications. Students completing the course

should be able to read and write VDM specifications,
demonstrate that a specification meets a requirement and
demonstrate that a design meets a specification.

At the time of writing, seven Foundation courses and eight
Perspective courses have been run. Eighty people, from STC and other
organisations, have attended the former and about sixty-five more
have attended the latter. The course programme, although developed
for internal purposes, has recently been made publicly available
through STC IDEC. This initiative has been supported by Professor
C.B. Jones and by Mr. D. Talbot, the Director of Software Engineering
for the Alvey Programme, since it is seen as highly compatible with
the Alvey Strategy in software engineering.

A particular feature of the course is the Material in the Foundation
course is based upon the book by C.B. Jones, "Software Development -
A Rigorous Approach" [JON80]. The course concentrates on developing
familiarity with the notation and confidence in its use. This is
achieved through a series of lectures, exercise sessions, student
presentationa and discussions in which attendees take a substantial
specification problem in a workshop in the second week in small teams.

Despite many initial reservations the majority of students have left
the course with the conviction that VDM provides a powerful technique
for introducing formal methods into the specification phase of the
software life cycle. What impact this will have on their work within
projects has yet to be analysed.

On the early courses no specific entry requirements were established
and this showed that students with a weak mathematical background do
experience difficulty with some of the course material. Of the
students who attended the first Foundation courses about 10% have
encountered varying difficulties in handling the notation. This has
been sufficient to impair their ability to use the notation within a
wider context of ideas.

To overcome this problem a one day course covering the elements of
Discrete Mathematics was set up and this is presented about one week
prior to the delivery of each Foundation course. A self test
procedure has now been developed which attempts to assess an
individual's familiarity with elementary Discrete Mathematics.

This test will allow individuals to decide, for themselves, whether
they can attend the VDM Foundation course directly or should avail
themselves of either the one day introductory course in Discrete
Mathematics or a more extensive treatment of the subject.

The later courses showed an improved "success rate" in this regard,
approaching 100%. In order to assist those people who have attended
the Foundation Course in their initial VDM applications, consultancy
services are available and their use is encouraged.

5.   LANGUAGE DEVELOPMENT AND SUPPORT TOOLS

Language Development activities have been concentrated in two main
timescales, short-term and medium term.

In the short-term, it was recognised that there was an immediate need
for facilities to allow the specification process to be carried out
'in-the-large' and for designs to be documented alongside the
specifications that they implement. STC IDEC consequently undertook
the development of an extended design language with the following
features:

(i)   It is possible to represent (almost) all of the VDM
         specification language taught in the programme of courses.

(ii)   A "module" facility is provided which allows large
         specifications to be developed in self-contained units with
         tight control over the scopes of names and well-defined
         interfaces.

(iii)   A programming language-like pseudo-code is provided for
         expressing designs within the same modules as their
         specifications.

This approach taken has been heavily influenced by work in IBM's
Boblingen Laboratory on the SLAN-4 languge [BEI83] and is based on
the assumption that, in the short-term, VDM will be used mainly as a
specification aid leading into more established and less formal
approaches to design. (This assumption is due mainly to two factors
- firstly, that improved specification is the most significant and

practicable benefit that formal methods can bring at present, secondly, that to introduce more rigorous design techniques requires more powerful automated tools than are currently available outside research establishments).

In the medium term, it was recognised that in order to extend the VDM specification language in a coherent and uniform way, and in order to build more powerful behaviourally-oriented support tools, it would be necessary to improve the standard of definition of the existing VDM specification language. Consequently, a joint activity was started by STL and the University of Manchester to define for STC a VDM "Reference Language" to be used as the standard within STC. To date, documents describing the concrete syntax, abstract syntax, type model and context conditions of the Reference Language have been issued and further work in the area of formal semantics is underway.

In the area of support tools, STC IDEC has produced a UNIX-based tool to perform syntax checking and (partial) type checking for the pseudo-code based language described above. In the medium term, it is intended to develop more extensive toolsets for VDM based around the VDM Reference Language, and a UK Alvey-funded project has just commenced for this purpose, in which STC, ICL, and Manchester University are taking part.

6. MAINTENANCE AND CO-ORDINATION ACTIVITIES

When it became apparent that there was wide interest in VDM across a number of STC units, a VDM Co-ordination and Maintenance Committee was established to support the controlled introduction of the method into STC. The membership is drawn from all actively involved units (i.e. those who are applying VDM or who have sent individuals on VDM courses). The terms of reference of the committee include:

- To develop and publish company standards for VDM and to implement change control procedures for such standards.

- To act as a qualification body for VDM support tools.

- To advise on courses, curricula and other matters related to the education and training required to introduce VDM into development centres.

- To disseminate information regarding the development and use of VDM by publishing occasional reports and by organising workshops and conferences.

- To co-ordinate interaction between STC units and external consultants with respect to VDM.

- To provide a general query/response service to established and prospective users.

The Committee has been active for about 18 months to date and has achieved positive results in all the above areas. In particular, standards have been established for the concrete and abstract syntax of the language as used within the company, and for a type model and context conditions.

7. ASSESSMENT OF VDM EXPERIENCE

In addition to training a substantial number of software engineers in the method and its language, we have now had experience of applying it to a number of typical problems in the information technology industry. These include aspects of advanced office communication systems, such as electronic mail, a data-base of personal calendars, and user access control. Case studies have also been carried out in a more conventional telecommunications problem and a real-time control system.

In general we have found the method particularly effective as an intellectual tool for analysing the problem and synthesising its specification. Deficiencies in the first statements and conception of the problem's requirements appear to be highlighted earlier in the software development process, enabling remedial action (or indeed reconsideration of the project's viability) to take place after a smaller developmental investment. Our experience is that the overwhelming majority of practising software engineers in a high technology industry can be taught the method in a practicable time-frame : here we believe the workshop component of the course to be particularly valuable.

On first adopting the VDM, different levels can be identified and progressively used by an organisation new to the method:

(i)   Formulating data types, the system state, and operations with their signatures.

(ii)   Formulating pre- and post-conditions of operations, and data-type system state invariants.

(iii)   Identifying the obligations of proof of correctness of the specfication and its requirements.

(iv)   Carrying out proofs by rigorous argument in specification reviews.

(v)   Carrying out formal proofs.

The first levels serve as a good communication medium between the roles in the development process, and the later levels would increase further the confidence we may feel in the quality of the final poduct. In STC we have carried levels (i) to (iii) and to some extent (iv) also. We have not attempted level (v) to date.

Weaknesses of the method evinced by our experience so far are:

(a)   For large systems and where a team of people is working on the specification, there is a need for dividing the specification up in a modular and well-structured way. The language does not provide a clear way of doing this.

(b)   The language does not support the communication aspects of specifying concurrent systems or the dynamic aspects of sequential systems whose functionality changes. However, it can solve the majority of specification problems with such systems, and the concurrency aspects have to be expressed in some separate way.

We have also felt the need for some support tools, and are taking active steps regarding this.

8. CONCLUSIONS

VDM, as a method for formal specification, can be successfully introduced into an industrial organisation, if appropriate levels of investment are made in the areas of:

(i)   Evaluation, by case studies, of the suitability of the method for the application area of interest. The evaluation criteria should be properly defined, monitored and assessed.

(ii)   Training for staff, of a professional quality.

(iii)   Consultancy, as appropriate to particular needs, by skilled and experienced personnel.

(iv)   General support, for example, by developing and implementing corporate standards.

(v)   Support tools in the longer term, such as a specification oriented database and a syntax-directed structure editor, which would add to the effectiveness of the method.

9. FURTHER WORK

We perceive that further work would be beneficial in the following areas:

(i)   Complete the semantics definition.

(ii)   Develop a means of formulating modular specifications in a semantically well defined way.

(iii)   Consider how to approach the specification of concurrent systems.

422

10. ACKNOWLEDGEMENTS

The results described above reflect the work of a number of people in
STC, including P.N. Hudson who developed the STC IDEC Design
Language, and B.Q. Monahan of STL who has done substantial work on
the definitions of the syntax and semantics of the VDM Reference
Language. We also greatly appreciate the contribution of Professor
C.B. Jones who has supported us thoughout with his advice and
encouragement.

11. REFERENCES

BEI83   Beichter F, Herzog O, Petzsch H.
         SLAN-4: A Language for the Specification and Design of Large
         Software Systems.
         IBM Journal of Research and Development, Vol. 27, No. 6,
         November 1983.

BJO82   Bjorner D, Jones C.B.
         Formal Specification and Software Development.
         Prentice Hall, 1982.

JON80   Jones C.B.
         Software Development: A Rigorous Approach
         Prentice Hall, 1980.

PRE83   Prehn S, Hanson I.O, Palm S.U, Gobel P.
         Formal Methods Appraisal: Final Report
         ESPRIT Preparatory Study Report, June 1983.

EDP SYSTEM DEVELOPMENT METHODOLOGY:

AUDITABILITY AND CONTROL

Avi Rushinek and Sara Rushinek
University of Miami
School of Business Administration
Coral Gables, FL 33124/USA

ABSTRACT

This study is both a replication and an extension of prior work on system development. By expanding on the previous information with more updated information, a better description of the system development process is obtained.

First, the audit of system development is explained. Then two normative models of the process are described, pointing out the advantages of each. Finally, the major phases of the system development process are presented and the authors' personal views and experiences are expressed.

INTRODUCTION

System development is a relatively new method of dealing with the problems of an organization. As such, the development of good systems is still in the experimental stage. There are few formal rules to follow, and basic insight and experience still have an essential role in determining the quality of the resulting design. Therefore, the authors have found that what distinguishes a good system from a bad system is the success of the end result.

Each organization is unique, and a system must be specifically tailored to meet the organization's specific needs and desires. In this concept of an organization, the organization is regarded as a communication system closed on the users' (of the output) needs and wants. As an example, the first step is to assess the users'needs. Then products, processes, and distribution methods are planned so as to meet these desires effectively and efficiently. The planning information flows to operations when the plans are carried out and the product (goods or service) is produced. The product is then promoted so that users will be aware of its existence and how it will serve their needs. Finally, the product is distributed to them, at which time the needs and desires of users are filled. This closed-loop communication system should operate continuously if the organization is to be efficient. The example illustrates how the design of a system must constantly rely on feedback. As users' needs change, the changes should be discovered as quickly as possible by management, plans revised, and operations changed accordingly to best serve the revised needs (Litecky, 1981).

Auditing The System Development Process

An auditor may evaluate the system development process in two ways. One, as a member of the system development team (Hannye, 1977). Another, in an ex post review capacity when the system developement process is evaluated. The two types of audit have different objectives and use different methods to gather evidence (Parker, 1977)

In the participation audit, the objectives are to ensure for a specific application system that controls are built into the system to safeguard assets, ensure data integrity, and achieve system effectiveness and efficiency. The primary method for the auditor to collect evidence is by observing the activities of the other members of the development team. This evidence is then evaluated against the auditor's model of the system development process.

In the review audit, the objectives are to reduce the extent of substantive testing needed for application systems and to make recommendations for improving the system development process. To collect evidence, the auditor uses interviews, observations, and a review of standards to obtain general and then detailed information on the system development process. He then evaluates this information to form a basis for hypothesizing strengths and weaknesses that may exist and to design compliance tests. Finally, the auditor selects a sample of application systems to determine whether the hypothesized strengths and weaknesses do actually exist (Davis, 1981).

Normative Models of the System Development Process

According to Caputo (1981), when auditing the system development process, the auditor must seek answers to two basic questions. First, do system design personnel perform all the activities necessary for the design and implementation of high-quality information systems? Second, are these activities performed well? In order to be able to answer these questions, the auditor needs a model to use as a basis for thinking about, evaluating, and approaching the audit of the system development life cycle approach and the socio-technical approach. The quality of the systems the auditors design depends on the appropriateness of the model used (Cerullo, 1981).

System Development Life Cycle Approach (SDLC)

The life cycle approach is the traditional method of systems development. The SDLC is a technique used to divide the system development process into a small number of distinct tasks with formal management control points placed between and during each phase. The objectives in using an SDLC technique are two-fold: to provide a proper and responsive communications channel among users, EDP auditors, hardware planning personnel, top management, and the data processing personnel responsible for developing the application systems.

Another method that is being used is to set up control points within each of the phases (Cerullo, 1981). During the development of the system, all requirements specified at each control point must be satisfied before that phase or the next phase can be continued. Basically two types of control points are used in this SDLC: those affecting the quality of systems being developed from a computer processing point of view and those used to interface users and others outside the data processing department.

The life cycle approach arose out of the belief that a successful system development process relied on appropriate managerial and technical applications. A history of technical and managerial problems, such as cost overruns, inadequate economic evaluations, inadequate system design, management abdication, poor communication and inadequate direction brought about the development of the new approach. In those cases, the life cycle approach is the perfect solution to help overcome those problems. Each separate phase of the life cycle must be defined and glaos set accordingly. The authors believe that careful planning and feedback to assure that the plans are followed is of utmost importance.

Sociotechnical Design Approach

Because the life cycle approach dealt exclusively with the technical aspects of a system, a new approach was developed to deal more effectively with behavioral problems that exist (Holley and Cash, 1981). Systems naturally degrade through lack of use, apathy, and sabotage. This approach arose as an answer to questions as to why behavioral problems occur and how they could be corrected.

The sociotechnical system is a process which optimizes the two systems: technological and social. The technological system's objective is task accomplishment while the social system's objective is to achieve a high quality of working life for the users of the system. Problems arise from neglecting the social system when implementing the new technical system.

The sociotechnical approach does not completely negate the importance of project management techniques and the traditional life cycle approach; rather, it makes use of those and adds to it the social approach. Thus, the sociotechnical approach is a more encompassing one, that believes that the life cycle approach is deficient when it comes to dealing with behavior problems. (Scott, 1979).

Evaluating the Major Phases in the System Development Process

A somewhat new approach has been advocated for the system development process. This approach, known as the normative model, includes the activities of the life cycle and sociotechnical approaches (Holley and Cash, 1981). There are ten major phases in the normative model of the system development process. They include 1) problem recognition, 2) management of the change process, 3) entry and feasibility assessment, 4) diagnosis and information analysis, 5) system design, 6) program development, 7) procedure and forms development, 8) acceptance testing, 9) conversion and 10) operation, maintenance and audit. If there are problems with the application of any of these activities, the auditor is responsible for determining the effects of the quality of the application system produced (Dowell and Hall, 1981).

Management of the Change Process

Management of the change process is necessary throughout the entire system development process. This requires formal project controls and change facilitating aspects. The formal project controls may include budgeting, exception reporting and checkpoints.

Change facilitating aspects include unfreezing the organization, implementing the change, and then refreezing the organization.

Management proceeds to unfreeze the organization by preparing the organization for the change. They must inform the system users of the need for the change, the methodology of the change and what is expected from each of the users in terms of ability to adapt to the change. Feedback should be provided in this instance to the organization in terms of the user's attitudes and behaviors. Similarly, data processing managers must establish quality control procedures within their organization to ensure that they do it right the first time (Davis, 1981). Among several of the important aspects of getting the change implemented correctly are education, participatory decision making, and command.

Once the organization has been prepared for the change, the actual changeover takes place. At this time, the users and the organization are ready and should know what to expect in terms of the adjustment process. Once the change is complete, and the new system is functioning, the organization undergoes the refreezing process. Positive feedback on the new system ensures adaptation of the system by the system users. Refreezing prevents the system's users from resuming their old patterns of system usage. If the users are discovered to have their own private information systems, then the refreezing activities may not have proceeded properly and taken full effect.

Entry and Feasibility Assessment

The entire change process is begun when the system designer establishes entry into the organization. The entry phase is used to unfreeze the organization and to develop cooperation among the users. Group meetings would be an effective method to ensure proper entry. The entry phase is important because it is during this time that the systems designers help show the users the faults of the old system and the needs for the new one. Unless the designer is able to truly convince the users of the need for change, there cannot be a successful changeover. If this is the case, then the hopes and plans for a new system may have to be forgotten.

Once the system users are convinced of the need for the change, a feasibility evaluation of the new system is needed to ensure it will be productive and will evaluate the programmers' testing of the change, evaluate the validity of the change, examine operating instructions, and generally review all program changes before final implementation in the production system (Stanford Research Institute, 1977). The four bases for evaluating feasibility under the normative model approach include technical feasibility, operational feasibility, economic feasibility and behavioral feasibility. There is a need to ensure that technology available is sufficient to support the proposed project. Also, with regard to the technology available, there must be the ability to acquire more and develop it sufficiently.

It is necessary to constantly review the feasibility of the system. New information is always gathered and, therefore, it must be reviewed. However, if the project is relatively small, feasibility analysis may be focused on at the conclusion of the development process. Feasibility may be difficult to determine in the beginning of the development process, since little is known about the system and the facts are still vague and difficult to determine. The objective of this entry and feasibility analysis to ensure the imposition of the new system upon the users was only advocated when the benefits outweigh the costs.

Diagnosis and Information Analysis

A proper diagnosis and information analysis is necessary to understand the social and technical systems currently existing and to develop the strategies for the new system. In order to have a basis for managing the change process, diagnosis is necessary. Strategies establish objectives and goals that help to point the design process in the right direction. Strategies may be developed through the information analysis.

In order to have an understanding of the existing conditions, the present organization is studied. The EDP auditor, user, and the project leader review the project organization, the arrangements with the user for communication, and the plans and work program for the design. This central point helps the project leader to establish a good working relationship with the user to ensure that the system reflects user requirements (Stanford Research Institute, 1977).

In addition, the designer must study the coordinating mechanism of the organization, and the willingness of the organization to change. Some of the major coordinating mechanisms advocated include: direction, organizational job design, selection, training, appraisal and developments, communication and control, and a reward system.

Also, strategic requirements need to be formulated, as they indicate the objectives and goals expected to be accomplished by the organization. Without the objectives and goals, there may be system failures that could have otherwise been avoided. Strategic requirements simply involve task requirements. They may be general or broad objectives or more specific. Once the strategic issues are evident, information systems can be designed to receive full benefits. There are many design types and by having knowledge of strategies, these designs may be evaluated effectively. Once information has been obtained on the previous system, the currently existing system can be evaluated. Although there was already a determination of feasibility, a more detailed information package enables a more suitable institution of the proposed system. Before we can even start to consider systems development, we should understand the entire data processing spectrum and its short and long-range plans, and document an understanding of what presently takes place and what will take place (Davis, 1981).

System Design

System design has meant the design of the information processing system; however, this concept of system design is inadequate. The concept which this paper proposes is a full concept, one that involves both the design of the social and technical aspects of the system and the set of coordinating mechanisms. The methodology of the sociotechnical system design is called action research. The designer establishes a collaborative mode whereby users jointly share the responsibility for design functions instead of the system designer imposing a system design on users.

In the design of the system, the designer again needs some basis for thinking about the organization and the change process to be implemented (Scott and Booker, 1979). It is useful for the designer to think about the organization in terms of four major sets of interacting variables; task, technology, structure, and human-social. For example, the technical system design establishes relationships within and between the first three sets of variables; the social system design establishes relationships within the human-social set; the sociotechnical system design establishes relationships within and between the four sets of variables.

There are other relationships that are also important when considering the design process, such as environmental uncertainty, organizational structure, and the information processing capabilities of the organization.

Coordinating mechanisms existing between the social and technical systems focus on three things: job design, organization design, and control. Job design consists of the traditional model in which individuals are more interested in what they earn rather than what they do. The human relations model focuses more on the context in which the job is performed and the human resources model is self-directing and controlling. In organization design the designer sometimes faces the choice of selecting an appropriate structure for the users.

Information processing system design involves the design of the information flow, design of the data base, design of the decision support system, preparation of program specifications and preparation of hardware/software specifications. Developments in both the hardware and software systems require a continual updating and strengthening of the technical expertise of the auditor who works with his clients' EDP systems (Jancura and Nance, 1981). As such, the EDP auditor should have a wide spectrum of technical knowledge and competence.

If the system requires hardware and software not currently available in the installations, hardware and software specifications must be prepared for the additional resources required.

Program Development

When the system design phase has been completed, the next phase in the system development process is program development. This involves a) designing; which entails the tasks of organizing the project, documenting the data base files, designing source documents in detail, and preparing program run writeups, b) flowcharting, c) coding, d) compiling, e) testing, and f) documenting. Generally the audit staff itself is involved in program development (Tashji, 1981).

Acceptance Testing

The purpose of acceptance testing is to identify as many errors and deficiencies in the system as possible prior to its implementation.

Normal processing attempts should also be made to try to crash the system to determine its tolerance to errors and ability to respond to exceptional circumstances.

According to the authors, it is very important from an auditor's viewpoint that the testing and documentation of test results be carefully planned and executed. One of the outcomes of the testing phase should be a test-bed of data for individual programs, and the overall system that should be properly recorded and maintained.

The conversion phase consists of organizing the project, conversion, monitoring system performance, and the final acceptance of system (Stanford Research Center, 1980). The conversion process may occur in one of three ways. First, the old system may stop totally and the new system takes over immediately. Second, both systems may run in parallel for a period, performing different functions, and with both outputs being utilized. Third, both the systems may run in parallel, performing the same functions, with the old system being used. Changeover to a new system will entail personnel training, installing new hardware and software, converting the files and programs, and scheduling operations and test running. The auditor is especially concerned with maintaining data integrity during the conversion process. There might be some tradeoffs between the integrity of data taken up on the system and the need to get the system running. When data is converted from one storage medium or one data structure to another, control totals must be developed to help identify any data corruption that occurs during the changeover process or any errors that exist in the data already.

During the operation of a system three types of changes may be needed: processing errors may be discovered that require correction; changes in the system environment may necessitate system modification; changes may be made to improve processing efficiency. The system should be reviewed on a regular basis by a team consisting of management, users, and auditors (Litecky, 1981).

Postaudit ensures that both the users as well as the organization have adapted to the changes.

The controls and techniques governing the system development process are important because the adequacy and effectiveness of controls included in computer application systems are heavily affected by the methods and procedures used during the system development process. To ensure the accuracy, completeness, and validity of data being processed by complex computer applications systems, internal auditors must consider an entire system of controls that encompass data preparation, data entry, data communications, data processing and data distribution (Davis, 1980).

Personal Views and Experiences

The authors' personal views and experiences confirm the theoretical notions as they are described in this paper. However, in real life, they appear to be implemented simultaneously, without such a clear distinction among these approaches. For example, the normative model coexists frequently with the SDLC approach. We as auditors are deeply committed to the use of specific norms as prescribed by professional bodies and standards such as the American Institute of Certified Public Accountants (AICPA) and their Generally Accepted Auditing Principles (normative approach). Likewise, we find ourselves breaking a system's development into the smallest possible segments, simply because it is otherwise uncontrollable.

Although these approaches seem to be rather comprehensive, they underestimate the importance of the review of the software requirements. It is the opinion of the authors that these are the most notorious source of frustration, anxiety and numerous problems. The review should thus be included as a control checkpoint prior to hardware requirements. Many times it is the software that determines the hardware requirements. For example, certain software packages will run only on certain operating systems or on a limited number of systems. For instance, Lotus Development Corporation markets a spreadsheet called "LOTUS 1-2-3", which is configured to run only on IBM Personal Computers and its clones. In the event that a user must use this software, this automatically narrows the hardware options.

As a final note, the authors suggest the software required should be thoroughly investigated prior to considering hardware requirements as a major control break point. (See Figure 2 for an illustration).

Summary, Conclusions and Implications

This paper reports on two aspects of the system development process: 1) the different models that exist and 2) the major phases that are an integral part of all models.

The information presented on the two different normative models - the system development life cycle approach and the sociotechnical design approach - pointed out the benefits and problems of each. Then the ten phases were explained as they pertain to the process of system development.

The implications of this information as it relates to the auditor are significant. The auditor must have an extensive knowledge of computer systems, as well as the ability to visualize the needs of the entity he is auditing. These are not only technical needs; social and behavioral needs are also very important.

The system development process is one that will always be upgraded and innovated on, based on the changing needs of the EDP auditor. Some of the others who have added to the models discussed include Dowell (1981), Hannye (1977), Holley (1981), Scott (1979), Barker (1977), and Tashji (1981). However, the articles that were written have gone beyond the scope of this text. Attention need be made to them as they further discuss the various other information available on accounting information systems development in EDP auditing.

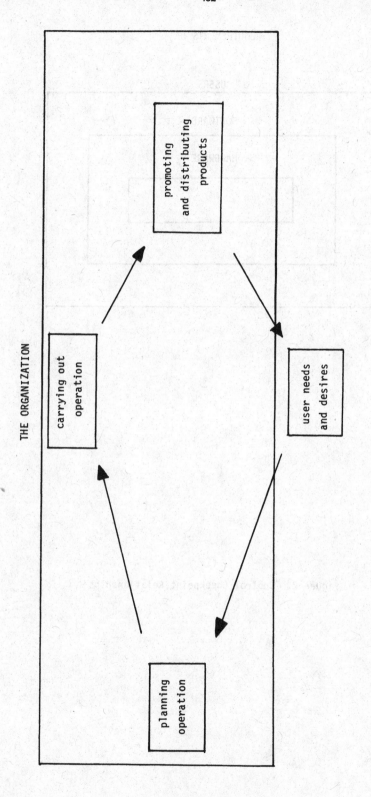

THE ORGANIZATION

promoting and distributing products

carrying out operation

user needs and desires

planning operation

Figure 1. Systems Development Process

REQUIREMENTS OF:

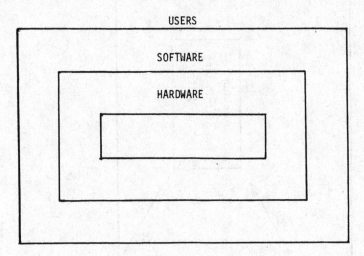

Figure 2. Control Checkpoint Relationships

References

Caputo, Charles A., "Managing the EDP Audit Function, Part 1". The Internal Auditor, (February, 1981), pp. 73-77.

Cerullo, Michael J., "Levels of Computer and Information Systems Knowledge Needed by Public Accountants". The National Public Accountant, (January, 1981), pp.19-23.

Davis, Keagle W., "The Information Systems Auditor of the 1980's". Management Accounting, (March, 1981), pp. 40-47.

Dowell, Dwayne C., and James Arthur Hall, "EDP Controls with Audit Cost Implications" Journal of Accounting, Auditing and Finance, (Fall, 1981), pp. 30-40.

Hannye, George L., "Auditors and EDP'ers Benefit From Association in the Systems Development Process". Internal Auditor, (December, 1977), pp. 67-70.

Holley, Charles L., and Daniel M. Cash, "Evaluations of EDP Systems Development". Journal of Systems Management, (June, 1981), pp. 16-21.

Jancura, Elise G., and James J. Nance, "Proficiency Levels for EDP Auditors". Journal of Accountancy, (February, 1981), pp. 39-41.

Litecky, Charles R., "Corporate Strategy and MIS Planning". Journal of Systems Management, (January, 1981), pp. 36-39.

Parker, Robert G., "The Auditor's Role in Systems Development". Canadian Chartered Accountant, (September, 1977), pp. 56-58.

Scott, Ronald L., and Jon A. Booker, "A Three-Phased Approach to the Systems Development Audit". Internal Auditor, (June, 1979), pp. 26-31.

Stanford Research Institute, "Application System Development Controls". Systems Auditability and Control-Control Practices, (September, 1977), pp. 99-109.

Stanford Research Institute, "System Development Life Cycle". Systems Auditability and Control-Audit Practices, (September, 1980), pp. 197-200.

Tashji, Gabriel G., "The EDP Auditor's Role in System Application Development". Internal Auditor, (December, 1981), pp. 45-53.

EXPERIENCES WITH OBJECT ORIENTED PROGRAMMING

Karl-Heinz Alws, Ingrid Glasner-Schapeler

Standard Elektrik Lorenz AG, ZT/FZSD

Postfach 40 07 49

D-7000 Stuttgart 40

Abstract

The object oriented programming paradigm has been applied to the development of syntax-directed structure editors. The principal features of our implementation are presented, which is derived from a grammar for structured control flow documents. Experiences we gained show that object oriented programming is a valuable programming paradigm, in particular with respect to software reusability and maintainability.

1.0 Introduction

Due to the ever increasing demand for software systems and to their increasing complexity, the process of software development has received a lot of attention.

Novel approaches to programming promise new ways to cope with the problems involved. One of these approaches currently under research is object oriented programming. It is claimed that it provides advances towards the following goals:

- o to improve reusability of code
- o to improve maintainability of software systems
- o to support rapid prototyping

In order to evaluate the object oriented programming technique, we decided to apply it to a particular task, namely the development of syntax-directed structure editors. We first developed a graphical structure editor for a variant of Nassi-Shneiderman diagrams. Then we tried to reuse as much code as possible for a pseudo code editor.

This paper is to communicate the experiences we gained. As the vehicle for our implementation, we used the programming language OOPC (Object Oriented Precompiler to C) [Cox, 1983] .

In the following we first give an overview of the object oriented programming paradigm. Then we briefly describe the behavior required from the structure editors, and provide some detail about their object oriented implementation. Finally, we discuss problems encountered, and derive conclusions related to the claims mentioned above.

2.0 Object Oriented Programming

The definition of "object" used in this paper is adopted from Smalltalk 80 [BYTE, 1981] resp. from OOPC [Cox, 1983]. An object consists of both data and the procedures necessary to handle that data. Objects know how to manipulate themselves. This is quite different from the conventional programming approach with its distinction between passive data and active programs.

An object corresponds to some real-world entity. E.g. considering a CAD system for automatic layout computation of printed board assemblies, any particular IC would be represented by an object. In a traditional approach to software development an overall software system would have to know how to draw the shapes of the various device types after having placed them. In the object oriented approach all knowledge about drawing is contained in the objects themselves, and the overall system only has to know that each object can be drawn, not how the drawing is performed.

Communication among objects is established by means of messages. Access to and modification of an object is possible only by sending it a message. All processing takes place inside objects and is triggered by message sending. Messages are represented by expressions composed from an identification of the receiver, a selector string, and optionally some arguments. The receiving object responds to a message by performing the appropriate actions via a routine determined by the message selector. The set of message selectors to which an object can react provides a clean and simple interface for the object. Nothing else has to be known to other objects in order to communicate with it.

Every object is an instance of some class. New objects, i.e. new instances of a class, are created by sending a message to the class itself. The class defines the methods, i.e. the routines available for manipulation of its instances, and thus determines the repertoire of messages that its instances understand. The class also defines names for "instance variables" which occur in all its instances and capture the status information specific to a certain object.

Classes are organized in an inheritance hierarchy. When a class is defined as subclass of an existing one, the new class automatically inherits the procedural and structural information associated with the superclass. Some of this may be not defined in the superclass itself, but inherited from a still more general class, i.e. information is actually inherited from a chain of superclasses. The inherited knowledge may be augmented and specialized by the subclass by definition of additional variables and/or routines. A method inherited from the superclass can also be overridden in its subclasses by locally defining a method with the same name.
An example for an inheritance tree is given in Figure 1.
The inheritance mechanism allows for class libraries from which applications can be built by defining specific subclasses.

Message sending as implemented in OOPC differs from a conventional subroutine call in that the binding of the message to the routine to be executed is dynamic, performed at runtime instead of by the compiler. Methods are identified by a method selector string. When an object receives a message, the message selector is matched against the set of method selectors associated with the class of the receiver; if necessary, search continues along the superclass chain, thus implementing inheritance of methods. Dynamic message binding has the advantage that the class of the message receiver does not have to be known in advance.

OOPC is based upon the Smalltalk object concept. It translates object oriented programs containing class definitions and message passing expressions into code of the C programming language. OOPC also supplies a library of classes implementing several basic kinds of data structure (e.g. linked lists). A very important feature provided by this library is a general object save/restore capability which is made possible by dynamic message binding. It allows any collection of objects to be written to a file and read in again in structured form, so that no application-specific parsing and unparsing routines are required.

3.0 User's View of the Structure Editors

The graphical structure editor (GSE) and pseudo code editor (PCE) support
software engineers during the detailed design phase of software development.
They allow for interactive construction of structured control flow documents.
The control flow is represented graphically by a variant of Nassi-Shneiderman
diagrams [Nassi and Shneiderman, 1973]. A diagram is composed of graphical
constructs (blocks), each of them representing an activity, which is described
by pieces of text inside the block.

There are two categories of blocks: simple blocks and composite blocks.
Simple blocks only contain text, whereas composite blocks contain other blocks
in analogy to the structured statements of a programming language, e.g.
conditional (if), selection (case), iteration (loop).

Diagrams are constructed according to two basic principles of structured
programming: sequencing of blocks, and nesting of blocks.

A sample diagram is given in Figure 2.

The graphical structure editor (GSE) is a specialized syntax-directed editor
possessing knowledge about the structure of Nassi-Shneiderman diagrams. A
syntax-directed editor knows about the syntactic structure of the objects which
it maintains and manipulates. It uses this knowledge to prevent modifications
that would introduce syntactic errors.

The pseudo code editor (PCE) is syntax-directed like the GSE, and provides the
same command interface. It is required to deal with documents written in a
pseudo code notation which is logically equivalent to the graphical notation of
Nassi-Shneiderman diagrams. I.e. the pseudo code constructs correspond to the
building blocks of diagrams and are combined according to the abovementioned
rules (sequencing, nesting).

Figure 3 shows the pseudo code document corresponding to the Nassi-Shneiderman
diagram in Figure 2.

A common disk file format for documents capturing only the structural
information of a design document is used by both editors. Since each of the
editors can generate the appropriate display representation, a document can be
created as diagram by the GSE, saved, and, in a subsequent session, manipulated
as pseudo code by the PCE (and vice versa).

4.0 Implementation of the Structure Editors

The operation of both GSE and PCE is directed by the syntactical structure of the diagram or pseudo code, respectively, to be edited. This is achieved by internally representing documents in both editors as abstract syntax trees. These syntax trees are constructed according to the following context-free grammar which is common to GSE and PCE:

```
diagram      ::= {block}
block        ::= primitblock | emptyblock |
                 caseblock | ifblock |
                 loopblock
primitblock  ::= Text
loopblock    ::= Text {block}
ifblock      ::= Text alternative alternative
caseblock    ::= Text {alternative}
emptyblock   ::= "empty"
alternative  ::= Text {block}
```

The notation {x} denotes an arbitrary number of occurences of x (at least one). The symbol Text is a terminal symbol of the grammar and represents some character string.

Each node of a syntax tree, i.e. each structural unit of a design document, is implemented as a separate object. The objects modelling a design document are instances of classes roughly corresponding to the syntactic categories of the underlying grammar.

E.g., each if-block occuring in a diagram is an instance of class IF_BLOCK. An if-block object knows where it is placed in the syntax tree, and which diagram components (i.e., which other objects) are nested within the if-block. It also contains knowledge about its display representation.
A certain set of message selectors is understood by all if-block objects, e.g. "delete" and "draw".
The corresponding instance variables and methods are in part defined locally within class IF_BLOCK, in part inherited from its superclass chain.

The class hierarchy in the object oriented implementation of GSE was quite naturally derived from the syntax rules for Nassi-Shneiderman diagrams.

The methods and the instance variables realizing the manipulations of the internal representation, like deleting nodes from or inserting nodes into a tree, are the same for all different kinds of syntactical units that may occur as nodes in a syntax tree. Therefore, such methods are contained in the upper, more general classes of the inheritance hierarchy. These classes also define the instance variables realizing the links between tree nodes.

On the other hand, methods and instance variables related to the external (graphical) representation as displayed to the user of the GSE are specific to the various kinds of blocks. Such methods are responsible for computing the layout information (height, width, position on the screen) associated with a block, and for generating its shape (as an ensemble of graphical symbols). Being different for different kinds of syntactical units, these methods and instance variables are defined in the lower classes of the inheritance tree.

Figure 4 shows the resulting class organization. (Alternatives occur as components of if-blocks and case-blocks.)

The grammar underlying the internal representation of documents is the same for GSE and PCE. Therefore, the class hierarchy looks the same for both editors, i.e. there is no difference concerning the class names and the subclass relationships between classes.

Furthermore, the editors have the same command interface and thus perform the same operations on the internal document representation (syntax tree). Because the upper classes are concerned with this internal representation only, they are identical for GSE and PCE. The corresponding code, developed during implementation of the GSE, could thus be reused without any modifications in the PCE implementation.

The classes in the lower part of the class hierarchy, however, had to be developed anew, since they deal with the external representation of design documents which, for PCE, is in the form of pseudo code, as opposed to the diagrammatic representation used by the GSE.

Figure 4 may be misleading in that it suggests that only a small portion of the GSE code could be reused for the PCE. However, the small number of upper level classes contain the bulk of code. The methods to be added by the lower level classes are rather simple. The OOPC source code for each of the editors consists of about 5700 lines of code (not including comment lines). About 4300 lines of code are common to both GSE and PCE. Thus, only about 1400 lines of specialized code had to be written in order to implement the PCE, which means that 3/4 of the GSE could be reused.

When developing the new specialized classes of the PCE, we had to take care that they present the same message interface as the corresponding GSE classes, in order to guarantee compatibility with the reused general classes. Instances of the new classes must be able to react to all messages that may be sent to them from within some method defined in an upper level class, e.g. to a "draw" message issued by the "delete" method defined in class NODE.

Apart from the distinction between upper level and lower level classes dictated by the distinction between display representation and internal representation, introduction of additional subclass relationships was motivated by our desire to exploit the inheritance mechanism wherever possible. E.g., class EMPTY_BLOCK is defined as subclass of class PRIMIT_BLOCK. Thus, the fact that empty blocks are displayed in the same fashion as primitive blocks is simply reflected by not defining in class EMPTYBLOCK specific methods dealing with the display representation, but making use of appropriate methods inherited from class PRIMIT_BLOCK.

A commonly used programming technique is to define a quite general "default method" on a high level in the hierarchy, and to override this method in a descendant class by defining a specialized method with the same selector. A general method "textinsert", for example, is defined in class FIXNODE, which performs all necessary actions (linkage and layout update and redisplay) when a new text string is inserted into a block. The text insertion operation is not admissible for empty blocks; their text must always be the string "empty". The implementation of this restriction is by defining a special method "textinsert" for class EMPTY_BLOCK, which does nothing but issue an error message.

The strong correspondence between class hierarchy and grammar for structured control flow documents is crucial for the simple implementation of syntax checking, the most important feature of the syntax-directed structure editors. A possible document modification, e.g. replacing a construct by a different one, is syntactically admissible only if the new construct is an instance of the type of construct required at this position. E.g., a case-block in the body of a loop may be replaced by some other kind of block, but not by an alternative (since alternatives occur as components of if-blocks and case-blocks only).

Using object oriented programming, the implementation of the necessary syntax checks was straightforward. In OOPC, each object can reply to a message asking whether it is an instance of (some subclass of) a certain class. E.g., a primitive block knows that it is an instance of a subclass of BLOCK and therefore can be placed at any position in a document where blocks are admissable.

By choosing a hierarchy of classes that reflects the syntactical relationships as defined by the grammar, the inheritance mechanism can thus be exploited in order to guarantee, in an easy way, that design documents constructed with GSE or PCE are always syntactically correct.

5.0 Problems and Suggestions

In implementing the structure editors as collections of OOPC classes, we have encountered several problems. Some of these problems just indicate a lack of certain language features in OOPC, or of tools to support the object oriented design methodology, some of them, however, are of a more fundamental nature.

In OOPC, each class has exactly one superclass, i.e. the graph of the subclass relation for a collection of classes is always a tree. Sometimes, though, the ability to define more than one superclass for a new class, the possibility to arrange classes in a lattice, is desirable.

For example, one often needs linked lists composed of objects of a certain kind. The elements of such lists must exhibit both the behavior of list elements in general as well as the behavior of the special kind of entities from which the list is composed. It is not possible, though, to define in OOPC a class that can inherit properties from both a generic "list element" class and from another class unrelated to lists. A somewhat clumsy solution is to implement each (conceptual) list element by two objects connected via a pointer. The first object is an instance of a generic class which provides variables and methods characteristic of linked lists, the second object is an instance of the class that deals with the specific properties of the objects in the list. The disadvantages of this solution are additional storage and runtime overhead. Using OOPC, they could be avoided only by redefining data and procedures common to all kinds of singly linked lists within each of the corresponding specialized classes, which, however, means giving up the advantages of inheritance.
The availability of multiple superclasses is a language feature missing in OOPC, but provided by many object oriented programming languages, including later versions of Smalltalk.

For applications realized by some larger collections of classes, the subclass relationships between classes and the induced inheritance may become hard to keep track of. Specialized cross reference tools would be desirable to support both the design and implementation and the debugging of object oriented application software.

An "inheritance checker" should display the superclass chain for a given class. It should also list the instance variables and methods available to this class via inheritance, and indicate for each of these the superclass from which it is inherited. Such an inheritance checking tool would be particularly valuable if multiple superclasses are allowed, i.e. if there may exist several superclass chains for each class.

Conversely, given a method selector, as occuring in a message, one might want to get an overview of all classes that define a method with that name. Note that each path in the inheritance tree (or lattice, respectively) may contain more than one method definition corresponding to a given selector. An example for such a situation, occuring in the structure editor implementation, is shown in the following figure:

```
        NODE        defines    "evalWidth"
          |
        BLOCK       redefines "evalWidth"
          |
    CASE_BLOCK
```

Undesirable effects may result when, in designing class CASE_BLOCK, the software developer relies on inheritance of method "evalWidth" from class NODE, forgetting that this method was redefined in class BLOCK in a fashion not suitable for class CASE_BLOCK.

In addition to tools checking static relationships between the entities defined for an object oriented application, object-level debugging requires special runtime support in order for the programmer to see the effects of dynamic message binding. Dynamic message binding means that the method executed in response to a message is determined not at compile time, but during program execution. Therefore, objects can send messages to other objects without having to know which class the receiver is an instance of. Instance variables that are pointers to other objects need not be "typed" with a specific class, but are uniformly defined as "OBJ" in OOPC.

This, however, makes it hard for application programmers to check the soundness of their implementation. For each class, they have to make sure that its instances know how to react in each context where they may occur. This means that for each message that may be sent to an instance of some class, a corresponding method has to be available (either directly, or via inheritance). But because of dynamic binding, it is impossible to construct a cross-reference tool showing all message selectors that instances of a certain class must be able to respond to. Related design errors cannot be detected by the compiler, but will, in general, show up during test runs of the program, i.e. rather late in the program life cycle.

Such errors can in part be prevented by implementation of default methods for all selectors occuring in some message. The definition of a default method has to be contained in a class that is a common ancestor of all classes of which instances are expected to receive a message with the corresponding selector. For example, in the structure editor implementation, a default method "draw" has been defined in class GRBOX, since we expect "draw"-messages to be sent to any kind of structural unit. The default method technique cannot, however, be applied for applications in which the only common ancestor of all relevant classes is a class taken from some given library which the application programmer cannot augment at will by additional methods.

When implementing the PCE, we tried to reuse as much code as possible from the GSE implementation of which a first version had already been completed. We expected this to be achieved in a straightforward manner, as described in the previous section, because of the conceptual subdivision of the class hierarchy into upper level classes, handling the internal representation of edited documents, and lower level classes, handling the display representation. However, in practice, this division was not so clear-cut.

It turned out that also in the general, upper level classes, code had to be included that is needed by only one of the editors. This was in many cases due to the fact that attached to each object representing a syntactical unit there is a second object which contains the data relevant to the external layout of the unit (height, width, etc.). Since the external representation of syntactical units is different for GSE and PCE, these "layout objects" are instances of different classes: of class GSEUNIT for GSE, and of class PCEUNIT for PCE.

This construction leads to the following problems:

1. Whenever a syntactical unit (e.g. a caseblock) is created during an editor session, a corresponding layout object has to be generated as well. In order to maximally exploit the inheritance mechanism to avoid replication of code, the method for layout object generation which is common to all kinds of syntactical units is incorporated in class GRBOX. Therefore this class, though placed very high in the inheritance hierarchy, contains code related to the external representation of documents.

   On the other hand, we wanted to use identical definitions of class GRBOX for GSE and PCE, since most of the methods of GRBOX are the same for both editors. Therefore, the method for layout object generation defined in GRBOX had to be given the ability to determine which is the current editor, in order to decide whether a GSEUNIT or PCEUNIT has to be created.

The general problem demonstrated by this example is a conflict between the objectives of

o code reuse within a specific application (e.g. GSE), by virtue of inheritance, which implies defining methods as high in the class hierarchy as possible

o code reuse across applications, in the form of reusing complete class definitions, which implies keeping higher level classes as general as possible

Both objectives can be given equal consideration by introducing additional intermediate layers into the class hierarchy. This, however, increases the runtime of the resulting object oriented programs, since the search path for the method to be executed in response to a message becomes fairly long.

2. As mentioned above, a diagram can be created by the GSE and, in some later editing session, manipulated by the PCE. In our implementation we used the general save/restore mechanism provided by the OOPC system. This mechanism always stores on file the complete set of objects referenced by any object to be saved. In particular, saving a diagram created by GSE implies that all associated layout objects, i.e. instances of class GSEUNIT, are written to the file. When this file is read for subsequent use by PCE, the PCE must be able to handle these GSEUNITs, though it will immediately substitute them by instances of PCEUNIT in the restored document. Thus, the PCE must know the structure of GSEUNITs. The only way to circumvent this problem would have been to implement our own specialized save/restore mechanism instead of using the mechanism already implemented.

6.0 Conclusions

Most of the problems we had with our implementation of the structure editors were due to the fact that none of the programmers involved in this project had any previous experience with the object oriented programming paradigm. For example, we had not sufficiently taken care of keeping the classes in the upper layers of the inheritance hierarchy as general as possible, which forced us to modify some of the GSE code in order to reuse it for PCE. But now, having gained first experiences with object oriented programming, we expect to better exploit its advantages in subsequent projects. In particular, we appreciate the advances in reusability and maintainability achieved by object oriented programming.

Object oriented programs are necessarily modular and clearly structured, as collections of classes arranged in an inheritance hierarchy. All knowledge about a certain kind of object is isolated in the corresponding class definition, with only its message interface visible from outside. Therefore, extending or modifying an existing implementation is fairly easy. Side effects introduced by changes are limited.

The inheritance mechanism provides a natural means to avoid code redundancy, and thus helps to keep consistency problems arising in the process of implementing changes to a minimum.
By factoring out common properties of several kinds of objects and associating these with fairly general "base classes", class libraries can be created which may be used by several different applications.
Specialized cross-reference tools for inheritance checking would be useful, especially during the software design phase and for debugging.

The object oriented approach seems to be particularly suitable for prototype development.
The logical subdivision of the application world into a collection of entities, which is induced by the problem to be solved, directly carries over into the object-oriented implementation: each entity is modeled by an object (or by several related objects). Therefore, once problem analysis has been performed, a first approximation of the projected software system already exhibiting most of the desired behavior can be implemented in a fairly straightforward fashion. Further improved versions will be derived from such prototype software. Since object classes are characterized by their functional interface, not by their internals, it is easy to replace these program components by functionally equivalent ones whose implementation puts more emphasis on runtime efficiency. Also, detail of program behavior can easily be added by introducing new classes as subclasses of existing ones.

Object oriented programming offers major advantages for finding design errors resulting from inadequate problem decomposition. Since there is such a close correspondence between the problem structure as perceived by the software designer and the structure of the implementation, the design can be verified by testing the resulting code.

The OOPC system supplies rudimentary object level debugging facilities, in particular the option to have a message log be produced at runtime which records each message sent. If full object level debugging is provided, the software engineer can deal with his problem on a very high conceptual level only throughout the whole process of software development.

On the whole, we have made the experience that object oriented programming brought great leverage to our specific task of implementing syntax-directed structure editors, and we think that it is a valuable general programming paradigm that we would like to become widely used.

7.0 Figures

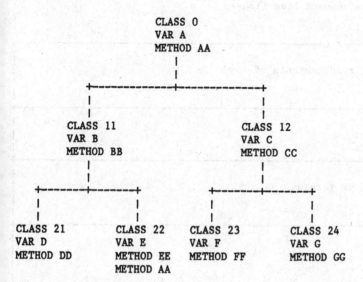

Along with each class name, this figure lists the locally defined data structures (variables) and methods (routines).

CLASS 21 inherits all data structures and methods (routines) defined by its superclass chain CLASS 11 - CLASS 0 and augments this information with variable D and method DD.

CLASS 22 also inherits all data definitions and methods of its superclasses. Method AA, however, which is defined in CLASS 0, has been overridden by a new method with the same name in CLASS 22.

Figure 1: Example for Inheritance Hierarchy of Classes

```
+------------------------------------------------------------------------+
|                                                                        |
| initialize and process command line flags                             |
|                                                                        |
|                                                                        |
+------------------------------------------------------------------------|-
|                                                                        |
| open or create files, read contents if any                            |
|                                                                        |
|                                                                        |
+------------------------------------------------------------------------+
|                                                                        |
| while not exit condition                                              |
|                                                                        |
|   +----------------------------------------------------------------+   |
|   |                                                                |   |
|   | Read a command from terminal                                  |   |
|   |                                                                |   |
|   |                                                                |   |
|   +----------------------------------------------------------------+   |
|   |                                                                |   |
|   | which command?                                                 |   |
|   |                                                                |   |
|   |         |        |               |                    |       |   |
|   | APPEND  | INSERT |    DELETE     |     UNDELETE       | EXIT  |   |
|   +---------+--------+---------------+--------------------+-------+   |
|   |         |        |               |                    |       |   |
|   | append  | insert | save element in| restore element on| raise |   |
|   | a new   | a new  | DELETE BUFFER  | its place          | exit  |   |
|   | element | element|               |                    | condition|
|   |         |        +---------------+--------------------+       |   |
|   |         |        |               |                    |       |   |
|   |         |        | delete element| clear DELETE BUFFER|       |   |
|   |         |        |               |                    |       |   |
|   |         |        |               |                    |       |   |
+---+---------+--------+---------------+--------------------+-------+   |
|                                                                        |
| terminate                                                             |
|                                                                        |
|                                                                        |
+------------------------------------------------------------------------+
```

Figure 2: Example for Diagram Generated with GSE

```
b e g i n
   initialize and process command line flags
e n d
b e g i n
   open or create files, read contents if any
e n d
l o o p
w h i l e  while not exit condition
   b e g i n
      Read a command from terminal
   e n d
   c a s e  which command? i s
      w h e n  APPEND = >
         b e g i n
            append a new element
         e n d
      w h e n  INSERT = >
         b e g i n
            insert a new element
         e n d
      w h e n  DELETE = >
         b e g i n
            save element in DELETE BUFFER
         e n d
         b e g i n
            delete element
         e n d
      w h e n  UNDELETE = >
         b e g i n
            restore element on its place
         e n d
         b e g i n
            clear DELETE BUFFER
         e n d
      w h e n  EXIT = >
         b e g i n
            raise exit condition
         e n d
   e n d c a s e
e n d l o o p
b e g i n
   terminate
e n d
```

Figure 3:   Example for Pseudo Code Generated with PCE

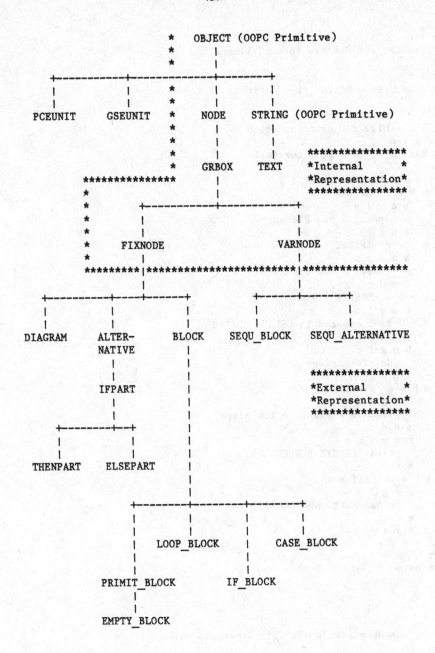

Figure 4: Class Hierarchy Implementing GSE and PCE

8.0 <u>References</u>

BYTE Magazine, Special Issue on SMALLTALK 80, Vol.6, No.8, August 1981.

Cox,B. The Object Oriented Precompiler. Programming SMALLTALK 80 Methods in C Language. ACM SIGPLAN Notices, Vol.18, No.1, 1983

Nassi,I. and Shneiderman,B. Flowchart Techniques for Structured Programming. ACM SIGPLAN Notices, Vol.8, No.8, 1973

AUTHOR INDEX